Cooking, Eating, Thinking

Cooking, Eating, Thinking

TRANSFORMATIVE PHILOSOPHIES OF
FOOD

edited by
Deane W. Curtin and Lisa M. Heldke

INDIANA
UNIVERSITY
PRESS
Bloomington and Indianapolis

The paper used in this publication meets the minimum requirements of
American National Standard for Information Sciences—Permanence of Paper
for Printed Library Materials, ANSI Z39.48-1984.

Manufactured in the United States of America

Library of Congress Cataloging-in-Publication Data

Cooking, Eating, Thinking : transformative philosophies of food /
edited by Deane W. Curtin and Lisa M. Heldke.
    p.   cm.
Includes bibliographical references and index.
ISBN 0-253-31599-9. — ISBN 0-253-20704-5 (pbk.)
1. Food—Philosophy. 2. Philosophy. I. Curtin, Deane W.
II. Heldke, Lisa M. (Lisa Maree), date.
B105.F66M35 1992
100—dc20   91-23622

1 2 3 4 5   96 95 94 93 92

To my family,
Rita, Evan, and Ian
D.C.

C O N T E N T S

Acknowledgments

To our student workers we are grateful for their careful, responsible work on the production end of this project; to Kathy Kjaglien, Holiday Lindahl, and Heath Philippi, thanks for the many hours spent photocopying, doing library searches, and sending out mailings. Thanks to Jillayne Jablonski and Chris Marshall for doing the bulk of the work communicating with publishers concerning permission to reprint, and to William Voelker for his work on the index. And thanks to Jeanie Reese for her careful work editing and proofing the manuscript.

Many people have contributed ideas, suggestions for readings, musings, thought-provoking questions, quibbles, enthusiastic encouragement, and other forms of stimulation that have shaped the direction this book has taken. Thanks to Ellie Beach, Jay Benjamin, Susan Bordo, Ann Braude, Jose Cabezon, Greg Gehrman, Sandra Harding, the Heldkes (Richard, Carol, Barb, and Sybil), Jeremy Iggers, Dennis Johnson, Sarah Verone Lawton, Doug Leonard, Bob Moline, Bruce Norelius, John Olson, Naomi Scheman, Art Simon, Allen Wall, Cynthia Sundberg Wall, and Dave Zauhar.

Particular thanks go to those individuals who read and discussed with us numerous drafts of our essays, and who provided other forms of intellectual, moral and gastronomic support: Rita Curtin and Stephen Kellert.

During 1989–90, we received a Faculty Development Grant from Gustavus Adolphus to support work on this book. Thanks to Gustavus for that grant. In the summer of 1989, we traveled and studied in India, a trip which had a significant impact on our thinking about food and development issues. That trip was funded by a Hewlett-Mellon Presidential Discretionary Grant from Gustavus. Thanks to John Kendall, then president at Gustavus, for giving us this opportunity.

"Playfulness, 'World'-Travelling, and Loving Perception," by María Lugones, was first published in *Hypatia*, Volume 2, Number 2, Summer 1987.

"The Indian Background" and "The Buddha's Conception of Personhood" from *The Principles of Buddhist Psychology*, by David Kalupahana, 1987. Reprinted by permission of State University of New York Press.

"Food Rules and the Traditional Sexual Ideology" from *Food, Sex and Pollution: A New Guinea Religion*, by Anna S. Meigs. Copyright © 1984 by Rutgers, the State University, reprinted by permission of Rutgers University Press.

"How to Stuff a Pepper," from *Carpenter of the Sun*, Poems by Nancy Willard, by permission of Liveright Publishing Corporation. Copyright © 1974 by Nancy Willard.

Excerpts from *Culture and Cuisine*, by Jean François Revel, translation copyright © 1982 by Doubleday, a division of Bantam Doubleday Dell Publishing Group, Inc. Used by permission of the publisher.

"Fushuku-hampō" ("Meal-time Regulations"), by Dōgen, from *Zen Is Eternal Life*, 3rd edition, revised, translated by Reverend Master Jiyu Kennet, 1987. Reprinted by permission of Shasta Abby Press.

"Verses of Sen-No-Rikyu" from *Cha-No-Yu*, by A. L. Sadler, 1962. Reprinted by permission of Charles E. Tuttle Co., Inc.

Excerpts from *American Fried: Adventures of a Happy Eater*, by Calvin Trillin, copyright © 1974 by Calvin Trillin. Used by permission of Doubleday, a division of Bantam Doubleday Dell Publishing Group, Inc.

"Becoming Vegetarian" from *Animal Liberation*, by Peter Singer, copyright © 1990. Published by Harper and Row. Reprinted by permission.

"Two Full of Butter," from *The Rig Veda: An Anthology*, translated by Wendy Donger O'Flaherty.

Excerpts from Genesis and Leviticus from *The New English Bible*. Copyright © The Delegates of the Oxford University Press and The Syndics of the Cambridge University Press 1971, 1970. Reprinted by permission.

Excerpt from *Gorgias*, by Plato. Translation by W.D. Woodhead (1953) by permission of Thomas Nelson and Sons, Edinburgh and New York, publishers.

"The Perfect Pie," by Al Sicherman, 1989. Reprinted with permission of the *Star and Tribune*, Minneapolis-St. Paul.

Excerpt from *Probabilistic Metaphysics*, by Patrick Suppes, 1984. Reprinted by permission of Basil Blackwell Publishers.

"Recipes for Theory Making," by Lisa M. Heldke, first published in *Hypatia*, Volume 3, Number 2, 1988.

Excerpt from *The Sexual Politics of Meat: A Feminist-Vegetarian Critical Theory*, by Carol J. Adams. Copyright © 1990 by Carol J. Adams. Reprinted by permission of the Continuum Publishing Company.

Excerpt from *Buffalo Bird Woman's Garden: Agriculture of the Hidatsa Indians*, by Gilbert L. Wilson, reprinted edition by Minnesota Historical Society Press, St. Paul, 1987.

Excerpts from "Instruction for the Tenzo" from *Moon in a Dewdrop: Writings of Zen Master Dōgen*, copyright © 1985 by Dōgen. Reprinted by permission of North Point Press.

Excerpt from *Zami: A New Spelling of My Name*, by Audre Lorde, 1982. Reprinted by permission of The Crossing Press.

Excerpts from *Vibration Cooking: or The Travel Notes of a Geechee Girl*, by Verta Mae Smart-Grosvenor, copyright © 1970 by Verta Grosvenor.

"Myths About Hunger" from *Food, Poverty and Power*, by Anne Buchanan, 1982. Reprinted by permission of Spokesman.

"Development, Ecology and Women" from *Staying Alive: Women, Ecology and Development*, by Vandana Shiva, 1988. Reprinted by permission of Zed Books.

"Are My Hands Clean?" words and music by Bernice Johnson Reagon. Published by Songtalk Publishing Co. and reprinted by permission.

"Women Whose Lives Are Food, Men Whose Lives Are Money" and "American Independence" reprinted by permission of Louisiana State University Press from *Women Whose Lives Are Food, Men Whose Lives Are Money*, by Joyce Carol Oates. Copyright © 1978 by Joyce Carol Oates.

"A Modest Proposal," from *Satires and Personal Writings*, by Jonathan Swift, Oxford University Press.

"Meeting the Expectations of the Land," excerpted from *Altars of Unhewn Stone*, copyright © 1987 by Wes Jackson. Published by North Point Press and reprinted by permission.

"Revolutionary Letter #42" and "Revolutionary Letter #55" from *Revolutionary Letters Etc 1966-1978*. Copyright © 1971, 1979 by Diane Di Prima. Published by City Lights Books and reprinted by permission.

"Thanksgiving Dinner During Pelting Season," by Mary Moran, from *A Gathering of Spirit: A Collection by North American Indian Women*, edited by Beth Brant. Published by Firebrand Books, Ithaca, New York, and reprinted by permission.

"The Pleasures of Eating" excerpted from *What Are People For?* copyright © 1990 by Wendall Berry. Published by North Point Press and reprinted by permission.

Introduction

Normally an anthology comes "after the fact"; it provides a retrospective view of territory that has already been mapped. This anthology departs from that convention. It attempts to establish the existence of a philosophical subject matter and to provide various ways of approaching that subject matter by offering new readings of a number of texts—religious, philosophical, anthropological, culinary, poetic, economic. We intend for this work to stand as a multi-voiced argument for the existence of a domain of philosophic inquiry; it is a *reader* in the philosophy of food.

Understanding food philosophically not only legitimates new categories of inquiry (the epistemology of food and the ontology of food, for example), but also holds the potential to provide further illumination of traditional philosophical problems (such as the relation between thought and practice or mind and body, and the concept of a person). It challenges the primacy that certain concepts and methods have tended to hold in western philosophy (the predominance of theory—abstract and eternal—over practice—concrete and temporal—being one important example). Furthermore, thinking about food philosophically enables productive new thinking about urgent issues in the politics of food: the role of agribusiness in the economies of dominated countries, trade friction resulting from the use of growth hormones and pesticides, and policy decisions on food distribution that widen the gap between wealthy and poor.

One might well ask why the philosophy of food does not already exist as a domain of philosophical discourse on a par with epistemology, metaphysics, or aesthetics. Why have philosophers not treated food as a proper subject for philosophical inquiry, equal in importance to subjects like the nature of knowledge or of the human soul? Philosophers have traditionally concerned themselves with questions of human value. Yet western philosophers have persistently ignored—or marginalized—one of the most common and pervasive sources of value in human experience—our relations with food.[1]

One important feature of an explanation for this philosophical neglect of food is clear. In many, if not most cultures, food production and preparation activities are women's work and/or the work of slaves or lower classes. Certainly this is true of Euro-American cultures, and to that extent it is not difficult to determine why western philosophers have not considered food a properly philosophical topic. Western philosophies, like the cultures in which they emerge, historically have discounted the value of women's activities. Quilts were considered crafts rather than fine arts; women's writing was considered introspective and recreational; work was defined in a way that excluded reproductive labor and unpaid activities in the home. The case has been similar for food and cooking. Those philosophers who have talked about food have tended to use it merely anecdotally, as an example of humans' base bodily nature, or have forced our experience of it into inappropriate categories.

Our interest in food, however, goes deeper than explicating the claim that many western philosophers have simply been sexist in the most transparent way. Thinking about food philosophically, we argue, can also reveal that the basic projects of western philosophical inquiry have been skewed. Our tradition has tended to privilege questions about the rational, the unchanging and eternal, and the abstract and mental; and to denigrate questions about embodied, concrete, practical experience. For example, the way in which the concept of personal identity has classically been approached by philosophers is by assuming the self to be a discrete, disembodied ego, and then asking for the logical conditions of its self-identity through time. By contrast, taking the production and preparation of food as an illuminating source, we might formulate a conception of the person which focuses on our connection with and dependence on the rest of the world. Personhood, then, might be thought of as an unfolding *process*, with identity conditions which evolve over time. Might such perennial philosophical knots as the mind/body problem, the problem of our knowledge of the external world, and the problem of other minds be untied in the context of a food-centered philosophy of human being?

Our use of the philosophical tradition in this reader treats the tradition as philosophy-become-popular-culture. That is, we address the western philosophical tradition not as an independent, academic body of texts and "ideas," but as sets of attitudes and practices that have come to shape the everyday lives of ordinary people. Several of the texts we include explicate connections between abstract philosophical concepts and people's ordinary life experiences. For example, Susan Bordo's article in Section One describes anorexia as a kind of Cartesian psychopathology. Bordo's point is not that anorexics are "Cartesians" in some self-conscious way, but that the Cartesian categories of body and mind can be interpreted as working in their lives. Through a process of coming to understand how these categories operate in her life, the anorexic can begin to return herself to health. Wes Jackson's essay in Section Four also explores philosophy as it has become popular culture. He describes the destructive relationship between U.S. farmers and the soil as emerging from a subject/object conception of the relation between humans and the environment, and he traces this conception back to Descartes, Bacon, and other philosophers.

We intend for this book to be a challenge to action as much as it is to be a book for philosophical contemplation. We write from a suspicion of the legitimacy of the theory/practice dichotomy. This suspicion is manifested in explicit arguments against the dichotomy found in the book (particularly in Section Three), and also in our commitment throughout the book to suggest concrete ways in which theoretical concepts do and should inform our actions in the world.

INTENDED AUDIENCE

Given that this reader is intended to serve as a multifaceted argument for the existence of a sphere of philosophical inquiry, we hope it will be of interest to academics in several disciplines in a way that a typical anthology is not. The "core" discipline is philosophy; the work may have particular appeal for philosophers working in social theory, feminist theory, and environmental ethics, but might also be of interest to philosophers working on alternative approaches to traditional subject areas like epistemology, aesthetics, and even metaphysics.

The work is not only directed toward academics; we also intend it to be used as a course text. In fact, the project arose in the context of our work to develop food-centered educational experiences for students in India. We realized, in searching for appropriate reading material, that there was no convenient text we could use to introduce students to a range of philosophical issues concerning food.

Finally, we like to imagine that the book will appeal to people who are neither academics nor students, but simply people who like to read—for new ideas, for new theoretical/practical perspectives on life, for pleasure. We have selected many writings which are simply fun to read, and we hope that people will allow themselves to have fun reading the book.

ABOUT THE TEXTS SELECTED

Though we use the European philosophical tradition as our point of departure, we also use Japanese Buddhist, Native American, African-American, Indian, and other "nonwestern" texts. In choosing the selections to be included in the reader, it was important to us to draw upon the thoughts of a broad spectrum of cultures. We believed that it was important to reveal some of the many ways in which food is central for humans' lives. When we began this project, we expected that we would find writings on food in any culture we might choose to explore—and we were correct. By presenting a sampling of this rich diversity, we intend both to show the potential that food has as a topic for philosophical conversation, and to reveal the inadequacy and incompleteness of traditional western philosophical thinking on the subject.

Furthermore, our desire to represent a variety of cultures is due to our political commitment to speak to/from the lives of those traditionally excluded from western philosophy—those who are not white and/or not men.

Given the history of western philosophical representation—given the perspectives that historically have been represented—our priority has been to include views from those less often heard from. We have attempted to do so with firsthand accounts, or with "secondhand" accounts in which the distance between the author and the persons being written about is smaller, not greater.[2]

In choosing selections, we also wished to include work from several disciplinary homes, and written in a variety of literary forms. Part of our motivation for doing so was that the ideas we wished to represent were not to be found in traditional philosophy texts. Thus, the reader employs a multidisciplinary approach; we include writings by novelists, anthropologists, poets, social critics, and economists as well as by traditional philosophers.

ON COLLABORATION

This reader represents our commitment to "coresponsible inquiry."[3] It is a collaborative effort on several levels. First, it represents a collaboration between us, its editors. Each section introduction, though principally authored by one of us, was read and critiqued by the other innumerable times. We worked together to locate and select readings to be excerpted. The work has emerged in its present form in large part because of the ongoing conversations we've had about it. The positions at which we've arrived bear the mark of each other's thought in deep structural ways.

The reader is also a kind of collaboration among us and the authors represented here. Through our introductory essays, we have attempted to engage in conversations with those authors in ways that acknowledge and utilize our own cultural particularity, but that also attempt to expand upon and critique our own cultural perspectives. The selections we've chosen manifest the interests and backgrounds of its editors—philosophers trained in traditional western thought. While we both were trained in traditional philosophy, we have also made serious efforts to move beyond that tradition to critique and augment it. Curtin brings to the book an interest in Buddhist philosophy and Heldke brings an interest in feminist theory.

Furthermore, it is a collaboration between us, the editors, and the many friends, students, family members, and colleagues who have worked with us, providing their labor, suggestions, conversation, enthusiasm, encouragement, and recipes. Their roles in the creation of this final product cannot be overestimated.

Finally, the reader is a collaboration between all those whose works are printed here, and all those who read it. The ideas developed here are significant insofar as they provide food for thought and action for those who read them. We invite readers to use them, and to make this a genuine collaboration by explaining their ideas to us.

STRUCTURE

The book is divided in four sections, each of which consists of an original introductory piece by Curtin or Heldke, followed by a set of readings from previously printed texts. Given the constructive nature of the reader, these introductory essays are quite substantial. They serve as invitations to read the reprinted texts in new ways—specifically, as facets of arguments for, and sketches of, philosophies of food.

The first two sections address relatively abstract issues of human personhood and values, while the last two explore issues concerning human activity and social policy. By first developing accounts of less familiar food issues, we prepare the way for understanding more familiar social and political issues in enhanced ways. It is our contention that issues of food and politics are closely connected to the issues of food and personhood and food and value. Developing an understanding of less familiar food issues can reshape our thinking about the political dimensions of food in important ways.

We do not mean to suggest that an understanding of the issues explored in Sections One through Three is *necessary* for a "proper" understanding of political issues involving food; there is no ontological or epistemological hierarchy governing the ordering of topics here, and we do not suggest that something like a "food metaphysics" is necessarily prior to a "food politics." Indeed, traditional philosophical hierarchies of subjects—metaphysics before epistemology, and both before aesthetics and ethics, for example—may well be ineffective for philosophical explorations of food. A food-based perspective reveals interrelations and interdependence among philosophical topics that enables them to be approached from any of various starting points.

NOTES

1. This is not entirely true. As Curtin will suggest in Section One, there has always been a philosophy of food; there have always been philosophers who have taken food seriously. However, their writings on food have tended to be accorded only marginal importance in the western philosophical canon.

2. Note that by "firsthand" we do not mean "untheoretical"; we are not using the experiences of, say, Hidatsa women as the "raw data" about which we then theorize.

3. See the introduction to Section Four for a discussion of coresponsible inquiry.

SECTION ONE

DEANE W. CURTIN

Food/Body/Person

Something for the industrious. . . . So far, everything that has given color to existence still lacks a history: or, where could one find a history of love, of avarice, of envy, of conscience, of piety, or of cruelty? . . . Does anyone know the moral effects of food? Is there a philosophy of nourishment? (The ever-renewed clamor for and against vegetarianism is sufficient proof that there is no such philosophy as yet.)

Nietzsche

I. ASKING THE RIGHT QUESTIONS

Nietzsche's questions are mischievous, unsettling, and if taken seriously, transformative. To address them seriously would be to embark on a philosophical journey that would leave very little in philosophy untouched. Nietzsche probably understood that philosophical neglect of food is not just a curious accident, but that there are deep structural reasons why the main strands of the western philosophical tradition *cannot* take food seriously. To do so would call into play the very questions asked by that tradition, as well as the philosophical methods used to answer them.

Philosophers in the dominant western tradition have been uninterested in those aspects of life that "give color to existence," those common, everyday experiences that, as we say, "add spice to life." Rather, they have confined their attention to those aspects they thought could be ordered by "theories" (where theory-making is understood to be the activity of reducing temporal events to abstract, disembodied, atemporal schemata), and to those kinds of values that are defined as public, masculine, and universal. Our relations to aspects of life that can only be understood as concrete and embodied (primary among them our relations to food) have been marginalized. They have been pushed to the periphery of what is regarded as important.

The purpose of this introductory essay is to begin to claim food as an important philosophical subject by exploring the ways in which food structures what counts as a person in our culture. That is, it addresses one of the subjects that has been regarded as "important" by western philosophers, a proper subject for theorizing (personhood), but it then asks what might have been said about personhood if our relations to marginalized aspects of life had been taken seriously. In adopting this strategy, it attempts to disrupt the transcendentalizing patterns of philosophical thinking by beginning with the possibility that some aspects of our experience are valuable just because they are physical, transitory, and completely ordinary. Part of the task will be to reconstruct what can be meant by "ordinary" since in the philosophical language we have inherited it can only be used in contrast to "something better." For now, the word can be taken to indicate a project: learning how to value the experiences of marginalized persons, as well as the marginalized experiences of dominant persons.

There is a dynamic between those who marginalize and those whose lives are marginalized. While everyone eats, some are enabled by the conceptual scheme[1] of a dominant philosophical culture to bracket off those food-related aspects of their experiences, to leave them unspoken and unacknowledged. Thus they literally do not experience themselves in these roles. They are not regarded, and do not understand themselves, as being defined by their eating practices. In marginalizing the lives of women, manual laborers, and persons of color (those who have been defined as responsible for food), dominant persons also marginalize the aspects of their own lives that are "ordinary" and "bodily." Attention to the experiences of marginalized persons reveals those aspects of *all* persons that have been marginalized.[2]

I begin by rehearsing one version of the standard philosophical account of personhood in terms of an autonomous and disembodied mind, or mental substance. I then consider the contemporary effects of this self-conception on the food-based self-understandings of women arguing that it has, quite literally, resulted in illness. This is a reason for suspicion about the dominant concept of personhood. I then argue that there are alternative, healthy ways of understanding personhood that learn from the food-related experiences of women. The position I endorse draws from the recognition of ourselves as inherently relational and temporal. It seeks to learn how to value "ordinary everydayness," and holds that there is no single way to construct personhood. Rather, persons are defined multiply through defining processes of experience. Finally, I bring feminist concerns into dialogue with Buddhist understandings of the self, suggesting that both approaches have pointed out important connections between a relational concept of personhood and the way one commits to participating in and valuing the world. Throughout, I shall be particularly interested in carrying out Nietzsche's mischievous intent by judging these accounts of the self in terms of how well they can account for our relations to food.

II. PERSON AS SUBSTANCE

In the *Phaedo* dialogue, Plato depicts Socrates as asking, "Do you think that it is right for a philosopher to concern himself with the so-called pleasures connected with food and drink," with other bodily pleasures such as sex, and "with smart clothes and shoes and other bodily adornments?" The answer could not be more unequivocal: "the true philosopher despises them." The body, according to Plato, confuses the mind in its pursuit of the absolutely true. It is the cause of war when riches are acquired "because we are slaves in its service." The philosopher's soul therefore "ignores the body and becomes as far as possible independent, avoiding all physical contacts and associations as much as it can in its search for reality" (*Phaedo*, 24–27*). Since death is the final release of the soul from the body, the true philosopher does not regret the death of his[3] body; rather, he anticipates it fondly.

Philosopher-kings of Plato's *Republic*, intellectuals determined to escape the prison of the body, must climb out of the image-world of the cave to gain illumination from the "Sun," the Form of the Good. The Form of the Good is the universal and unchanging source of all morality and all real knowledge (Plato 1961, Book 7). Theorizing requires him to leave behind the unruly world in which people eat. With work of the mind taking the philosopher elsewhere, work of the hand must be left to those who are not able to govern, philosophize, or fight in battle. Back in the cave, the artisan class must "get the meal on the table" somehow; just how is not a matter of interest to the philosopher. That's the work of women, slaves, and free manual laborers.

Plato's powerful metaphor of man struggling against his body toward the universal expresses what Theodor Adorno called the logic of identity (Adorno, 3–57). According to the logic of identity, a theoretical account is complete only when all elements in a domain of inquiry have been reduced to a common, atemporal scheme. Plato does this primarily through his determination to represent the world in terms of exclusive dualisms, dualisms that answer to the dominant metaphor of the pristine brightness of the Platonic heaven versus the dim, dusty cave: mind/body, self/other, culture (philosophy)/nature, good/evil, reason/emotion. "Ordinary" life in the cave is a dangerous illusion; it comes to have definition only by exclusion, through its opposition to the "extraordinary" life of the philosopher.

Two features of this movement toward dualistic thought have been inimical to serious philosophical interest in food. These dualisms are distinctions of *ontological kind* and of *value*. Ontological separateness of each of the dualistic pairs guarantees their non-interaction; it also buttresses the idea that one of the pairs is the kind of thing that is autonomous and, therefore, fully real. (Things like self, culture, good, mind, and reason.)

The other term in the dualistic pair is understood as dependent and, therefore, neither fully real nor fully knowable.

Philosophers define substances as autonomous and independent entities, just the kind of entity about which one can have a theory. This concept has been employed to answer two of the most basic philosophical questions in the western philosophical tradition: What is it to exist? and What is knowledge? Substances are defined as *independent* both metaphysically and epistemologically. Ontologically, they are fully real because they can exist apart from dependence on any other thing. Substances make knowledge possible because explanations terminate in them; they are the explanation for other things, while requiring no further explanation themselves.[4] In essence, substances are the kind of entity that must exist if there can be theorizing according to the logic of identity. Substances are made to be reducible to atemporal schemata.

It is plain, however, that the search for autonomy has systematically tended to exclude serious philosophical attention to those things that are *not* substances and can only be understood as deeply relational—things like our relations to food.[5] Because of their very ordinariness and their unqualified time-boundedness, food practices are *ontologically* not the kinds of things philosophical theories are designed to explain.

The second feature of dualistic thought that has tended to silence philosophical interest in food is that the dualisms are not only dualisms of ontological kind, but also of value.[6] The true self is defined in terms of the soul, which can remain identical through time, autonomous, and "independent" (*Phaedo*, 25*) of the decay and dissolution of the body. Each dualistic pair places the first of the pair on a higher ontological and normative rank than the second. The first exists and has value only by excluding and marginalizing the second. Food, those who are defined as responsible for the growing and preparation of food, and those (bodily) aspects of the lives of all persons that inevitably concern food, are constructed as the kinds of things that are normatively inferior.

We have paid a dear price for this understanding of what it means to be a person. It implies an understanding of human life pervaded by conflict: my "self" against my body; my reason against my emotions and desires (including my desire to eat); my moral rights against the rights of others; culture (the products of mind) against nature (where nature needs to be transformed into culture to provide food); theory (philosophy) against practice (agriculture). While this model has dominated in our culture, its metaphors, as Nietzsche said, are by now "illusions about which one has forgotten that this is what they are; metaphors which are worn out and without sensuous power" (Nietzsche 1954b, 47). To accept the centrality of the ordinary is not to learn how to live happily in Plato's cave. That would be to accept Plato's categories simply by reversing his normative hierarchy. Rather, it is to go beyond his reductionist dualism and value the ordinary as meaningful in itself.

I do not claim that the alternative explored here is *logically* superior to the received view, since, at this level, the persuasiveness of entire sets of metaphors is what we find compelling. There are, however, more or less *healthy* conceptions of personhood available to us. (I am speaking literally here.) I suggest that a consideration of our culture's popular attitudes toward the body and food indicates that the radical separation of mind and body, and an understanding of ourselves as nonrelational and disembodied, leads to illness. Such a consideration of popular culture also suggests that the categories of Platonic (and Cartesian) philosophy are not just a relic of the past. Seemingly abstract philosophical categories have a demonstrable effect on popular culture today.

III. HEALTH AND PERSONHOOD

Susan Bordo argues that the Cartesian estrangement from the body is misconceived if we think of it only as a conceptual puzzle about whether we can really know the "external world." She regards anorexia nervosa and other eating disorders as the psychopathological crystallization of culture, a process she explains partly in terms of the effects of Cartesian philosophy on popular culture. (Like Platonic philosophy, Cartesian philosophy is committed to the logic of identity and to the prioritization of the mind, or soul, over the body.) Anorexia nervosa is a disorder, like hysteria in Victorian times, that came to be, and continues to be made possible, through particular cultural conditions. Like hysteria, its impact is felt primarily by women, who constitute 90 percent of its victims. An anorexic typically feels alienation from her body and the hunger "it" feels. Bordo quotes one woman as saying she ate because "my stomach wanted it." The starvation of the body is motivated by the dream to be "without a body," to achieve "absolute purity, hyperintellectuality and transcendence of the flesh" (34 and 35*). Self-denial is taken to confer a sense of nonbodily purity deeply reminiscent of Plato.

Kim Chernin's "Confessions of an Eater" vividly draws out these ideas experientially. As Chernin comes to understand the causes of her eating disorder she says, "This hunger I feel, which drives me to eat more than I need, requires more than the most perfectly mixed handful of almonds and raisins. It requires, in whatever form is appropriate, the evolution and expression of self" (Chernin, 62*). "What I wanted from food" she says, "was companionship, comfort, reassurance, a sense of warmth and wellbeing that was hard for me to find in my own life, even in my own home. And now that these emotions were coming to the surface, they could no longer be easily satisfied with food. I was hungering, it was true; but food apparently was not what I was hungering for" (61*).

Chernin begins to understand that her food obsession is not fundamentally an obsessive relationship to food, but a faulty construction of personhood which shows itself through food. She is obsessive when she pits herself, understood as her will, against the body. When she loses weight, she celebrates by buying new clothes for "it," only to regain the weight. She finally experiences a breakthrough when she overcomes her estrangement from her body, when she is able to accept herself (her *body*) as her *self*: "My body, my hunger and the food I give to myself, which have seemed like enemies to me, now have begun to look like friends. And this, it strikes me, is the way it should be; a natural relationship to oneself and the food that nourishes one. Yet, this natural way of being does not come easily to many women in our culture"(59*).

The consequence of what Chernin calls a "natural relationship" with herself is a "reconciliation within the self," which shows itself in "a yearning for permission to enjoy the sensuous aspects of the self" (64*). She concludes, "my alienation from my body was the key to understanding my troubled relationship to food, to my appetite, and to my very identity as a woman" (66*). What she had been taught to regard as trivial, a woman's relationship to food, comes to be seen as the key to establishing herself as a healthy person. The issue is control, but unlike the obsessive contest of will against body, healthy control—the power to direct one's life—comes from accepting herself as body.

IV.   TOWARD A SYMPATHETIC UNDERSTANDING OF FOOD

Though compulsive eating is a disease of the twentieth century, the logic of Chernin's illness has been repeated over and over again in western philosophy: philosophical themes have been invented to reassure us that we are not utterly temporal beings. These themes have been disseminated and popularized resulting in deep and often unspoken attitudes toward aspects of experience that are "beneath" the level of philosophical attention. In consequence, food has usually been regarded as an uncomfortable counterexample that has to be twisted to the purposes of transcendentalizing philosophy. At worst, its relationship to our lives has remained completely unspoken.

Feminist philosophy can be seen partly as a process of learning how to value the ordinary experiences of women's lives, experiences that have been defined by patriarchal culture as trivial. But feminist philosophy need not be exclusively by women for women. Men, too, who are allowed to express themselves as bodily creatures only in a hypermasculine atmosphere such as that of the football playing field (an atmosphere in which tears and bodily embraces do not risk one's manliness), can learn from the food-based experiences of women. In a patriarchal culture, where women's entire lives are trivialized and privatized, certain aspects of men's lives are also trivialized and privatized.

Food, which has been defined as trivial, should be important to women and men for the same reason Chernin discovered it was important to her.

Through sympathetic attention to food, a sense of ourselves as bodily creatures can be revealed, and with that a sense of the value of the most ordinary (and vitally important) aspects of our experience.

We can learn something about what it means to be a healthy person by paying attention to the agency of women's transformative experiences. If anorexia nervosa is an illness made possible by, and resulting from, a Cartesian estrangement from the body, I believe this constitutes an objection to the view of ourselves as mental substances. And if it is possible to enter into a direct relationship to food, thereby achieving a new sense of personhood as relational and bodily, this constitutes a reason for regarding the alternative as better. Through really attending to who we are when we grow, prepare, and eat food, we can learn to be healthy persons.

When in the *Gorgias,* for example, Plato dismissed cooking as a mere knack designed to produce bodily gratification, he was obviously speaking as a philosopher rather than as a cook. It is possible to begin with a commitment to radical dualism, and then to force that dualism onto our attitudes about food. But it would be difficult to begin with a careful and sympathetic account of cooking, eating, and growing food and end up with radical dualism as an adequate account of those experiences.

Consider some aspects of eating and cooking. Eating is like childbirth in the way it threatens a sense of self as absolutely autonomous. A fetus is part of a woman's body, but it will become separate. Even when separate, though, the child remains related to the mother physically and emotionally. The mother's body is food for the child. Speaking of Julia Kristeva's reading of the relation between the child and the mother's body, Kelly Oliver says, "For Kristeva, the abject is that which points up the arbitrariness of borders. And the border at stake in this primary relationship is the border between the mother's body and the infant's" (Oliver, 71*).

Similarly, edibles that are classified as food in a particular cultural context have a way of threatening the borders of an autonomous self. All edibles are not counted as food. There are many things one might eat, in the sense that they could provide bodily sustenance, but which do not count as food in a particular culture, e.g., human flesh, dogs, or snakes. The classification of something as food means it is understood as something made to become part of who we are. Classifying an edible as food means we have foreknowledge that it will become us bodily, and that it will be expelled. Food stands in a special relationship to the self that is different from the merely edible. Taking the category "food" seriously leads to a suspicion that the absolute border between self and other which seems so obvious in the western tradition is nothing more than an arbitrary philosophical construction.

Consider, as well, the kind of socializing of self that occurs in the kitchen, one of those domains that have been dismissed from philosophical attention as trivial. Breadbaking, as anyone knows who has experience that goes beyond opening a package of Rhodes frozen bread dough, is hardly to be thought of as a process of mind applying abstract rules to "matter." A recipe, as Lisa Heldke argues, is hardly a theory, where theory is defined in contradistinction to practice. An experienced baker can interpret a recipe as a set of practical guidelines which need to be adapted to local conditions. (You do not add as much water to the flour on a humid July afternoon as on a frigid Minnesota January morning.) This knowledge is contextual and bodily. One needs the right kind of physical experience and skills—what Heldke calls "bodily knowledge"—to know how to read the gluten in the dough to determine if it has risen sufficiently. Becoming an accomplished bread baker is best achieved under the guidance of a master baker. A cookbook can hint at how to cook but it is no substitute for the "hands on" tutelage of a master. Culinary knowledge is social knowledge. Cooking is a "thoughtful practice."

The product of cooking, too, is best regarded as something to share. Mealtimes are special in human culture because they are (or at least were) the principal daily means of developing community feeling. We often hear the lament that modern life has become so busy that no one has time to sit down together for a meal. While it may be increasingly difficult to accomplish, we still nostalgically regard an "old-fashioned" meal together as highly desirable.

As Wes Jackson forcefully argues, agriculture suffers as well by the way our culture has forced it into a dualistic mold. There is a general perception, he reports, that "agriculture is in trouble." Often it is said that "something needs to be done about the farm problem" (Jackson, 360*). He traces this perception to the Cartesian assumption that parts are independent of the whole, that parts are individual, autonomous entities. This allows us to talk about "the environment" as something "apart from us." But, "We were, after all, made from the environment. We are maintained by it. The subject-object dualism has given us the notion that it is possible to isolate parts of the environment we don't like" (366*). The dualist conceptual scheme alienates us from nature and objectifies it. Jackson concludes, "Agriculture in the largest sense cannot be repaired independently of culture and society" (368*).

Careful attention to a wide range of growing, cooking, and eating practices repeatedly suggests that Plato was wrong to dismiss cooking as a mere knack and to dismiss eating as a necessary evil. As a practice, it simply does not fit Plato's neat "either/or" choice of art or knack. He was wrong to think that food affects only the body as distinct from the mind. In fact, cooking requires an artful blending of the mental and physical, of "theory" and practice. As sustenance, food is as much mental and spiritual as it is physical. Far from supporting the model of radical dualism, cooking provides as clear an example as we have of what might be called a body/mind working together in unison, engaged in a thoughtful practice which ministers to the whole person, an ordinary being in an ordinary context.

V. PARTICIPATORY AND OBJECTIFIED RELATIONS TO FOOD

Our confusing modern relations to food, I believe, can best be understood by reference to the distinction between two ways of understanding relations: as *participatory* or *objectified*. The substance project for personhood, which stresses autonomy and independence, must understand our relations to food as *objectified;* food is understood as "other." Obviously, even substances have to stop to eat, as Plato noted unhappily, but because of the dual nature of substances as mind and body, food is understood merely as fuel that recharges the body while leaving the mind untouched. Substances have relations to food, but such relations are indirect, external. Therefore, they are not understood as defining what it means to be a person. By the term "objectified relation," then, I intend to characterize the substance project's implied understanding of the relation of mental substance to food: while a relation exists between a substance and food, this relationship is not considered to be defining. A mental substance can enter into such external relations without losing its independence.

In contrast, sympathetic attention to the experiences of women as reported by Bordo and Chernin leads to the conclusion that we stand in a *participatory* relationship to what we choose to count as food, and that to neglect such testimony endangers our health. We become persons through connecting in relation to other beings. Our connections with food partially define who we are.

I understand a "participatory relation" to be a defining relation.[7] An agent is understood not in terms of essential, internal, and immutable qualities, but gradually *becomes* a person through relational openness to others. We are defined by our relations to the food we eat. To account for our openness to food requires a relational understanding of self. We are what we eat.

First, we are what we eat in a most literal, bodily way. Our bodies literally are food transformed into flesh, tendon, blood, and bone. Perhaps the most succinct way to express this is in terms of illness resulting from certain food practices. In the United States men who eat an average meat-based diet have a fifty percent chance of dying of a heart attack. The male American vegan (one who eats no dairy products, eggs, meat or fish) has a four percent risk of death from heart attack (T. Gordon 1971; M. Hardinge 1962). American girls who eat an average amount of meat experience early menstruation, which has been associated with high cancer rates. Chinese women who eat a vegetable- and grain-based diet start menstruating three to six years later than American women and rarely suffer these cancers.[8] It is undeniable that our bodies are what we eat.

Second, we are what we eat socially and politically. Anorexia nervosa is a disease made possible by conditions of contemporary cultural life that predominantly affect women. It is also a disease of the twentieth century in that it is a result of culturally enforced expectations about the shape of women's bodies.

The social and political embodiment of food can be seen as well in the effects of consumer cultures on developing societies. These effects include ecological devastation and destruction of local food economies that are transformed into export economies. As we have seen in the last ten years, an increase in food exports from developing countries to consumer countries is consistent with increased starvation in exporting countries. Land once used to feed local people with locally affordable food that connected with local traditions is now used to grow expensive export crops.[9] We need not be conscious of these effects of our eating practices in order for them to define us, and to affect who we are.

Third, we are what we eat symbolically and spiritually.[10] A Christian who mindfully partakes of the "body and blood of Christ" in communion, a Hindu who follows Ayurvedic practices, or a Jew who observes the ancient koshering laws of Leviticus, is expressing something deep about who that person is and about what it means to belong to a spiritual community. The same is true of the Ihalmiut, who symbolically apologize to the caribou for killing it; of the Japanese, whose Shinto festival atones for the killing of insects caused by the planting of holy food, rice; and of the Hopi's relationship to blue corn.

I am making two claims about the distinction between participatory and objectified (or defining and nondefining) relations, one ontic, the other epistemic. Ontologically, I am claiming that we are, in fact, constituted as persons by the food we eat, and by what we will count as food. This is so whether we know it or not. It is unhealthy to think of ourselves as autonomous entities that only enter into nondefining relations. Epistemically, I am claiming that, though it is better for a person's health to have a relational understanding of self, it is certainly possible not to understand oneself in this way. Indeed, I have been saying that most of western philosophical culture and the popular culture engendered by it do not include such a self-understanding.

VI. THE OBJECTIFICATION OF FOOD

If I am correct that our relations to food are defining, but that we live in a dominant culture which does not—indeed cannot because of its philosophical language—understand them as defining, we should expect to find powerful cultural pressures that objectify food, that make it seem nondefining. Philosophical ideas get translated into popular culture through a variety of mechanisms. Such mechanisms are not hard to find.

The "food as fuel" idea, a popular expression of the idea that food is nondefining, is powerfully present in our culture. In a fast-food culture, self-definition does not come through food, but through other commitments. Technology (another of those normative dualisms when paired with science) as the mechanism of social progress and control, and correlated values, such as speed and reproducibility, define us. Food does not define technology. Rather, food practices are technological practices. As Martin Heidegger said, "Agriculture is now the mechanized food industry." Heidegger's analysis of technology includes the idea that modern technology "order[s] the real as standing-reserve" (Heidegger 1977, 296 and 300). Food is not produced as food, but as an industrial reserve having no other status than as a reserve. It thereby loses its inherent quality as food and becomes like stores of oil or iron ore: a neutral (objectified) thing that can be manipulated in the service of technology. Food is understood as a means to some other end. That end is thought to define what the practice is and who we are; food is not defining. Because food is experienced as objectified, it is not understood as self-defining; food practices do not become transparent to us. Driving through the fast-food pick-up lane is something we *do*; it would be frightening to think it defines who we *are*.

In particular, the attitude toward nonhuman animals as a standing-reserve, as something external to us and absolutely different, is powerfully reinforced by political and economic agendas. Faced with declining demand for beef, an advertising campaign of the American Beef Council presents Hollywood celebrities endorsing the slogan, beef is "Real Food for Real People." Traditionally red meat has been considered food for men. (Significantly, two of the rare active roles that men traditionally play in food preparation are grilling meats outside, and ceremonially carving the meats—prepared by women—before a holiday feast.) Though to expand market appeal some women have been included as role-models, the appeal remains principally directed to men. Gender (being a "real man") is connected with eating red meat. This plays off the unspoken (and false) assumption that to build muscle a man must eat muscle. There is a connection to the body here, principally to the bodies of athletes and movie stars as models of masculinity. But it is a body defined by the media for its own purposes, a body cut off from responsibility for the reality of turning a living being into "meat." The gender identity of those who do not eat red meat is implicitly questioned: if you do not eat "real food," you must not be a "real person." In such advertising campaigns, food is used as a means to discipline a consumer group, to define what counts as a person in terms of sales potential for its product.

Even our language is complicit with the tendency to externalize food by distancing us from violence, and, more generally, from the reality of what we will count as food. Meat words in English often have a positive connotation that is reinforced by television advertising: "Where's the beef?", an expression that became part of popular culture through a fast-food advertisement, has been used as a political weapon during a presidential campaign in order to question the substance of an opponent's position.

To be without "beef" is to be weak, vulnerable. On the other hand, to say that someone "vegetates" in front of the TV, or is a "vegetable," is to connote weakness and vulnerability.

Examples such as these can be gathered at will. Briefly, I am suggesting that the modern technology of food, reinforced by advertising, forcefully shields us from the act of violence committed in killing animals for food (or being indirectly responsible for killing animals) while at the same time it implicitly attacks the value of nonflesh foods. It shields us from the reality of the food. We do not see that what we will count as food is a *choice*. Our true relationship to food is obscured. Food is thereby objectified. We see the effects of the logic of identity operating here. Given only the categories of absolute identity and difference, other animals can only be regarded as utterly different and foreign. Therefore, it is thought that they can be used for the benefit of the autonomous agent. The logic of identity leaves no room for respect for difference.

The conflict inherent in these forces by which the modern self is constructed is plain: while our symbolic and spiritual self-definition through food is attacked so that we do not *experience* food participatorily, food remains unalterably defining of who we are both physically and politically. To ignore this is to risk both physical and political health. This situation calls to mind an analogy Socrates often used to characterize untenable positions: what worse could one say about a position than that it leads to ill health, whether moral, psychosocial (anorexia nervosa), or physical (heart disease)? Granted, one can adopt such a position from ignorance, but can it really be adopted with full knowledge of its consequences? That is tantamount to saying one wants to be ill. I agree with Socrates that this is incoherent.

In Section Two, I shall suggest that a possible response to the recognition of ourselves as defined by the food we eat, particularly in the context of a dominant, industrialized country which objectifies food, is what I shall call "contextual moral vegetarianism." This is a kind of vegetarianism whose rationale does not come from universal moral laws, but from a response to a specific context of ordinary experience.

VII. TWO WAYS OF CONSTRUCTING A PARTICIPATORY SELF

A. FEMINIST THEORY AND THE POLITICS OF ORDINARY EXPERIENCE

While I have been arguing that women's experiences of food can help us to reconceptualize what it means to be a person, I do not want to eulogize women's experiences, nor to minimize the fact that the kitchen has often been the locus of women's oppression. It is through the kitchen, after all, that the logic of identity has been enforced, thus privatizing and marginalizing the experiences of many women.

A relational model of self may often suggest that the interests of others should, in certain contexts, come before one's own. It suggests that knowing what to do in a particular situation requires empathetic projection into another's life. The potential vulnerability of this position is that putting the other in front of oneself creates a situation in which there is potential for abuse. Women have been defined as "naturally" altruistic; men have often been described as "naturally" aggressive and egoistic.[11] This unfortunate distinction has tended to make Platonic categories out of the social constructions of a dominating culture. The example of the wife who selflessly cares for her husband (who cares only about himself) is only too well known. The demand to "get the food on the table" by 5:30 every day *"no matter what"* betrays a flight from the temporal ebb and flow of ordinary life that women generally do not have the luxury to ignore. Healthy personhood cannot be achieved through the dissolution of self, but through achieving the power to choose the defining relations through which one becomes a person.

In a society that oppresses women by privatizing their lives, it does no good to suggest that women should go on selflessly providing care if social structures make it all too easy to abuse that care. The philosophical intention to learn from women's experiences of themselves as relational must be understood as part of a radical political agenda that allows for development of contexts in which caring can be nonabusive. The participatory sense of self, the willingness to empathetically enter into the world of others and care for them, can be expanded and developed as a matter of feminist political awareness so that it includes those outside the already established circle of trusting relationships. Its goal is not just to make a "private" understanding of self "public" (to allow women to act like men), but to help undercut the public/private distinction. Its goal is not just to make dependent beings independent, but to develop contexts that are genuinely interdependent and participatory.

There is an important distinction between the person understood as either independent substance or dependent attribute (both of which only make sense within the logic of identity) and the relational self. A dependent self really has no sense of self, but is defined through utter dependence on a person defined as independent. By contrast, the relational self *is* a self. However, unlike the autonomous self, she recognizes that self-definition is a participatory, not an autonomous, process. The goal of this section and the next is to clarify what the participatory self is if neither independent nor dependent.

María Lugones addresses the issue of operating from a relational understanding of self in a patriarchal culture in "Playfulness, 'World'-Travelling, and Loving Perception."[12] She writes as an American Latina in a predominantly White/Anglo culture, and "stresses a particular feature of the outsider's existence: the outsider has necessarily acquired flexibility in shifting from the mainstream construction of life where she is constructed as an outsider to other constructions of life where she is more or less 'at home.' " She emphasizes that "this flexibility is necessary for the outsider but it can also be willfully exercised by the outsider or by those who are at ease in the mainstream. I recommend this willful exercise which I call 'world'-travelling and I also recommend that the willful exercise be animated by an attitude that I describe as playful" (Lugones, 85*). She recommends playful world-travelling to anyone who seeks to understand the ways we dominate others, but also for understanding how we oppress ourselves.

Following the work of Marilyn Frye in *The Politics of Reality* (1983), Lugones distinguishes arrogant perception from loving perception. Arrogant perception attempts to "graft the substance" of one person to another. It recognizes the one as being defined by and living only through the other, e.g., women who are grafted to the substance of their husbands; servants who are grafted to the substance of their "masters." Loving perception sympathizes with the interests of the other while recognizing the other's difference. Unlike arrogant perception, which insists on defining love in terms of identification, loving perception accepts difference.

As a Latina who travels from a world in which she feels "at home" to worlds constructed by others, Lugones is also aware of being constructed differently in different worlds. She notices this through finding that attributes which do apply to her in one world, e.g., playfulness, do not apply in other worlds where she does not feel comfortable. In contrast to the person who has the self-perception of inhabiting only one world (a person who feels comfortable in a dominant culture) and therefore has a *"fixed conception of him or herself"* (96*), a person who moves playfully from one world to another recognizes that "I am a plurality of selves" constructed differently in different worlds (95*). Coming to understand the self as plural through world-travelling has immediate consequences for how one acts:

> the playful attitude involves openness to surprise . . . openness to self-construction or reconstruction and to construction or reconstruction of the "worlds" we inhabit playfully. Negatively, playfulness is characterized by uncertainty, lack of self-importance, absence of rules or a not taking rules as sacred, a not worrying about competence and a lack of abandonment to a particular construction of oneself, others, and one's relation to them. (97*)

This "lack of abandonment" to any one construction of self as *the* correct construction is a kind of power. A multiply constructed self has an understanding of and control over one's life that the autonomous self lacks.

The autonomous self defines power as the ability to control himself, exclude others from controlling him, and, yet, to be able to control others. The tension here is that the autonomous self desires power over others that he would not accept over himself. He seeks to control without being controlled. And, if I am correct that the understanding of self on which this idea of power is based is illusory, then it follows this is a kind of power that cannot be achieved. Nothing short of the power of a god would be enough.

In contrast, the participatory self sees through the deadly seriousness of this illusion. She playfully refuses to abandon herself to the illusion that there is a single construction of the self, and that she can become fully a person by becoming autonomous. Her power is not absolute, but comes precisely from accepting ordinary life as it is: pervaded by uncertainty, where rules are helpful but not sacred, and where no single construction of self can adequately capture what it means to be a person.

There is a moral impact of this lack of abandonment of the self to any one construction. The relational person sees that in order to care for others, we need to care for ourselves. In order really to bring something to a relationship, one needs to be a healthy self. The assumption of the substance project that, being autonomous, care for oneself is independent of care for others, is a moral illusion based on an unhealthy conception of personhood. The issue of egoism versus altruism, which has been so important and vexing for traditional moral philosophy, becomes a nonissue. It is based on a mistaken conception of what it means to be a person.

Lugones describes very well the kind of politicized, participatory process by which one chooses the self one becomes. Personhood is not inscribed in Platonic heaven. Healthy personhood comes from having the power to choose the relations through which one will be defined. Careful attention to the variety of food practices in which we engage highlights the ordinariness of this process. We come to see, as Wendell Berry has said, that "eating is an agricultural act. Eating ends the annual drama of the food economy that begins with planting and birth." He adds, "Most eaters, however, are no longer aware that this is true" (374*).

I would only add (as does Berry himself) that eating is also a political act. By being mindful of the ways food comes to our tables, we can become aware of the fact that to be healthy, to really care for oneself, one needs to care for others. And caring for others is really to care for oneself. We should make the effort to know where our food comes from and decide whether to be part of that process. To care for oneself is to care for the migrant laborers whose daily, bodily work provides our food. To care for migrant laborers is truly to care for oneself.

B. THE NON-SUBSTANTIAL SELF

Like feminist philosophy, Buddhist philosophy resists the logic of identity and celebrates the plural self. The early Buddhist philosophy of personhood describes a middle way according to which personhood is neither independent nor dependent, neither substance, nor mere nothing. Rather, persons are *co-dependent.* Like feminist philosophy, Buddhist philosophy is concerned to expose the moral and political dangers inherent in thinking of oneself as autonomous. According to early Buddhist philosophy, the substance construction of self is not just a mistake of philosophers, but a basic human delusion and the principal cause of suffering.

David Kalupahana interprets the earliest Buddhist texts as arguing for "an adventure in non-substantialism."[13] The Buddha was reacting against "the Upanisadic thinkers in India who propounded a notion of an eternal self (*ātman*) which prefigured the speculations of both Descartes and Kant in the Western world" (Kalupahana, 7). Like Immanuel Kant, these thinkers held that, over and above the empirical self, there is a transcendental self that is not conditioned by experience, but, rather, conditions, and is the precondition of empirical experience. The Buddha reacted against the theory of an autonomous, transcendent self by proposing a series of sophisticated phenomenological arguments. The most significant for my purposes is his description of the human being as a "psychophysical personality," and its further analysis into "five aggregates." The very term, "psychophysical personality," or "*nāmarūpa*" (literally mind/matter), recalls the Buddha's resistance to the idea that mind and body can be analyzed into distinct substances. "He was not prepared to assume that mind (*nāma*) can have independent status or existence. It is always associated with a body or a physical personality" (102*). When pressed to explain *nāma* he termed it "contact with concepts." Similarly, *rūpa* is "contact with resistance" (102*). Mind and matter are not "things" or "stuff," but processes of experience. In contrast to the substance philosopher who tries to show that mind and body are ultimately independent of one another, the Buddha's project is to show their codependence and their utter temporality.[14]

In a move somewhat reminiscent of David Hume, the Buddha contended that when he closely examined himself trying to find what made him a person, he found only the five aggregates. He found no substantial self; nothing remains absolutely identical or autonomous through time. The substance philosopher mistakes continuity of experience for identity. There is no autonomous self; everything that comes to be is co-dependent.

The five aggregates are *rūpa* (material form), *vedanā* (feeling or sensation), *saññā*(perception), *sankhārā* (dispositions), and *viññāna* (consciousness). Of these, the last two are particularly important here because *sankhārā* is "*the* factor that contributes to the individuation of a person," and *viññāna* is intended to explain the feeling of continuity of a person who is individuated by dispositions (*sankhārā*) (105 and 106*). That is, these two aggregates account for our feelings of individuality and continuity (just what the substance project most wanted to account for), our feeling of being a self, without justifying any further inference to a substantial self. There is no identity of the kind required by the logic of identity for a complete account of self. Aggregates are contingently connected processes of ordinary experience.

The Buddha's understanding of dispositions is particularly suggestive in relation to food. A disposition is "that which processes material form, feeling, perception, disposition [itself] and consciousness into their particular forms." Dispositions "groom our physical personality" and determine the nature of our future personality, but they also mould our physical surroundings, "even our amenities of life, housing, clothing, utensils, and in a major way, our towns, cities, etc., our art and architecture, our culture and civilization . . . "(105*). Dispositions are mind/matter determinants of what we make. They are not mind acting on a Cartesian "external" and foreign world, but are inherently involved in it—they *participate* in it—in a relation of co-dependence. As we give definition to the world, it defines us. The substance philosopher takes these relational activities and recasts them as projects of an autonomous will. In the process, our participatory relations to food are recast as objectified.

Unlike Hume, however, who stops short having pointed out that when he introspects he does not find a substantial self, the Buddha draws an important moral consequence from the understanding of self as co-dependent. The tendency to mistake simple continuity of personhood for personal identity is not just the mistake of transcendentalizing philosophers; it is a fundamental human mistake caused by the delusion that the nontemporal is more real than the temporal. It is the mistake of thinking that Plato's heaven is the source of true knowledge and values, rather than the "river" of ordinary life.[15] Whether we intend to do good or evil, when we mistake who we are, our actions will produce illness. Only by coming to see ourselves as being defined multiply, provisionally, and in relation to others through a range of defining relationships can we be morally healthy.

Feminist philosophy and early Buddhist philosophy agree that a self-understanding as a substance which abandons itself to the illusion that it inhabits only one "world," leads to unhealthy participation in the world. They agree, further, that there is a connection between thinking of oneself participatorily and a playful, yet mindful, way of acting in the world that does not give itself over to a single construction of self. Sections Two and Four further explore the connection between self-conception and practice, between the participatory self and co-responsible action.

VIII. GATHERING THE HARVEST

In the preceding section I have written suggestively about two radical critiques of self that are widely divergent in terms of cultural origin, time of authorship, and specific philosophical agendas. I am not contending that there is some hidden unity between them, but that, brought into dialogue with one another, they can powerfully suggest new perspectives on a philosophy of food.

In Buddhist and feminist perspectives we find conscious critiques of the substance project and direct connections to a philosophy of food. *Nāmarūpa* and the feminist "plurality of selves" retain a sense of self, but embrace the idea that definition of the self is a participatory process of mutuality and co-dependence; we come to be as persons by shaping the world according to our dispositions, as it reciprocally shapes us.

From the affirmation of a relational self, there are important moral implications, not just about our right to do this or that (our right to claim a sphere of autonomy for the autonomous self), but about the very meaning of an appropriate project for a human life. In the humble values of the kitchen we can find deep meaning about the value of life. It is not "somewhere else," in some transcendent realm made secure by absolute knowledge. We find meaning in ordinary everydayness: in an empathetic conversation, in willingness to travel to other worlds, and in being mindful about relations to what we will count as food. Had western philosophers begun their educations in the kitchen, perhaps it would not have seemed so important to escape the ordinariness of Plato's Cave to attain a glimpse of the meaning of life.

NOTES

References to texts printed in this anthology are followed by an asterisk (*). Other page references refer to citations in the list of references.

1. By a conceptual scheme I mean a set of beliefs and attitudes that connect to practices and structure what can be thought and done in a particular culture. By a dominating conceptual scheme, I mean a conceptual scheme that depends on a normative hierarchy to privilege certain ways of thinking and acting by marginalizing, trivializing, and privatizing other ways of thinking and acting. Such a conceptual scheme is couched in what Theodor Adorno calls the "logic of identity" (Adorno 1973, "Introduction"), the deep assumption that to give a rational account is to reduce the objects of thought to a common, universal measure. The logic of identity reveals "an unrelenting urge to think things together in a unity, to formulate a representation of the whole, a totality" (Young 1987, 60–61). A dominating conceptual scheme is not the invention of any single individual, nor need one be aware of the fact that it provides structures for domination and oppression either to take advantage of them or to suffer from them.

2. I am conscious of being a male and writing about the experiences of women. I do not intend to *tell* women about their experiences (as if that were possible); rather, I write with the spirit that we can all learn from the experiences of women.

3. Gender specific language, where used here, is intentional.

4. One need not be a dualist to support the substance project. One could say that only matter counts as a candidate for substance, or only mind, or that substance has aspects of both the mental and the physical. However, the dominant tradition, the one that has had the greatest impact on our understanding of what it means to be a person, has employed a dualist concept of substance. I think there are reasons for this. Principal among them is that the substance project is reductionist in its attempt to count only one kind of reality as fully real. Conceptual power is gained by having an inferior kind of reality that stands as constant reminder and reinforcement of the difference. When I use the term "substance" I intend it to be understood as shorthand for this dualistic version of substance that has been at the core of the western understanding of personhood.

5. As Heldke discusses in Section Three (IIb, "Temporality"), some important philosophers, especially Plato, have referred to food. But while there have been remarks about food in the standard philosophical tradition, there has been no philosophy of food. That, as I am arguing here, is not an accident.

6. I do not suggest that it is never useful to distinguish between kinds of things, nor that there are no hierarchies of value. The problem with these particular dualisms based on the logic of identity is that they allow us to value only those aspects of experience that support a logic of identity. They tend to marginalize, trivialize, and privatize (literally, to exclude from the realm of what is publicly discussable) precisely those persons who are typically associated with the body: women, laborers, and those who have been classified as "outsiders," particularly persons of color.

7. While not all relations *are* defining for all persons at all times, any relations *could be* defining if they are brought within the moral/aesthetic narrative of a life, if they operate within a style of living. For a very interesting analogous case, see Danto 1981, chapter 7. He rejects the Platonic theory that there is some eternal artmaking quality (such as representation or form), but argues that commonplace objects can become artworks when they take on (among other qualities) a style.

8. Cornell University study by T. Colin Campbell as reported May 8, 1990, *Minneapolis Star and Tribune*.

9. See Section Four, especially "Women, Development and Ecology," "The Pleasures of Eating" (implicitly), "Are My Hands Clean?" and "Myths About Hunger."

10. See Section Two, especially "The Two Full of Butter," "Leviticus," "Verses of Sen-No-Rikyu," "Meal-Time Regulations."

11. See Blum 1973.

12. See Benhabib 1987; Blum 1973; Ferguson 1988; Holler 1990 for other feminist constructions of personhood.

13. See Kalupahana 1987, 144. (Not in the selection included in this volume.)

14. See Yuasa 1987 for a contemporary eastern mind-body theory. He notes that whereas western philosophy has generally concerned itself with the analysis of categories of being that are taken to *exist*, eastern philosophy has generally been concerned with *cultivation* of what might come to exist. Yuasa says, "What might we discover to be the philosophical uniqueness of eastern thought? One revealing characteristic is that personal "cultivation" (*shugyō*) is presupposed in the philosophical foundation of the Eastern theories. To put it simply, true knowledge cannot be obtained simply by means of theoretical thinking, but only through "bodily recognition or realization" (*tainin* or *taitoku*), that is, through the utilization of one's total mind and body. Simply stated, this is to "learn with the body," not the brain. Cultivation is a practice that attempts, so to speak, to achieve true knowledge by means of one's total mind and body" (25–26).

15. The choice of metaphors is interesting. Whearas Plato thinks of ordinary experience as a life condemned to a dark cave, the Buddhist tradition often depicts it in terms of a flowing river.

R E F E R E N C E S

Adorno, Theodor. *Negative Dialectics.* New York: Continuum, 1973.
Benhabib, Seyla. "The Generalized and the Concrete Other: The Kohlberg-Gilligan Controversy and Feminist Theory." *Feminism as Critique: On the Politics of Gender.* Ed. Seyla Benhabib and Drucilla Cornell. Minneapolis: University of Minnesota, 1987:77–95.

Blum, Larry, Marcia Homiak, Judy Housman, and Naomi Scheman. "Altruism and Women's Oppression." *Philosophical Forum* 5 (Fall-Winter 1973): 222–247.

Danto, Arthur. *The Transfiguration of the Commonplace: A Philosophy of Art.* Cambridge: Harvard University Press, 1981.

Ferguson, Ann. "A Feminist Aspect Theory of Self." *Science, Morality and Feminist Theory.* Ed. Marsha Hanen and Kai Nielsen, *Canadian Journal of Philosophy* Supplementary Volume 13 (1988): 339–356.

Frye, Marilyn. *The Politics of Reality: Essays in Feminist Theory.* Trumansburg, NY: Crossings Press, 1983.

Gordon, T. "Premature Mortality from Coronary Heart Disease: The Framington Study." *Journal of the American Medical Association.* 215 (1971): 1617.

Hardinge, M. "Nutritional Studies of Vegetarians: IV. Dietary Fatty Acids and Serum Cholesterol Levels." *American Journal of Clinical Nutrition* 10 (1962): 522.

Heidegger, Martin. "The Question Concerning Technology." *Basic Writings.* Ed. David Farrell Krell. San Francisco: Harper and Row, 1977:284–317.

Holler, Linda. "Thinking with the Weight of the Earth: Feminist Contributions to an Epistemology of Concreteness." *Hypatia* 5, no. 1 (1990): 1–23.

Hume, David. *Enquiries Concerning the Human Understanding and Concerning the Principles of Morals.* 2nd ed. Ed. L. A. Selby-Bigge. Oxford: Oxford University Press, 1902.

Kalupahana, David J. *The Principles of Buddhist Psychology.* Albany: State University of New York Press, 1987.

Nietzsche, Friedrich. "The Gay Science." *The Portable Nietzsche.* Ed. Walter Kaufmann. New York: Viking Press, 1954a: 93–102.

———. "On Truth and Lie in an Extra-Moral Sense." *The Portable Nietzsche.* Ed. Walter Kaufmann. New York: The Viking Press, 1954b: 42–47.

Plato. "Republic." Eds. Edith Hamilton and Huntington Cairns. Princeton: Princeton University Press, 1961: 575–844.

Young, Iris Marion. "Impartiality and the Civic Public: Some Implications of Feminist Critiques of Moral and Political Theory." *Feminism as Critique: On the Politics of Gender.* Ed. Seyla Benhabib and Drucilla Cornell. Minneapolis: University of Minnesota, 1987:57–76.

Yuasa, Yasuo. *The Body: Toward an Eastern Mind-Body Theory.* Trans. Shigenori Nagatomo and Thomas P. Kasulis. Albany: State University of New York Press, 1987.

Matins (excerpt)

Marvelous Truth, confront us
at every turn,
in every guise, iron ball,
egg, dark horse, shadow,
cloud
of breath on the air,

dwell
in our crowded hearts
our steaming bathrooms, kitchens full of
things to be done, the
ordinary streets.

Thrust close your smile
that we know you, terrible joy.

from *PHAEDO*

Do we believe that there is such a thing as death?

Most certainly, said Simmias, taking up the role of answering.

Is it simply the release of the soul from the body? Is death nothing more or less than this, the separate condition of the body by itself when it is released from the soul, and the separate condition by itself of the soul when released from the body? Is death anything else than this?

No, just that.

Well then, my boy, see whether you agree with me. I fancy that this will help us to find out the answer to our problem. Do you think that it is right for a philosopher to concern himself with the so-called pleasures connected with food and drink?

Certainly not, Socrates, said Simmias.

What about sexual pleasures?

No, not at all.

And what about the other attentions that we pay to our bodies? Do you think that a philosopher attaches any importance to them? I mean things like providing himself with smart clothes and shoes and other bodily ornaments; do you think that he values them or despises them—in so far as there is no real necessity for him to go in for that sort of thing?

I think the true philosopher despises them, he said.

Then it is your opinion in general that a man of this kind is not concerned with the body, but keeps his attention directed as much as he can away from it and toward the soul?

Yes, it is.

So it is clear first of all in the case of physical pleasures that the philosopher frees his soul from association with the body, so far as is possible, to a greater extent than other men?

It seems so.

And most people think, do they not, Simmias, that a man who finds no pleasure and takes no part in these things does not deserve to live, and that anyone who thinks nothing of physical pleasures has one foot in the grave?

That is perfectly true.

Now take the acquisition of knowledge. Is the body a hindrance or not, if one takes it into partnership to share an investigation? What I mean is this. Is there any certainty in human sight and hearing, or is it true, as the

poets are always dinning into our ears, that we neither hear nor see anything accurately? Yet if these senses are not clear and accurate, the rest can
hardly be so, because they are all inferior to the first two. Don't you agree?

Certainly.

Then when is it that the soul attains to truth? When it tries to investigate
anything with the help of the body, it is obviously led astray.

Quite so.

Is it not in the course of reflection, if at all, that the soul gets a clear
view of facts?

Yes.

Surely the soul can best reflect when it is free of all distractions such as
hearing or sight or pain or pleasure of any kind—that is, when it ignores
the body and becomes as far as possible independent, avoiding all physical
contacts and associations as much as it can, in its search for reality.

That is so.

Then here too—in despising the body and avoiding it, and endeavoring
to become independent—the philosopher's soul is ahead of all the rest.

It seems so.

Here are some more questions. Simmias. Do we recognize such a thing
as absolute uprightness?

Indeed we do.

And absolute beauty and goodness too?

Of course.

Have you ever seen any of these things with your eyes?

Certainly not, said he.

Well, have you ever apprehended them with any other bodily sense? By
'them' I mean not only absolute tallness or health or strength, but the real
nature of any given thing—what is actually is. Is it through the body that
we get the truest perception of them? Isn't it true that in any inquiry you
are likely to attain more nearly to knowledge of your object in proportion
to the care and accuracy with which you have prepared yourself to understand that object in itself?

Certainly.

Don't you think that the person who is likely to succeed in this attempt
most perfectly is the one who approaches each object, as far as possible,
with the unaided intellect, without taking account of any sense of sight in
his thinking, or dragging any other sense into his reckoning—the man who
pursues the truth by applying his pure and unadulterated thought to the
pure and unadulterated object, cutting himself off as much as possible
from his eyes and ears and virtually all the rest of his body, as an impediment which by its presence prevents the soul from attaining to truth and
clear thinking? Is not this the person, Simmias, who will reach the goal of
reality, if anybody can?

What you say is absolutely true, Socrates, said Simmias.

All these considerations, said Socrates, must surely prompt serious philosophers to review the position in some such way as this. It looks as though this were a bypath leading to the right track. So long as we keep to the body and our soul is contaminated with this imperfection, there is no chance of our ever attaining satisfactorily to our object, which we assert to be truth. In the first place, the body provides us with innumerable distractions in the pursuit of our necessary sustenance, and any diseases which attack us hinder our quest for reality. Besides, the body fills us with loves and desires and fears and all sorts of fancies and a great deal of nonsense, with the result that we literally never get an opportunity to think at all about anything. Wars and revolutions and battles are due simply and solely to the body and its desires. All wars are undertaken for the acquisition of wealth, and the reason why we have to acquire wealth is the body, because we are slaves in its service. That is why, on all these accounts, we have so little time for philosophy. Worst of all, if we do obtain any leisure from the body's claims and turn to some line of inquiry, the body intrudes once more into our investigations, interrupting, disturbing, distracting, and preventing us from getting a glimpse of the truth. We are in fact convinced that if we are ever to have pure knowledge of anything we must get rid of the body and contemplate things by themselves with the soul by itself. It seems, to judge from the argument, that the wisdom which we desire and upon which we profess to have set our hearts will be attainable only when we are dead, and not in our lifetime. If no pure knowledge is possible in the company of the body, then either it is totally impossible to acquire knowledge, or it is only possible after death, because it is only then that the soul will be separate and independent of the body. It seems that so long as we are alive, we shall continue closest to knowledge if we avoid as much as we can all contact and association with the body, except when they are absolutely necessary, and instead of allowing ourselves to become infected with its nature, purify ourselves from it until God himself gives us deliverance. In this way, by keeping ourselves uncontaminated by the follies of the body, we shall probably reach the company of others like ourselves and gain direct knowledge of all that is pure and uncontaminated— that is, presumably, of truth. For one who is not pure himself to attain the realm of purity would no doubt be a breach of universal justice.

Something to this effect, Simmias, is what I imagine all real lovers of learning must think themselves and say to one another. Don't you agree with me?

Most emphatically, Socrates.

Very well, then, said Socrates, if this is true, there is good reason for anyone who reaches the end of this journey which lies before me to hope that there, if anywhere, he will attain the object to which all our efforts have been directed during my past life. So this journey which is now ordained for me carries a happy prospect for any other man also who believes that his mind has been prepared by purification.

It does indeed, said Simmias.

And purification, as we saw some time ago in our discussion, consists in separating the soul as much as possible from the body, and accustoming it to withdraw from all contact with the body and concentrate itself by itself, and to have its dwelling, so far as it can, both now and in the future, alone by itself, freed from the shackles of the body. Does not that follow?

Yes it does, said Simmias.

Is not what we call death a freeing and separation of soul from body?

Certainly, he said.

And the desire to free the soul is found chiefly, or rather only, in the true philosopher. In fact the philosopher's occupation consists precisely in the freeing and separation of soul from body. Isn't that so?

Apparently.

Well then, as I said at the beginning, if a man has trained himself throughout his life to live in a state as close as possible to death, would it not be ridiculous for him to be distressed when death comes to him?

It would, of course.

SUSAN BORDO

Anorexia Nervosa: Psychopathology as the Crystallization of Culture

Historians long ago began to write the history of the body. They have studied the body in the field of historical demography or pathology; they have considered it as the seat of needs and appetites, as the locus of physiological processes and metabolisms, as a target for the attacks of germs or viruses; they have shown to what extent historical processes were involved in what might seem to be the purely biological base of existence; and what place should be given in the history of society to biological "events" such as the circulation of bacilli, or the extension of the lifespan. But the body is also directly involved in a political field; power relations have an immediate hold upon it; they invest it, mark it, train it, torture it, force it to carry out tasks, to perform ceremonies, to emit signs.
— Michel Foucault, *Discipline and Punish*

I believe in being the best I can be,
I believe in watching every calorie . . .
— "Crystal Light" commercial

Psychopathology, as Jules Henry has said, "is the final outcome of all that is wrong with a culture."[1] In no case is this more strikingly true than in the case of anorexia nervosa and bulimia, barely known a century ago, yet reaching epidemic proportions today. Far from being the result of a superficial fashion phenomenon, these disorders reflect and call our attention to some of the central ills of our culture—from our historical heritage of disdain for the body, to our modern fear of loss of control over our futures, to the disquieting meaning of contemporary beauty ideals in an era of female presence and power.

Changes in the incidence of anorexia[2] have been dramatic.[3] In 1945, when Ludwig Binswanger chronicled the now famous case of Ellen West, he was able to say that "from a psychiatric point of view we are dealing here with something new, with a new symptom." In 1973, Hilde Bruch, one of the pioneers in understanding and treating eating disorders, could still say that anorexia was "rare indeed."[4] In 1984, it was estimated that as many as one in every 200–250 women between the ages of thirteen and twenty-two suffers from anorexia (*TO*, p.1), and that anywhere from 12 to 33 percent of college women control their weight through vomiting, diuretics, and laxatives.[5] The New York Center for the Study of Anorexia and Bulimia reports that in the first five months of 1984 it received 252 requests for treatment, compared to 30 requests received in all of 1980.[6] Even allowing for increased social awareness of eating disorders and a greater willingness to report the illness, these statistics are startling and provocative. So, too, is the fact that 90 percent of all anorexics are women, and that of the 5,000 people each year who have their intestines removed to lose weight 80 percent are women.[7]

Anorexia nervosa is clearly, as Paul Garfinkel and David Garner call it, a "multidetermined disorder,"[8] with familial, psychological and possibly biological factors[9] interacting in varying combinations in different individuals to produce a "final common pathway."[10] Over the last several years, with growing evidence, not only of an overall increase in frequency of the disease, but of its higher incidence in certain populations,[11] attention has begun to turn, too, to cultural factors as significant in the pathogenesis of eating disorders. Until very recently, however, the most that one could expect in the way of cultural or social analysis, with very few exceptions,[12] was the (unavoidable) recognition that anorexia is related to the increasing emphasis that fashion has placed on slenderness over the last fifteen years. This, unfortunately, is only to replace one mystery with another, more profound mystery than the first.

What we need to ask is *why* our culture is so obsessed with keeping our bodies slim, tight, and young that when 500 people were asked, in a recent poll, what they feared most in the world, 190 replied "getting fat."[13] So, too, do we need to explore the fact that it is women who are most oppressed by what Kim Chernin calls "the tyranny of slenderness,"[14] and that this particular oppression is a post-1960s, post-feminist phenomenon. In the 1950s, by contrast, with the women once again out of the factories and safely immured in the home, the dominant ideal of female beauty was exemplified by Marilyn Monroe—hardly your androgynous, athletic, adolescent body type. At the peak of her popularity, Monroe was often described as "femininity incarnate," "femaleness embodied"; last term, a student of mine described her as "a cow." Is this merely a change in what size hips, breasts, and waist are considered attractive, or has the very idea of incarnate femaleness come to have a different meaning, different associations, the capacity to stir up different fantasies and images, for the culture of the 1980s? These are the sorts of questions that need to be addressed if we are to achieve a deep understanding of the current epidemic of eating disorders.

The central point of intellectual orientation for this paper is expressed in its subtitle. I take the psychopathologies that develop within a culture, far from being anomalies or aberrations, as characteristic expressions of that culture, as the crystallization, indeed, of much that is wrong with it. For that reason they are important to examine, as keys to cultural self-diagnosis and self-scrutiny. "Every age," says Christopher Lasch, "develops its own peculiar forms of pathology, which express in exaggerated form its underlying character structure."[15] The only thing with which I would disagree in this formulation, with respect to anorexia, is the idea of the expression of an underlying, unitary cultural character structure. Anorexia appears less as the extreme expression of a character structure than as a remarkably overdetermined *symptom* of some of the multifaceted and heterogeneous distresses of our age. Just as it functions in a variety of ways in the psychic economy of the anorexic individual, so a variety of cultural currents or streams converge in anorexia, find their perfect, precise expression in it.

I will call those streams or currents "axes of continuity": *axes* because they meet or converge in the anorexic syndrome; *continuity* refers to the fact that when we place or locate anorexia on these axes, its family resemblances and connections with other phenomena emerge. Some of these axes represent anorexia's *synchronicity* with other contemporary cultural practices and forms—bodybuilding and jogging, for example. Other axes will bring to light *historical* connections: for example, between anorexia and earlier examples of extreme manipulation of the female body, such as corseting, or between anorexia and long-standing traditions and ideologies in Western culture, such as our Greco-Christian traditions of dualism. The three axes that I will discuss in this paper (although they by no means exhaust the possibilities for cultural understanding of anorexia) are *the dualist axis, the control axis, and the gender/power axis.*[16]

Throughout my discussion, it will be assumed that the body, far from being some fundamentally stable, acultural constant to which we must *contrast* all culturally relative and institutional forms, is constantly "in the grip," as Foucault puts it, of cultural practices. Not that this is a matter of cultural *repression* of the instinctual or natural body. Rather, there *is* no "natural" body. Cultural practices, far from exerting their power *against* spontaneous needs, "basic" pleasures or instincts, or "fundamental" structures of body experience, are already and always inscribed, as Foucault has emphasized, "on our bodies and their materiality, their forces, energies, sensations, and pleasures."[17] Our bodies, no less than anything else that is human, are constituted by culture.

The malleability of the body is often but not exclusively a matter of the body-as-experienced (the "lived body," as the phenomenologists put it) rather than the physical body. For example, Foucault points to the medicalization of sexuality in the nineteenth century, which recast sex from a family matter into a private, dark, bodily secret that was appropriately investigated by doctors, psychiatrists, school educators, etc. The constant probing and interrogation, Foucault argues, ferreted out, eroticized, and solidified all sorts of sexual types and perversions, which people then experienced (although they hadn't originally) as defining their bodily possibilities and pleasures. The practice of the medical confessional, in other words, in its constant foraging for sexual secrets and hidden stories, actually *created* new sexual secrets—and eroticized the acts of interrogation and confession, too.[18] Here, social practice changed people's *experience* of their bodies and their possibilities. Similarly, as we shall see, the practice of dieting—of saying "no" to hunger—contributes to the anorexic's increasing sense of hunger as a dangerous eruption, which comes from some alien part of the self, and to a growing intoxication with controlling that eruption.

Although the malleability of the body is frequently a matter of the body-as-experienced, the *physical* body can also be an instrument and medium of power. Foucault gives the classic example of public torture during the ancien régime, through which "the sovereign's power was literally and publicly inscribed on the criminal's body in a manner as controlled, scenic and well-attended as possible."[19] Similarly, the nineteenth-century corset appears, in addition to the actual physical incapacitation it caused the wearer, as a virtual emblem of the power of culture to impose its designs on the female body.

Indeed, women's bodies in general have historically been more vulnerable to extremes in both forms of cultural manipulation of the body. When we later turn to consider some aspects of the history of medicine and fashion, the social manipulation of the female body emerges as an absolutely central strategy in the maintenance of power relations between the sexes over the last hundred years. This historical understanding must deeply affect our understanding of anorexia, and of our contemporary preoccupation with slenderness.

This is *not* to say that I take what I am doing here to be the unearthing of a long-standing male conspiracy against women, or the fixing of blame on *any* particular participants in the play of social forces. In this, I once again follow Foucault, who reminds us that although a perfectly clear logic may characterize historical power relations, with perfectly decipherable aims and objectives, it is nonetheless "often the case that no one was there to have invented" these aims and strategies, either through choice of individuals or through the rational game plan of some presiding "headquarters."[20] This does not mean that individuals do not *consciously* pursue goals that advance their own positions, and advance certain power positions in the process. But it does deny that in doing so, they are directing the overall movement of relations, or engineering their shape. They may not even know what that shape is. Nor does the fact that power relations involve the domination of particular groups—say, prisoners by guards, females by males, amateurs by experts—entail that the dominators are in control of the situation, or that the dominated do not sometimes advance and extend the situation themselves.[21] Nowhere, as we shall see, in this more clear than in the case of anorexia.

THE DUALIST AXIS

I will begin with the most general and attenuated axis of continuity—the one that begins with Plato, winds its way to its most lurid expression in Augustine, and finally becomes metaphysically solidified and "scientized" by Descartes. I am referring, of course, to our dualistic heritage: the view that human existence is bifurcated into two realms or substances—the bodily or material on the one hand, and the mental or spiritual on the other. Despite some fascinating historical variations, which I will not go into here, the basic imagery of dualism has remained fairly constant. Let me briefly describe its central features; they will turn out, as we will see, to constitute the basic body imagery of the anorexic.

First, the body is experienced as alien, as the not-self, the not-me. *It* is "fastened and glued" to me, "nailed" and "riveted" to me, as Plato describes it in the *Phaedo*.[22] For Descartes, it is the brute material envelope for the inner and essential self, the thinking thing—ontologically distinct from it, as mechanical in its operations as a machine, comparable to animal existence.

Second, the body is experienced as *confinement* and *limitation:* a "prison," a "swamp," a "cage," a "fog"—all images that occur in Plato, Descartes, and Augustine—from which the soul, will, or mind struggles to escape. "The enemy ['the madness of lust'] held my will in his power and from it he made a chain and shackled me," says Augustine.[23] In all three, images of the soul being "dragged" by the body are prominent. The body is "heavy, ponderous," as Plato describes it,[24] it exerts a downward pull.

Third, the body is the *enemy*, as Augustine explicitly describes it time and again, and as Plato and Descartes strongly suggest in their diatribes against the body as the source of obscurity and confusion in our thinking. "A source of countless distractions by reason of the mere requirement of food," says Plato, "liable also to diseases which overtake and impede us in the pursuit of truth: it fills us full of loves, and lusts, and fears, and fancies of all kinds, and endless foolery, and in very truth, as men say, takes away from us the power of thinking at all. Whence come wars, and fightings, and factions? Whence but from the body and the lusts of the body."[25]

Finally, whether as an impediment to reason or as the home of the "slimy desires of the flesh" (as Augustine calls them), the body is the locus of all that threatens our attempts at *control*. It overtakes, it overwhelms, it erupts and disrupts. This situation, for the dualist, becomes an incitement to battle the unruly forces of the body, to show it who is boss; for as Plato says, "Nature orders the soul to rule and govern and the body to obey and serve."[26] All three, Plato, Augustine, and, most explicitly, Descartes provide instructions, rules, or models of how to gain control over the body,[27] with the ultimate aim of learning to live without it. That is: to achieve intellectual independence from the lure of its illusions, to become impervious to its distractions, and most importantly, to kill off its desires and hungers. Once control has become the central issue for the soul, these are the only possible terms of victory, as Alan Watts makes clear:

> Willed control brings about a sense of duality in the organism, of consciousness in conflict with appetite. . . . But this mode of control is a peculiar example of the proverb that nothing fails like success. For the more consciousness is individualized by the success of the will, the more everything outside the individual seems to be a threat—including . . . the uncontrolled spontaneity of one's own body. . . . Every success in control therefore demands a further success, so that the process cannot stop short of omnipotence.[28]

Dualism here appears as the offspring, the by-product, of the identification of the self with control, an identification that Watts sees as lying at the center of Christianity's ethic of antisexuality. The attempt to subdue the spontaneities of the body in the interests of control only succeeds in constituting them as more alien, and more powerful, and thus more needful of control. The only way to win this no-win game is to go beyond control, is to kill off the body's spontaneities entirely. That is: to cease to *experience* our hungers and desires.

This is what may anorexics describe as their ultimate goal. "[I want] to reach the point," as one put it, "when I don't need to eat at all" (*ED*, p. 84). Kim Chernin recalls her surprise when, after fasting, her hunger returned: "I realized [then] that my secret goal in dieting must have been the intention to kill off my appetite completely" (*TS*, p. 8).

It is not usually noted, in the popular literature on the subject, that anorexic women are as obsessed with *hunger* as they are with being slim. Far from losing her appetite, the typical anorexic is haunted by her appetite (in much the same way as Augustine describes being haunted by sexual desire) and is in constant dread of being overwhelmed by it. Many describe the dread of hunger—"of not having control, of giving in to biological urge," to "the craving, never satisfied thing"[29] as the "original fear" (as one puts it—*GC*, p. 4), or, as Ellen West describes it, "the real obsession." "I don't think the dread of becoming fat is the real . . . neurosis," she writes, "but the constant desire for food. . . . [H]unger, or the dread of hunger, pursues me all morning. . . . Even when I am full, I am afraid of the coming hour in which hunger will start again." Dread of becoming fat, she interprets, rather than being originary, served as a "brake" to her horror of her own unregulatable, runaway desire for food ("EW," p. 253). Bruch reports that her patients are often terrified by the prospect of taking just one bite of food, lest they never be able to stop (ED, p. 253). (Bulimic anorexics, who binge on enormous quantities of food—sometimes consuming up to 15,000 calories a day [*TO*, p. 6] indeed *cannot* stop.)

For these women, hunger is experienced as an alien invader, marching to the tune of its own seemingly arbitrary whims, disconnected from any normal self-regulating mechanisms. How could it be so connected? (For it is experienced as coming from an area *outside* the self.) One patient of Bruch's says she ate breakfast because "my stomach wanted it" (*ED*, p. 270), expressing here the same sense of alienation from her hungers (and her physical self) that Augustine expresses when he speaks of his "captor," "the law of sin that was in my member."[30] Bruch notes that this "basic delusion," as she calls it, "of not owning the body and its sensations" is a typical symptom of all eating disorders. "These patients act," she says, "as if for them the regulation of food intake was outside [the self]" (*ED*, p. 50). This experience of bodily sensation as foreign, strikingly, is not limited to the experience of hunger. Patients with eating disorders have similar problems in identifying cold, heat, emotions, and anxiety as originating in the self (*ED*, p. 254).

While the body is experienced as alien and outside, the soul or will is described as being trapped or confined in an alien "jail," as one woman puts it.[31] A typical fantasy, as it is for Plato, is of total liberation from the bodily prison: "I wish I could get out of my body entirely and fly!"[32] "Please dear God, help me. . . . I want to get out of my body, I want to get out!"[33] Ellen West, astute as always, sees a central meaning of her self-starvation in this "ideal of being too thin, of being *without a body*" ("EW," p. 251; emphasis added).

Anorexia is not a philosophical attitude; it is a debilitating affliction. Yet quite often a highly conscious and articulate scheme of images and associations—one could go so far as to call it a metaphysics—is presented by these women. The scheme is strikingly Augustinian, with evocations of Plato. This is not to say, of course, that anorexics are followers of Plato or Augustine, but that in the anorexic's "metaphysics" elements are made explicit, historically grounded in Plato and Augustine, that run deep in our culture.[34] As Augustine often speaks of the "two wills" within him,"one the servant of the flesh, the other of the spirit," who "between them tore my soul apart,"[35] so the anorexic describes a "spiritual struggle," a "contest between good and evil" (*Solitaire* p. 109), often conceived explicitly as a battle between mind or will and appetite or body. "I feel myself, quite passively," says West, "the stage on which two hostile forces are mangling each other" ("EW," p. 343). Sometimes there is a more aggressive alliance with mind against body: "When I fail to exercise as often as I prefer, I become guilty that I have let my body 'win' another day from my mind. I can't wait 'til this semester is over. . . . My body is going to pay the price for the lack of work it is currently getting. I can't wait!"[36]

In this battle, thinness represents a triumph of the will over the body, and the thin body (that is, the nonbody) is associated with "absolute purity, hyperintellectuality and transcendence of the flesh. My soul seemed to grow as my body waned; I felt like one of those early Christian saints who starved themselves in the desert sun. I felt invulnerable, clean and hard as the bones etched into my silhouette."[37] Fat (i.e., becoming *all* body) is associated with the "taint" of matter and flesh, "wantonness" (*Solitaire*, p. 109), mental stupor and mental decay.[38] One woman describes how after eating sugar she felt "polluted, disgusting, sticky through the arms, as if something bad had gotten inside."[39] Very often, sexuality is brought into this scheme of associations, and hunger and sexuality are psychically connected. Cherry Boone O'Neill describes a late-night binge, eating scraps of leftovers from the dog's dish:

> I started slowly, relishing the flavor and texture of each marvelous bite. Soon I was ripping the meager remains from the bones, stuffing the meat into my mouth as fast as I could detach it.
>
> [Her boyfriend surprises her, with a look of "total disgust" on his face.]
>
> I had been caught red-handed . . . in an animalistic orgy on the floor, in the dark, alone. Here was the horrid truth for Dan to see. I felt so evil, tainted, pagan. . . . In Dan's mind that day, I had been whoring after food.[40]

A hundred pages earlier, she had described her first romantic involvement in much the same terms: "I felt secretive, deceptive, and . . . tainted by the ongoing relationship" (which never went beyond kisses).[41] Sexuality, similarly, is "an abominable business" to Aimée Liu; for her, staying reed-thin is seen as a way of avoiding sexuality, by becoming "androgynous," as she puts it (*Solitaire*, p. 101). In the same way, Sarah, a patient of Levenkron's, connects her dread of gaining weight with "not wanting to be a 'temptation' to men" (*TO*, p. 122). In Aimée Liu's case, and in Sarah's, the desire to appear unattractive to men is connected to anxiety and guilt over earlier sexual abuse. Whether or not such episodes are common to many cases of anorexia,[42] "the avoidance of any sexual encounter, a shrinking from all bodily contact," according to Bruch, is characteristic.[43]

THE CONTROL AXIS

Having pointed to the axis of continuity from Plato to anorexia, we should feel cautioned against the impulse to regard anorexia as expressing en-

tirely modern attitudes and fears. Disdain for the body, the conception of it
as an alien force and impediment to the soul, is very old in our Greco-
Christian traditions (although it has usually been expressed most forcefully
by male philosophers and theologians rather than adolescent women!).
But although dualism is as old as Plato, in many ways contemporary culture
appears *more* obsessed than previous eras with the control of the unruly
body. Looking now at contemporary American life, a second axis of continuity emerges on which to locate anorexia. I will call it the *control axis.*

The anorexic, typically, experiences her life as well as her hungers as
being out of control. She is torn by conflicting and contradictory expectations and demands, wanting to shine in all areas of student life, confused
about where to place most of her energies, what to focus on, as she develops into an adult. Characteristically, her parents expect a great deal of her
in the way of individual achievement (as well as physical appearance, particularly her father), yet have made most important decisions for her (*GC,*
p. 33). Usually, the anorexic syndrome emerges, *not* as a conscious decision to get as thin as possible, but as the result of her having begun a diet
fairly casually, often at the suggestion of a parent, having succeeded splen-
didly in taking off five or ten pounds, and then having gotten *hooked* on
the intoxicating feeling of accomplishment and control.

Recalling her anorexic days, Aimée Liu recreates her feelings:

> The sense of accomplishment exhilarates me, spurs me to continue on and
> on. It provides a sense of purpose and shapes my life with distractions from
> insecurity. . . . I shall become an expert [at losing weight]. . . . The constant
> downward trend [of the scale] somehow comforts me, gives me visible proof
> that I can exert control. [Solitaire, p. 36]

The diet, she realizes, "is the one sector of my life over which I and I alone
wield total control."[44]

The frustrations of starvation, the rigors of the constant exercise and
physical activity in which anorexics engage, and the pain of the numerous
physical complications of anorexia do not trouble the anorexic; indeed,
her ability to ignore them is further proof to her of her mastery of her
body. "Energy, discipline, my own power will keep me going," says Liu.
"Psychic fuel. I need nothing and no one else, and I will prove it. . . .
Dropping to the floor, I roll. My tailbone crunches on the hard floor. . . . I
feel no pain. I will be master of my own body, if nothing else, I vow"
(*Solitaire,* p. 123). And from one of Bruch's patients: "*You make of your
own body your very own kingdom where you are the tyrant, the absolute
dictator*" (*GC,* p. 65).

Surely we must recognize in this last honest and explicit statement a
central modus operandi for the control of contemporary bourgeois anxiety.
Consider compulsive jogging and marathon running, often despite shin-
splints and other painful injuries, with intense agitation over missed days

or not meeting goals for particular runs. Consider the increasing popularity of triathlon events like the "Iron Man," which appear to have no other purpose than to allow people to find out how far they can push their bodies before collapsing. Consider lawyer Mike Frankfurt, who runs ten miles every morning: " . . . *To run with pain is the essence of life.*"[45] Or the following excerpts from student journals:

> . . . [T]he best times I like to run are under the most unbearable conditions. I love to run in the hottest, most humid and steepest terrain I can find. . . . For me running and the pain associated with it aren't enough to make me stop. I am always trying to overcome it and the biggest failure I can make is to stop running because of pain. Once I ran five of a ten-mile run with a severe leg cramp but wouldn't stop—it would have meant failure.[46]

> When I run I am free. . . . The pleasure is closing off my body—as if the incessant pounding of my legs is so total that the pain ceases to exist. There is no grace, no beauty in the running—there is the jarring reality of sneaker and pavement. Bright pain that shivers and splinters sending its white hot arrows into my stomach, my lung, but it cannot pierce my mind. I am on automatic pilot—there is no remembrance of pain, there is freedom—I am losing myself, peeling out of this heavy flesh. . . . Power surges through me.[47]

None of this is to dispute that the contemporary concern with fitness has nonpathological, nondualist dimensions as well. Particularly for women, who have historically suffered from the ubiquity of rape and abuse, from the culturally instilled conviction of our own helplessness, and from lack of access to facilities and programs for rigorous physical training, the cultivation of strength, agility, and confidence has a clearly positive dimension. Nor are the objective benefits of daily exercise and concern for nutrition in question here. My focus, rather, is on a subjective stance, increasingly more prominent over the last five years, which, although preoccupied with the body and deriving narcissistic enjoyment from its appearance, takes little pleasure in the *experience* of embodiment. Rather, the fundamental identification is with mind (or will), ideals of spiritual perfection, fantasies of absolute control.

Not everyone, of course, for whom physical training is a part of daily routine exhibits such a stance. Here, an examination of the language of female bodybuilders is illustrative. Bodybuilding is particularly interesting because on the surface it appears to have the very opposite structure from anorexia: The bodybuilder is, after all, building the body *up*, not whittling it down. Bodybuilding develops strength. We imagine the bodybuilder as someone who is proud, confident, and, perhaps most of all, conscious of and accepting of her physicality. This, is indeed, how some female bodybuilders experience themselves:

> I feel. . . . tranquil and stronger [says Lydia Cheng]. Working out creates a high everywhere in my body. I feel the heat. I feel the muscles rise, I see them

blow out, flushed with lots of blood. . . . My whole body is sweating, and there's few things I love more than working up a good sweat. That's when I really feel like a woman.[48]

Yet a sense of joy in the body as active and alive is *not* the most prominent theme among the women interviewed by Trix Rosen in *Strong and Sexy*. Many of them, rather, talk about their bodies in ways that are disquietingly resonant with typical anorexic themes.

There is the same emphasis on will, purity, and perfection: "I've learned to be a stronger person with a more powerful will . . . pure concentration, energy and spirit." "I want to be as physically perfect as possible." "Body-building suits the perfectionist in me." "My goal is to have muscular perfection."[49] Compulsive exercisers—who Dinitia Smith, in an article for *New York*, calls "The New Puritans"—speak in similar terms: Kathy Krauch, a New York art director who bikes twelve miles a day and swims two and a half, says she is engaged in "a quest for perfection." Such people, Smith emphasizes, care little about their health: "They pursue self-denial as an end in itself, out of an almost mystical belief in the purity it confers."[50]

Among bodybuilders, as for anorexics, there are the same unnerving conceptualizations of the body as alien, the not-self:

I'm constantly amazed by my muscles. The first thing I do when I wake up in the morning is look down at my "abs" and flex my legs to see if the "cuts" are there. . . . My legs have always been my most stubborn part, and I want them to develop so badly. Every day I can see things happening to them. . . . I don't flaunt my muscles as much as I thought I would. I feel differently about them; they are my product and I protect them by wearing sweaters to keep them warm.[51]

Most strikingly, there is the same emphasis on *control*, on feeling one's life to be fundamentally out of control, and on the feeling of accomplishment derived from total mastery of the body. That sense of mastery, like the anorexic's, appears derived from two sources. First, there is the reassurance that one can overcome all physical obstacles, push oneself to any extremes in pursuit of one's goals (which, as we have seen, is a characteristic motivation of compulsive runners, as well). Second, and most dramatic (it is spoken of time and again by female bodybuilders), is the thrill of being in total charge of the shape of one's body. "Create a masterpiece," says *Fit*. "Sculpt you body contours into a work of art." As for the anorexic—who literally cannot *see* her body as other than her inner reality dictates and who is relentlessly driven by an ideal image of ascetic slenderness—so too a purely mental conception comes to have dominance over the bodybuilder's life: "You visualize what you want to look like . . . and then create the form." "The challenge presents itself; to rearrange things."[52] "It's up to you to do the chiseling; you become the master sculptress." "What a fantasy, for your body to be changing! . . . I keep a picture in my mind as I work out of what I want to look like and what's happened to me already."[53] The technology of dictating to nature one's own chosen design for the body is at the center of the bodybuilder's mania, as it is for the anorexic.

The sense of security derived from the attainment of this goal appears, first of all, as the pleasure of control and independence. "Nowadays," says Michael Sacks, associate professor of psychiatry at Cornell Medical College, "people no longer feel they can control events outside themselves— how well they do in their jobs or in their personal relationships, for example—but they can control the food they eat and how far they can run. Abstinence, tests of endurance, are ways of proving their self-sufficiency."[54] In a culture, moreover, in which our continued survival is often at the mercy of "specialists," machines, and sophisticated technology, the body takes on a special sort of vulnerability and dependency. We may live longer than ever before, but the circumstances surrounding illness and death may often be perceived as more alien, inscrutable, and arbitrary than ever before.

Our contemporary body fetishism, however, expresses more than a fantasy of self-mastery in an increasingly unmanageable culture. It also reflects our alliance *with* culture against all reminders of the inevitable decay and death of the body. "Everybody wants to live forever" is the refrain from the theme song of *Pumping Iron*. The most youth-worshipping of popular television shows, *Fame*, opens with a song that begins, "I want to live forever." And it is striking that although the anorexic may come very close to death (and 15% do indeed die), the dominant experience throughout the illness is of *invulnerability*.

The dream of immortality is, of course, nothing new. But what is unique to modernity is that the defeat of death has become a scientific fantasy rather than a philosophical or religious mythology. We no longer dream of eternal union with the gods; we build devices that can keep us alive indefinitely, and we work on keeping our bodies as smooth and muscular and elastic at forty as they were at eighteen. We even entertain dreams of halting the aging process completely: "Old age," according to Durk Pearson and Sandy Shaw, authors of the popular *Life Extension*, "is an unpleasant and unattractive affliction."[55] The megavitamin regime they prescribe is able, they claim, to prevent and even to *reverse* the mechanisms of aging.

Finally, it may be that in cultures characterized by gross excesses in consumption, the "will to conquer and subdue the body" (as Chernin calls it—*TS*, p. 47) expresses an aesthetic or moral rebellion. Anorexics initially came from affluent families, and the current craze for long-distance running and fasting is largely a phenomenon of young, upwardly mobile professionals (Dinitia Smith calls it "Deprivation Chic"). To those who are starving *against* their wills, of course, starvation cannot function as an expression of the power of will. At the same time, we should caution against viewing anorexia as a trendy illness of the elite. Rather, powerlessness is its most outstanding feature.

THE GENDER/POWER AXIS

Ninety percent of all anorexics are women. We do not need, of course, to know that particular statistic to realize that the contemporary "tyranny of slenderness" is far from gender neutral. Women are more obsessed with their bodies than men, less satisfied with them,[56] and permitted less latitude with them by themselves, by men, and by the culture. In a recent *Glamour* poll of 33,000 women, 75% said that they thought they were "too fat." Yet by Metropolitan Life Insurance tables—themselves notoriously affected by cultural standards—only 25% of these women were heavier than the specified standards, and a full 30% were *below*.[57] The anorexic's distorted image of her body—her inability to see it as anything but "too fat"—while more extreme, is not radically discontinuous from fairly common female misperceptions.

Consider, too, actors like Nick Nolte and William Hurt, who are permitted a certain amount of softening, of thickening about the waist, while still retaining romantic lead status. Individual style, wit, the projection of intelligence, experience, and effectiveness still go a long way for men, even in our fitness-obsessed culture. But no female can achieve the status of romantic or sexual ideal without the appropriate *body*. That body, if we use television commercials as a gauge, has gotten steadily leaner over the past ten years.[58] What used to be acknowledged as extremes required of high-fashion models is now the dominant image that beckons to high school and college women. Over and over, extremely slender women students complain of hating their thighs or their stomachs (the anorexic's most dreaded danger spot); often, they express concern and anger over frequent teasing by their boyfriends: Janey, a former student, is 5'10" and weighs 132 pounds. Yet her boyfriend calls her "Fatso" and "Big Butt" and insists she should be 110 pounds because "that's what Brooke Shields weighs." He calls this "constructive criticism," and seems to experience extreme anxiety over the possibility of her gaining any weight: "I can tell it bothers her yet I still continue to badger her about it. I guess that I think that if I continue to remind her things will change faster. . . . "[59] This sort of relationship—within which the woman's weight has become a focal issue—is not at all atypical, as I've discovered from student journals and papers.

Hilde Bruch reports that many anorexics talk of having a "ghost" inside them or surrounding them, "a dictator who dominates me," as one woman describes it; "a little man who objects when I eat" is the description given by another (*GC*, p. 58). The little ghost, the dictator, the "other self " (as he is often described) is always male, reports Bruch. The anorexic's *other* self—the self of the uncontrollable appetites, the impurities and taints, the flabby will and tendency to mental torpor—is the body, as we have seen. But it is also (and here the anorexic's associations are surely in the mainstream of Western culture) the *female* self. These two selves are perceived as at constant war. But it is clear that it is the male side—with its associated values of greater spirituality, higher intellectuality, strength of will—being expressed and developed in the anorexic syndrome.[60]

What is the meaning of these gender associations in the anorexic? I propose that there are two levels of meaning. One has to do with fear and disdain for traditional female *roles* and social limitations. The other has to do, more profoundly, with a deep fear of "The Female," with all its more nightmarish archetypal associations: voracious hungers and sexual insatiability. Let us examine each of these levels in turn.

Adolescent anorexics express characteristic fears about growing up to be mature, sexually developed, potentially reproductive women. "I have a deep fear," says one, "of having a womanly body, round and fully developed. I want to be tight and muscular and thin."[61] If only she could stay thin, says another, "I would never have to deal with having a woman's body; like Peter Pan I could stay a child forever."[62] The choice of Peter Pan is telling here—what she means is, stay a *boy* forever. And indeed, as Bruch reports, many anorexics, when children, dreamt and fantasized about growing up to be boys.[63] Some are quite conscious of playing out this fantasy through their anorexia: Adrienne, one of Levenkron's patients, was extremely proud of the growth of facial and body hair that often accompanies anorexia, and especially proud of her "skinny, hairy arms" (*TO*, p. 82). Many patients report, too, that their fathers had wanted a boy, were disappointed to get "less than" that,[64] or had emotionally rebuffed their daughters when they began to develop sexually (*TO*, pp. 103, 45).

In a characteristic scenario, anorexia will develop just at the beginning of puberty. Normal body changes are experienced by the anorexic, not surprisingly, as the takeover of the body by disgusting, womanish fat. "I grab my breasts," says Aimée Liu, "pinching them until they hurt. If only I could eliminate them, cut them off if need be, to become as flat-chested as a child again" (*Solitaire*, p. 79). She is exultant when her periods stop (as they do in *all* cases of anorexia) (*GC*, p. 65). The disgust with menstruation is typical: "I saw a picture at a feminist art gallery," says another woman; "there was a woman with long red yarn coming out of her, like she was menstruating. . . . I got that *feeling*—in that part of my body that I have trouble with . . . my stomach, my thighs, my pelvis. That revolted feeling."[65]

Many anorexics appear to experience anxiety over falling into the lifestyle they associate with their mothers. It is a prominent theme in Aimée Liu's *Solitaire*. One woman describes her feeling that she is "full of my mother . . . she is in me even if she isn't there" in nearly the same breath as she complains of her continuous fear of being "not human . . . of ceasing to exist" (*GC*, p. 12). And Ellen West, nearly a century earlier, had quite explicitly equated becoming fat with the inevitable (for a woman of her time) confinements of domestic life and the domestic stupor she associates with it:

> Dread is driving me mad . . . the consciousness that ultimately I will lose everything; all courage, all rebelliousness, all drive for doing; that it—my little world—will make me flabby, flabby, and fainthearted and beggarly. . . . ["EW," p. 243]

Several of my students with eating disorders reported that their anorexia had developed after their families had dissuaded or forbidden them from embarking on a traditionally male career.

Here anorexia finds a true sister-phenomenon in the epidemic of female invalidism and "hysteria" that swept through the middle and upper middle classes in the second half of the nineteenth century. It was a time that, in many ways, was very like our own, especially in the conflicting demands that women were newly confronting: the opening up of new possibilities, the continuing grip of the old expectations. On the one hand, the old preindustrial order, with the father at the head of a self-contained family production unit, had given way to the dictatorship of the market, opening up new, nondomestic opportunities for working women; on the other, it also turned many of the most valued "female" skills—textile and garment manufacture, food processing—out of the home and over to the factory system.[66] In the new machine economy, the lives of middle-class women were far emptier than they had been before.

It was an era, too, that had been witnessing the first major feminist wave: In 1840, the World Anti-Slavery Conference had been held, at which the first feminists spoke loudly and long on the connections between the abolition of slavery and women's rights. 1848 saw the Seneca Falls Convention. In 1869, John Stuart Mill published his landmark work, "On the Subjection of Women." And in 1889, the Pankhursts formed the Women's Franchise League. But it was an era, too (and not unrelatedly, as I shall argue later) when the prevailing ideal of femininity was the delicate, affluent lady, unequipped for anything but the most sheltered domestic life, totally dependent on her prosperous husband, providing a peaceful and comfortable haven for him each day after his return from the labors of the public sphere.[67] In a now famous 1883 letter, Freud, criticizing John Stuart Mill, writes:

> It really is a still-born thought to send women into the struggle for existence exactly as men. If, for instance, I imagine my gentle sweet girl as a competitor it would only end in my telling her, as I did seventeen months ago, that I am fond of her and that I implore her to withdraw from the strife into the calm uncompetitive activity of my home.[68]

This is exactly what male doctors *did* do when women began falling ill, complaining of acute depression, severe headaches, weakness, nervousness, and self-doubt.[69] Among them were such noted feminists and social activists as Charlotte Perkins Gilman, Jane Addams, Elizabeth Cady Stanton, Margaret Sanger, leading English abolitionist Josephine Butler, and German suffragist Hedwig Dohm. "I was weary of myself and sick of asking what I am and what I ought to be," recalls Gilman, who later went on to write a fictional account of her mental breakdown in the chilling novella *The Yellow Wallpaper.* Her doctor, the famous female specialist S. Weir Mitchell, instructed her, as Gilman recalls, to "live as domestic a life as possible. Have your child with you all the time. . . . Lie down an hour every day after each meal. Have but two hours intellectual life a day. And never touch pen, brush or pencil as long as you live."[70]

Freud, who favorably reviewed Mitchell's 1887 book and who advised that psychotherapy for hysterical patients be combined with Mitchell's rest cure ("to avoid new psychical impressions"),[71] was as blind as Mitchell to the contribution that isolation, boredom, and intellectual frustration made in the etiology of hysteria. Nearly all of the subjects in *Studies in Hysteria* (as well as the later "Dora") are acknowledged to be unusually intelligent, creative, energetic, independent, and often highly educated. Freud even comments, criticizing Janet's notion that hysterics were "physically insufficient," on the characteristic coexistence of hysteria with "gifts of the richest and most original kind."[72] Yet Freud never makes the connection (which Breuer had begun to develop)[73] between the monotonous domestic lives these women were expected to lead after their schooling was completed, and the emergence of compulsive daydreaming, hallucinations, dissociations, and hysterical conversions.

Charlotte Perkins Gilman does. In *The Yellow Wallpaper* she describes how a prescribed regime of isolation and enforced domesticity eventuates, in her fictional heroine, in the development of a full-blown hysterical symptom, madness, and collapse. The symptom, the hallucination that there is a woman trapped in the wallpaper of her bedroom, struggling to get out, is at once both a perfectly articulated expression of protest and a completely debilitating idée fixe that allows the woman character no distance on her situation, no freedom of thought, no chance of making any progress in leading the kind of active, creative life her body and soul crave.

So too for the anorexic. It is indeed essential to recognize in this illness a dimension of protest against the limitations of the ideal of female domesticity (the "feminine mystique," as Betty Friedan called it) that reigned in America throughout the 1950s and early 1960s—the era when most of their mothers were starting homes and families. This was, we should recall, the era of the return to "normalcy" following World War II, an era during which women had been fired en masse from the jobs they had held during the war and shamelessly propaganized back into the full-time job of wife and mother. It was an era, too, when the "fuller figure," as Jane Russell now calls it, came into fashion once more, a period of "mammary madness"[74] (or "resurgent Victorianism," as Lois Banner calls it),[75] that glamorized the voluptuous, large-breasted woman. This remained the prevailing fashion tyranny until the late 1960s and early 1970s.

But we must recognize that the anorexic's "protest," like that of the classical hysterical symptom, is written on the bodies of anorexic women, and *not* embraced as a conscious politics, nor, indeed, does it reflect any social or political understanding at all. Moreover, the symptoms themselves function to preclude the emergence of such an understanding: the idée fixe—staying thin—becomes at its farthest extreme so powerful as to render any other ideas or lifeprojects meaningless. Liu describes it as "all-encompassing" (*Solitaire*, p. 141). West writes that "I felt all inner development was ceasing, that all becoming and growing were being choked, because a single idea was filling my entire soul" ("EW," p. 257).

Paradoxically—and often tragically—these pathologies of female "protest" (and we must include agoraphobia here, as well as hysteria and anorexia)[76] actually function as if in collusion with the cultural conditions that produced them. The same is true for more moderate expressions of the contemporary female obsession with slenderness. Women may feel themselves deeply attracted by the aura of freedom and independence suggested by the boyish body ideal of today. Yet, each hour, each minute that is spent in anxious pursuit of that ideal (for it does not come "naturally" to most mature women) is *in fact* time and energy diverted from inner development and social achievement. As a feminist protest, the obsession with slenderness is hopelessly counterproductive.

It is important to recognize, too, that the anorexic is terrified and repelled, not only by the traditional female domestic role—which she associates with mental lassitude and weakness—but by a certain archetypal image of the female: as hungering, voracious, all-needing, and all-wanting. It is this image that shapes and permeates her experience of her own hunger for food as insatiable and out-of-control, which makes her feel that if she takes just one bite, she won't be able to stop.

Let's explore this image. Let's break the tie with food and look at the metaphor: Hungering. Voracious. Extravagantly and excessively needful. Without restraint. Always wanting. Always wanting too much affection, reassurance, emotional and sexual contact and attention. This is how many women frequently experience themselves, and, indeed, how many men experience women. "Please, please God, keep me from telephoning him," prays the heroine in Dorothy Parker's classic "The Telephone Call," experiencing her need for reassurance and contact as being as out of control and degrading as the anorexic experiences her desire for food. The male counterpart to this is found in someone like Paul Morel in Lawrence's *Sons and Lovers*: "Can you never like things without clutching them as if you wanted to pull the heart out of them?" he accuses Miriam as she fondles a flower. "Why don't you have a bit more restraint, or reserve, or something. . . . You're always begging things to love you, as if you were a beggar for love. Even the flowers, you have to fawn on them."[77] How much psychic authenticity do these images carry in 1980s America? One woman in my class provided a stunning insight into the connection between her perception of herself and the anxiety of the compulsive dieter: "You know," she said, "the anorexic is always convinced she is taking up too much space, eating too much, wanting food too much. I've never felt that way, but I've often felt that I was *too much*—too much emotion, too much need, too loud and demanding, too much *there*, if you know what I mean."[78]

The most extreme cultural expressions of the fear of woman-as-too-much—which almost always revolve around her sexuality—are strikingly full of eating and hungering metaphors. "Of woman's unnatural, *insatiable* lust, what country, what village doth not complain?" queries Burton in *The Anatomy of Melancholy*. "You are the true hiennas," says Walter Charleton, "that allure us with the fairness of your skins, and when folly hath brought us within your reach, you leap upon us and *devour* us."[79]

The mythology/ideology of the devouring, insatiable female (which, as we have seen, is the internalized image the anorexic has of her female self) tends historically to wax and wane. But not without rhyme or reason. In periods of gross environmental and social crisis, such as characterized the period of the witch-hunts in the fifteenth and sixteenth centuries, it appears to flourish.[80] "All witchcraft comes from carnal lust, which is in women *insatiable*," say Kramer and Sprenger, authors of the official witch-hunters' handbook, *Malleus Malificarum*. For the sake of fulfilling the "*mouth* of the womb . . . [women] consort even with the devil."[81]

Anxiety over women's uncontrollable hungers appears to peak, as well, during periods when women are becoming independent and asserting themselves politically and socially. The second half of the nineteenth century saw a virtual "flood" (as Peter Gay calls it) of artistic and literary images of the dark, dangerous, and evil female: "sharp-teethed, devouring" Sphinxes, Salomés, and Delilahs, "biting, tearing, murderous women." "No century," claims Gay, "depicted woman as vampire, as castrator, as killer, so consistently, so programmatically, and so nakedly as the nineteenth."[82] No century, too, was as obsessed with female sexuality and its medical control. Treatment for excessive "sexual excitement" and masturbation included placing leeches on the womb (*TS*, p. 38), clitoridectomy, and removing of the ovaries (also recommended for "troublesomeness, eating like a ploughman, erotic tendencies, persecution mania, and simple 'cussedness' ").[83]

It is in the second half of the nineteenth century, too, despite a flurry of efforts by feminists and health reformers, that the stylized "S-curve," which required a tighter corset than ever before, comes into fashion.[84] "While the suffragettes were forcefully propelling all women toward legal and political emancipation," says Amaury deRiencourt, "fashion and custom imprisoned her physically as she had never been before."[85] Described by Thorstein Veblen as a "mutilation, undergone for the purpose of lowering the subject's vitality and rendering her permanently and obviously unfit for work,"[86] the corset indeed did just that. In it, a woman could barely sit or stoop, was unable to move her feet more than six inches at a time, and had difficulty keeping herself from regular fainting fits. The connection was often drawn in popular magazines between enduring the tight corset and the exercise of self-restraint and control. The corset is "an ever present monitor," says one 1878 advertisement, "of a well-disciplined mind and well-regulated feelings."[87] Today, of course, we diet to achieve such control.

It is important to emphasize that, despite bizarre and grotesque examples of gross physical manipulation and external control (clitoridectomy, Chinese foot binding, the removal of bones from the rib cage in order to fit into the tight corset), such control plays a relatively minor role in the maintenance of gender power relations. For every historical image of the dangerous, aggressive woman, there is a corresponding fantasy—an ideal femininity, from which all threatening elements have been purged—that women have mutilated themselves *internally* to attain. In the Victorian era, at the same time as operations were being performed to control female sexuality, William Acton, Krafft-Ebing, and others were proclaiming the official scientific doctrine that woman are naturally passive and "not very much troubled with sexual feelings of any kind."[88] Corresponding to this male medical fantasy was the popular artistic and moral theme of woman-as-ministering-angel: sweet, gentle, domestic, without intensity or personal ambition of any sort.[89] Peter Gay suggests, correctly, that these ideals must be understood as a reaction-formation to the era's "pervasive sense of manhood in danger,"[90] and argues that few women actually fit the "insipid goody" (as Kate Millett calls it)[91] image. What Gay forgets, however, is that most women *tried*—lower classes as well as middle were affected by the "tenacious and all-pervasive" ideal of the perfect lady[92]—and that many women did manage to achieve depressingly effective results.

On the gender/power axis the female body appears, then, as the unknowing medium of the historical ebbs and flows of the fear of woman-as-too-much. That, as we have seen, is how the anorexic experiences her female, bodily self: as voracious, wanton, needful of forceful control by her male will. Living in the tide of cultural backlash against the second major feminist wave, she is not alone in these images. Christopher Lasch, in *The Culture of Narcissism*, speaks of what he describes as "the apparently aggressive overtures of sexually liberated women" that "convey to many males the same message—that women are *voracious, insatiable*," and call up "early fantasies of a possessive, suffocating, *devouring* and castrating mother" (emphasis added).[93]

Our contemporary beauty ideals, on the other hand, seem purged, as Kim Chernin puts it, "of the power to conjure up memories of the past, of all that could remind us of a woman's mysterious power" (*TS*, p. 148). The ideal, rather, is an "image of a woman in which she is not yet a woman":

Darryl Hannah as the lanky, newborn mermaid in *Splash*; Lori Singer (appearing virtually anorexic) as the reckless, hyper-kinetic heroine of *Footloose*; The Charlie Girl; "Cheryl Tiegs in shorts, Margaux Hemingway with her hair wet, Brooke Shields naked on an island";[94] the dozens of teen-age women who appear in Coke commercials, in jeans commercials, in chewing gum commercials.

The images suggest amused detachment, casual playfulness, flirtatiousness without demand, and lightness of touch. A refusal to take sex, death, or politics too deadly seriously. A delightfully unconscious relationship to her body. The twentieth century has seen this sort of feminine ideal before, of course: When, in the 1920s, young women began to flatten their breasts, suck in their stomachs, bob their hair, and show off long, colt-like legs, they believed they were pursuing a new freedom and daring that demanded a carefree, boyish style.[95] If the traditional female hourglass suggested anything, it was confinement and immobility. Yet the flapper's freedom, as Mary McCarthy's and Dorothy Parker's short stories brilliantly reveal, was largely an illusion—as any obsessively cultivated sexual style must inevitably be. Although today's images may suggest androgynous independence, we need only consider who is on the receiving end of the imagery in order to confront the pitiful paradox involved.

Watching the commercials are thousands of anxiety-ridden women and adolescents (some of whom are likely the very ones appearing in the commercials) with anything *but* an unconscious relation to their bodies. They are involved in an absolutely contradictory state of affairs, a totally no-win game: caring desperately, passionately, obsessively about attaining an ideal of coolness, effortless confidence, and casual freedom. Watching the commercials is a little girl, perhaps ten years old, who I saw in Central Park, gazing raptly at her father, bursting with pride: "Daddy, guess what? I lost two pounds!" And watching the commercials is the anorexic, who associates her relentless pursuit of thinness with power and control, but who in fact destroys her health and imprisons her imagination. She is surely the most startling and stark illustration of how cavalier power relations are with respect to the motivations and goals of individuals, yet how deeply they are etched on our bodies, and how well our bodies serve them.

N O T E S

This essay, like all intellectual projects, has been a collaborative enterprise. All of the many students, friends, and colleagues who have discussed its ideas with me, suggested articles and resources, commented on earlier versions, shared personal experiences, or allowed me to glimpse their own fears and angers have collaborated with me on this project, have made its development possible. In particular, I owe a large debt to the students of my metaphysics and "Gender, Culture, and Experience" classes, whose articulate and honest journals I have drawn on in these pages, and whose work often pushed forward my own. Here, I would single out Christy Ferguson, Vivian Conger, and Nancy Monaghan, whose research on Victorian and early twentieth-century ideals of femininity contributed insights and information that proved significant to this paper. Although many people have commented on earlier drafts, Lynne Arnault, Mario Moussa, and Nancy Fraser were especially helpful in providing systematic and penetrating criticisms and editorial suggestions for the final version.

Since this essay first appeared in 1985, there has been an explosion of published material, media attention, and clinical study devoted to eating disorders. At the same time, my own thinking on the subject has evolved, as the essay itself has evolved into further essays and ultimately into a book, *Food, Fashion and Power*, currently in progress. I have not incorporated new statistics or studies into this piece, although many of them strongly bear out observations and interpretations offered here. Nor have I attempted to revise the essay in light of changes in my own perspective. Instead, I have chosen to let the essay stand in its original form, as an initial mapping of a complex, culturally live domain, about which we are learning new things all the time.

1. Jules Henry, *Culture Against Man* (New York: Knopf, 1963).

2. Throughout this paper, the term "anorexia" will be used to designate a general class of eating disorders within which intake-restricting (or abstinent) anorexia and bulimia/anorexia (characterized by alternating bouts of gorging and starving and/or gorging and vomiting) are distinct subtypes (see Hilde Bruch, *The Golden Cage: The Enigma of Anorexia Nervosa* [New York: Vintage, 1979], p. 10 [cited parenthetically in the text as *GC*]; Steven Levenkron, *Treating and Overcoming Anorexia Nervosa* [New York: Warner Books, 1982], p. 6 [cited parenthetically in the text as *TO*]; R.L. Palmer, *Anorexia Nervosa* [Middlesex, U.K.: Penguin, 1980], pp. 14, 23–24; Paul Garfinkel and David Garner, *Anorexia Nervosa: A Multidimensional Perspective* [New York: Brunner/Mazel, 1982], p. 4). Although there are striking and fascinating differences in personality traits and personal history characteristic of these two subgroups of anorexics (see Levenkron, pp. 65–66; Garfinkel and Garner, pp. 40–55), I will concentrate on those images, concerns, and attitudes largely common to both. Where a difference seems significant in terms of the themes of this essay, I will indicate the relevant difference in a note rather than overcomplicate the main argument of the text. This procedure is not to be taken as belittling the importance of these differences in the understanding and treatment of eating disorders. Rather, separate and extended discussion of such differences will appear elsewhere in my work.

3. Although throughout history there have been scattered references to patients who sound as though they may have been suffering from self-starvation, the first medical description of anorexia as a discrete syndrome was made by W. W. Gull in an 1868 address at Oxford. Six years later, Gull began to use the term "anorexia nervosa"; at the same time, E. D. Lesegue independently described the disorder (Garfinkel and Garner, pp. 58–59). Although cases have been recorded ever since then, researchers are in almost universal agreement that the evidence suggest a striking increase in frequency over the last twenty years (see Garfinkel and Garner, p. 100, for an exhaustive list of studies suggestive of this; also Bruch, p. vii; Levenkron, p. xvi). So startling is the increase in rate of occurrence, and so rare was it formerly, that Bruch, in 1978, suggests it can in a sense be regarded as "a new disease."

4. Ludwig Binswanger, "The Case of Ellen West," in *Existence*, ed. Rollo May (New York: Simon and Schuster, 1958), p. 288 (cited parenthetically in the text as

"EW"). Hilde Bruch, *Eating Disorders* (New York: Basic Books, 1973), p. 4 (cited parenthetically in the text as *ED*).

5. Susan Squire, "Is the Binge-Purge Cycle Catching?" *Ms.*, October 1983; *Anorexia/Bulimia Support*, Syracuse, New York.

6. Dinitia Smith, "The New Puritans," *New York*, June 11, 1984, p. 28.

7. Kim Chernin, *The Obsession: Reflections on the Tyranny of Slenderness* (New York: Harper and Row, 1981), pp. 63, 62 (cited parenthetically in the text as *TS*).

8. Garfinkel and Garner. *Anorexia Nervosa*, pp. 186–213.

9. Anorexics characteristically suffer from a number of physiological disturbances, including amenorrhea (cessation of menstruation) and abnormal hypothalamic function (see Garfinkel and Garner, pp. 58–89, for an extensive discussion of these and other physiological disorders associated with anorexia; also, Eugene Garfield, "Anorexia Nervosa: The Enigma of Self-Starvation," *Current Contents*, August 6, 1984, pp. 8–9). Researchers are divided, with arguments on both sides, as to whether hypothalamic dysfunction may be a primary cause of the disease, or whether these characteristic neuroendocrine disorders are the result of weight loss, caloric deprivation, and emotional stress. The same debate rages over abnormal vasopresin levels discovered in anorexics, recently touted in tabloids all over the United States as the "explanation" of anorexia and key to its cure. Apart from such debates concerning a possible biochemical predisposition to anorexia, research continues, as well, exploring the role of biochemistry as possibly contributing to the self-perpetuating nature of the disease, and the relation of the physiological effects of starvation to particular experiential symptoms, such as the anorexic's preoccupation with food (see Bruch, *The Golden Cage*, pp. 7–12; Garfinkel and Garner, *Anorexia Nervosa*, pp. 10-14).

10. Garfinkel and Garner, *Anorexia Nervosa*, p. 189.

11. Initially, anorexia was found to predominate among upper-class white families. There is, however, widespread evidence that this is now rapidly changing (as we might expect; no one in America is immune to the power of popular imagery). The disorder has become more equally distributed in recent years, touching populations (e.g., blacks and East Indians) previously unaffected, and all socioeconomic levels (Garfinkel and Garner, *Anorexia Nervosa*, pp. 102-3). There remains, however, the overwhelming disproportion of women to men (ibid., pp. 112–13).

12. Kim Chernin's book *The Obsession*, whose remarkable insights inspired my interest in anorexia, was the first outstanding exception to the lack of cultural understanding of eating disorders. Since the writing of this essay, Chernin's second book on eating disorders, *The Hungry Self* (New York: Harper and Row, 1985) and Susie Ohrbach's *Hunger Strike* (New York: W. W. Norton, 1986) have appeared. Both contribute significantly to our cultural understanding of anorexia.

13. Chernin, *The Obsession*, pp. 36–37. My use of the term "our culture" may seem overly homogenizing here, disrespectful of differences among ethnic groups, socioeconomic groups, subcultures within American society, etc. It must be stressed here that I am discussing ideology and images whose power is *precisely* the power to homogenize culture. Even in pre-mass media cultures, we see this phenomenon: the nineteenth-century ideal of the "perfect lady" tyrannized even those classes who couldn't afford to realize it. With television, of course, a massive deployment of images becomes possible, and there is no escape from the mass shaping of our fantasy lives. Although they may start among the wealthy and elite ("A woman can never be too rich or too thin"), media-promoted ideals of femininity and masculinity quickly and perniciously "trickle down" to everyone who owns a TV or can afford a junk magazine or is aware of billboards. Recent changes in the incidence of anorexia among lower-income groups (see note 11) bear this out.

14. Until very recently, this dimension was largely ignored or underemphasized, with a very few notable exceptions. Kim Chernin and Susie Ohrbach (*Fat Is a Femi-*

nist Issue) were ground-breakers in exploring the connections between eating disorders and images and ideals of femininity. Robert Seidenberg and Karen DeCrow (*Women Who Marry Houses: Panic and Protest in Agoraphobia*) provide a very brief, interesting discussion, the value of which is marred, however, by some fundamental errors concerning the typical pattern of the disorder. Hilde Bruch touches these issues, but only barely, in her otherwise excellent work on eating disorders. Lately, however, there has been a veritable explosion of creative work, both theoretical and therapeutic, confronting the connections between eating disorders and the situation of women. Shortly after this paper was completed, I attended the Third Annual Conference of the Center for the Study of Anorexia and Bulimia (New York, November 17–18, 1984), which was devoted entirely to the theme of "The Psychology of Women and the Psychotherapy of Eating Disorders." Institutes such as The Women's Therapy Institute in New York have developed techniques of treatment that are specifically grounded in a feminist reconstruction of object-relations theory (see Luise Eichenbaum and Susie Ohrbach, *Understanding Women: A Feminist Psychoanalytic Approach* [New York: Basic Books, 1983]). And new perspectives are emerging all the time, from ideological quarters as diverse as experimental psychology and Jungian analysis (see, for example, Angelyn Spignesi, *Starving Women* [Dallas, Tex: Spring Publications, 1983]).

15. Christopher Lasch, *The Culture of Narcissism* (New York: Warner Books, 1979), p. 88.

16. I choose these three primarily because they are where my exploration of the imagery, language, and metaphor produced by anorexic women led me. Delivering earlier versions of this essay at colleges and conferences, I discovered that one of the commonest responses of members of the audiences was the proffering of further axes; the paper presented itself less as a statement about the ultimate "meaning" or causes of a phenomenon than as an invitation to continue my "unpacking" of anorexia as a crystallizing formation. Yet the particular axes chosen have more than a purely autobiographical rationale. The dualist axis serves to identify and articulate the basic body imagery of anorexia. The control axis is an exploration, but focuses on the question "Why Now?" The gender/power axis continues this exploration, but focuses on the question "Why Women?" The sequence of axes takes us from the most general, most historically diffuse structure of continuity—the dualist experience of self—to ever narrower, more specified "arenas" of comparison and connection. At first, the connections are made without regard to historical context, drawing on diverse historical sources to exploit their familiar coherence in an effort to sculpt the "shape" of the anorexic experience. In this section, too, I want to suggest that the Greco-Christian tradition provides a particularly fertile soil for the development of anorexia. Then, I turn to the much more specific context of American fads and fantasies in the 1980s, considering the contemporary scene largely in terms of popular culture (and therefore through the "fiction" of homogeneity), without regard for gender difference. In this section, the connections drawn point to a historical experience of self common to both men and women. Finally, my focus shifts to consider not what connects anorexia to other general cultural phenomena, but what presents itself as a rupture from them, and what forces us to confront how ultimately opaque the current epidemic of eating disorders remains unless it is linked to the particular situation of women.

The reader will notice that the axes are linked thematically as well as through their convergence in anorexia: e.g., the obsession with control is linked with dualism, and the gender/power dynamics discussed implicitly deal with the issue of control (of the feminine) as well. Obviously the notion of a "crystallizing formation" requires further spelling out: e.g., more precise articulation of the relation of cultural axes to each other and elaboration of general principles for the study of culture suggested by this sort of analysis. I have chosen not to undertake this project within this essay, however, but to reserve it for a more extended treatment of the relationship between psychopathology and culture. The inevitable complexity of such a theoretical discussion would divert from the concrete analysis that is the focus of the essay.

17. Michael Foucault, *The History of Sexuality*, vol. 1 (New York: Vintage Books, 1980), p. 155.

18. Ibid., pp. 47–48.

19. Hubert L. Dreyfus and Paul Rabinow, *Michael Foucault: Beyond Structuralism and Hermeneutics* (Chicago: University of Chicago Press, 1983), p. 112.

20. Foucault, *History of Sexuality*, p. 95.

21. Michael Foucault, *Discipline and Punish* (New York: Vintage Books, 1979), p. 26.

22. Plato, *Phaedo*, in *The Dialogues of Plato*, trans. Benjamin Jowett, 4th ed. rev. (Oxford: Clarendon Press, 1953), 83d.

23. St. Augustine, *The Confessions*, trans. R. S. Pine-Coffin (Middlesex, U.K.: Penguin Books, 1961), p. 164.

24. *Phaedo*, 81d.

25. *Phaedo*, 66c. For Descartes on the body as a hindrance to knowledge, see *Conversations with Burman*, trans. John Cottingham (Oxford: Clarendon Press, 1976), p. 8, and *Passions of the Soul* in *Philosophical Works of Descartes*, trans. Elizabeth Haldane and G. R. T. Ross (Cambridge: Cambridge University Press, 1969), Vol. 1, p. 353.

26. *Phaedo*, 80a.

27. Indeed, the Cartesian "rules for the direction of the mind," as carried out in the *Meditations* especially, are actually rules for the transcendence of the body—its passions, its senses, the residue of "infantile prejudices" of judgment lingering from that earlier time when we were "immersed" in body and bodily sensations.

28. Alan Watts, *Nature, Man and Woman* (New York: Vintage, 1970), p. 145.

29. Entry in student journal, 1984.

30. Augustine, *Confessions*, p. 164.

31. Entry in student journal, 1984.

32. Aimée Liu, *Solitaire* (New York: Harper and Row 1979), p. 141 (cited parenthetically in the text as *Solitaire*).

33. Jennifer Woods, "I Was Starving Myself to Death," *Mademoiselle*, May 1981, p. 200.

34. Why they should emerge with such clarity in the twentieth century and through the voice of the anorexic is a question answered, in part, by the following two axes.

35. Augustine, *Confessions*, p. 165.

36. Entry in student journal, 1983.

37. Woods, "Starving Myself," p. 242.

38. "I equated gaining weight with happiness, contentment, then slothfulness, then atrophy, then death." (From case notes of Binnie Klein, MSW, to whom I am grateful for having provided parts of a transcript of her work with an anorexic patient.) See also Binswanger, "The Case of Ellen West," p. 343.

39. Klein, case notes.

40. Cherry Boone O'Neill, *Starving for Attention* (New York: Dell, 1982), p. 131.

41. Ibid., p. 49.

42. A Minnesota study of high school students determined that one in every ten anorexics was a victim of sexual abuse. Comments by and informal discussion with therapists at the Third Annual Conference for the Study of Anorexia and Bulimia bear these findings out; therapist after therapist remarked on the high incidence of early sexual violence and incest in anorexic patients.

43. Bruch, *The Golden Cage*, p. 73. The same is not true of bulimic anorexics, who tend to be sexually active (Garfinkel and Garner, *Anorexia Nervosa*, p. 41). Bulimic anorexics, as seems symbolized by the binge/purge cycle itself, stand in a somewhat more ambivalent relationship to their hungers than do abstinent anorexics.

44. Liu, *Solitaire*, p. 46. In one study of female anorexics, 88% of the subjects questioned reported that they lost weight because they "liked the feeling of will power and self-control" (G. R. Leon, "Anorexia Nervosa: The Question of Treatment Emphasis, " in M. Rosenbaum, C. M. Franks, and Y. Jaffe, eds., *Perspectives on Behavior Therapy in the Eighties* [New York: Springer, 1983], pp. 363–77). For an insightful and stimulating discussion of the contemporary conception of health as linked to self-control, discipline, and self-denial, see Robert Crawford, "A Cultural Account of 'Health'—Self-Control, Release, and the Social Body," in John B. Mc-Kinlay, ed., *Issues in the Political Economy of Health Care* (New York: Tavistock, 1984.

45. Smith, "The New Puritans." p. 24.

46. Entry in student journal, 1984.

47. Entry in student journal, 1984.

48. Trix Rosen, *Strong and Sexy* (New York: Putnam, 1983), p. 108.

49. Ibid., pp. 62, 14, 47, 48.

50. Smith, "The New Puritans," pp. 27, 26.

51. Rosen, *Strong and Sexy*, pp. 61–62.

52. Ibid., p. 72.

53. Ibid., p. 61. This fantasy is not limited to female bodybuilders. John Travolta describes his experience training for *Staying Alive*: "[It] taught me incredible things about the body . . . how it can be reshaped so you can make yourself over entirely, creating an entirely new you. I now look at bodies almost like pieces of clay that can be molded." ("Travolta: 'You really can make yourself over,' " *Syracuse Herald*, Jan. 13, 1985.)

54. Smith, "The New Puritans," p. 29.

55. Durk Pearson and Sandy Shaw, *Life Extension* (New York: Warner, 1982), p. 15.

56. Sidney Journard and Paul Secord, "Body Cathexis and the Ideal Female Figure." *Journal of Abnormal Social Psychology* 50: 243–46; Orland Wooley, Susan Wooley, and Sue Dyrenforth, "Obesity and Women—A Neglected Feminist Topic," *Women's Studies Institute Quarterly* 2(1979):81–92. Student journals and informal conversations with women students certainly have borne this out. See also Garfinkel and Garner, *Anorexia Nervosa*, pp. 110–15.

57. "Feeling Fat in a Thin Society," *Glamour*, February 1984, p. 198.

58. The same trend is obvious when the measurements of Miss America winners are compared over the last fifty years (see Garfinkel and Garner, *Anorexia Nervosa*, p. 107). Recently, there is some evidence that this tide is turning, and that a more solid, muscular, and athletic style is emerging as the latest fashion tyranny.

59. Entry in student journal, 1984.

60. This is one striking difference between the abstinent anorexic and bulimic anorexic: In the binge-and-vomit cycle, the hungering female self refuses to be annihilated, is in constant protest (to the great horror, of course, of the male self, who must negate every indulgence with a cleansing purge).

61. Entry in student journal, 1983.

62. Entry in student journal, 1983.

63. Bruch, *The Golden Cage*, p. 72; Bruch, *Eating Disorders*, p. 277. Others have fantasies of androgyny: "I want to go to a party and for everyone to look at me and for no one to know whether I was the most beautiful slender woman or handsome young man" (as reported by therapist April Benson, panel discussion, "New

Perspectives on Female Development," Third Annual Conference of the Center for the Study of Anorexia and Bulimia, New York, 1984).

64. See, for example, Levenkron's case studies; O'Neill, *Starving for Attention*, p. 107; Susie Ohrbach, *Fat Is a Feminist Issue* (New York: Berkley, 1978), pp. 174–75.

65. Klein, case study.

66. See, among many other works on this subject, Barbara Ehrenreich and Deirdre English, *For Her Own Good* (Garden City, N.Y.: Doubleday, 1979), pp. 1–29.

67. See Martha Vicinus, ed., *Suffer and Be Still* (Bloomington: Indiana University Press, 1972), pp. x–xi.

68. Ernest Jones, *Sigmund Freud: Life and Work* (London: Hogarth Press, 1956), vol. 1, p. 193.

69. On the nineteenth-century epidemic of female invalidism and hysteria, see Ehrenreich and English, *For Her Own Good*; Carroll Smith-Rosenberg, "The Hysterical Woman: Sex Roles and Conflict in Nineteenth-Century America," *Social Research* 39, no. 4 (Winter 1972): 652–78; Ann Douglas Wood, "The 'Fashionable Diseases': Women's Complaints and Their Treatment in Nineteenth Century America," *Journal of Interdisciplinary History*, 4 (Summer 1973): 25–52.

70. Ehrenreich and English, *For Her Own Good*, pp. 2, 102.

71. Sigmund Freud and Joseph Breuer, *Studies on Hysteria* (New York: Avon, 1966), p. 311.

72. Ibid., p. 141; see also p. 202.

73. See especially ibid., pp. 76 (Anna O.), 277, 284.

74. Marjorie Rosen, *Popcorn Venus* (New York: Avon, 1973).

75. Lois Banner, *American Beauty* (Chicago: University of Chicago Press, 1983), pp. 283–85. Christian Dior's enormously popular full skirts and cinch-waists, as Banner points out, are strikingly reminiscent of Victorian modes of dress.

76. On the protest dimension in anorexia, see Chernin, *The Obsession*, pp. 102–3; Seidenberg and DeCrow, *Woman Who Marry Houses*, pp. 88–97; Bruch, *The Golden Cage*, p. 58; Ohrbach, *Hunger Strike*, pp. 97–115. For an examination of the connections between hysteria, agoraphobia, and anorexia, see Susan Bordo, "The Body and the Reproduction of Femininity," in Alison Jaggar and Susan Bordo, eds., *Gender/Body/Knowledge: Feminist Reconstructions of Being and Knowing* (New Brunswick, N.J.: Rutgers University Press, 1988).

77. D. H. Lawrence, *Sons and Lovers* (New York: Viking, 1958), p. 257.

78. This experience of oneself as "too much" may be more or less emphatic, depending on variables such as race, religion, socioeconomic class, sexual orientation, etc. Eichenbaum and Ohrbach (*Understanding Women: A Feminist Psychoanalytic Approach*) emphasize, however, how frequently their clinic patients, non-anorexic as well as anorexic, "talk about their needs with contempt, humiliation, and shame. They feel exposed and childish, greedy and insatiable" (p. 49). Eichenbaum and Ohrbach trace such feelings, moreover, to infantile experiences that are characteristic of all female development, given a division of labor within which women are the emotional nurturers and physical caretakers of family life. Briefly (and this sketch cannot begin to do justice to their rich and complex analysis): mothers unwittingly communicate to their daughters that feminine needs are excessive, bad, and must be contained. The mother will do this out of a sense that her daughter will have to learn this lesson in order to become properly socialized into the traditional female role of caring for others—of feeding others, rather than feeding the self—and also because of an unconscious identification with her daughter, who reminds the mother of the "hungry, needy little girl" in herself, denied and repressed through the mother's *own*, "education" in being female: "Mother comes to be frightened by her daughter's free expression of her needs, and unconsciously acts toward her infant daughter in the same way she acts internally toward the little-

girl part of herself. In some ways the little daughter becomes an external representation of that part of herself that she has come to dislike and deny. The complex of emotions that results from her own deprivation through childhood and adult life is both directed inward in the struggle to negate the little-girl part of herself and projected outward onto her daughter" (p. 44). Despite a real desire to be totally responsive toward her daughter's emotional needs, the mother's own anxiety limits her capacity to respond. The contradictory messages she sends out convey to the little girl "the idea that to get love and approval she must show a particular side of herself. She must hide her emotional cravings, her disappointments and her angers, her fighting spirit. . . . She comes to feel that there must be something wrong with who she really is, which in turn must mean that there is something wrong with what she needs and what she wants. . . . This soon translates into feeling unworthy and hesitant about pursuing her impulses" (pp. 48–49). Once she has grown up, of course, these feelings are reinforced by cultural ideology, further social "training" in femininity, and the likelihood that the men in her life will regard her as "too much" as well, having been schooled by their own training in masculine detachment and autonomy.

(With boys, who do not stir up such intense identifications in the mother and who she knows, moreover, will grow up into a world that will meet their emotional needs [i.e., the son will eventually grow up to be looked after by his future wife, well-trained in the feminine arts of care], mothers feel much less ambivalent about the satisfaction of needs, and behave much more consistently in their nurturing. Boys therefore grow up, according to Eichenbaum and Ohrbach, with an experience of their needs as legitimate, appropriate, worthy of fulfillment.)

The male experience of the "woman-as-too-much" has been developmentally explored, as well, in Dorothy Dinnerstein's much-discussed *Mermaid and the Minotaur* (New York: Harper and Row, 1970). Dinnerstein argues that it is the woman's capacity to call up memories of helpless infancy, primitive wishes of "unqualified access" to the mother's body, and "the terrifying erotic independence of every baby's mother" (p. 62) that is responsible for the male fear of what he experiences as "the uncontrollable erotic rhythms" of the woman. Female impulses, a reminder of the autonomy of the mother, always appear on some level as a threatening limitation against his own. This gives rise to a "deep fantasy resentment" of female impulsivity (p. 59) and, on the cultural level, "archetypal nightmare visions of the insatiable female" (p. 62).

79. Quoted in Brian Easlea, *Witch-Hunting, Magic and the New Philosophy* (Atlantic Highlands, N.J.: Humanities Press, 1980), p. 242.

80. See Peggy Reeve Sanday, *Female Power and Male Dominance* (Cambridge: Cambridge University Press, 1981), pp. 172–84.

81. Easlea, *Witch-Hunting*, p. 8.

82. Peter Gay, *The Bourgeois Experience*, vol. 1, *Education of the Senses* (New York: Oxford University Press, 1984), pp. 197–201, 207.

83. Ehrenreich and English, *For Her Own Good*, p. 124.

84. Banner, *American Beauty*, pp. 86–105, 149–150. It is significant that these efforts failed, in large part, because of their association with the woman's rights movement. Trousers, such as those proposed by Amelia Bloomer, were considered a particular badge of depravity and aggressiveness, the *New York Herald* predicting that bloomer women would end up in "lunatic asylums or perchance in the state prison" (p. 96).

85. Amaury deRiencourt, *Sex and Power in History* (New York: David McKay, 1974), p. 319. The metaphorical dimension here is as striking as the functional, and it is a characteristic feature of female fashion: the dominant styles always decree, to one degree or another, that women *should not take up too much space*, that the territory we occupy should be limited. This is as true of cinch-belts as it is of foot-binding.

86. Quoted in deRiencourt, *Sex and Power in History*, p. 319.

87. Christy Ferguson, "Images of the Body: Victorian England" (philosophy research project, LeMoyne College, 1983).

88. Quoted in E. M. Sigsworth and T. J. Wyke, "A Study of Victorian Prostitution and Venereal Disease," in Vicinus, *Suffer and Be Still*, p. 82.

89. See Kate Millett, "The Debate Over Women: Ruskin vs. Mill," and Helen E. Roberts, "The Painter's View of Women in the First Twenty-five Years of Victoria's Reign," in Vicinus, *Suffer and Be Still*.

90. Gay, *Education of the Senses*, p. 197.

91. Vicinus, *Suffer and Be Still*, p. 123.

92. Ibid., p. x.

93. Lasch, *The Culture of Narcissism*, p. 343.

94. Charles Gaines and George Butler, "Iron Sisters," *Psychology Today*, November 1983, p. 67.

95. Some disquieting connections can be drawn, as well, between the anorexic and the flapper, who, according to Banner, *American Beauty*, expressed her sensuality "not through eroticism but through constant vibrant movement." The quality that marked the sex appeal of the 1920s—the "It" made famous by Clara Bow—was characterized by "vivacity, fearlessness and a basic indifference to men" (p. 279), qualities high on the list of anorexic values.

KIM   CHERNIN

Confessions of an Eater

What a surprising effect food has on our
organisms. Before I ate, I saw the sky,
the trees, and the birds all yellow, but
after I ate, everything was normal to my
eyes. . . . I was able to work better. My
body stopped weighing me down. . . . I
started to smile as if I was witnessing a
beautiful play. And will there ever be a
drama more beautiful than that of eating? I felt that I was eating for the first
time in my life.

Carolina Maria de Jesus

She got up at once, went to get a mag-
nificent apple, cut a piece and gave it to
me, saying: "Now Mama is going to
feed her little Renée. It is time to drink
the good milk from Mama's apples."
She put the piece in my mouth, and
with my eyes closed, my head against
her breast, I ate, or rather drank, my
milk. A nameless felicity flowed into my
heart. It was as though, suddenly, by
magic, all my agony, the tempest which
had shaken me a moment ago, had
given place to a blissful calm. . . .

Renee, *Autobiography of a
Schizophrenic Girl*

I remember the first time I ate compulsively. I was seventeen years old,
not yet an introspective person. I had no language or vocabulary for what
was happening to me. The issue of compulsive eating had not yet become
a matter of public confession. Looking back I can say: "That was the day
my neurosis began." But at the time, if I knew the word at all, I would not
have known to apply it to myself.

I was in Berlin, sitting at the breakfast table with my American room-mate and our German landlords. I remember the day vividly: the wind blows, the curtain lifts on the window, a beam of sunlight crosses the room and stops just at the spout of the teapot. A single, amber drop becomes luminous at the tip of the spout. I feel that I am about to remember something and then, unaccountably, I am moved to tears. But I do not cry. I say nothing, I look furtively around me, hoping this wave of strong feeling has not been observed. And then, I am eating. My hand is reaching out. And the movement, even in the first moments, seems driven and compulsive. I am not hungry. I had pushed away my plate moments before. But my hand is reaching and I know that I am reaching for something that has been lost. I hope for much from the food that is on the table before me but suddenly it seems to me that nothing will ever still this hunger—an immense implacable craving that I do not remember having felt before.

Suddenly, I realize that I am putting too much butter on my breakfast roll. I am convinced that everyone is looking at me. I put down the butter knife. I break off a piece of the roll and put it in my mouth. But it seems to me that I am wolfing it down. That I am devouring it.

I notice, with alarm, that Olga is beginning to clear the table. Unable to control myself, I lurch forward, reach out for another roll and pull the butter plate closer to myself. Everyone laughs and I am mortified. I am blushing the way I have not blushed since I was twelve or thirteen years old. I feel trapped and I want to go on eating. I *must* go on eating. And yet I feel an acute and terrible self-consciousness.

While Olga looks away and Rudi bends over to take something from the mouth of his child, I stuff the two rolls in my pocket, stand up from the table, and leave the room.

Once out of the house I begin running. And as I run I eat. I break the pieces of the roll without taking them from my pocket; I keep the broken portion covered with my hand. Making an apparently casual gesture I raise my hand to my mouth. Smoothly, as if I have practiced this many times, I drop the portion of bread into my mouth. And I continue to run.

Suddenly, as I fly by, I catch a glimpse of myself in the reflecting surface of a store window, looking for all the world as if a tempestuous spirit had been unleashed upon this quiet, bourgeois town. My hair is floating up in wisps, there is something frantic in my face. Perhaps it is a look of astonishment that the body I see there is so very slender when I imagine that it is terribly fat. And then I am violently parted from my own reflection as I race around the corner and stand still for a moment, staring down the street.

I see one of those stations where you can get a sausage, a paper plate, mustard, a white roll. You don't have to enter the restaurant. you can take the thing from an open window, carry it over to a table, stand outside, and dip the sausage in mustard, using your hands. No utensils, no formalities, no civilized behaviors. I slow down and walk up to the window, making every effort to appear at ease. But there is someone in line before me. Suddenly, a wave of tremendous anger and frustration comes over me. I think, if I do not control myself, I shall take this man by the shoulders and shove him aside.

I don't want to wait, I can't wait, I can't bear waiting. I must eat now, at this moment, without delay. I fumble in my pocket for another bit of roll. The pocket is empty. I am kicking at the ground, nudging a small stone about on the pavement. It seems to me, as I become aware of this gesture, that I am pawing the earth. I am terrified now that I will lose control completely—start swearing or muttering or even yelling at the man. I have seen such things before: people who sit speaking to themselves on subways, who burst out yelling for no apparent reason, while everyone laughs. I look down at my coat—it is covered with crumbs. My shoes look shabby. All at once I feel that I am filthy—a gross and alien creature at the edge of unbearable rage. I don't know what to do with myself, the man in front of me still talking to the woman behind the window, his sausage steaming on the counter before him and he does not reach out to take it in his hands. . . .

It is a cold day. I become aware of this as I stand, pawing the ground, watching the steam rise from the sausage. And I know exactly what I am doing when I suddenly dart forward, grab the plate and begin to run. I do not look back over my shoulder, I run with a sudden sense of release, as if I have finally cut the restraint that has been binding me. I hear the man's voice call out. "*Verdammtes Mädel,*" it says. "You damn girl." And then he begins to laugh. I too am laughing as I dart around a corner and stand with my back pressed to a cement building, urgently dipping the sausage into the mustard, stuffing large chunks of it into my mouth. And then I am crying. . . .

And so I ran from bakery to bakery, from street stall to street stall, buying cones of roasted chestnuts, which made me frantic because I had to peel away the skins. I bought a pound of chocolate and ate it as I ran. I never went to the same place twice. I acquired a mesh bag and carried supplies with me, wrapped in torn pieces of newspaper. When I felt tired, I sat down on benches, spread out my food next to me, tried to move slowly, as if I were enjoying a picnic, felt constrained by this pretense, darted the food into my mouth, ran on. . . .

In a few weeks I was planning to return to America. The summer vacation, which had lasted for more than seven months, had finally come to an end. I was out of of money; I was tired of traveling, I should have returned home to start college months before. But I knew that I could not go home fat. I looked down at parts of my body—at my wrists, at my ankles, at my calves. There was always something wrong with them, something that could be improved or perfected. How could I know then that the time would never come when I would regard myself as sufficiently slender? How indeed could I possibly imagine that one day I would weigh less than ninety pounds and still be ashamed to go out in a bathing suit? The future was completely dark. I had no idea that this episode of compulsive eating would become a typical event in my life over the next twenty years. It never occurred to me that a whole generation of women would become familiar with this unfortunate experience of their appetites and their bodies, or that I myself would one day weave their experience and my own into a book. At the time my thoughts were riveted upon the shame I felt. I considered going to the movies but I felt so self-conscious that I walked on down the street, feeling that I was a woman of perverse, almost criminal tendencies. I thought that in this obsession with food I was completely alone.

Twenty years later there is laughter. The event has become a story; I tell it to friends and we all smile knowingly. I write it down on the page and I marvel at that young woman running about the streets so frantically, that tempestuous gobbler with her wild eyes. But what has happened during the twenty years? What cycle, beginning that day in Berlin, has now almost accomplished itself, so that today I can sit at my typewriter and dare to look back? Or stand and look at myself in the mirror without considering how I might change this body I see? For it has happened during the last years (and from this I come by degree to believe in miracles) that I have been able to sit down at a meal without computing the calories involved, without warning my appetite about its excess, without fearing what might happen if I took pleasure from my plate. My body, my hunger and the food I give to myself, which have seemed like enemies to me, now have begun to look like friends. And this, it strikes me, is the way it should be; a natural relationship to oneself and the food that nourishes one. Yet, this natural way of being does not come easily to many women in our culture. Certainly it has not come easily to me.

Indeed, if I think back ten years or eight or nine, or to any period of my life, I find that I know exactly how much I weighed, whether I had recently gained or lost weight, exactly what clothes I was able to wear. These facts remain where so many other details have been forgotten. And of course, even in the act of recollection, I hasten to assure anyone who is listening that I was never really fat. Sometimes too slender, I would stand in front of a mirror, practically knocking against my own bones. At other times, when I had gained weight, I would grow attached to a particular pair of blue jeans and Chinese shirt. If an occasion required me to change out of these I felt extremely uncomfortable. These clothes, which I had grown accustomed to, seemed to hide me; anything else I might have changed into would be, I felt, a revelation of how fat I had become. Finally, I acquired a bright colored Mexican poncho; draped in this covering garment, I felt protected from judgments about my immense weight. But that was when I weighed 120 pounds. Surely even the weight charts consider that normal for a woman five feet four-and-a-half inches tall?

During those years my body and my appetite usually inspired me with a sense of profound uneasiness. True, for a week or two after losing weight I would feel that my body had become a celebration. I would rush out and buy new clothes for it, eager to have it testify to this triumph of my will. Inevitably, however, the weight would return. Mysteriously, the willpower would give way to desire. "An extra grape," I'd say, "and I've gained it all back again."

My hunger filled me with despair. It would always return, no matter how often I resolved to control it. Although I fasted for days, or went on a juice diet, or ate only vegetables, always, at the end of this fast, my hunger was back. The shock I would feel made me aware that my secret goal in dieting must have been the intention to kill off my appetite entirely.

When I write about this now it reminds me of the way people in the nineteenth century used to feel about sexuality and particularly about masturbation. I had these same feelings about masturbating when I was a little girl. Then, too, it seemed to me that a powerful force would rise up from my body and overcome my moral scruples and all my resistance. I would give in to it with a sense of voluptuous release, followed by terrible shame. Today, I begin to see that there is a parallel here. A woman obsessed with losing weight is also caught up in a terrible struggle against her sensual nature. She is trying to change and transform her body, she is attempting to govern, control, limit and sometimes even destroy her appetite. But her body and her hunger are, like sexual appetite, the expression of what is natural in herself; it is a futile, heartbreaking and dismal struggle to be so violently pitted against them. Indeed, this struggle against the natural self is one of the essential and hidden dramas of obsession.

Such an understanding did not come to me at all, however, when I was rushing about eating food, or going on diets, or swallowing diuretics, or staring at myself in the mirror, or pinching my waist, or using tape measures to measure the size of my wrists or ankles. For ten or eleven years after that episode in Berlin I felt that my obsession with food and weight was steadily growing more extreme. Finally, I was passing through a period when I found it very difficult to control my eating. Every day, when I woke up, my first thought was about food. Frequently, I could not make it even as far as lunch without eating a pound of candy. When I weighed myself I was filled with alarm by the needle creeping up the scale. "The scale is broken," I would say to myself. "It just wants to pay me back for kicking it," I would explain, not knowing whether or not I actually believed this nonsense. When I went past a mirror I would put my hands over my eyes, frightened of what I might behold there. I even hid from the toaster and the curved surface of a large spoon or the fender of a polished car. In that mood the world seemed filled with reminders that I was not as slender as the woman on the magazine cover, that I, in spite of all my will and effort, was not now able to make myself lean and gaunt.

One night, during this time, I woke around midnight, wondering how I could possibly be hungry, since I had eaten a great deal that day. I lay in bed, hoping I would not get up and go into the kitchen. But I was still hoping this as I made my way down the hallway, walking on tiptoe although I was alone in the house and there was no one to hear me. I opened the refrigerator; there had been a party at my house the day before and much of the food had remained behind. There were, I recall, neatly wrapped packages of feta and grape leaves, a basket of black figs, a few slices of green melon with prosciutto folded across the top, a carefully sliced piece of *boeuf* Wellington, and several chunks of halvah, rising up from a plate of sliced strudel that was flaking off bits of its dough. These were, without question, my most beloved foods and now as I looked at them I was suddenly faced with the necessity of choice. Which should I eat first? I went through several complex computations, persuading myself I would like the halvah better if I ate it after the feta, would not really want the *boeuf* Wellington if I had eaten the strudel first.

In truth, I really wasn't the least bit interested in these foods. Did I want to rush out then and find something in a late-night market? The donut shop perhaps? Or the ice cream store where you could get extra portions of butterscotch? But these foods too seemed to be lacking something. I went to the window of my bedroom and looked out into the garden, trying still to figure out what it was I wanted to eat. But now suddenly, for the first time in my life, I realized that what I was feeling was not hunger at all. I was restless, that was true; I had awakened feeling lonely, I was sad at being alone in the house, and I was frightened: the creaking of stairs, the noise of wind blowing in the window sounded like footsteps to me or like a door opening. What I wanted from food was companionship, comfort, reassurance, a sense of warmth and well-being that was hard for me to find in my own life, even in my own home. And now that these emotions were coming to the surface, they could no longer be easily satisfied with food. I was hungering, it was true; but food apparently was not what I was hungering for.

Recently, I came across a poem which would have helped me greatly if I could have read it years ago. It is by June Jordan and it contains an astonishing insight into the relationship between feeling and hunger:

> Nothing fills me up at night
> I fall asleep for one or two hours then
> up again my gut
> alarms
> I must arise
> and wandering into the refrigerator
> think about evaporated milk homemade vanilla ice cream
> cherry pie hot from the oven with Something like Vermont
> Cheddar Cheese disintegrating luscious
> on the top while
> mildly

I devour almonds and raisins mixed to mathematical
criteria or celery or my very own sweet and sour snack
composed of brie peanut butter honey and
a minuscule slice of party size salami
on a single whole wheat cracker *no salt added* . . .

The poem, as it continues, observes the complex social and personal reasons for anger, for loneliness, for the lack of self-love, those emotions which become hunger and rise up from the gut, driving us back to the refrigerator late at night. And it concludes:

Maybe when I wake up in the middle of the night
I should go downstairs
dump the refrigerator contents on the floor
and stand there in the middle of the spilled milk
and the wasted butter spread beneath my dirty feet
writing poems
writing poems . . . [1]

This shift from literal to symbolic understanding is always overwhelming. The poet, distilling the learning of years, dumps out this food that cannot satisfy the complex hunger that is driving her, and stands there writing her poem. And so I learn from her: this hunger I feel, which drives me to eat more than I need, requires more than the most perfectly mixed handful of almonds and raisins. It requires, in whatever form is appropriate, the evolution and expression of self.

Not that this shift to the symbolic will change overnight the way anyone feels about her body or its food. Many times over these years I have continued to wake late at night and have gone back to the refrigerator. I did not dump out its contents. I stood plotting the perfect sequence of food, perplexed at the growing dissatisfaction I felt when I finally began to eat; guilty the next morning, of course, but increasingly driven to reflect upon my experience. For I had the first clue into the resolution of this problem of obsession. I could no longer take it literally. Now, whenever I began to hate my body, or feel fear about the size of my appetite, whenever I began to long for food, I would ask myself what these fears and longings meant.

This research into the meaning of hunger went on for many years, during which I began to talk seriously with other women about their problems with weight. Slowly, it began to occur to me that my understanding of our condition was producing material worthy to become a book. At times, I was excited by this prospect of presenting a careful and detailed analysis of the cultural and pychological meanings of our obsession; at other times I felt that I did not want to continue with this undertaking because its subject matter seemed so trivial to me.

Imagine, I said to myself, spending the next years of your life writing about a woman's problem with her weight. Imagine using all your intellect and all your skill to analyze the reasons for an obsession with food. The obsession had always seemed so petty to me that I could not at times bear the idea that my whole life had already been swallowed up by this preoccupation.

One day, returning from the library, I suddenly realized that this whole idea of triviality was itself revealing. I had been reading Cocteau's book about his addiction to opium and had felt in its writer a distinct sort of pride. "I am speaking of the real smokers," he had written in what seemed to me a remarkably revealing passage. "The amateurs feel nothing, they wait for dreams and risk being seasick; because the effectiveness of opium is the result of a pact. If we fall under its spell, we shall never be able to give it up."[2] I was aware that no woman with a weight problem would make this distinction between the real obsessive and the amateur, for she would see herself, not as a member of an elite fraternity ("the nurses only know the counterfeit smokers, the elegant smokers, those who combine opium, alcohol, drugs . . . "), but as a being afflicted with a dreadful problem she cannot transcend and cannot control. For her, there could be no pride in this, no feeling that her addiction to food exalted her. And yet, Cocteau was able to claim precisely this exaltation for the opium addict. "The addict," he wrote, "can become a masterpiece. A masterpiece which is above discussion. A perfect masterpiece, because it is fugitive, without form and without judges."[3] Opium, I understood, opened the doors to a higher imaginative life; whatever disadvantages the addiction held for the addict, the glamour of this surrender to the higher self placed the addict above the condition of the average mortal. But the woman who surrendered to her obsession with food—who would ever assert this on her behalf? And yet, I reasoned, there must be in this obsession of ours the same deep promptings, the same longings and dissatisfactions, which drove a man to become addicted to opium, to make this pact, to fall under its spell, and never be able to give it up. Our insistence—my own insistence—that our obsession was trivial, was no doubt merely a resistance to what these deeper promptings might reveal.

Some indication of the very great significance of eating can be found in the story of G. T. Fechner, which is told by James Hillman in *The Dream and the Underworld*.[4] Fechner, the founder of psychophysics, was highly regarded by Freud for his work on dreams. But after years of productive work, at the age of thirty-nine, Fechner began to experience a breakdown. His eyes failed and he finally went blind. He also "fell into melancholic isolation, lost control over his thoughts, hallucinated tortures, and his alimentary tract broke down." He remained in this unfortunate condition for three years. Twice, however, he was "miraculously healed: once when a woman friend dreamed of preparing him a meal of Bauerschinken, a heavily spiced raw ham cured in lemon juice and Rhine wine." When she took this dish to him he ate it, against his better judgment, and discovered that his appetite and digestion were both restored. And he was healed also on another occasion when suddenly one morning at dawn "he found that he was able to bear the light and even hungered for it." From this moment his recuperation began, his eyesight returned and he lived on, in good health, for another forty-four years.

As it happened, I was reading this story quite recently in a Berkeley coffee shop. When I looked up from my book I caught sight of several perfectly sliced pieces of Italian rum chocolate cake behind the glass counter next to the espresso machine. I found myself wondering whether I would be able to immerse myself again in the story of old Fechner and prove once more the power of my will to resist my appetite, when the significance of the tale I had just read came home to me. Suddenly, it seemed no accident that Hillman had spoken of Fechner's *hunger* for light. For Fechner, I thought, had been cured precisely by the return of his appetite, when his melancholic withdrawal from the world was superseded by desire. Thus, he begins to eat and his alimentary tract is cured. He begins to hunger for light and his vision is restored. Was it possible, I wondered, that Fechner had been suffering from a severe and controlling attitude towards sensual existence, like so many other intellectual men of the nineteenth century? If so, it made sense that he was healed by giving himself permission to eat, since this permission would have represented a profound reconciliation with instinctual life, a willingness to gratify rather than control desire.

This reflection came upon me as something distinctly new and it made me aware that our obsession had in it as much potential "exaltation" as the surrender to opium. It, too, might be seen as a quest for reconciliation within the self. Opium, perhaps, opened the doors to the higher, imaginative life; but I could now see that our obsession with food expressed a yearning for permission to enjoy the sensual aspects of the self.

This insight had an immediate impact upon my own relationship to food. For the first time in my conscious life I began to imagine appetite as a healthful, natural aspect of myself. I imagined standing up from my table, holding my head high, and walking across the room. In my fantasy I stood calmly in line, not swearing under my breath about the man taking too much time in front of me. Then, I requested the man who worked behind the counter to fill up a tray for me, with two pieces of Italian rum chocolate cake, a large cup of hot chocolate, with espresso and whipped cream. I intended to go sit by myself at a table near the door, letting everyone who passed by look in at me, peacefully eating, not devouring, taking my time, giving myself permission to gratify my appetite.

But now, before I could enact this fantasy. my eyes fell upon the oranges stacked up in an informal pyramid at the top of the counter. The light from the window must have been falling upon them, because they were burnished with a vivid and beautiful glow. I was so fascinated by them that I forgot my conflict about eating; I stared at the oranges, entranced by their roundness. And suddenly I was aware that I had seen them like this when I was a child, on my first trip to California. What a vision that had been as the train passed by the orchard and I shook my mother by the shoulder. "Mama, look," I cried out, waking the old lady drowsing on the seat in front of us, "in California the oranges grow on trees."

This early sense of wonder and delight came to me again now; I looked at the fruit as if it were the gift of a divine being or were itself divine. And now suddenly I realized that my hunger had vanished. I felt that I was being filled with my own joy in the beauty of the world. Everything I looked at now had this same quality of fullness and abundance that gleamed from the oranges stacked in their pyramid across the room. A friend stopped at my table, setting down her tray and bending over to kiss me on the cheek. "You're glowing," she said. "I could practically see you from the other side of the street." She offered me a brioche, which I accepted. But at the first bite I found that I was already satisfied. I took a sip of her coffee, sat back in my chair. "You look," she said, "as if you've swallowed the canary." "Yes," I replied, "I feel as if I'd just eaten the whole world."

For many weeks after that time I found that whenever I was in conflict about food what I needed was permission to eat. If I was in fact able to let myself eat for pleasure, the terrible conflict abated and with it the sense of an insatiable hunger. Frequently, as I observed this conflict over food, I noticed that the permission to eat was closely linked to a delight in life, a sense of joy and abundance, an awareness of some unexpected meaning or beauty. And frequently, too, there were memories of childhood. Occasionally, walking down the street with a salted pretzel from the street stand at the edge of the college campus, I would feel that I had little legs and hands, that I was walking in the Bronx with my mother, tasting everything for the first time. In this state of delight, it never took a great deal of food to satisfy my hunger. However plain or simple it was, to me it seemed exactly the pleasure and satisfaction I had been looking for. The moral to draw from this seemed clear. There was a state of mind and being in which food became a simple, uncomplicated sensual pleasure. But if I were lacking this state, if I simply could not give myself permission to eat, food would not satisfy me, no matter how excellent it was or how much of it I consumed in compulsive rebellion against my own prohibition.

The process of understanding, which over the years was gradually changing my relationship to food, had one last dramatic insight in store for me. This one occurred during a time in my life when I no longer ate compulsively, but would still experience periods of anxiety about my body, feeling that suddenly, overnight I had become fat. On this occasion I was lying in bed counting over the calories I'd eaten during the day. My attention was vaguely focused upon my body, which was filling me with a sense of extreme dissatisfaction. Now, I reverted to a fantasy about my body's transformation from this state of imperfection to a consummate loveliness, the flesh trimmed away, stomach flat, thighs like those of the adolescent runner on the back slopes of the fire trail, a boy of fifteen or sixteen, running along there one evening in a pair of red trunks, stripped to the waist, gleaming with sweat and suntan oil, his muscles stretching and relaxing, as if he'd been sent out there to model for me a vision of everything I was not and could never be. I don't know how many times this fantasy of transformation had occupied me before, but this time it ended with a sudden eruption of awareness, for I had observed the fact that the emotions which prompted it were a bitter contempt for the feminine nature of my own body. The sense of fullness and swelling, of curves and softness, the awareness of plenitude and abundance, which filled me with disgust and alarm, were actually the qualities of a woman's body.

With this knowledge I now got up and went to look at myself in the mirror. For the first time I was able to perceive the transparent film of expectation I placed over my image in the looking glass. I had never seen myself before. Until now, all I had been able to behold was my body's failure to conform to an ideal. Now, I realized that what I had called fat in myself, and considered gross, was this body of a woman. And it was beautiful. The thighs, too large for an adolescent boy, were appropriate to a woman's body. Hips rounding, belly curved, what had driven me to deny this evidence that I was a woman?

For a long moment I stood before my own image, coming to knowledge of myself. Suddenly, I saw all that I was supposed to be but was not—taller, more ethereal, more refined, less hungry, not so powerful, much less emotional, more subdued, not such a big talker; a more generous, loving, considerate, nurturant person; less selfish, less ambitious, and far less given to seeking pleasure for myself.

Now, however, all this came into question: Who, I wondered, had made up this ideal for women? Who had imposed it and why hadn't I seen through it before? Why, for that matter, did I imagine a slender body would bring me these attainments, even if I decided I actually wanted them for myself? And why, finally, wasn't I free simply to throw off this whole coercive system of expectation and be myself—eating, lusting, laughing, talking, taking?

It was a moment of clear vision and it would, I knew, organize the ideas and impressions I had been gathering around a central theme. For now I could no longer doubt that my alienation from my body was the key to understanding my troubled relationship to food, to my appetite, and to my very identity as a woman. I knew also that I would have to go further—to understand, for instance, why so many women of my generation could not tolerate their bodies. I would have to ask why our culture held up before us an ideal image that was appropriate only to an adolescent. I needed to understand whether this inappropriate ideal was part of a much larger coercion exercised against the full and natural development of women.

A book comes into being at that juncture where a personal problem, which has caused great distress, has begun to resolve itself, so that the deeper meanings and wider issues of the problem are apparent. Certainly, I was now beginning to experience a vivid transformation in my way of seeing and hearing. Now, listening to women talk about their problems of weight, I felt myself understanding on many levels at the same time. I went to the same places as before, I listened often to the same women talking, recorded again and again the power of this obsession over their lives, but now I was asking new questions, following different leads, translating everything into a new structure of meaning. And therefore, when a woman said to me one day, "I have rarely had a moment of peace about my body. All my life, no matter what else is going on, I have felt an uneasiness. A sense that something was about to get out of control. That I needed to keep watch. That something about me needed changing," I reached for my notebook and went out to gather evidence that might show how widespread was this uneasiness about the body and its urges. For this obsession, I felt, might well be considered one of the most serious forms of suffering affecting women in America today.

N O T E S

1. June Jordan, *Passion*, Boston, 1980.
2. Jean Cocteau, *Opium: The Diary of a Cure*, London, 1957.
3. Ibid.
4. James Hillman, *The Dream and the Underworld*, New York, 1979.

KELLY OLIVER

Nourishing the Speaking Subject: A Psychoanalytic Approach to Abominable Food and Women

In this essay, I take a different approach than most of the other pieces in this collection. I use a psychoanalytic approach in order to analyze the relationship between food and the individual in Western culture. In addition, focusing on what is usually our first food, mother's milk, I diagnose some of the ways in which patriarchal Western cultures "purify" this food by disassociating it from the "impure" material body, the body of woman. Like other approaches taken in this collection, this psychoanalytic account reveals some aspects of the relationship between food and women and their oppression. More than uncovering patriarchal myths about these relations, using the work of Julia Kristeva, I suggest ways that we might reconceive the relationship between mother's milk and our subjectivity which challenge the Christian discourse on maternity and which may found a new ethics, what Kristeva calls "herethics."

Psychoanalytic literature, particularly the work of Julia Kristeva, can provide important insights into the relationship between food and the ways in which we become social individuals. This literature reminds us that the first food that most of us receive comes from our mothers' bodies. It reminds us that our first relationship with another person is founded on a bodily relationship whereby one body feeds another. Whether or not the infant is breast-fed, usually its feeding is associated with the mother. In addition, Freud was the first to suggest that the infant takes pleasure in feeding from its mother's body. Even the infant does not merely eat in order to live but takes pleasure in eating. This pleasure ensures that the infant takes nourishment and stays alive. In addition, this pleasure is the pleasure of its communion with the maternal body and maternal love.

Julia Kristeva suggests that we become subjects, more precisely speaking subjects, because of, and in response to, the primary pleasure of eating. She maintains that the infant's nourishing relationship to the maternal body puts in motion a material logic which prefigures and sets up the logic of the psyche. According to Kristeva, the logic of our first eating becomes the logic of speaking and loving. Kristeva compares the infant's relationship of the breast to the subsequent relationship of "the speech of the other," that is, the language which pre-exists the infant. In addition, she suggests that there is an identification with the maternal body which prefigures the identification with an other in a love relationship.

Kristeva suggests that this early identification is a reduplication of a pattern. Kristeva explains, following Freud, that the archaic identification with the mother's breast is a preobjectal identification. The infant *becomes* the breast through its incorporation. According to Kristeva, this breast is not an object for the infant but a "model," a "pattern" (1983, 25). The infant's identification with this model or pattern of/through incorporation is not the *imitation* of an object, or even a pattern. Rather, Kristeva describes this identification as a *reduplication* of the pattern.[1] This suggests that this archaic identification, a strange identification indeed, is biological. It is what Kristeva calls "semiotic." For Kristeva, the semiotic is the place where nature meets culture and drives are inscribed in signifying processes. The semiotic always recalls the maternal body because it is this body which provides the most fundamental and powerful example of the seam between nature and culture.

For Kristeva, the child's relation to the maternal body and its first nourishment set up an archaic pattern which is reduplicated on level after level until we have the speaking subject. Thus, this archaic semiotic identification with the mother's breast becomes the first in a series of reduplications. It prefigures and sets in motion the logic of object identifications in all object relations, including both discourse and love (1983, 25).

The infant's incorporation of the breast sets up the logic of the subsequent incorporation of "the speech of the other" (1983, 26). For Kristeva, this substitution is both literal and metaphorical. There is a logic or pattern which is reduplicated in the move from breast to speech. In this sense, speech is an analogue of the breast. While nursing, the infant takes in the milk from the mother, incorporates the food from the other, and makes this food part of itself. This same pattern is repeated with language and social customs. The child takes language from the other and makes this language part of itself. Kristeva explains that through incorporating the speech of the other the infant incorporates the pattern of language and thereby identifies with the other. In fact, it is the incorporation of the patterns of language which enables the infant to communicate and thus commune with others. And through the ability to "assimilate, repeat, and reproduce" words, the infant becomes like the other: a subject (1983, 26). According to Kristeva, the operator within this process is the logic of reduplication, which is put in motion by the first identifications with the mother's body and sets up the logic of the psyche, repetition. So, the logic of reduplication itself becomes a pattern reduplicated by the psyche.

For Kristeva, the speaking subject is not born solely from the mother's giving of the breast. As important as the giving is the taking away. The mother regulates the infant's first nourishment. Although in the beginning the infant "takes" itself for an extension of its mother's body, a body which exists solely for its own gratification, eventually the infant must be weaned. The infant must take up its existence as a separate subject. It must see that its mother has a separate existence and that her body does not exist solely for its gratification. According to Kristeva, the infant must substitute speech for its mother's breast. It takes pleasure in the materiality of speech just as it did in the materiality of its mother's body. One oral satisfaction takes over for another. Most simply, this substitution takes place when the child realizes that its mother is a separate being who can leave and does not merely exist for its own gratification. At this time, the child must learn to translate its needs into demands in language. It must ask for what it wants because it knows now that its needs are not automatically met. It is through this process that the child also learns that it is a separate subject.[2]

Thus in addition to the logic of reduplication, which is repeated in both the incorporation of the breast and speech, on another level, the move from breast to speech is an organic evolution of the psyche through which speech is "literally" substituted for the breast. If we can no longer have the breast to satisfy our needs, we have to settle for a second rate substitute, language. Language is second-rate because, according to Lacanian theory, once the child is separated from the maternal body, which met all of its needs, it must, but never can, say what it wants. It cannot say what it wants because its desire is always beyond language. And this is why we keep talking.

In order to explain how the infant separates itself from the maternal body, Kristeva develops the notion of abjection in *Powers of Horror* (1980). Abjection

> is an extremely strong feeling which is at once somatic and symbolic, and which is above all a revolt of the person against an external menace from which one wants to keep oneself at a distance, but of which one has the impression that it is not only an external menace but that it may menace us from inside. So it is a desire for separation, for becoming autonomous and also the feeling of an impossibility of doing so— (1980a, 135–36)

The abject is something repulsive that both attracts and repels. It holds you in spite of your disgust. It fascinates. In Kristeva's account, it is not a "lack of cleanliness or health that causes abjection but what disturbs identity, system, order" (1980, 4).

The abject is what is on the border, what doesn't respect borders. It is "ambiguous," "in-between," "composite" (1980, 4). It is neither one nor the other. It is undecidable. The abject is not a "quality in itself." Rather, it is a relationship to a boundary and represents what has been "jettisoned out of that boundary, its other side, a margin" (1980, 69). The abject is what threatens identity. It is neither good nor evil, subject nor object, ego nor unconscious, nature nor culture, but something that threatens the distinctions themselves. The abject is not an object that corresponds to an ego; rather, it is what is excluded by the superego: "To each ego its object, to each superego its abject" (1980, 2).

Thus, although every society is founded on the abject—that is, constructing boundaries and jettisoning the antisocial—every society may have its own abject. In all cases, the abject threatens the unity/identity of both society and the subject. It calls into question the boundaries upon which they are constructed. The abject threat comes from what has been prohibited by culture, what has been prohibited so that the culture can be. For Kristeva, in Western culture, the prohibition which founds, and yet undermines, society is the prohibition against the maternal body.[3] It is what is off limits.

For Kristeva, the abject is that which points up the arbitrariness of borders. And the border at stake in this primary relationship is the border between the mother's body and the infant's. It is food, what is taken into the body, along with excrement, what is expelled from the body, which calls into question the borders of the body. How can we be bodies separated from our mothers when it is her body which we eat? Her fluids become ours. How can we imagine ourselves as separate bodies when we eat that which is not-us, which in turn becomes us? How can we imagine ourselves as separate bodies when we expel part of us, which in turn becomes not-us?

According to Kristeva, we can become separated from our mothers, weaned, only by abjecting their bodies. This body "having been the mother, will turn into an abject. Repelling, rejecting; repelling itself, rejecting itself. Ab-jecting" (1980, 13). The child tries to separate but feels that it is impossible. The mother is made abject to facilitate the separation from her. At this point the mother is not-yet-object and the child is not-yet-subject. The child in this abject relation to its mother is not yet separated from her but no longer identical with her. The abject-mother takes the place of Other, which will be occupied by the object-mother once the child becomes a subject proper.

Abjection, then, is a kind of crisis in identity. It is the "realization" that the primary identification with the mother is a "seeming," a fake. It is the beginnings of separation from the mother. Or, as Kristeva maintains, it is the separation before the beginning, before the beginning of subjectivity proper. For this abjection which forces separation is founded in birth itself:

Abjection preserves what existed in the archaism of pre-objectal relationship, in the immemorial violence with which a body becomes separated from another body in order to be. . . . the heterogeneous flow, which portions the abject and sends back abjection, already dwells in a human animal that has been highly altered. . . . Significance is indeed inherent in the human body. (1980, 10)

Human life, human society, is founded on the abject separation of one body from another at birth. This separation, like subsequent ones, is labored but necessary. The prototypical abject experience may be the experience of birth itself. It is at the birth of the child, and not before, that the identity of the human subject is most visibly called into question. Birth is an unruly border between mother and child. Before the umbilical cord is cut, who can decide? Is there one or are there two? In this case, there is neither one nor two, but something in between.

Maternity threatens borders. In addition, the most archaic boundaries of the clean and proper self, of course, are those regulated by the maternal authority, in particular anal and oral drives. Food, not yet the body, is taken in through the mouth. Feces, no longer the body, is expelled through the anus. The boundaries between body and not-body are controlled by the mother.

What this analysis suggests, then, is that a pattern is set up and repeated which moves from the corporeal "logic" of the maternal body to the cultural logic of language. The nourishing maternal womb and identity of mother and child before birth is repeated after birth with the nourishing maternal breast. The separation of child from the maternal body at birth is repeated when the child is weaned. This exchange between the child and the maternal body, between subject and other/object, is repeated in social exchange and interaction. According to Kristeva, this logic of separation founds Western culture. If the patterns of our language and symbolic systems repeat the pattern which begins within the maternal body, it will be interesting and useful to analyze the traditional discourses surrounding that maternal body, which, in fact, in Western culture, repress the primary relationship to this nourishing body.

As I have indicated earlier, according to Kristeva, both the subject and society depend on the repression of this maternal authority. Culture, which sets up a parceling order, represses the parceling order set up by the maternal authority over the infant's body (1980, 72). It is corporeal nourishment and waste, originally regulated by the mother, which represents a threat from beyond the borders of culture (1980, 70). However, culture maintains its borders through ritual. Kristeva argues that by means of a system of ritual exclusions, through available language, culture looks back toward the archaic experience of maternal authority and makes of it a partial-object. The ritual does not turn the pre-objectal abject into an object; rather, it treats the abject as a type of partial-object. These rituals are more re-enactments than symbolizations. As such, they never really secure the borders of culture. Rather, according to Kristeva, these rituals "illustrate the boundary between semiotic authority and symbolic law" (1980, 73). They point to the weak spots in culture. Just as waste is expelled from the healthy body, the abject is expelled from healthy society. There comes a point, however, where the body itself becomes waste, the corpse, and society becomes barbaric, genocidal.[4] Our rituals, violent in themselves, are flimsy protection against disintegration.

In *Powers of Horror*, following Mary Douglas's analysis, Kristeva presents an interesting account of biblical dietary prohibitions and rituals, which set up the borders of the clean and proper subject against the abject. On Kristeva's reading, these dietary regulations prohibit those foods which call into question borders. They prohibit the undecidable abject. These prohibitions protect us from our first food, from the nourishing maternal body, the body without borders, the undecidable abject body. These dietary prohibitions protect us from drowning in mother's milk, that which is neither child nor mother but somehow both.

Kristeva's analysis centers on the book of Leviticus. In Leviticus various prohibitions are listed. Kristeva divides those prohibitions into three categories of abomination: "1) Food taboos; 2) corporeal alteration and its climax, death; 3) the feminine body and incest" (1980, 93). Kristeva argues that all of these prohibitions follow the same logic of separation. She maintains that the food taboos identify those "foods" that call into question separation, or identity, as impure or unclean. For example, the blood of animals is not to be eaten because blood is the life of an animal and to eat both the dead flesh and its life is to mix two elements from different orders, flesh and blood, death and life (1980, 96–98).[5] Also, many fish, birds, and insects are unclean because they cannot be linked to only one element—sea, heaven, or earth. Those which partake of a mixture of elements, and thereby call into question their borders, are impure and not to be eaten (1980, 98). "The pure," says Kristeva, "will be that which conforms to an established taxonomy; the impure, that which unsettles it, establishes intermixture and disorder" (1980, 98).

The biblical prohibitions against the female body, like some dietary prohibitions, have to do with blood. Kristeva points out that Leviticus 12:2 specifies that the woman in childbirth will be impure because of the accompanying blood. Because of her impurity the mother must perform rituals to ensure that the child is not also impure (1980, 99). Because of blood, all potentially fertile women are impure. Bodily fluids, especially blood, call into question the borders of the body and even the borders between life and death. Once again it is the undecidable, the unsettling, the threat to identity, which is abject. The dietary prohibition against cooking an animal in its mother's milk indicates an explicit connection between abominable food and maternal nourishment (Exodus 23:19, 34:26; Deuteronomy 14:21). Once the offspring has been separated from its mother, it must remain separated. The bond between the mother and her baby, milk, must be broken (1980, 105). In addition, to boil the offspring in its mother's milk blurs the boundary between life and death. The mother's milk which nourishes and gives life cannot also be that which brings death. In this case, which is more contaminating, life-bringing milk, or death-bringing fire? Ultimately, Kristeva suggests that all of the dietary prohibitions, like this one, may cover over the separation from the maternal body upon which they are founded:

> Dietary abomination has thus a parallel—unless it be a foundation—in the abomination provoked by the fertilizable or fertile feminine body (menses, childbirth). Might it be that dietary prohibitions are a screen in a still more radical separation process? Would the dispositions . . . be an attempt to keep a being who speaks to his God separated from the fecund mother? In that case, it would be a matter of separating oneself from the phantasmatic power of the mother, that archaic Mother Goddess who actually haunted the imagination of a nation at war with the surrounding polytheism. (1980, 100)

The fundamental separation through which the nation of Moses defines itself is the separation from the fecund mother who is worshipped by other nations. The rituals of separation are repeated over and over again in different forms on various levels of culture. Some of the primary rituals involve maintaining the separation of the child from its mother's milk. This milk poses a threat not only to the identity of the child as an autonomous being, but also to the nation itself as a monotheistic patriarchy.

On the level of personal archeology, separation from the mother's milk is fundamental to establishing an autonomous individual. In Western culture, the repression of this bonding fluid and its abjection are central to our conception of personhood. Persons are autonomous and rational. They have overcome any animal nature and stepped surefootedly into culture. Mother's milk is a threat to both autonomy and rationality insofar as it recalls our animality. Western culture sustains itself by establishing borders between abject corporeal nature, which oozes and flows and defies categorization, on the one side, and civilized society composed of clean and proper individuals on the other. Kristeva describes the biblical symbolization of the child's necessary weaning and entry into culture proper:

> A phantasmatic mother who also constitutes, in the specific history of each person, the abyss that must be established as an autonomous (and not encroaching) *place* and *distinct* object, meaning a *signifiable* one, so that such a person might learn to speak. At any rate, that evocation of defiled maternality, in Leviticus 12, inscribes the logic of dietary abomination within that of a limit, a boundary, a border between the sexes, a separation of feminine and masculine as foundation for the organization that is "clean and proper," "individual," and, one thing leading to another, signifiable, legislatable, subject to law and morality. (1980a, 100)

Language, law, and morality, in Western culture, are based on the abjection of the maternal. The maternal body, the body without borders, must be excluded or at least subdued, so that the borders of both society and the individual can be established. Kristeva points out that in the New Testament this abject threat no longer comes from the outside. Rather, it is internalized. Now the enemy, the abject, is within. Still, the New Testament must provide ways of covering over this abject threat—the threat from corporeality, ultimately maternal blood and milk—which serve to buttress the borders of culture and keep it from slipping into nature. In the New Testament, the impure is absorbed within the pure. In this way, the pure triumphantly retains its borders by encompassing all that is.

Christ becomes a symbol for this incorporation. Christ is born out of a woman. However, he seems to be born without blood. Certainly he is conceived without the mess of the body. He is a human being, but not contaminated by the intermingling of the sexes. Christ's mother, Mary, is a virgin, who symbolizes a well maintained separation between the sexes. Although Christ is the intermingling of God and human, the holy absorbs the unholy. Still, Christ's unholy body must die, not a normal death, but a death that is a new life and therefore retains the integrity of an eternal God. Christ's blood and body are symbolically eaten during Christian rituals in which their purity purifies the sinner's blood and body.

Likewise, the Virgin Mary does not die at all. She is transported directly to heaven. Her pure body is never compromised by the impurity of death. Her body does not become an abominable rotting corpse. In addition, fluids from her body are pure. Her tears and milk redeem maternity and subdue any threat that it poses. Her purity provides an antidote for the abject mother. God can love abject mothers and all abominable women only through the purity of the Virgin Mary.

Traditionally, in western Christian culture, the religious discourse of the Virgin Mary has provided the dominant discourse on maternity. Kristeva argues that this discourse absorbs the abject mother, which is necessary to the child's separation. What Kristeva describes as the "cult of the virgin" has been used by a paternal symbolic in order to cover up the unsettling aspects of maternity and the mother-child relationship (1976a). The "cult of the virgin" controls maternity and mothers by doing violence against them. Like sacrifice, the cult of the virgin contains the violence of semiotic drives by doing violence to them. The virgin's only pleasure is her child, who is not hers alone but everyone's, while her silent sorrow is hers alone. Kristeva maintains that the image of the virgin covers over the tension between the maternal and the symbolic.

In the biblical stories, the virgin is impregnated by the Word, the Name of the Father, God. This, argues Kristeva, is a way of ensuring paternity and fighting off the remnants of matrilinear society. After all, it is the name of the father which guarantees paternity and inheritance. According to Kristeva, the cult of the virgin is the reconciliation of matrilinearism and the unconscious needs of the primary identification with the mother, on the one hand, "and on the other the requirements of a new society based on exchange and before long on increased production which require the contribution of the superego and rely on the symbolic paternal agency" (1976a, 259). This symbolic paternal agency, then, both guarantees, and is

founded on, the exchange and control of women and children through the
Name of the Father.[6]

The mother is a threat to the symbolic. She not only represents, but is, a
strange fold between culture and nature which cannot be fully incorporated by the symbolic (1976a, 259). However, the symbolic attempts a
complete incorporation of the mother with her strange fold and her outlaw
jouissance (complete pleasure, sexual and otherwise) through the cult of
the virgin. First, the virgin birth does away with the "primal scene" and the
mother's *jouissance*, which might accompany it. The virgin's is an immaculate conception. According to Kristeva, this fantasy of the immaculate conception is a protection against a fantasy that is too much for the child to
bear: "that of being supernumerary, excluded from the act of pleasure [the
primal scene] that is the origin of its existence" (1987, 42). Thus, rather
than be excluded from the mother's *jouissance*, the child excludes the
mother's *jouissance* with the fantasy of the virgin birth. This is all the more
striking with Kristeva's claim that "virgin" is a mistranslation of "the
Semitic term that indicates the sociolegal status of a young unmarried
woman" (1976a, 236–37). The *jouissance* of the young unmarried woman
is a *jouissance* that is not confined within the social sanctions of marriage.
It is an outlaw *jouissance* that does not come under paternal control, the
remnants of a matrilinear society where the resulting child can only take
the name of the mother. The *jouissance* of this young unmarried woman
and her "bastard" child present a threat to the paternal function of the
symbolic. The image of virgin, however, controls this threat. The virgin has
no *jouissance* and her body is marked with the Name of the Father. There
is no mistake about paternity here in spite of the fact that in the biblical
story Joseph becomes Mary's husband.

The power of the mother in a matrilinear society, the power of the
child's primary relationship/identification with the mother, and the power
of the mother as the authority over the child's body, are all condensed into
the symbol of the virgin mother. The mother's power is brought under
paternal control. According to Kristeva, it is domesticated: "[i]t is as if
paternity were necessary in order to relive the archaic impact of the maternal body on man . . . in order somehow to admit the threat that the male
feels as much from the possessive maternal body as from his separation
from it—a threat that he immediately returns to that body" (1975a, 263).

Man returns the threat to the maternal body through the cult of the
virgin. The maternal body is allowed only joy in pain. Her body has only
ear, milk, and tears (1976a, 248–49). The sexed body is replaced by the
"ear of understanding," the Virgin Mary of the Catholic Church (1976a,
257). In this way, the virgin covers over the maternal fold between the
biological and cultural. There is nothing biological going on here. The
virgin covers over both the bodily connection between mother and child
and the separation of child from mother that gives way to the child's entry

into the symbolic. The virgin's maternity, and her relation to her child, is purely spiritual. Otherwise, the god-child is contaminated.

However, Kristeva suggests that the silent ear, milk, and tears "are metaphors of nonspeech, of a 'semiotics' that linguistic communication does not account for." Thus, the virgin mother becomes the representative of a "return of the repressed" semiotic (1976a, 249). Although the virgin can control the maternal semiotic, it cannot contain the semiotic. According to Kristeva, Christianity, with its virgin birth, both unravels and protects the paternal function (1987, 40). Like sacrifice, the violence of the drives returns within the very ritual which attempts to repress it. The maternal semiotic is focused in the symbol of the virgin, and its threat to the symbolic order is thereby controlled.

The virgin's child, the god-child, strangely enough, is Freud's fantasy. According to Freud the child is the woman's satisfaction. And what of the mother? What of her satisfaction? Kristeva suggests that Freud's account of motherhood as either an attempt to satisfy penis-envy (baby=penis) or a reactivated anal drive (baby=feces) is merely a male fantasy. With regard to the complexities of maternal experience, claims Kristeva, "Freud offers only a massive nothing, which, for those who might care to analyze it, is punctuated with this or that remark on the part of Freud's mother, proving to him in the kitchen that his own body is anything but immortal and will crumble away like dough; or the sour photograph of Marthe Freud, the wife, a whole mute story . . . " (1976a, 255).

Traditional psychoanalytic theory cannot properly account for maternity. Kristeva argues that because within Western culture we are left with an inadequate religious discourse of maternity, which is itself crumbling, women are abjected. Kristeva partially accounts for women's oppression by locating it in this misplaced abjection. This is why in "Stabat Mater" and other essays, Kristeva begins to suggest another discourse on maternity, one in which the mother is "alone of her sex" (1976). The mother is not synonymous with woman. To separate from the maternal body is not to separate from woman or even the mother. Rather, in Kristeva's scenario, we separate from the maternal body in order to love the mother, women, and all others.

Within our culture, for the child who needs to become an autonomous subject, the maternal body is threatening even while it is fascinating and sublime. The 'subject' discovers itself as the impossible separation/identity of the maternal body. It hates that body but only because it can't be free of it. That body, the body without borders, the body out of which this abject subject came, is impossible (1980, 6). It is a horrifying, devouring body.[7] It is a body that evokes rage and fear.

Kristeva says in an interview that the maternal body enrages because it carries the child: "if there is a sort of rage against mothers it is not only because they take care of the child, it's because they carry it in their bodies" (1980a, 138). The rage is directed not just against the outside of the maternal body which nourishes and weans; it is also directed against the inside of the maternal body, and especially the inside that becomes outside, the child among other things. The child, the male child, feels rage against his mother because her carrying him in her womb compromises his identity. How can he become a man when 'he' was once a woman? He was once part, now the "expelled waste," of a woman's body. Even more curiously, how can he become a man and love a woman, that abject and threatening body 'represented' by his mother?[8]

In *Powers of Horror*, Kristeva describes how the child, there always the male child, must split his mother in order to take up his masculine gender identity. The mother is split in two: the abject and the sublime (1980a, 157). Making the mother abject allows the male child to separate from his mother and become autonomous. However, if the mother is only abject, then she becomes the phobic object and the child himself becomes abject. The oedipal situation, then, would be thrown out of alignment, on the border of disappearing altogether. If the mother remains abject, she never becomes the object, and certainly not the object of love. The phobic substitutes the sign, in a denial of sexual difference, for the absent object (1980a, 45). The mother must also be made sublime so that the male child can take her, a woman, as an object of love. However, if she is only sublime, the child will not separate from her. He will have no subject or object identity whatsoever, no primary repression and thus no secondary repression. In other words, the Other will have been completely foreclosed, never set up, and the child will be psychotic. He will still be unable to love a woman, or anyone else. For the psychotic, there is no one else, no object, no other(s). The sublime and abject must come together under the auspices of the paternal in order to produce the object of love.[9] The child can overcome the abject mother only through a "third" agency, traditionally associated with the Father who threatens castration (1975a, 263).

However, Kristeva argues that the castration threat is not enough to motivate the child's move away from the maternal body. After all, if all we have to look forward to is a world of threats, why would any of us leave the safe haven of the maternal body? Although this "third party" brings with it the need to symbolize (1980a, 118, 44; 1981, 314), it is not the authoritarian father of traditional psychoanalysis. Rather, as Kristeva suggests in *Tales of Love*, it is the loving mother-father conglomerate (put into operation through the mother's love) who helps the child overcome abjection.

So, the son splits the mother, has his cake and eats it too, but what about the daughter? Whereas the son splits the mother in order to unify himself, if the daughter splits the mother, she splits herself. In addition, the female does not have to divide the mother in order to take up her feminine gender identity. Rather, taking up her gender identity requires that she abandon her mother as love object for the father (1980b, 137). Now it would seem that for the female the mother need only be abject.

However, when the female makes her mother abject in order to reject her, she also makes herself abject, rejects herself, and not just temporarily. Kristeva maintains that when women do embrace the abject or even make themselves abject, it is in order to please a man, perhaps a pervert turned on by abjection (1980a, 54; 1980b, 136). Kristeva claims that feminine perversion is very rare. This, she says, is because of the difficulty women have in "combat" with their mothers (1980b, 136–37).

In an interview, Kristeva identifies two ways that a woman can "get rid" of her mother. One possibility is that she doesn't ever get rid of her mother. Rather, she carries with her "this living corpse," the mother's body which no longer nourishes (1980b, 137). Usually, however, claims Kristeva, women close their eyes to this corpse. They forget about it. And they certainly don't eroticize it (1980b, 137). The other alternative is that a woman forms a defense against the mother. Feminism is one such defense. Presumably, politics, art, and science are others. If a woman enters this "combat" with her mother without any such defense, Kristeva warns that it can lead to "fairly serious forms of psychosis" (1980b, 137).

For both sexes, the battle to become autonomous is a battle with the mother. Primal repression, for both sexes, is a repression of the identification with the mother's body. In the traditional psychoanalytic account, primal repression is replaced and strengthened by a secondary repression, language. Language, as the traditional story goes, comes through the Law of the Father, which guarantees that the primary prototype of the object, the mother, is signifiable even while she is desiring. Kristeva suggests that if we look closely at this thesis—that the mother is the first object—we see that "no sooner sketched out, such a thesis is exploded by its contradictions and flimsiness" (1980a, 32). For behind this mother-object is the mother's body—filled with drives and pre-objects—the body which must be abjected so that the child can take an object.

Because our traditional discourses on motherhood do not distinguish between the abject mother and all women, they perpetuate the denigration of women. Within these discourses we reject the mother's breast as abject and thereby reject all women as abject. Once again a part of women, the nourishing breast, stands in for the whole of women. What we need, then, is a discourse on motherhood which explains how we can wean ourselves from the nourishing breast, the maternal body, in order to become individuals without excluding or denying all women. More radically, perhaps we need to rethink the need for autonomy which turns the nourishing breast and mother's milk into a threat. Perhaps we need a new discourse on motherhood which can found a new conception of the individual and society, and, in the end, a new conception of ethics.

In the essay "Stabat Mater" from *Tales of Love*, Kristeva begins to imagine a new discourse on motherhood and the resulting ethics which she calls "herethics." "Herethics" is an ethics founded on the relationship between the mother and child. This ethics sets up one's obligations to the other as obligations to the self and obligations to the species. It is an ethics which is not merely a social relation enforced by law. It is not an ethics founded on prohibition but on love. According to Kristeva, the social relation can be founded on love rather than prohibition. It is a matter of living with, and learning to love, the other within us (the unconscious). Kristeva suggests that if we can learn to live with the other in ourselves, then we can learn to live with others in our society. If we can learn to love the stranger in ourselves, then we can learn to love the strangers outside of ourselves. The other, then, is not so radically other, and ethics may be possible. Significantly, the first model of this other who is not so other is found in the experience of maternity.

"Herethics" is founded on the ambiguity in maternity and birth between subject and object positions.[10] Maternity is the embodiment of the social relation based on the love of the other within the self. Pregnancy, says Kristeva, is an "institutionalized psychosis": "Am I me or it?"[11] The other cannot be separated from the self. The other is identical to the self. It is not in its place—the place of the other. It is, rather, in the place of the subject. This inability to separate self from other is a symptom of psychosis, the fundamental "psychosis" upon which any relationship is built. Pregnancy is the only place where this psychosis is socially acceptable.[12] "In a double-barreled move," claims Kristeva, "psychotic tendencies are acknowledged, but at the same time they are settled, quieted, and bestowed upon the mother in order to maintain the ultimate guarantee: symbolic coherence" (1975, 238).

Maternity is a bridge between nature and culture, the drives and signification. The mother's body is the "pivot of sociality," "at once the guarantee and a threat to its stability" (1977, 297). Thus, maternity is impossible for culture. Kristeva defines the maternal as "the ambivalent principle that is bound to the species, on the one hand, and on the other stems from an identity catastrophe that causes the Name to topple over into the unnameable that one imagines as femininity, nonlanguage, or body" (1976, 235). If we understand the concept of mother as defined by drives, we are born out of something nonsocial and nonsymbolic; the concept of mother is lost. This is because the mother cannot be on the side of the drives, or we are born out of something nonsocial and nonsymbolic and we lose the mother. Yet, she cannot straddle the drives and culture for the same reason. And she cannot be completely within culture or we lose the child. Western culture can deal with the mother only as myth and fantasy (the virgin mother, the denigrated woman) which covers over this psychotic process and undecidable identity.[13]The mother, however, 'knows' better:

For a mother. . . . [t]he other is inevitable, she seems to say, turn it into a God if you wish, it is nevertheless natural, for such an other has come out of myself. . . . The "just the same" of motherly peace of mind . . . gnaws, on account of its basic disbelief, at culture's allmightiness. It bypasses perverse negation ("I know, but just the same") and constitutes the basis of the social bond in its generality, in the sense of "resembling others and eventually the species." (1976, 262)

The mother's other, rather than the radically separated, unreachable Other, is a natural other. "Turn it into a God if you wish," but it is not transcendent; it is real. The mother has bodily proof of this. For the mother this relationship with the other is not a struggle for recognition. It is not a battle—either me or you, subject or object. It is not a battle to separate. The child really is/was part of the mother's flesh. And her own flesh exists for the sake of the child, because at the limit, it does not and cannot "exist for itself." This other is not yet autonomous; it depends on the subject. As such, it threatens the "allmightiness" of cultural Laws or religion, which require an autonomous and inaccessible Other.[14]

The mother, however, gains access to what is off-limits, excluded from culture. She 'knows' better. She knows that there is no radically separated Other. The other is the flesh of her flesh, natural, loved. Whereas the perverse negation, the fetishism, necessary to maintain the Law of language and society ("I know that the word is not the thing, but just the same"; "I know that the other is not me, but just the same") constitutes the social bond through force of law, the mother's "just the same" is its reverse (cf. 1980, 37). The mother negates the Law even while ensuring its generation. She realizes that the other is the same, that the separation is not absolute. In the face of the culture and its autonomous individual, she says "just the same, I know." The mother's "just the same" constitutes the social bond through love, not force. However, this "just the same" threatens to do away with difference and "it can crush everything the other (the child) has that is specifically irreducible" (1976, 263). In other words, it threatens to do away with the culture. It threatens psychosis. This is why even if the culture denies the existence of the mother, she cannot, for the sake of her child, deny the existence of culture. She must wean the child. She must instigate the break-up of their primary symbiosis. She must be silent about what she 'knows' because she knows better.[15]

The child must separate from its mother's body in order to be an autonomous being. It cannot remain dependent on her. In fact, it must abject its mother's body so that it might love its mother. Until it can separate itself from the maternal body, it cannot love any other. Until it can separate from the maternal body, there is no other. However, it is the mother's love which supports the move into society, the move from maternal milk to speech. It is this love which fills language with meaning. Is it possible, then, that the primary identification with the mother is repressed because it is a reunion with the mother's love, which is founded on, yet mistaken for, a union with the mother's body?

The maternal body is abjected if necessary, but only for the sake of what motivates the bond in the first place: maternal love. In terms of the phallocentric discourse, this love is narcissism without a properly separated Other. Yet, according to Kristeva, without this narcissism discourse is empty, meaningless, mourning the loss of love. So, rather than exclude mother's milk as the abominable and impure fluid which threatens the disintegration of culture into nature, we can imagine mother's milk as the fluid which nourishes both the speaking subject and society. We can create a new discourse in which mother's milk is a symbol for a social bond based on love of an other as oneself. We can imagine mother's milk as a bonding fluid which founds ethics beyond the Law. Mother's milk becomes the food of an outlaw love which gives birth to a new ethics.

NOTES

Thanks to Lisa Heldke and Deane Curtin for their helpful comments on an earlier draft of this essay.

1. This reduplication, however, is not an imitation. And, because it is not an imitation, it does not presuppose an already constructed ego in relation with an already constructed object. It is not one being imitating another, the child imitating its object.

2. At this stage, Kristeva accepts Lacan's account of the "mirror stage," in which the child first recognizes itself as a body with defined borders and begins to separate itself from objects, including its primary object, Mom.

3. Whether it is the oedipal prohibition against incest formulated by Freud, the prohibition against the mother's desire or *jouissance* formulated by Lacan, or the prohibition against the semiotic *chora* formulated by Kristeva, all of these prohibitions are directed against the maternal body (1980, 14).

4. Cf. Lacan 1955, 232.

5. See Genesis 9:4 and Leviticus 10:18.

6. Cf. Lacan 1977, 207; Kristeva 1980c.

7. Cf. 1980, 39. Kristeva argues that becoming abject is the body's defense against cannibalism: if it is disgusting, it won't be eaten (1980, 78–79).

8. Here I would like to point out that this is why, according to Freud, the fetishist, usually male, fetishizes his mother and not just any woman. He denies that his mother has no penis because, once part of that penisless body, his own identity as male is threatened.

9. See 1983, 368. This splitting of the mother is complicated by another possibility central to Kristeva's discussion of Celine in *Powers of Horror*. There she argues that the abject can *become* sublime (1980a, 59). The phobic can sexualize the abject and take sexual pleasure in it. This eroticized abject is the 'object' of perverts and artists.

10. Here I think that Kristeva covers over one of her own foremothers, Simone de Beauvoir. Kristeva criticizes existential feminist notions of motherhood without mentioning Beauvoir.

11. 1977, 297. Kristeva's discussion of the pregnant maternal body is the central focus, around the time of her own pregnancy (which led to the birth of her son in

1976), in two essays: "Motherhood According to Giovanni Bellini" (1975), and "Stabat Mater" (1976).

12. Even this is problematic—witness Kristeva's account of the cult of the virgin mother and, I might add, the rhetoric of anti-abortion crusaders in the U.S. who argue that the foetus is a unified subject in its own right.

13. Kristeva is careful to limit her analysis to Western culture. However, she does not address differences within Western culture. And, therefore, it seems that she suggests that her generalizations might apply to different ethnic groups within Judeo-Christian culture. Kristeva maintains that while she is a social scientist concerned with generalizations, she is equally concerned with the individual in his or her particularity.

14. It is this radical separation that opens the gap between signifier and signified and produces the symbolic.

15. 1976, 260. This, of course, poses problems for feminist mothers. In order to ensure that their children are socially well-adjusted, mothers must initiate them into a patriarchal culture which may denigrate or deny existence of the mother.

R E F E R E N C E S

Kristeva, Julia
1975. "From One Identity to Another," in *Desire in Language*, translated by Thomas Gora, Alice Jardine, and Leon Roudiez; edited by Leon Roudiez, New York: Columbia Press.
1975a. "Motherhood According to Giovanni Bellini," in *Desire in Language*, translated by Thomas Gora, Alice Jardine, and Leon Roudiez, edited by Leon Roudiez, New York: Columbia Press.
1975b. "The Subject in Signifying Practice," *Semiotext(e)* 1(3):19–34.
1976. "The Father, Love, and Banishment," in *Desire in Language*, translated by Thomas Gora, Alice Jardine, and Leon Roudiez, edited by Leon Roudiez, New York: Columbia Press.
1976a. "Stabat Mater," in *Tales of Love*, translated by Leon Roudiez, New York: Columbia Press, 1987.
1976b. "China, Women and the Symbolic," *Sub-Stance*, 13.
1976c. "Signifying Practice and Mode of Production," *Edinburgh Review* 1.
1977. "Place Names," in *Desire in Language*, translated by Thomas Gora, Alice Jardine, and Leon Roudiez, edited by Leon Roudiez, New York: Columbia Press.
1980. *Desire in Language*, translated by Thomas Gora, Alice Jardine, and Leon Roudiez, edited by Leon Roudiez, New York: Columbia Press.
1980a. *Powers of Horror*, translated by Leon Roudiez, New York: Columbia Press, 1982.
1980b. "Interview with Julia Kristeva," in *Women Analyze Women*, edited by Elaine Baruch and Lucienne Serrano, New York: NYU Press, 1988.
1981a. "The Maternal Body," *m/f* 5/6.
1983. *Tales of Love*, translated by Leon Roudiez, New York: Columbia Press, 1987.
1986. "An Interview with Julia Kristeva," by Edith Kurweil, *Partisan Review*, 53 (2):216–229.

1986a. "An Interview with Julia Kristeva," by I. Lipowitz and A. Loselle, *Critical Texts* 3, 3.

1987. *Au commencement etait l'amour*, translated by Arthur Goldhammer as *In the Beginning Was Love: Psychoanalysis and Faith*, New York: Columbia Press, 1988.

1987a. *Soleil Noir: Depression et Melancolie*, Gallimard: Paris.

1987b. "La Femme Tristesse," *L'Infini*, 17:5–9.

1987c. "La Vierge De Freud," *L'Infini*, 18:23–30.

Lacan, Jacques

1954–1955. *The Seminars of Jacques Lacan: The Theory of the Ego in Psychoanalytic Theory and Practice*, "Freud's Papers on Techniques," edited by Jacques A. Miller, New York; Norton.

1977. *Ecrits: A Selection*, London: Tavistock.

Playfulness, "World"-Travelling, and Loving Perception

This paper weaves two aspects of life together. My coming to consciousness as a daughter and my coming to consciousness as a woman of color have made this weaving possible. This weaving reveals the possibility and complexity of a pluralistic feminism, a feminism that affirms the plurality in each of us and among us as richness and as central to feminist ontology and epistemology.

The paper describes the experience of 'outsiders' to the mainstream of, for example, White/Anglo organization of life in the U.S. and stresses a particular feature of the outsider's existence: the outsider has necessarily acquired flexibility in shifting from the mainstream construction of life where she is constructed as an outsider to other constructions of life where she is more or less 'at home.' This flexibility is necessary for the outsider but it can also be willfully exercised by the outsider or by those who are at ease in the mainstream. I recommend this willful exercise which I call "world"-travelling and I also recommend that the willful exercise be animated by an attitude that I describe as playful.

As outsiders to the mainstream, women of color in the U.S. practice "world"-travelling, mostly out of necessity. I affirm this practice as a skillful, creative, rich, enriching and, given certain circumstances, as a loving way of being and living. I recognize that much of our travelling is done unwillfully to hostile White/Anglo "worlds." The hostility of these "worlds" and the compulsory nature of the "travelling" have obscured for us the enormous value of this aspect of our living and its connection to loving. Racism has a vested interest in obscuring and devaluing the complex skills involved in it. I recommend that we affirm this travelling across "worlds" as partly constitutive of cross-cultural and cross-racial loving. Thus I recommend to women of color in the U.S. that we learn to love each other by learning to travel to each other's "worlds."

On the other hand, the paper makes a connection between what Marilyn Frye has named "arrogant perception" and the failure to identify with persons that one views arrogantly or has come to see as the products of arrogant perception. A further connection is made between this failure of identification and a failure of love, and thus between loving and identifying with another person. The sense of love is not the one Frye has identified as both consistent with arrogant perception and as promoting unconditional servitude. "We can be taken in by this equation of servitude with love," Frye (1983, 73) says, "because we make two mistakes at once: we think, of both servitude and love that they are selfless or unselfish." Rather, the identification of which I speak is constituted by what I come to characterize as playful "world"-travelling. To the extent that we learn to perceive others arrogantly or come to see them only as products of arrogant perception and continue to perceive them that way, we fail to identify with them—fail to love them—in this particularly deep way.

IDENTIFICATION AND LOVE

As a child, I was taught to perceive arrogantly. I have also been the object of arrogant perception. Though I am not a White/Anglo woman, it is clear to me that I can understand both my childhood training as an arrogant perceiver and my having been the object of arrogant perception without any reference to White/Anglo men, which is some indication that the concept of arrogant perception can be used cross-culturally and that White/Anglo men are not the only arrogant perceivers. I was brought up in Argentina watching men and women of moderate and of considerable means graft the substance[1] of their servants to themselves. I also learned to graft my mother's substance to my own. It was clear to me that both men and women were the victims of arrogant perception and that arrogant perception was systematically organized to break the spirit of all women and of most men. I valued my rural 'gaucho' ancestry because its ethos has always been one of independence in poverty through enormous loneliness, courage and self-reliance. I found inspiration in this ethos and committed myself never to be broken by arrogant perception. I can say all of this in this way only because I have learned from Frye's "In and Out of Harm's Way: Arrogance and Love." She has given me a way of understanding and articulating something important in my own life.

Frye is not particularly concerned with women as arrogant perceivers but as the objects of arrogant perception. Her concern is, in part, to enhance our understanding of women "untouched by phallocratic machinations" (Frye 1983, 53), by understanding the harm done to women through such machinations. In this case she proposes that we could understand women untouched by arrogant perception through an understanding of what arrogant perception does to women. She also proposes an understanding of what it is to love women that is inspired by a vision of women unharmed by arrogant perception. To love women is, at least in part, to perceive them with loving eyes. "The loving eye is a contrary of the arrogant eye" (Frye 1983, 75).

I am concerned with women as arrogant perceivers because I want to explore further what it is to love women. I want to explore two failures of love: my failure to love my mother and White/Anglo women's failure to love women across racial and cultural boundaries in the U.S. As a consequence of exploring these failures I will offer a loving solution to them. My solution modifies Frye's account of loving perception by adding what I call playful "world"-travel.

It is clear to me that at least in the U.S. and Argentina women are taught to perceive many other women arrogantly. Being taught to perceive arrogantly is part of being taught to be a woman of a certain class in both the U.S. and Argentina, it is part of being taught to be a White/Anglo woman in the U.S. and it is part of being taught to be a woman in both places: to be both the agent and the object of arrogant perception. My love for my mother seemed to me thoroughly imperfect as I was growing up because I was unwilling to become what I had been taught to see my mother as being. I thought that to love her was consistent with my abusing her (using, taking for granted, and demanding her services in a far reaching way that, since four other people engaged in the same grafting of her substance onto themselves, left her little of herself to herself) and was to be in part constituted by my identifying with her, my seeing myself in her: to love her was supposed to be of a piece with both my abusing her and with my being open to being abused. It is clear to me that I was not supposed to love servants: I could abuse them without identifying with them, without seeing myself in them. When I came to the U.S. I learned that part of racism is the internalization of the propriety of abuse without identification: I learned that I could be seen as a being to be used by White/Anglo men and women without the possibility of identification, i.e., without their act of attempting to graft my substance onto theirs, rubbing off on them at all. They could remain untouched, without any sense of loss.

So, women who are perceived arrogantly can perceive other women arrogantly in their turn. To what extent those women are responsible for their arrogant perceptions of other women is certainly open to question, but I do not have any doubt that many women have been taught to abuse women in this particular way. I am not interested in assigning responsibility. I am interested in understanding the phenomenon so as to understand a loving way out of it.

There is something obviously wrong with the love that I was taught and something right with my failure to love my mother in this way. But I do not think that what is wrong is my profound desire to identify with her, to see myself in her; what is wrong is that I was taught to identify with a victim of enslavement. What is wrong is that I was taught to practice enslavement of my mother and to learn to become a slave through this practice. There is something obviously wrong with my having been taught that love is consistent with abuse, consistent with arrogant perception. Notice that the love I was taught is the love that Frye (1983, 73) speaks of when she says "We can be taken in by this equation of servitude with love." Even though I could both abuse and love my mother, I was not supposed to love servants.

This is because in the case of servants one is and is supposed to be clear about their servitude and the "equation of servitude with love" is never to be thought clearly in those terms. So, I was not supposed to love and could not love servants. But I could love my mother because deception (in particular, self-deception) is part of this "loving." Servitude is called abnegation and abnegation is not analyzed any further. Abnegation is not instilled in us through an analysis of its nature but rather through a heralding of it as beautiful and noble. We are coaxed, seduced into abnegation not through analysis but through emotive perception. Frye makes the connection between deception and this sense of "loving" clear. When I say that there is something obviously wrong with the loving that I was taught, I do not mean to say that the connection between this loving and abuse is obvious. Rather I mean that once the connection between this loving and abuse has been unveiled, there is something obviously wrong with the loving given that it is obvious that it is wrong to abuse others.

I am glad that I did not learn my lessons well, but it is clear that part of the mechanism that permitted my not learning well involved a separation from my mother: I saw us as beings of quite a different sort. It involved an abandoning of my mother while I longed not to abandon her. I wanted to love my mother, though, given what I was taught, "love" could not be the right word for what I longed for.

I was disturbed by my not wanting to be what she was. I had a sense of not being quite integrated, my self was missing because I could not identify with her, I could not see myself in her, I could not welcome her world. I saw myself as separate from her, a different sort of being, not quite of the same species. This separation, this lack of love, I saw, and I think that I saw correctly as a lack in myself (not a fault, but a lack). I also see that if this was a lack of love, love cannot be what I was taught. Love has to be rethought, made anew.

There is something in common between the relation between myself and my mother as someone I did not use to be able to love and the relation between myself or other women of color in the U.S. and White/Anglo women: there is a failure of love. I want suggest here that Frye has helped me understand one of the aspects of this failure, the directly abusive aspect. But I also think that there is a complex failure of love in the failure to identify with another woman, the failure to see oneself in other women who are quite different from oneself. I want to begin to analyze this complex failure.

Notice that Frye's emphasis on independence in her analysis of loving perception is not particularly helpful in explaining this failure. She says that in loving perception, "the object of the seeing is another being whose existence and character are logically independent of the seer and who may be practically or empirically independent in any particular respect at any particular time" (Frye 1983, 77). But this is not helpful in allowing me to understand how my failure of love toward my mother (when I ceased to be her parasite) left me not quite whole. It is not helpful since I saw her as logically independent from me. It also does not help me to understand why the racist or ethnocentric failure of love of White/Anglo women—in particular of those White/Anglo women who are not pained by their failure—should leave me not quite substantive among them. Here I am not particularly interested in cases of White women's parasitism onto women of color but more pointedly in cases where the failure of identification is the manifestation of the "relation." I am particularly interested here in those many cases in which White/Anglo women do one or more of the following to women of color: they ignore us, ostracize us, render us invisible, stereotype us, leave us completely alone, interpret us as crazy. All of this *while we are in their midst.* The more independent I am, the more independent I am left to be. Their world and their integrity do not require me at all. There is no sense of self-loss in them for my own lack of solidity. But they rob me of my solidity through indifference, an indifference they can afford and which seems sometimes studied. (All of this points of course toward separatism in communities where our substance is seen and celebrated, where we become substantive through this celebration. But many of us have to work among White/Anglo folk and our best shot at recognition has seemed to be among White/Anglo women because many of them have expressed a *general* sense of being pained at their failure to love.)

Many times White/Anglo women want us out of their field of vision. Their lack of concern is a harmful failure of love that leaves me independent from them in a way similar to the way in which, once I ceased to be my mother's parasite, she became, though not independent from all others, certainly independent from me. But of course, because my mother and I wanted to love each other well, we were not whole in this independence. White/Anglo women are independent from me, I am independent from them, I am independent from my mother, she is independent from me, and none of us loves each other in this independence.

I am incomplete and unreal without other women. I am profoundly dependent on others without having to be their subordinate, their slave, their servant.

Frye (1983, 75) also says that the loving eye is "the eye of one who knows that to know the seen, one must consult something other than one's own will and interest and fears and imagination." This is much more helpful to me so long as I do not understand Frye to mean that I should not consult my own interests nor that I should exclude the possibility that my self and the self of the one I love may be importantly tied to each other in many complicated ways. Since I am emphasizing here that the failure of loves lies in part in the failure to identify and since I agree with Frye that one "must consult something other than one's own will and interests and fears and imagination," I will proceed to try to explain what I think needs to be consulted. To love my mother was not possible for me while I retained a sense that it was fine for me and others to see her arrogantly. Loving my mother also required that I see with her eyes, that I go into my mother's world, that I see both of us as we are constructed in her world, that I witness her own sense of herself from within her world. Only through this travelling to her "world" could I identify with her because only then could I cease to ignore her and to be excluded and separate from her. Only then could I see her as a subject even if one subjected and only then could I see at all how meaning could arise fully between us. We are fully dependent on each other for the possibility of being understood and without this understanding we are not intelligible, we do not make sense, we are not solid, visible, integrated; we are lacking. So travelling to each other's "worlds" would enable us to *be* through *loving* each other.

Hopefully the sense of identification I have in mind is becoming clear. But if it is to become clearer, I need to explain what I mean by a "world" and by "travelling" to another "world."

In explaining what I mean by a "world" I will not appeal to travelling to other women's worlds. Rather I will lead you to see what I mean by a "world" the way I came to propose the concept to myself: through the kind of ontological confusion about myself that we, women of color, refer to half-jokingly as "schizophrenia" (we fell schizophrenic in our goings back and forth between different "communities") and through my effort to make some sense of this ontological confusion.

"WORLDS" AND "WORLD" TRAVELLING

Some time ago I came to be in a state of profound confusion as I experienced myself as both having and not having a particular attribute. I was sure I had the attribute in question and, on the other hand, I was sure that I did not have it. I remain convinced that I both have and do not have this attribute. The attribute is playfulness. I am sure that I am a playful person. On the other hand, I can say, painfully, that I am not a playful person. I am not a playful person in certain worlds. One of the things I did as I became confused was to call my friends, far away people who knew me well, to see whether or not I was playful. Maybe they could help me out of my confusion. They said to me, "Of course you are playful" and they said it with the same conviction that I had about it. Of course I am playful. Those people who were around me said to me, "No, you are not playful. You are a serious woman. You just take everything seriously." They were just as sure about what they said to me and could offer me every bit of evidence that one could need to conclude that they were right. So I said to myself: "Okay, maybe what's happening here is that there is an attribute that I do have but there are certain worlds in which I am not at ease and it is because I'm not at ease in those worlds that I don't have that attribute in those worlds. But what does that mean?" I was worried both about what I meant by "worlds" when I said "in some worlds I do not have the attribute" and what I meant by saying that lack of ease was what led me not to be playful in those worlds. Because you see, if it was just a matter of lack of ease, I could work on it.

I can explain some of what I mean by a "world." I do not want the fixity of a definition at this point, because I think the term is suggestive and I do not want to close the suggestiveness of it too soon. I can offer some characteristics that serve to distinguish between a "world," a utopia, a possible world in the philosophical sense, and a world view. By a "world" I do not mean a utopia at all. A utopia does not count as a world in my sense. The "worlds" that I am talking about are possible. But a possible world is not what I mean by a "world" and I do not mean a world-view, though something like a world-view is involved here.

For something to be a "world" in my sense it has to be inhabited at present by some flesh and blood people. That is why it cannot be a utopia. It may also be inhabited by some imaginary people. It may be inhabited by people who are dead or people that the inhabitants of this "world" met in some other "world" and now have in this "world" in imagination.

A "world" in my sense may be an actual society given its dominant culture's description and construction of life, including a construction of the relationships of production, of gender, race, etc. But a "world" can also be such a society given a non-dominant construction, or it can be such a society or *a* society given an idiosyncratic construction. As we will see it is problematic to say that these are all constructions of the same society. But they are different "worlds."

A "world" need not be construction of a whole society. It may be a construction of a tiny portion of a particular society. It may be inhabited by just a few people. Some "worlds" are bigger than others.

A "world" may be incomplete in that things in it may not be altogether constructed or some things may be constructed negatively (they are not what 'they' are in some other "world"). Or the "world" may be incomplete because it may have references to things that do not quite exist in it, references to things like Brazil, where Brazil is not quite part of that "world." Given lesbian feminism, the construction of 'lesbian' is purposefully and healthily still up in the air, in the process of becoming. What it is to be a Hispanic in this country is, in a dominant Anglo construction purposefully incomplete. Thus one cannot really answer questions of the sort "What is a Hispanic?", "Who counts as Hispanic?", "Are Latinos, Chicanos, Hispanos, black dominicans, white cubans, korean-columbians, italian-argentinians hispanic?" What is it to be a 'hispanic' in the varied so-called hispanic communities in the U.S. is also yet up in the air. We have not yet decided whether there is something like a 'hispanic' in our varied "worlds." So, a "world" may be an incomplete visionary non-utopian construction of life or it may be a traditional construction of life. A traditional Hispano construction of Northern New Mexican life is a "world." Such a traditional construction, in the face of a racist, ethnocentrist, money-centered anglo construction of Northern New Mexican life is highly unstable because Anglos have the means for imperialist destruction of traditional Hispano "worlds."

In a "world" some of the inhabitants may not understand or hold the particular construction of them that constructs them in that "world." So, there may be "worlds" that construct me in ways that I do not even understand. Or it may be that I understand the construction, but do not hold it of myself. I may not accept it as an account of myself, a construction of myself. And yet, I may be *animating* such a construction.

One can "travel" between these "worlds" and one can inhabit more than one of these "worlds" at the very same time. I think that most of us who are outside the mainstream of, for example, the U.S. dominant construction or organization of life are "world travellers" as a matter of necessity and of survival. It seems to me that inhabiting more than one "world" at the same time and "travelling" between "worlds" is part and parcel of our experience and our situation. One can be at the same time in a "world" that constructs one as stereotypically latin, for example, and in a "world" that constructs one as latin. Being stereotypically latin and being simply latin are different simultaneous constructions of persons that are part of different "worlds." One animates one or the other or both at the same time without necessarily confusing them, though simultaneous enactment can be confusing if one is not on one's guard.

In describing my sense of a "world," I mean to be offering a description of experience, something that is true to experience even if it is ontologically problematic. Though I would think that any account of identity that could not be true to this experience of outsiders to the mainstream would be faulty even if ontologically unproblematic. Its ease would constrain, erase, or deem aberrant experience that has within it significant insights into non-imperialistic understanding between people.

Those of us who are "world"-travellers have the distinct experience of being different in different "worlds" and of having the capacity to remember other "worlds" and ourselves in them. We can say "That is me there, and I am happy in that "world." So, the experience is of being a different person in different "worlds" and yet of having memory of oneself as different without quite having the sense of there being any underlying "I." So I can say "that is me there and I am so playful in that "world." I say "That is *me* in that "world" not because I recognize myself in that person, rather the first person statement is non-inferential. I may well recognize that that person has abilities that I do not have and yet the having or not having of the abilities is always an "I have . . . " and "I do not have . . . ", i.e., it is always experienced in the first person.

The shift from being one person to being a different person is what I call "travel." This shift may not be willful or even conscious, and one may be completely unaware of being different than one is in a different "world," and may not recognize that one is in a different "world." Even though the shift can be done willfully, it is not a matter of acting. One does not pose as someone else, one does not pretend to be, for example, someone of a different personality or character or someone who uses space or language differently than the other person. Rather one is someone who has that personality or character or uses space and language in that particular way. The "one" here does not refer to some underlying "I." One does not *experience* any underlying "I."

BEING AT EASE IN A "WORLD"

In investigating what I mean by "being at ease in a 'world,'" I will describe different ways of being at ease. One may be at ease in one or in all of these ways. There is a maximal way of being at ease, viz. being at ease in all of these ways. I take this maximal way of being at ease to be somewhat dangerous because it tends to produce people who have no inclination to travel across "worlds" or have no experience of "world" travelling.

The first way of being at ease in a particular "world" is by being a fluent speaker in that "world." I know all the norms that there are to be followed, I know all the words that there are to be spoken. I know all the moves. I am confident.

Another way of being at ease is by being normatively happy. I agree with all the norms, I could not love any norms better. I am asked to do just what I want to do or what I think I should do. At ease.

Another way of being at ease in a "world" is by being humanly bonded. I am with those I love and they love me too. It should be noticed that I may be with those I love and be at ease because of them in a "world" that is otherwise as hostile to me as "worlds" get.

Finally one may be at ease because one has a history with others that is shared, especially daily history, the kind of shared history that one sees exemplified by the response to the "Do you remember poodle skirts?" question. There you are, with people you do not know at all. The question is posed and then they all begin talking about their poodle skirt stories. I have been in such situations without knowing what poodle skirts, for example, were and I felt so ill at ease because it was not *my* history. The other people did not particularly know each other. It is not that they were humanly bonded. Probably they did not have much politically in common either. But poodle skirts were in their shared history.

One may be at ease in one of these ways or in all of them. Notice that when one says meaningfully "This is *my* world," one may not be at east in it. Or one may be at ease in it only in some of these respects and not in others. To say of some "world" that it is "*my* world" is to make an evaluation. One may privilege one or more "worlds" in this way for a variety of reasons: for example because one experiences oneself as an agent in a fuller sense that one experiences "oneself" in other "worlds." One may disown a "world" because one has first person memories of a person who is so thoroughly dominated that she has no sense of exercising her own will or has a sense of having serious difficulties in performing actions that are willed by herself and no difficulty in performing actions willed by others. One may say of a "world" that it is "my world" because one is at ease in it, i.e., being at ease in a "world" may be the basis for the evaluation.

Given the clarification of what I mean by a "world," "world"-travel, and being at ease in a "world," we are in a position to return to my problematic attribute, playfulness. It may be that in this "world" in which I am so unplayful, I am a different person than in the "world" in which I am playful. Or it may be that the "world" in which I am unplayful is constructed in such a way that I could be playful in it. I could practice, even though that "world" is constructed in such a way that my being playful in it is kind of hard. In describing what I take a "world" to be, I emphasized the first possibility as both the one that is truest to the experience of "outsiders" to the mainstream and as ontologically problematic because the "I" is identified in some sense as one and in some sense as plurality. I identify myself as myself through memory and I retain myself as different in memory. When I travel from one "world" to another, I have this image, this memory of myself as playful in this other "world." I can then be in a particular "world" and have a double image of myself as, for example, playful and as not playful. But this is a very familiar and recognizable phenomenon to the outsider to the mainstream in some central cases: when in one "world" I animate, for example, that "world's" caricature of the person I am in the other "world." I can have both images of myself and to the extent that I can materialize or animate both images at the same time I become an ambiguous being. This is very much a part of trickery and foolery. It is worth remembering that the trickster and the fool are significant characters in many non-dominant or outsider cultures. One then sees any particular "world" with these double edges and sees absurdity in them and so inhabits oneself differently. Given that latins are constructed in Anglo "worlds" as stereotypically intense—intensity being a central characteristic of at least one of the Anglo stereotypes of latins—and given that many latins, myself included, are genuinely intense, I can say to myself "I am intense" and take a hold of the double meaning. And furthermore, I can be stereotypically intense or be the real thing and, if you are Anglo, you do not know when I am which *because* I am Latin-American. As Latin-American I am an ambiguous being, a two-imaged self: I can see that gringos see me as stereotypically intense because I am, as a Latin-American, constructed that way but I may or may not *intentionally* animate the stereotype or the real thing knowing that you may not see it in anything other than in the stereotypical construction. This ambiguity is funny and is not just funny, it is survival-rich. We can also make the picture of those who dominate us funny precisely because we can see the double edge, we can see them doubly constructed, we can see the plurality in them. So we know truths that only the fool can speak and only the trickster can play out without harm. We inhabit "worlds" and travel across them and keep all the memories.

Sometimes the "world"-traveller has a double image of herself and each self includes as important ingredients of itself one or more attributes that are *incompatible* with one or more of the attributes of the other self: for example being playful and being unplayful. To the extent that the attribute is an important ingredient of the self she is in that "world," i.e., to the extent that there is a particularly good fit between that "world" and her having that attribute in it and to the extent that the attribute is personality or character central, that "world" would have to be changed if she is to be playful in it. It is not the case that if she could come to be at ease in it, she would be her own playful self. Because the attribute is personality or character central and there is such a good fit between that "world" and her being constructed with that attribute as central, *she* cannot become playful, she is unplayful. To become playful would be for her to become a contradictory being. So I am suggesting that the lack of ease solution cannot be a solution to my problematic case. My problem is not one of lack of ease. I am suggesting that I can understand my confusion about whether I am or am not playful by saying that I am both and that I am different persons in different "worlds" and can remember myself in both as I am in the other. I am a plurality of selves. This is to understand my confusion because *it is to come to see it as a piece* with much of the rest of my experience as an outsider in some of the "worlds" that I inhabit and of a piece with significant aspects of the experience of non-dominant people in the "worlds" of their dominators.

So, though I may not be at ease in the "worlds" in which I am not constructed playful, it is not that I am not playful *because* I am not at ease. The two are compatible. But lack of playfulness is not caused by lack of ease. Lack of playfulness is not symptomatic of lack of ease but of lack of health. I am not a healthy being in the "worlds" that construct me unplayful.

PLAYFULNESS

I had a very personal stake in investigating this topic. Playfulness is not only the attribute that was the source of my confusion and the attitude that I recommend as the loving attitude in travelling across "worlds"; I am also scared of ending up a serious human being, someone with no multi-dimensionality, with no fun in life, someone who is just someone who has had the fun constructed out of her. I am seriously scared of getting stuck in a "world" that constructs me that way. A world that I have no escape from and in which I cannot be playful.

I thought about what it is to be playful and what it is to play and I did this thinking in a "world" in which I only remember myself as playful and in which all of those who know me as playful are imaginary beings. A "world" in which I am scared of losing my memories of myself as playful or have them erased from me. Because I live in such a "world," after I formulated my own sense of what it is to be playful and to play I decided that I needed to "go to the literature." I read two classics on the subject: Johan Huizinga's *Homo Ludens* and Hans-Georg Gadamer's chapter on the concept of play in his *Truth and Method*. I discovered, to my amazement, that what I thought about play and playfulness, if they were right, was absolutely wrong. Though I will not provide the arguments for this interpretation of Gadamer and Huizinga here, I understood that both of them have an agonistic sense of 'play.' Play and playfulness have, ultimately, to do with contest, with winning, losing, battling. The sense of playfulness that I have in mind has nothing to do with those things. So, I tried to elucidate both senses of play and playfulness by contrasting them to each other. The contrast helped me see the attitude that I have in mind as the loving attitude in travelling across "worlds" more clearly.

An agonistic sense of playfulness is one in which *competence* is supreme. You had better know the rules of the game. In agonistic play there is risk, there is *uncertainty*, but the uncertainty is about who is going to win and who is going to lose. There are rules that inspire hostility. The attitude of *playfulness is conceived as secondary to or derivative from play*. Since play is agon, then the only conceivable playful attitude is an agonistic one (the attitude does not turn an activity into play, but rather presupposes an activity that is play). One of the paradigmatic ways of playing for both Gadamer and Huizinga is role-playing. In role-playing, the person who is a participant in the game has a *fixed conception of him or herself*. I also think that the players are imbued with *self-importance* in agonistic play since they are so keen on winning given their own merits, their very own competence.

When considering the value of "world"-travelling and whether playfulness is the loving attitude to have while travelling, I recognized the agonistic attitude as inimical to travelling across "worlds." The agonistic traveller is a conqueror, an imperialist. Huizinga, in his classic book on play, interprets Western civilization as play. That is an interesting thing for Third World people to think about. Western civilization has been interpreted by a white western man as play in the agonistic sense of play. Huizinga reviews western law, art, and many other aspects of western culture and sees agon in all of them. Agonistic playfulness leads those who attempt to travel to another "world" with this attitude to failure. Agonistic travellers fail consistently in their attempt to travel because what they do is to try to conquer the other "world." The attempt is not an attempt to try to erase the other "world." That is what assimilation is all about. Assimilation is the destruction of other people's "worlds." So, the agonistic attitude, the playful attitude given western man's construction of playfulness, is not a healthy, loving attitude to have in travelling across "worlds." Notice that given the agonistic attitude one *cannot* travel across "worlds," though one can kill other "worlds" with it. So for people who are interested in crossing racial and ethnic boundaries, an arrogant western man's construction of playfulness is deadly. One cannot cross the boundaries with it. One needs to give up such an attitude if one wants to travel.

So then, what is the loving playfulness that I have in mind? Let me begin with one example: We are by the river bank. The river is very, very low. Almost dry. Bits of water here and there. Little pools with a few trout hiding under the rocks. But mostly is wet stones, grey on the outside. We walk on the stones for awhile. You pick up a stone and crash it onto the others. As it breaks, it is quite wet inside and it is very colorful, very pretty. I pick up a stone and break it and run toward the pieces to see the colors. They are beautiful. I laugh and bring the pieces back to you and you are doing the same with your pieces. We keep on crashing stones for hours, anxious to see the beautiful new colors. We are playing. The playfulness of our activity does not presuppose that there is something like "crashing stones" that is a particular form of play with its own rules. Rather *the attitude that carries us through the activity, a playful attitude, turns the activity into play.* Our activity has no rules, though it is certainly intentional activity and we both understand what we are doing. The playfulness that gives meaning to our activity includes uncertainty, but in this case the uncertainty is an *openness to surprise.* This is a particular metaphysical attitude that does not expect the world to be neatly packaged, ruly. Rules may fail to explain what we are doing. We are not self-important, we are not fixed in particular constructions of ourselves, which is part of saying that we are *open to self-construction.* We may not have rules, and when we do have rules, *there are no rules that are to us sacred.* We are not worried about competence. We are not wedded to a particular way of doing things. While playful we have not abandoned ourselves to, nor are we stuck in, any particular "world." We *are there creatively.* We are not passive.

Playfulness is, in part, an openness to being a fool, which is a combination of not worrying about competence, not being self-important, not taking norms as sacred and finding ambiguity and double edges a source of wisdom and delight.

So, positively, the playful attitude involves openness to surprise, openness to being a fool, openness to self-construction or reconstruction and to construction or reconstruction of the "worlds" we inhabit playfully. Negatively, playfulness is characterized by uncertainty, lack of self-importance, absence of rules or a not taking rules as sacred, a not worrying about competence and a lack of abandonment to a particular construction of oneself, others and one's relation to them. In attempting to take a hold of oneself and of one's relation to others in a particular "world," one may study, examine and come to understand oneself. One may then see what the possibilities for play are for the being one is in that "world." One may even decide to inhabit that self fully in order to understand it better and find its creative possibilities. All of this is just self-reflection and it is quite different from resigning or abandoning oneself to the particular construction of oneself that one is attempting to take a hold of.

CONCLUSION

There are "worlds" we enter at our own risk, "worlds" that have agon, conquest, and arrogance as the main ingredients in their ethos. These are "worlds" that we enter out of necessity and which would be foolish to enter playfully in either the agonistic sense or in my sense. In such "worlds" *we* are not playful.

But there are "worlds" that we can travel to lovingly and travelling to them is part of loving at least some of their inhabitants. The reason why I thing that travelling to someone's "world" is a way of identifying with them is because by travelling to their "world" we can understand *what it is to be them and what it is to be ourselves in their eyes.* Only when we have travelled to each other's "worlds" are we fully subjects to each other (I agree with Hegel that self-recognition requires other subjects, but I disagree with his claim that it requires tension or hostility).

Knowing other women's "worlds" is part of knowing them and knowing them is part of loving them. Notice that the knowing can be done in greater or lesser depth, as can the loving. Also notice that travelling to another's "world" is not the same as becoming intimate with them. Intimacy is constituted in part by a very deep knowledge of the other self and "world"-travelling is only part of having this knowledge. Also notice that some people, in particular those who are outsiders to the mainstream, can be known only to the extent that they are known in several "worlds" and as "world"-travellers.

Without knowing the other's "world," one does not know the other, and without knowing the other one is really alone in the other's presence because the other is only dimly present to one.

Through travelling to other people's "worlds" we discover that there are "worlds" in which those who are the victims of arrogant perception are really subjects, lively beings, resistors, constructors of visions even though in the mainstream construction they are animated only by the arrogant perceiver and are pliable, foldable, file-awayable, classifiable. I always imagine the Aristotelian slave as pliable and foldable at night or after he or she cannot work anymore (when he or she dies as a tool). Aristotle tells us nothing about the slave *apart from the master.* We know the slave only through the master. The slave is a tool of the master. After working hours he or she is folded and placed in a drawer till the next morning. My mother was apparent to me mostly as a victim of arrogant perception. I was loyal to the arrogant perceiver's construction of her and thus disloyal to her in assuming that she was exhausted by that construction. I was unwilling to be like her and thought that identifying with her, seeing myself in her necessitated that I become like her. I was wrong both in assuming that she was exhausted by the arrogant perceiver's construction of her and in my understanding of identification, though I was not wrong in thinking that identification was part of loving and that it involved in part my seeing myself in her. I came to realize through travelling to her "world" that she is not foldable and pliable, that she is not exhausted by the mainstream argentinian patriarchal construction of her. I came to realize that there are "worlds" in which she shines as a creative being. Seeing myself in her through travelling to her "world" has meant seeing how different from her I am in her "world."

So, in recommending "world"-travelling and identification through "world"-travelling as part of loving other women, I am suggesting disloyalty to arrogant perceivers, including the arrogant perceiver in ourselves, and to their constructions of women. In revealing agonistic playfulness as incompatible with "world"-travelling, I am revealing both its affinity with imperialism and arrogant perception and its incompatibility with loving and loving perception.

NOTE

1. Grafting the substance of another to oneself is partly constitutive of arrogant perception. See M. Frye (1983, 66).

REFERENCES

Frye, Marilyn. 1983. *The politics of reality: Essays in feminist theory.* Trumansburg, N.Y.: Crossing Press.
Gadamer, Hans-Georg. 1975. *Truth and method.* New York: Seabury Press.
Huizinga, Johan. 1968. *Homo ludens.* Buenos Aires, Argentina: Emecé Editores.

DAVID J. KALUPAHANA

The Indian Background

The Indian philosophical background, with a strongly substantialist meta-physic and a rigid social, political and moral structure founded upon that metaphysic, provided the Buddha with an opportunity to reflect seriously upon the questions regarding human experience and understanding. The substantialist metaphysic was presented as follows:

> In the beginning, this [world] was only the self (*ātman*) in the form of a person. Looking around he saw nothing else than the self. He first said 'I am.' There-fore, arose the name of 'I.' Therefore, even to this day when one is addressed he says that 'This is I' and then speaks whatever other names he may have.[1]

The self (*ātman*), so conceived, is the permanent and eternal reality unsmeared by all the change and fluctuations that take place in the world of experience. In fact, it is the basis of the unity of empirical experience of variety and multiplicity, of change and mutability, of past, present and future. The real self and the unreal or mutable self, the transcendental apperception and empirical consciousness are graphically presented with the parable of the "two birds" perched on one branch, the one simply watching and the other enjoying the fruit.[2]

The self-same *ātman* is next presented as *brahman*. This time it is not a simple *a priori* fact, but also the *a priori* value on the basis of which all other values in the world are to be judged. The passage reads as follows:

> Verily, in the beginning this [world] was *brahma*, one only. Being one, he was not developed. He created a still superior form, the *kṣatra*, even those who are *kṣatra* among gods: Indra, Varuna, Soma, Rudra, Parjanya, Yama, Mrtyu, Iśāna. Therefore, at the *rājasūya* ceremony, the *brahman* sits below the *ksa-triya*. Upon *kṣatra* alone does he confer his honor. This same thing, namely, *brahma*, is the source of the *kṣatra*. Therefore, even if the king attains su-premacy, he rests finally upon *brahma* as his own source. Whosoever injures him [i.e., *brahman*], he attacks his own source. He fares worse in proportion as he injures one who is better.
>
> . . . . . .
>
> He was not yet developed. He created a still superior form, *dharma*. This is the power of the *kṣatriya* class, namely, law. Therefore, there is nothing supe-rior than law. So a weak man controls a stronger man by law, just as if by a king. Verily, that which is law is truth (*satya*). Therefore, they say of a man who speaks the truth: "He speaks the law," or of a man who speaks the law: "He speaks the truth." Verily, both are the same.[3]

Having stated the law (*dharma*) and its absolute validity or truth (*satya*), and identifying both with the brahman class as the standard of value judgment, the passage goes on to explain the evolution of the two other classes in society, the *vaisya* and *śūdra*. There could be little doubt as to the implication of this passage. The source of the value-system is *brahman* and, as the source of everything else, it is inviolable. The four-fold caste system and the values attached to it are inviolable and irrevocable. A person's duty as a human being is determined by the nature of the caste to which he is born. Whatever other things he may do are subordinate to this primary duty. It is pre-ordained. That duty is to be performed whatever the consequences are. This is the notion of duty that came to be inculcated in the *Bhagavadgītā*, which made the reluctant Arjuna go to war. In other words, by performing that duty Arjuna was acting according to his 'conscience,' and as such, even if he were to destroy another human being, he would be free from any form of guilt.

The unity of *ātman* and *brahman* represents the wedlock between "consciousness of self" and "conscience," between the "starry heavens above" and the "moral law within." Even though presented in a very crude form, the implications and intentions of this theory are no more different from those of the elaborate system propounded by Kant.

The Buddha's teachings are embodied in the discourses included in the Pali Nikāyas and the Chinese Āgamas. Even some of the later Buddhists, who had questions regarding the nature of the teachings, openly admitted that these represented the original sources for the study of the Buddha's message. What is extremely significant is that among the doctrines taken up for criticism in these discourses, the concepts of *ātman* and caste are the most prominent, especially considering the frequency with which they are taken up for analysis and refutation by the Buddha. The former being the foundation of the latter, the Buddha spared no pains in refuting it, devoting more time to its negation than to a presentation of his own positive thesis, namely, "dependent arising" (*paṭiccasamuppāda*).

The Buddha's Conception of Personhood

While the Buddha utilized a variety of sophisticated arguments and methods to reject the conception of an *ātman* or a "transcendental appercep-tion," the most significant among these is the description of a human being as a "psychophysical personality" (*nāmarūpa*) and its further analysis into five aggregates (pañcakkhandha) or six elements (*cha-dhātu*). In this process he explained the nature and function of the so-called "transcendental apperception" and, instead of considering it as an indispensable foundation of epistemology, criticized it as the source of bondage and suffering.

THE PSYCHOPHYSICAL PERSONALITY

The first step toward rejecting the metaphysical self is the recognition of a psychophysical personality, generally referred to as *nāmarūpa*. In order to avoid the metaphysical problems that arise as a result of analyzing the personality into two distinct entities or substances as mind and matter, the Buddha carefully refrained from speaking of two entities as *nāma* and *rūpa*. He was not prepared to assume that mind (*nāma*) can have independent status or existence. It is always associated with a body or a physical personality. There could be no consciousness or mental activity unless it is located in such a personality.

The almost universal tendency to look upon mind and matter as two distinct entities, with matter existing on its own and mind, whenever it is present, reflecting such matter, was abandoned by the Buddha. He did not succumb to the "philosophic faith, bred like most faiths from an aesthetic demand," that is, the faith that "mental and physical events are, on all hands, admitted to present the strongest contrast in the entire field of being."[4] He was probably anticipating such reactions as those of the so-called scientific minds, referred to by James: "It is time for scientific men to protest against the recognition of any such thing as consciousness in a scientific investigation."[5] Yet, in explaining both mind and matter, he was prepared to recognize such things as contact and sensation as the "unscientific half" of existence, leaving himself with the problem of dealing with emotion later on. For this reason, when the question regarding the nature of mind (*nāma*) and matter (*rūpa*) was raised, he responded by saying that the so-called matter is "contact with resistence" (*patigha-samphassa*) and what is called mind is "contact with concepts" (*adhivacana-samphassa*).[6] In so doing, he was reducing both mind and matter to contact (*samphassa*) and, therefore, processes of experience rather that any kind of material-stuff or mind-stuff.

Such an explanation of both mind and matter avoids the so-called "automaton-theory" as well as the idea of "ghost in the machine." With it, the Buddha relinquishes any search for a mysterious *something* that determines the physical laws as well as the laws of thought. In short, it is an abandoning of all metaphysical criticisms that make all causes and conditions obscure. This is clearly expressed in the following statement of the Buddha:

In this case, monk, it occurs to someone: "What was certainly mine is certainly not mine (now); what might certainly be mine, there is certainly no chance of

my getting." He grieves, mourns, laments, beats his breast, and falls into disillusionment. Even so, monk, does there come to be *anxiety (paritassanā)*
about something objective that does not exist.

. . .   . . .

In this case, monk, the view occurs to someone: "This world is this self; after
dying I will become permanent, lasting, eternal, not liable to change, I will
stand fast like unto the eternal." He hears the doctrine as it is being taught by
the Tathāgata or by a disciple of the Tathāgata for rooting out all resolve for,
bias, tendency and addiction to the determination and conditioning of views,
for the appeasement of all views, for the appeasement of all dispositions, for
the relinquishing of all attachment, for the waning of craving, absence of lust,
cessation, and freedom. It occurs to him thus: "I will surely be annihilated, I
will surely be destroyed, I will surely not be." He grieves, mourns, laments,
beats his breast, and falls into disillusionment. Thus, monk, there comes to be
anxiety about something subjective that does not exist.[7]

For the Buddha, the dissatisfaction with what is given and the search for
something hidden in or behind experience, even though leading to metaphysical theories, is good evidence for the creativity of man when respond-
ing to experience whether that be subjective or objective. It also supports
the view that a human being is not merely a hapless object swayed to and
fro by the irresistible force of the "Outer World," but also one who is able
to exert similarly irresistible force upon that outer world and bring about
changes in it. Just as much as the world is dependently arisen (*patic-
casamuppanna*), it is also dispositionally conditioned (*sankhata*). The
realization that the world is dispositionally conditioned as well prompted
him to admit consciousness as a significant part of the human personality,
not a mere "epi-phenomenon." As will be shown later, the Buddha would
have no difficulty agreeing with William James, who defined consciousness as "at all times primarily a *selecting agency*. Whether it is in the
lowest sphere of sense, or in the highest of intellection, we find it always
doing one thing, choosing one out of several of the materials so presented
to its notice, emphasizing and accentuating that and suppressing as far as
possible all the rest. The item emphasized is always in connection with
some interest felt by consciousness to be paramount at the time."[8]

This view of consciousness, as will be shown later, leads to the recognition of the efficacy of consciousness even in the matter of dealing with the
physical world. Thus, the psychophysical personality admitted by the Buddha emphasizes the dependence of consciousness on the physical personality as well as the capacity on the part of the former to mould the latter
without being a mere receptacle of impressions.

THE FIVE AGGREGATES (PAÑCAKKHANDHA)

The next most popular description of the human personality is in terms of
the five aggregates or constituents. These are referred to as "aggregates of

grasping" (*upādānakkhandha*), for it is these aggregates that a person clings to as his personality. The five constituents are as follows:

(1) *Rūpa* or material form. Whether it stands for one's own physical body or whether it implies the experience of material objects, the definition of it provided by the Buddha makes it a function rather than an entity. It is so called because of the way in which (a person) is affected (*ruppatīti kho rūpaṃ*).[9] For example, the experience of cold or warmth, of wind and heat, of various forms of insect bites, etc., are listed as the way in which one is affected. In other words, unless the experience of such phenomena are available, it is meaningless to speak of material form. Neither is it appropriate to assume that such experiences are mere imaginations. It may be noted that Hume's "bundle of perceptions," in terms of which he was explaining away the belief in self, included such experiences as cold and warmth. Thus, earth (*paṭhavi*) represents solidity or roughness, water (*āpa*) fluidity, etc.[10] Apart from such experiences, the Buddha was reluctant to speak of any material elements.

Furthermore, "material form" (*rūpa*) as part of a human personality, becomes extremely important as a way of identifying that personality. While there are instances where the Buddha would speak of mental states or states of meditation which are immaterial (*arūpa*), it is difficult to come across any reference by him to a human person who is without a body or material form (*rūpa*).

(2) *Vedanā* or feeling or sensation is another important aspect or constituent of the personality. It accounts for emotions which are an inalienable part of a living person, whether he be in bondage or has attained freedom (*nibbāna*). Feeling consists of three types: the pleasant or the pleasurable (*manāpa, sukha*), the unpleasant or the painful (*amanāpa, dukkha*) and neutral (*adukkhamasukha*). Except in the meditative trance where all perceptions and feelings (or more specifically, "what has been felt") are made to cease (temporarily) and which, therefore, represents a non-cognitive state, feelings are inevitable in experience. However, the human responses to such feeling can always be restrained, for these responses consist of continuous yearning or thirsting for the feelings. Thus, a living person is expected to eliminate lust (*rāga*) or craving (*taṇhā*) that arise on the basis of pleasurable feelings.

(3) *Saññā* or perception stands for the function of perceiving (*sañjā-nātīti saññā*). It is not a percept that can be separated or isolated from other activities. Instead, it is a continuous process of perception, with flights as well as perchings, the latter being determined mostly by interest. Thus, we may continually return to our perchings ignoring the flights so much so that we carve out discrete objects out of the flux of experience and assume that they are the same objects existing independently of all experience.

As in the case of feelings, the perceptions are also related to all other constituents of the human personality. Thus, they are not atomic impressions that are compounded into complex entities as a result of the activities of mind such as imagination. Each one of our perceptions constitutes a mixed bag of memories, concepts, and dispositions as well as the material elements or the functions referred to by *rūpa.* A pure percept undiluted by such conditions is *not* recognized by the Buddha or any subsequent Buddhist psychologist who has remained faithful to the Buddha. A pure percept is as metaphysical as a pure *a priori* category.

(4) *Saṅkhāra* or dispositions explain why there cannot be pure percepts. In the Buddha's perspective, this is *the* factor that contributes to the individuation of a person, and therefore, of his perceptions. Almost everything including physical phenomena, come under the strong influence of this most potent cause of evolution of the human personality as well as its surrounding. Hence the Buddha's definition of disposition as "that which processes material form, feeling, perception, disposition [itself] and consciousness into their particular forms."[11]

What the Buddha was attempting to explain on the basis of dispositions, which is part of the conscious process, is what James endeavored to describe in relation to consciousness itself. Refuting the "automaton-theory," so popular with modern-day biologists, James argues that evolution is not a strictly physiological process. He says:

> Survival can enter into a purely physiological discussion only as an *hypothesis made by an onlooker* about the future. But the moment you bring in a consciousness into the midst, survival ceases to be a mere hypothesis. . . . *Real* ends appear for the first time now upon the world's stage. The conception of consciousness as a purely cognitive form of being, which is the pet way of regarding it in many idealistic-modern as well as ancient schools, is thoroughly anti-psychological, as the remainder of this book will show. Every actually existing consciousness seems to itself at any rate to be a *fighter for ends,* of which many, but for its presence, would not be ends at all. Its powers of cognition are mainly subservient to these ends, discerning which facts further them and which do not.[12]

For very valid reasons (to be explained later), the Buddha attributes such evolution to dispositions, rather than to consciousness in general. Indeed, the dispositions are responsible not only for the manner in which we groom our physical personality once we are in possession of it, but also in partly[13] determining the nature of a new personality that we may come to possess in the future. It is not merely the human personality that is moulded or processed by dispositions. Our physical surroundings, even our amenities of life, housing, clothing, utensils, and in a major way, our towns, cities, etc., our art and architecture, our culture and civilization, and in the modern world, even outer space come to be dominated by our dispositions. Karl Popper calls this the World Three.[14] For this very reason, the Buddha, when describing the grandeur in which a universal monarch lived, with palaces, elaborate pleasure gardens and all other physical comforts, referred to all of them as dispositions (*saṅkhāra*).[15]

Epistemologically, the dispositions are an extremely valuable means by which human beings can deal with the world of experience. In the absence of any capacity to know everything presented to the senses, dispositional tendencies function in the form of interest, in selecting material from the "big blooming buzzing confusion"[16] in order to formulate one's understanding of the world.

(5) *Viññāṇa* or consciousness is intended to explain the continuity in the person who is individuated by dispositions (*saṅkhārā*). Like the other constituents, consciousness depends upon them for existence as well as nourishment. It is not a permanent and eternal substance or a series of discrete momentary acts of conscious life united by a mysterious self. Thus, consciousness separated from the other aggregates, especially material form (*rūpa*), cannot function. It is said to act with other aggregates if thoughts were to occur.

The theory of aggregates provides an interesting parallel to the relationship between mind and body envisaged by James:

> The consciousness, which is itself an integral thing not made of parts, 'corresponds' to the entire activity of the brain, whatever that may be, at the moment. This is a way of expressing the relation of mind and brain from which I shall not depart during the remainder of the book, because it expresses the bare phenomenal fact with no hypothesis, and is exposed to no such logical objections as we have found to cling to the theory of ideas in combination.[17]

When consciousness is so explained, it is natural for someone to conclude that it is a substantial entity. This was the manner in which the substantialists responded to both the Buddha and William James, and as may be seen later, to Vasubandhu himself. Buddha's response was that consciousness is nothing more than the act of being conscious (*vijānātītiviññaṇam*).[18] So did William James assert when he insisted:

> To deny plumply that 'consciousness' exists seems so absurd on the face of it—for undeniably 'thoughts' do exist—that I fear some readers would follow me no further. Let me then immediately explain that I mean only to deny that the word stands for an entity, but to insist most emphatically that it does stand for a function.[19]

Thus, the analysis of the human personality into five aggregates is intended to show the absence of a psychic self (an *ātman*). James was literally agreeing with the Buddhas *anātma*-view when he underscored the non-substantiality of this phenomenal fact:

> *The bare PHENOMENON, however, the IMMEDIATELY KNOWN thing which on the mental side is in opposition with the entire brain-process is the state of consciousness and not the soul itself.*[20]

These five aggregates are not intended as the ultimately irreducible elements (*dharma*) of existence. Instead, they illustrate some of the most prominent functions that are involved whenever the human personality is the subject of discussion. At least four basic functions are represented by them. *Rūpa* or material form accounts for the function of identification; *vedanā* or feeling and *saññā* or perception represent the function of experience, emotive as well as cognitive; *saṅkhārā* or disposition stands for the function of individuation; *viññāṇa* or consciousness explains the function of continuity in experience. After denying a permanent and eternal self underlying or embodying these functions, the Buddha felt the need to explain the continuity in human experience. This leads him to the recognition of the "stream of consciousness" (*viññāṇa-sota*).

ABBREVIATIONS

D	*Dīgha-Nikāya*, ed. T. W. Rhys Davids and J. E. Carpenter, 3 volumes, London: PTS, 1890–1911.
ERE	William James, *Essays in Radical Empiricism*, ed. Frederick Burkhardt, Cambridge, Mass.: Harvard University Press.
M	*Majjhima-nikāya*, ed. V. Trenckner and R. Chalmers, 3 volumes, London: PTS, 1887–1901.
PP	William James, *The Principles of Psychology*, ed. Frederick Burkhardt, Cambridge, Mass.: Harvard University Press, 1981. (References in parentheses are to the original editions, New York: Henry Holt, 1908).
S	*Samyutta-nikāya*, ed. L. Feer, 5 volumes, London: PTS, 1884–1904.
SPP	William James, *Some Problems of Philosophy*, ed. Frederick Burkhardt, Cambridge, Mass.: Harvard, 1979.

NOTES

1. *Bṛhadāraṇyaka Upaniṣad*, 1.4.1.
2. *Muṇḍaka Upaniṣad*, 3.1.1.
3. *Bṛhadāraṇyaka Upaniṣad*, 1.4.11, 14.
4. William James, *PP*, p. 138 (I.134).
5. Ibid.
6. *D* 2.62.
7. *M* 1.136.
8. James, *PP*, p. 142 (I.139).
9. *S* 3.86.
10. Ibid.
11. Ibid., 3.87, *rūpaṃ rūpattāya*, . . . *vedanaṃ vedanattāya*, . . . *saññaṃ*

saññattāya, . . . saṅkhāraṃ saṅkhārattāya, . . . viññāṇaṃ viññaṇattāya abhisaṅkhatam abhisaṅkharotīti saṅkhāro.

12. *PP*, p. 144 (I.141).
13. *M* 1.265 which refers to *gandhabba*, which is another name for the combination of *saṅkhārā* and *viññāṇa*.
14. Karl R. Popper and John C. Eccles, *The Self and Its Brain*, New York: Springer International, 1977, pp. 36–47.
15. *D* 2.198.
16. James, *SPP*, p. 36.
17. *PP*, p. 177 (I.177).
18. *S* 3.86.
19. *ERE*, p. 4.
20. *PP*, p. 182 (I.182).

ANNA S. MEIGS

Food Rules and the
Traditional Sexual Ideology

To talk with a Hua male about why he does not eat a food is ultimately to talk with him about the nature of sexual differences. Most foods stand for sexual states, organs, and processes, and indigenous explanations of food rules are rife with sexual references. A question about a food rule immediately embroils ethnographer and consultant in the details of a complicated, multifaceted sexual ideology.

Here I shall examine only one facet of this ideology: the naive or common knowledge that males are superior, powerful, and pure, that females are inferior, malevolent, weak, and polluted. This general portrait of the sexual stereotypes was drawn by the first generation of New Guinea highlands ethnographers and continues to dominate the literature today. It was based on a relatively standard set of data: the residential segregation of the sexes, the existence of men's cults, the males' fear of menstrual and parturitional fluids, the various rituals to expel symbolically such substances from the bodies of men, and the rules of female avoidance in general.

These phenomena do exist among the Hua, and the eating rules and the metaphors associated with them provide strong new support for the description of New Guinea sexual ideology as one of overwhelming male superiority and power. But beneath the arrogant male ideological stance, the ground is soft. Careful study reveals a second facet to male thinking—an attitude of reproductive impotence and sexual inferiority.

The analysis presented in this chapter, although applicable to the entire set of food rules, derives from a detailed study of only one class of prohibitions, those enjoined upon a male initiate, the most vulnerable class of persons, and, therefore, the one most in need of protection through isolation from dangerous foods. These prohibitions may last a week, a month, a year, or until extreme old age. The following simplified catalog groups the prohibitions into eight main categories, which are summarized in table 1.

1. Things that are red. This prohibition includes all the reddish spinachlike vegetables, the two reddish taros (*koraiziziya* and *kai atve*), the reddish banana (*opne*), the red birds, the two reddish mushrooms (*arerua* and *kuhara*), and most important, the red pandanus. The oil of the pandanus is identified by male informants with menstrual blood (see also Lindenbaum 1976). The original pandanus is said to have been created out of refuse at the site of an abandoned menstrual hut.

The identification between the pandanus and menstrual blood is paralleled by that between the color red and the vagina. The insult "Your mother's red bird burns!" refers to her vagina. Male informants say that the vagina is like the red impatiens flower (Balsaminaceae *Impatiens hawkeri*). One man, who occasionally wore a blossom pasted to his nose, told me he did so because he liked women and sex.

2. Items that smell *be' ftu*. *Be' ftu*, the smell of a menstruating woman, is said by males to be like the smell of a number of rotting substances. (Buchbinder and Rappaport 1976 report a similar association between female sexuality and decay among the Maring of the Central Highlands.) Included in this class of prohibitions are certain species of possum, one mushroom (*zokoni*) that resembles the commonly eaten North American one, and two species of yam (*fanu hgu* and *ame'*).

3. Foods that male informants associate with a hole. Included are the birds and possums that live in holes in trees, a species of fish (*dgopo'*) that lives under rock overhangs, the mouse, and the possum species that live in holes in the ground. In addition, one mushroom (*dkugea'*) is forbidden because it grows in holes in trees.

TABLE 1

Categories of Prohibited Foods

Foods that are	Because of identification with
Red	Menstrual blood and vagina
Be' ftu in smell	Smell of menstruating woman
Associated with holes	vagina
Hairy	Pubic hair
Possum (or foods associated with	Female sexuality and fertility in general
Associated with the ground	Uncleanness and subordination in general and of women in particular
Dark on the interior	Ill health and fertility
Wild	Things inimical to males and their projects

Some informants identified the mouse holes with the vagina. My inference—that holes have vaginal connotations in certain eating contexts—receives confirmation in insults that play on the vaginal origin of the insulted person: "Are you something that came from an earth overhang? from a hole in the ground? from a hole in a tree? from a hole in the rocks?"

4. Things that informants claim are hairy. This prohibition includes all the furred animals with the exception of the pig, the birds that have particularly profuse facial plumage, and a vegetable (*fera okani*) that is said to be hairy.

Informants say that possum fur is like female pubic hair and that bird faces in which the mouth is surrounded by heavy plumage are like the female pudenda.

5. Possum. So potent is this taboo that a number of foods are forbidden

simply because of their resemblance to possum. For example, insufficiently cooked sweet potato is prohibited because its whiteness resembles that of possum eyes, traditional salt because of the cake was curved like a possum tail, pork from the bone because pig bones resemble possum bones, and a ground-growing mushroom (*knegu*) plus all water from the jungle because possums have polluted both with their urine and feces.

Male informants, when asked why they do not eat possum, usually answer, "Because I might become pregnant." One informant, however, answered, "Possum is the counterpart of women." Other informants confirmed this statement and some, when asked how possum was the female counterpart, volunteered that possum fur is like female pubic hair, that the holes in which possums live are like vaginas, that possums smell like menstruating women, or that the way one species of possum, the *hazubre'*, creeps out of trees is like the infant's emergence from the vagina.

6. Substances that informants associate with the ground. They include short sugarcanes, ground-growing mushrooms, birds that live or feed on the ground, pig feet, mouse, dog, and ground possums. What was taboo about the ground was difficult to elicit in reference to the food prohibitions themselves and emerged only in other contexts.

The ground is associated with uncleanness. The Hua, who have no latrines and undergarments for humans and stalls or pens for animals, maintain that the ground is heavily contaminated by human and animal waste. The ground-feeding animals, with which women are identified, are said to have interiors darkened by this waste, while the tree-feeding animals, with which men are identified, remain pure and white. In the residentially segregated past, the dirt floor of a woman's house was alleged to be especially contaminated. When crawling around inside these very low structures, males supported their hands with sticks to avoid contamination, according to informants. (A similar identification of the ground with pollution and of the arboreal heights and sky with purity has been reported in numerous New Guinea societies. See R. Bulmer 1967, Barth 1975.)

The ground is also associated with subordination. The relevant features are the uncleanness and the lowness of the ground. Women traditionally were compelled to hide their eyes and bend their bodies to the ground in an attitude of submission when men paraded the cult flutes. Female sleeping platforms were low, barely off the ground, in contrast to the greater elevation of the male platforms—a difference that male informants claim as a significant contrast between the sexes. (Barth 1975: 20 reports a similar low-high contrast between the houses belonging to females and those belonging to males among the Baktaman of New Guinea's Western District.) A standard response to a question about why a man should not eat a prohibited food is "Lest I be on the ground." Informants explain this statement as meaning "Lest I fail in my subsequent efforts and battles," in other words, "Lest I become subordinate."

Finally, the ground is associated with women indirectly because of their allegedly unclean and subordinate qualities and directly through various metaphors. Women are said to be like the ground-living toads while men are like birds. Nearly all female names are drawn from the ground-hugging plants, while male names are taken from the tall trees, birds, and mountains.

7. Substances that informants say are dangerous to eat because they have dark interiors. This class includes two species of taro (*ekremu'* and *kinarikogu*), mouse, dog, possum, the large birds, and the heart, liver, and intestines of the pig. (Possum, mouse, and dog appear in many of the prohibition classes. Being multiply prohibited, they are highly taboo.)

Informants were unable or unwilling to specify the dangerous characteristics of foods with dark interiors. I think it is fair to infer that their conception of this danger is related to their ideas about food and fertility. Darkness of blood is said to be a sign of bad health: blood darkens, thickens, and consequently begins to smell only with sickness and old age. The awesome state of fertility is associated by males with rotting, putrid, dark, and heavy matter. The interior of a woman's body, like a fertile soil, is said to exhibit these qualities. (The Maenge of New Britain also associate fertility with blackness, liquid, coolness, and rot, and infertility with whiteness, dryness, and hardness. See Panoff 1970b: 242.) These associations undoubtedly derive from observation of relative soil fertilities.

8. Wild things. In this class informants include the wild yams and taros, wild bananas, wild green vegetables, and wild red pandanuses, the white pandanus (of which all species are considered wild), and, again, the possum and mouse.

In all of the prohibited types discussed so far, informants made, or I was able to infer, an association between the prohibited aspect of the food and some aspect of the female body or social status. In the case of the prohibition on things that are wild, the association with women is secondary. The primary characteristics that the Hua attribute to wild biota in general are that they are unknown to and uncontrolled by humans. As such, they constitute a danger. Female reproductive powers fall into this class of mysterious, dangerous, and uncontrollable phenomena.

The assumption that female reproductive powers are essentially wild is implicit in the male view that the mere presence of certain categories of women destroys many cultural projects. A man making a bow, arrow, axe, or flute must do so at a distance from women. If a male makes an earth oven, he has to keep women away, for their presence would prevent the food from cooking. Similarly, butchered or cooked pork must be isolated from women, as their presence causes it to rot. This conception of the effect of women on cultural processes in general and on meat in particular is widespread. De Beauvior (1964: 149), for example, quotes the *British Medical Journal* in 1878: "It is an undoubted fact that meat spoils when touched by menstruating women."

ASSOCIATION OF ALIMENTARY AND SEXUAL SYSTEMS

These eight prohibition types suggest an intense male preoccupation with and anxiety about female fertility and sexuality and, in addition, a masculine insistence on the notion of feminine inferiority. Men deny women a political voice, rights in land, and authority over the products of their labor. They seek to impress their superiority on women through a number of symbolic devices. Significant among them are the well-known secret flutes, common throughout the highlands as one of the main cult items of the secret society of the men's house. Hua males claim that they traditionally killed women who so much as dared to look at these flutes, which men paraded openly through the community. Women and children were taught to believe that their sound came from weird birds.

A second symbolic device whereby men seek to reinforce their position of sexual superiority and political dominance is based on the reciprocal association of alimentary and sexual organs and processes, two body systems that are universally associated but whose mutual identification receives here an unusual degree of publicity. The identification of foods with sexual organs and substances has been demonstrated. The reverse identification, of sexual organs and substances with foods, receives considerable public elaboration in folktales, expressions of endearment, and insults.

In one tale a man cuts off one of his testicles, wraps it in vegetable leaves, and asks his wife to cook it. She cannot resist the delicious smells emanating from the packet and in his absence eats it. In a second tale a small bird discovers a house full of sleeping girls. He plays a trick on them by pasting an edible mushroom (*zokoni*) to their vaginas.

The expression "I will eat your blood" is one of the means by which a man indicates he would like to have intercourse with a woman. Certain insults play on the identification of stolen food with a part of the owner's anatomy, which the thief is then ordered to eat. Where the thief takes a wide range of items from a woman's garden, it is appropriate to say, "Burst open my pregnant womb and eat it." Where the thief steals the white pandanus, a woman can say, "Eat the fruit at the center of a woman's vagina." Where he takes the red pandanus, she can say, "Since you like pandanus, drink the clotted blood from my vagina." When the owner is male, the insults differ. For example, if the thief steals sugarcane, which is identified with semen in many contexts, the male can say, "Eat the semen in my penis."

Parallel to the identification between foods and sexual substances is that between the mouth and the vagina, which is allowed considerable public expression in Hua culture. A woman observing my naked two-year-old daughter eating an ear of corn said to her, fondly and laughingly, "Eat it with your vagina." A prohibition on males eating pork that has been formally given to a woman hinges on the identification of her vagina with her mouth. Men say that at the announcement of the woman's name before she receives the pork, her vagina answers, *ve* "yes?" Other informants say, *Kaummu'bo bu' bo bre* "Her vagina expresses its appreciation."

Consider the following two stories about facial hair. According to one, the Hua males originally had no facial hair. One day, however, they blew into the mouths of flutes into which women had stuffed their pubic hair. That pubic hair became the male beard. According to the second story, the variation in the density of men's beards is accounted for by a similar variation in the density of their mother's pubic hair.

Where facial hair is publicly associated with pubic hair, one would expect that the mouth might also be publicly associated with the vagina. A rule forbids initiates to eat any bird that has a very feathery face—in particular, three owl-like birds (*hazuifi'a, bume,* and *ktrupe*). These faces, in which a heavy plumage surrounds a mouth, are publicly said to resemble the female pudenda.

Where one finds public or semipublic association of the orifices of the upper and lower halves of the body and of the substances taken in at both, it is not surprising to find open and reciprocal association of feeding and sexual intercourse. The equation of these two acts comes from a transfer of two substances that males say occurs during intercourse. The first is *nu* (Pidgin English *gris*), which is for the Hua the essence of life and vitality. Men claim that the transfers of *nu* (semen and sweat) occurring in intercourse result in female gains in weight and vitality and corresponding male losses. The second substance is *vza bu'* "mouth steam, breath, air," conceived as the gaseous form of *nu*. So essential is *vza bu'* to growth and strength that initiates must undergo a period of silence to prevent its loss through speaking. During intercourse females take in the *vza bu'* that males breathe out; thus, according to male informants, the female's strength is increased while the male's is reduced.

In describing these transfers, my informants did not specifically say that sexual intercourse is like feeding. However, given the common association between the mouth and the vagina, between foods and sexual substances, and the attribution of a nutritive effect to sexual intercourse, it seems reasonable to claim an implicit association between feeding and sexual intercourse. This association is also implicit in the belief in oral conception. At least two of the most important male food taboos (the prohibitions on eating possum and on eating leafy green vegetables picked by certain categories of women) are obeyed in order to avoid oral conception.[1]

VALUES OF MALE AND FEMALE BODIES

Hua males use the association of the sexual and alimentary systems to make a particular statement about the relative value of male and female bodies.

Loss of *nu* causes the stunting of growth, aging, impotence, and weakness in general. The many manifestations of a person's *nu* include his or her blood, lymph, sweat, body oil, sexual or reproductive fluids, and any living thing that the person has invested great effort into growing, for example, children, pigs, and special garden produce. It is important to note that all *nu* substances are readily transferred between persons. Each act of *nu* transfer, whether through the medium of pig, garden produce, blood (which the Hua let from their veins and drank), sweat or body oil (both of which they rubbed on one another's bodies), or actual flesh (the Hua traditionally were cannibals) has two possible effects. It can cause the recipient's body *kosi-* "to grow, increase in weight, strength, and vitality" or *keva ro-* "to become stunted, dry out, wither, decrease in weight, strength, and health."

Whether a positive or negative value is attributed to any act of *nu* transfer is determined by the social relationship of the parties to the act. Where the social relationship is positive, the value attributed to the act is also positive. Where the social relationship is negative, the value attributed is also negative. For example, a man may eat or otherwise permit his body to come in contact with the *nu* substances of his real and classificatory fathers, mothers, grandparents, aunts, uncles, and siblings as long as he is enjoying the relationship of support and warmth that is expected to exist between them. A man may not eat or otherwise permit his body to come in contact with certain of the *nu* substances of his agemates or his real or classificatory cross-cousins (his relationships with both agemates and cross-cousins are typically competitive), or with any person of any category with whom he has a relationship of enmity.

The effects attributed to any act of *nu* transfer suggest that the Hua like to have physiological or body relationships mirror social ones. They like to express the expected or experienced emotional quality of a social relationship through a physical metaphor. To make that metaphor work, each body act must be represented as having an ambiguous value. The fact that the same act can have positive and negative physical effects permits it to reflect both the trust and the hostility common to social relationships.

The public and explicit identification of the alimentary and sexual acts, both of which are prototypical acts of *nu* transfer, allows the Hua to attribute to them the dual value posited for other acts of *nu* transfer. The value normally attributed to each act may be changed, enabling Hua males to perceive the act associated with their bodies as superior to the act associated with females bodies—at least within those contexts where these associations are made.

VALUES OF SEXUAL INTERCOURSE AND FEEDING

Although sexual intercourse and feeding are viewed as the prototypical acts of *nu* transfer, they are not normally assigned a dual value. Sexual intercourse is viewed as a negative act. According to males the sex act, although it increases the female's vitality, decreases the male's. Each act depletes the finite quantity of a man's *nu* and thus increases the rate at which he ages. Balding, which Hua males hide with small woven caps, is thought to be a direct result of sexual excess because semen is believed to originate in the head. Females deny that they profit from the receipt of semen and maintain instead that sexual intercourse releases menstrual flow, which women (but not men) think involves potentially dangerous losses of *nu*. Both sexes commonly express enthusiasm for the sexual and reproductive inactivity of old age.

Feeding is viewed as the opposite of sex. It is the quintessentially positive act, the one that best produces strength and health. In fact, feeding is the most morally positive act. A good person is, almost by definition, one who feeds others generously.

Sexual intercourse and feeding are associated not only with moral values but also with gender identifications. Sexual intercourse is viewed as a male act, as males in the "publicly prescribed" Hua view take the active part in it. Feeding, on the other hand, is viewed as a female act, as women are the feeders, and children and men are fed.

Where the male act of intercourse is the morally negative act and the female act of feeding is the morally positive act, the implication that females are, at least in this respect, morally superior is unavoidable. Reinterpretation of the male sexual act as similar to the female feeding act, and the female feeding act as similar to the male sexual act, achieves the usual duality in matters of *nu* transfer. The values usually attributed to these two acts in a daily context are reversed in this specialized context of male ritual and taboo.

My argument depends on a careful delineation of contexts. Certain kinds of comments and statements about a topic are appropriate in some contexts but not in others. For example, in North American society uninhibited and chauvinistic comments about the sexuality and status of females are appropriate, at least in some male's perspectives, in barracks, pubs, locker rooms, all-male card games, and so on. Similar comments are inappropriate in other all-male contexts, like board meetings, planning sessions, and church vestry meetings, where discussions of sex, if they occur at all, are inhibited and blatant chauvinism is avoided. Hua males also have a variety of attitudes and styles for talking about females and sex, each appropriate to certain contexts. If a stranger entered a Hua village and wanted to talk publicly about sex and feeding in an appropriate fashion in the normal course of the day, it would be correct for him or her to assume that sexual intercourse is a negative act in which the male has the initiative and that feeding is a positive act in which the female has the initiative. The Hua context in which these assumptions are not appropriate is the men's house. If this same stranger wanted to talk about these topics with the men in the men's house, he or she could talk about how males nourish females in the act of having sex with them, and about how females pollute and in some extreme cases impregnate males in the process of feeding them.

By reversing the functions normally attributed to the sexual and feeding acts—by making sex a feeding act and feeding a sexual act—the males reverse the values normally associated with each act, at least within the men's house context. In the process they make it possible to allocate to themselves, at least for the duration of the context, the role of moral superiority. It is a role that conforms with their preferred image of themselves as social benefactors, protectors of the community, supporters of its people. It also conforms with the much promoted image of females (other than consanguineal ones) as hostile and threatening to the community. This image makes some sense in a community that draws most of its wives from foreign groups, groups with whom there may now be a peaceful relationship but with whom wars were fought in the past and may be fought again in the future.

This reversal of the functions and values normally attributed to the alimentary and sexual acts is comparable to the role Buchbinder and Rappaport (1976) report for a Maring ritual in which males plant cultigens over a special earth oven that is identified with the vagina and its fertility. The ethnographers interpret this planting as a male attempt to assert authority and control not only over the vagina and its powers but also over the earth and its fruits, normally considered a female preserve. Lindenbaum (1976) reports a similar concern among Fore males to achieve a semblance of control over female fertility through ritual devices.

The Hua reversal enables males to say in the appropriate contexts that the female physical act of feeding is a negative act, just as female social acts are negative, and that the male act of copulation is a positive act, just as male social acts are positive. Body acts and relationships are made to mirror the preferred male conception of social acts and relationships. The physical or natural order has been reversed to bring it in line with the social order (or the preferred male conception of that order) and thus to strengthen this particular male conception or theory about social relations. Such a reversal and linking of different orders is not uncommon. Lévi-Strauss (1963) first described it in his definition of totemism as using logical relations perceived to exist in the world of nature to express relations among people in society. An example similar to the Hua case is provided by Rigby (1968), who describes how Gogo sex roles are temporarily reversed in a ritual in order to effect a parallel to the natural world. The Hua males, by reversing the values usually attributed to sex and feeding, strengthen a view of the relationship between the sexes that is flattering to them. This reversal, like the cult of the secret flutes, the ritual expulsion of female substance, the residential segregation of the sexes, and the exclusive male ownership of land and pigs, impresses a conception of women as inferior on members of the community. Such a conception is neither fully believed by the males nor fully accepted by the females. It exists as one of several ways of thinking about male-female relations. It is one in a set of competing ideologies, the expression of which is appropriate in some contexts but not in others.

NOTE

1. The Umeda of the New Guinea Sepik see eating, violence (hunting), and sexuality as alternative modes of a single basic activity, which is represented by one verb, *tadv* (Gell 1977:32). In dreams these modes are switched around. An instance of love-making in a dream has implications for the dreamer's real-life hunting. A man dreaming of his sister coming and giving him food prefigures his success in a real-life love affair.

BIBLIOGRAPHY

Barth, F. 1975. *Ritual and Knowledge among the Baktaman of New Guinea.* New Haven: Yale University Press.
Beauvoir, S. de. 1964 (1953). *The Second Sex.* New York: Knopf.
Buchbinder, G., and Rappaport, R.A. 1976 "Infertilitiy and Death among the Maring." In *Man and Woman in the New Guinea Highlands*, ed. P. Brown and G. Buchbinder. A.A.A. Special Publication 8. Washington, D.C.: American Anthropological Association.
Bulmer, R.N.H. 1967. "Why Is the Cassawary Not a Bird?" *Man* n.s. 2:5-25.
Lévi-Strauss, C. 1963. *Totemism.* Boston: Beacon Press.
Lindenbaum, S. 1972, "Sorcerers, Ghosts, and Polluting Women: An Analysis of Religious Belief and Population Control." *Ethnology* 11:241–253.
Panoff, F. 1970b. "Food and Faeces: A Melanesian Rite." *Man* n.s. 5:237–252.
Rigby, P. 1968. "Some Gogo Rituals of Purification: An Essay on Social and Moral Categories." In *Dialectic in Practical Religion*, ed. E.R. Leach. Cambridge: Cambridge University Press.

How to Stuff a Pepper

Now, said the cook, I will teach you
how to stuff a pepper with rice.

Take your pepper green, and gently,
for peppers are shy. No matter which side
you approach, it's always the backside.
Perched on green buttocks, the pepper sleeps
In its silk tights, it dreams
of sommersaults and parsley,
of the days when the sexes were one.

Slash open the sleeve
as if you were cutting a paper lantern,
and enter a moon, spilled like a melon,
a fever of pearls,
a conversation of glaciers.
It is a temple built to the worship
of morning light.

I have sat under the great globe
of seeds on the roof of that chamber,
too dazzled to gather the taste I came for.
I have taken the pepper in hand,
smooth and blind, a runt in the rich
evolution of roses and ferns.
You say I have not yet taught you

to stuff a pepper?
Cooking takes time.

Next time we'll consider the rice.

SECTION TWO

Recipes for Values

> In Buddhism, the most important pre-
> cept of all is to live in awareness, to
> know what is going on. To know what is
> going on, not only here, but there. For
> instance, when you eat a piece of bread,
> you may choose to be aware that our
> farmers, in growing the wheat, use
> chemical poisons a little too much. Eat-
> ing the bread, we are somehow co-re-
> sponsible for the destruction of our
> ecology. When we eat a piece of meat
> or drink alcohol, we can produce aware-
> ness that 40,000 children die *each day*
> in the third world from hunger and that
> in order to produce a piece of meat or a
> bottle of liquor, we have to use a lot of
> grain. Eating a bowl of cereal may be
> more reconciling with the suffering of
> the world than eating a piece of meat.
> (Hanh 1987, 65)

I. CONNECTING RELATIONAL SELVES WITH RELATIONAL VALUING

We come to be persons through defining processes of experience. Since there are many processes of experience that make up a complex human life, each of us is actually a multiplicity of persons. This introductory essay concerns the relation of these multiple selves to ways of participating mindfully in the world.

The substance project's understanding of personhood is clear about the relation of personhood to action. It requires a moral agent that stands apart from the world and applies moral rules to it. Ontologically distinct from the world of bodily actions, the moral agent comes to the world of moral actions antecedently unconnected, "fresh," and "untouched." This ap-proach to moral theory is expressed most notably by Immanuel Kant, who defined the moral in opposition to mere customs. Whereas we all preexist in a complex set of cultural customs, the moral agent, according to Kant, must consciously set these aside in order to judge solely according to moral duty, a transcultural criterion that originates in what he calls the "categorical imperative" (Kant 1988, 263).

By contrast, a participatory understanding of self understands the moral agent as already deeply connected to others in a complex pattern of defining relations. The question, then, is not into which (objectified) relations we want to enter from the outside, but, given the antecedent fact of connectedness, which defining relations can we conscientiously continue to affirm? As Thich Nhat Hanh says, a participatory understanding of self leads to an ethic "in awareness" of our ineluctable connectedness to others (65).

A feminist ethic of care and a Buddhist ethic of compassion affirm the participatory character of a healthy self. Both understand the process of living in terms of a context-specific moral/aesthetic narrative which is guided by an awareness of one's defining relations to others. Since both Buddhist and feminist ethics are pluralist and affirm difference as real, it will not be possible (or desirable) to give a set of necessary and sufficient conditions for an ethic of compassion or care. However, much can be said here to elucidate what might be called "boundary conditions" for such an ethic.[1]

In this section, I work out the transition from a food-based conception of personhood to a reoriented conception of value. First, I describe how a dualist hierarchy, which constructs food as objectified (external and nondefining), might value food.[2] I then characterize a participatory understanding of value through the idea of a direct or authentic presence to food. In contrast to an indirect relation to food (through the body which is regarded as external to the self), this is a way of focusing on and learning from the manner in which we are related to what we *choose* to count as food. It is not simply the ontological fact of relatedness, but a mindful focus on food.[3] This reveals that what we will count as food is a choice that reflects who we are morally. I then argue that an ethic of care or compassion is sympathetic to the idea of authentic presence to food. The connection between awareness of food and value has implications for the ways we value other human beings, and also for the ways we value other beings with which (with whom) we may enter into relations of compassion or care: nonhuman life, mountain ranges, oceans, and skies. One meaningful response to a recognition of ourselves as directly related to food is what I shall call contextual moral vegetarianism.

II. OBJECTIFIED FOOD VALUES

Reading Jean-François Revel, I have the impression that if Plato had written a philosophy of food it might have read very much like this. Revel is concerned to draw a distinction between "two sources of gastronomic art"

(1982, 151*), "a popular one," which "has the advantage of being linked to the soil, of being able to exploit the products of various regions and different seasons, in close accord with nature, of being based on age-old skills, transmitted unconsciously by way of imitation and habit, of applying methods of cooking patiently tested and associated with certain cooking utensils and recipients prescribed by a long tradition" (148*), and second, an "erudite" source, "based by contrast on invention, renewal, experimentation."

The popular source is the "peasant mother" of cuisine "prepared by the mother (or the humble family cook)"; the erudite source is the "galloping father" of cuisine prepared by "professionals that only chefs fanatically devoted to their art have the time and the knowledge to practice" (148 and 149*). Popular cuisine, being linked to the land and local practical traditions, is not exportable. Erudite cuisine, as something in which one is trained or educated, is exportable; it is a true international cuisine. Furthermore, popular cuisine is not an end in itself, but aims at "a perfecting of nutrition." Erudite cuisine is an end in itself, "a perfecting of cuisine itself" (150*). It is dedicated to food for food's sake.

Revel perfectly replicates Plato's distinction between practices that involve knowledge (erudite cuisine, which has intellectual rules that can be taught and applied elsewhere), and knacks or routines (popular cuisine, which is practical, must be shown rather than explained, and cannot be exported outside those craft traditions). Perhaps it is not intended as dismissively as Plato's, but Revel's distinction is, nonetheless, hierarchical. International cuisine is regarded as the summit of gastronomic experience.

This value hierarchy has been employed in similar ways in the philosophy of art and in moral theory. "Fine arts" include painting, sculpture, and literature, and (so it is often argued by formalists) are independent of national boundaries; "applied arts" include pottery and quilts, and cannot transcend the specific customs of a particular place. The distinction is even gender-based: fine arts and international cuisine are the "father," while applied arts and popular cuisine are the "mother."

Similarly, a common distinction in ethics, most notably expressed by Kant, is between proper moral judgments, which are intersubjective and transcultural because universal and rule-bound, and merely local cultural customs. "Duty," he says, "is the necessity of an action done from respect for law." Cultural customs are mere "anthropology" for Kant (1988, 253 and 260).

Appropriate to the normative distinction between kinds of cuisine, Revel understands himself analogously to an art critic or objective moralist who stands apart from what he judges. Distance provides objectively; it allows for judgment according to intersubjectively accepted standards: "fortunately or unfortunately—cuisine is a normative art in which, as with grammar, ethics, and medicine, description and prescription can scarcely be separated" (148*).

Revel's understanding of his critical relationship to food is deeply structured by his attitude that international cuisine, though certainly important to him, is essentially external to the critic who judges it. This is clear in his attitude that international cuisine is nutritionally external to the person who eats it. (One could hold such an opinion, but it would hardly be healthful.) It seems he arrives at an externalist position through the set of exclusive normative dualisms of the kind that were explored in Section One: self versus other; normative, intellectual, rule-based disciplines versus non-normative, affective, completely contextual practices; and male versus female. Revel's attitude is typical of a masculine perspective which seeks to maintain the self as an autonomous agent that acts at a distance from a world that is categorically distinct from the agent.[4] I now turn to an alternative way of valuing food.

III. AUTHENTIC, PRESENCE TO FOOD

Experience of food is temporal: the ground is cultivated and fertilized; the seeds are planted and cared for; the crops must be harvested, and processed for food. Fruits are ripe only for a day before they begin to rot. Most foods are seasonal (at least they were until the advent of "processed" frozen foods). Meal preparations include perusing menus, strategic planning to ensure the dishes will be ready at the same time, tasting, experimenting, and deciding how to present the meal. The meal is served in a proper order, which depends on the culture and is rarely altered: e.g., salad first (or last), entrée, dessert, coffee. When the meal is finished, the dishes must be cleared, cleaned, and returned to their proper places, ready for the next round of preparation, cooking, eating, and cleaning.

Food is experienced only briefly. Yet, far from being diminished in value because it is transient and contextual, its value is precisely that its "moment" comes and goes. To experience a raspberry fresh from the garden requires experiential knowledge of when to pick it, receptivity to the moment it is tasted, and a timely appreciation of its flavors and textures. We must be fully present in the moment. If we are distracted, or use that moment for some other purpose, we will miss the experience. (Part of our fascination with the plastic mock-ups of food that Japanese restaurants set in their windows as advertisements is that, while they look somewhat like food, they lack an essential property of food: change.)[5]

These observations serve to introduce the idea of an authentic presence to food. If we are to understand food in such a way that its flavor is not lost in abstractions, we must be willing to acknowledge our relations with it in such a way that they are not falsified by a theoretical bias for the abstract and the atemporal. We must draw out and highlight the appropriate and timely response to the present moment. We must learn to valorize the fleeting presence of *this*, here and now.

The Japanese philosopher Dōgen was deeply concerned with the relation of food to the understanding of personhood and value. During a trip to China in 1223 to study in the great Buddhist monasteries, he met a temple cook who reproached him for thinking that the Buddhist path could be pursued only in the Meditation Hall, that enlightenment is separate from ordinary life. The path to self-understanding could be found as well, he urged, by forming a mindful relationship to ordinary things like food.[6] When Dōgen returned to Japan he found in Buddhist temples a lack of understanding of the relationship of food to enlightenment. He quickly moved to establish the *tenzo*, the temple cook, as one of the most important positions in the temple after the abbott.

Dōgen offers a suggestion on how to start thinking about authentic presence to food. He begins the *Fushuku-hampō* ("Meal-Time Regulations"), a set of regulations for monks to help them realize their proper relations to food, by quoting from the *Vimalakirti Sutra*: "When one is identified with the food one eats one is identified with the whole universe; when we are one with the whole universe we are one with the food we eat" (153*). Dōgen understands our relations to food participatorily. We will see this, he thinks, if we focus on the everyday reality of our food.[7] Instead of the common experience of a meal as a race one runs to get on to more "important" matters, Dōgen suggests we slow the mind to the point that we experience what literally becomes us through a temporal process of eating. By slowing the mind we can be instructed by food about the inherent temporality and relationality of life.[8] Both the self and the food that becomes the self come together uniquely in each moment.

When Dōgen speaks about just being present to the rice he eats, he is not classifying this as a kind of experience, whether aesthetic or moral. He is not saying "Appreciate the snowy whiteness of the rice," nor is he saying "Recognize your duty to the food you eat." Such cognizing, even if necessary and appropriate at times, emphasizes separateness from the rice, which is being judged critically; interrelatedness is submerged. According to Dōgen, categories such as self versus other—the person eating versus the food eaten—are constructed only retrospectively.[9] They are constructed as absolute categories only in reflection on the experience; they are not found in the moment of experience.

Instead of adopting critical attitude, he is saying, "Be present to the experience; just eat the rice!" As Kim Chernin gives herself permission simply to eat her food and thereby discovers herself, so Dōgen is saying something very simple and ordinary like "Discover your ordinary self by just eating." Doing so mindfully will be transformative in a way that leads to new aesthetic, ontological, and ethical understandings.

Thomas Kasulis provides a phenomenological interpretation of Dōgen's use of the crucial Japanese phrase "genjokoan." Quoting Dumoulin (1990), he glosses it as "This physical world, just as it is, is genuine, patent reality." Kasulis continues, "As directly experienced, impermanence is the 'presence of things as they are' (*genjokoan*)" (Kasulis 1981,

84). Authentic presence to the rice one eats, then, can bring one into awareness of "genuine, patent reality" where reality is understood as the direct experience of impermanence.

The "knowledge" one comes to have through authentic presence to food is bodily and experiential. This is not conceptual knowledge prepared in advance and applied to the world. It is a kind of knowledge that comes to be for, and speaks authoritatively only to, the person or persons shaped definitively by a particular kind of experience. Kim Chernin's description of the long and agonizing process through which she learned to understand her eating disorder should be read as a description of this kind of process. When she experienced the breakthrough in self-understanding her bodily knowledge was incontestable within that context; it was warranted by her health. The process of seeking release from her disease was transformative. It resulted in becoming a new kind of person. This return to health was a process of cultivation.

Though Dōgen is asking that we experience food directly and hold off classifying it, there are numerous moral and aesthetic consequences that follow from acknowledging the mutual definition of self and food that occurs in mindful eating. Participatory self-definition may lead to living economically. If food is not the possession of an autonomous agent, if we understand ourselves to be defined partially by our relations to other human beings and to nonhuman beings, food becomes something to be consumed with others in mind. As Dōgen points out, "From both the rational and practical outlook, one should try never to waste a single grain of rice at mealtimes; the whole universe is completely identified with the meal" (161*).

There is the illness of the anorexic who starves herself in a tragic attempt to achieve nonbodily purity. But there is also the healthful response to food that comes from taking only what one needs, and from eating with others in mind. Such an authentic presence to food cultivates the idea that eating is an act *in relation* to others: *this* grain of rice here and now is irreplaceable.

Furthermore, one may come to see oneself as functioning most healthfully within a specific context, for example, by coming to understand that some foods are appropriate to that context, and just as importantly, that other foods are not. When the Japanese see themselves as defined in an important way by being a "rice culture,"[10] this says something about what it means—spiritually, culturally and economically—to be Japanese. There is a focus on and respect for a particular food that comes through exclusion as well as from inclusion, a focus that is lost in culture-hopping visits to the latest "ethnic" restaurant.

It is important to understand that the two food categories from which we normally operate both decontextualize food. "Food as technology" and "food as high art" can be regarded as two sides of the same view: either food is cheap, fast, and easily reproducible, or it is expensive, labor-intensive, and difficult to reproduce. For this reason, "ethnic" food is now being advertised as the new chic form of high cuisine. But this "elevation" in status destroys its true character. In fact, it is neither "high" nor "low." What makes food "ethnic" is its deep connections to a specific cultural context. It is ordinary food in context.

Wendell Berry was thinking of the sense in which food exists most appropriately within a context when he said, "The pleasure of eating should be an *extensive* pleasure, not that of a mere gourmet" (378*). The gourmet judges food "objectively" whereas the cook has an "extensive" relation to food as ordinary and contextual. Revel clearly represents the first approach. Many of the authors included in this volume—Dōgen, Sen-No-Rikyu, Calvin Trillin, Audre Lorde, and Verta Mae Smart-Grosvenor, to name several—represent an extensive understanding of food. They understand our relations to food as a moral/aesthetic structuring of ordinary experience. Ordinary experience is neither high nor low, neither exclusively moral nor aesthetic. It is healthy, everyday living.

The fundamental reorientation toward the ordinariness of life that occurs from "just eating" makes it difficult to distinguish categorically between the moral and the aesthetic—categories that seem so obvious to Kant and Revel. The way of participating in the world that results from a transformed sense of self is as usefully described by what would traditionally be regarded as aesthetic predicates as by traditional moral predicates. This reorientation does encounter new moral questions which cannot be raised usefully within dualist thinking, such as our moral relations to other animals, but it responds in ways that might be described as aesthetic. It is concerned with "economy" and with what is "appropriate" within a context. This is why a participatory self operates within a moral/aesthetic response to, and interaction with, a particular narrative context.[11]

Perhaps the most important result of authentic presence to food, though, is a sense of candor, transparency, and openness to the food we eat; a simple willingness to face the reality of what we are willing to count as food; an "accurate consciousness of the lives and the world from which food comes" (Berry, 378*). To regard what we will *count* as food as a *choice* moves us from an attitude that treats food only as an object, to the beginnings of a food practice that gradually and relationally becomes a conscious expression of who we are. Such transparency allows us to appreciate the process by which plant foods become part of us physically, politically, and spiritually. In particular, when we grant that eating is a moral issue we can ask a question that has been disallowed by a culture that marginalizes food: do we become violent literally (bodily) by being complicit in acts of violence done on our behalf to produce what we choose to count as food? This is the issue I explore next.

In summary, authentic presence to food is the direct experience of impermanence, of the physical world as "genuine, patent reality." It gives focus to our participatory relations with food and includes a way of understanding ourselves, an attitude toward food, and a way of acting: (1) It requires acceptance of ourselves, the food we eat, and our relations to food as time-bound and relational. We come to see ourselves as embodied, and our experiences as unfolding processes. (Disembodied egos do not get hungry; they send their bodies out for a pizza.) (2) Its "knowledge" is bodily and experiential. (3) It leads to economical living and (4) living within a context. (5) It does not distinguish absolutely between the moral and the aesthetic. (6) Through it we come to treat food—and through the agency of food—ourselves, and others with the *transparency,* openness, candor, that such a relation commands. We must be willing to name what we eat and to understand where it comes from. (7) In turn, transparency encourages a sense of *mutuality* or responsiveness—a willingness to enter into and be transformed by food—that leads to nonviolent practice, or, at least, to acceptance of responsibility within one's context for one's food practices.

IV. CONTEXTUAL MORAL VEGETARIANISM

A participatory self-understanding focused by an authentic presence to food includes, of course, the recognition that plant foods die to become food for us.[12] Mindfulness about food may encourage us to ritualize our healthful relatedness to plant foods. A conception of self as interdependent should celebrate contexts in which this becomes transparent: one may go outside on a summer morning to pick blueberries from the garden for a bowl of cereal and reflect on the way in which what is now (literally) outside will become internal.

One can also enter into a mindful relationship with animal flesh killed for food. The Ihalmiut, whose snowy domain and physical isolation rule out growing most plant foods, ritualize the violence of their food practices by symbolically "apologizing" to the caribou when it is claimed as food. Tibetans, who as Buddhists[13] have not been inclined toward vegetarianism, ritualize their consumption of flesh foods by a gift of their bodies to the birds. Human corpses are hacked to pieces and offered to the birds in "sky burials." (Thus they dramatically reveal their relational sense of person-hood: just as they count other bodies as food, they can also imagine their own bodies counting as food for others. This distinguishes such a practice from cannibalism, which objectifies the body of the "other.")[14] Closer to "home," Wendell Berry says, "Some, I know, will think it bloodthirsty or worse to eat a fellow creature you have known all its life. On the contrary, I think, it means that you eat with understanding and with gratitude" (378*).

The sincerity and transparency of these attitudes allow us to see what is often missed in a culture that marginalizes food. There is a moral question here: What do we become—bodily, politically, spiritually—by killing sentient life for food? In this culture, it is difficult even to raise the question without inviting contempt. A culture that defines the body as an evil impediment that blocks the struggle to realize our full human potential is deeply invested in thinking of (other!) animals as contemptible, and as unworthy of moral consideration. Furthermore, commitment to vegetarianism as a healthy way of living in relation to others is a kind of "bodily knowledge" that presupposes a process of experience in order for it to be compelling. Certainly, very few people have been "argued" into moral vegetarianism. However, the very contempt with which this question is treated, the feints and diversions one meets in seeking to raise it seriously, unmask the question's importance. To allow this as a serious question, as anything more than marginal and annoying, is to admit that the autonomous man is conceptually vulnerable.

By raising the question of the morality of our food choices, I am not suggesting that vegetarianism is the *only* answer compatible with an authentic presence to food. It is not. Unfortunately, vegetarianism is sometimes presented as the morally pure high ground, the stance of perfect nonviolence.[15] But there is no such thing as a life of perfect nonviolence. Boiling water to cook those homegrown, organic vegetables kills millions of microscopic organisms. To live is to commit violence.

Out of this awareness, the moral vegetarian should not think of violence as something *others* commit. Violence is committed by the most mindful of vegetarians every day. However, out of the recognition of one's eating practices as violent *can* come a bodily commitment to direct one's defining relations toward nonviolence whenever possible. Contextual moral vegetarianism should be understood not as a moral *state*, therefore, but as a moral *direction*.

A common objection to vegetarianism (sometimes lodged seriously, sometimes as an evasion) is hypothetical: "What if plants turn out to be sentient beings? As a vegetarian, would you, in that case, eat both plants and animals, or neither?" While I know of no good reason to think that plants are sentient beings, or that they will be discovered to be in the future, my point does not rest on whether all or no eating is violent. Grant for the sake of argument, if you will, that killing both plants and animals for food is violent (or, at least, that in growing plant food violence is committed); my point is that there is a *direction* toward less violence that can be taken in choosing to eat only plant foods. Killing animals for food[16] inflicts needless, conscious suffering. Eating plant foods, on any reasonable theory, inflicts little suffering. To refuse to decide on vegetarianism pending some future (unlikely) scientific discoveries is not a moral decision but an evasion of a moral issue—a simple refusal to be addressed by the question. At best it reveals the mistaken assumption that the fate of vegetarianism rests on whether it is the perfect moral response to the question of our relations to others.

Recognition of oneself as a participant in a relational network that includes other animals and plants does not mean we must think of ourselves as being the same as other members of the network. (Such thinking is

required only within the logic of identity.)[17] Recognition of others as genuinely different (though related) leads to a willingness to treat them in ways
that they may *not* treat us. I may refuse to kill a predator even if I know it
might kill me under certain circumstances.

Neither, however, does a commitment to vegetarianism mean one would
never kill a predator in self-defense, or in defense of innocent others. Vegetarianism is a commitment to eliminate violence wherever possible. Yet,
moral vegetarianism need not be understood as involving a willingness to
commit suicide, nor to stand aside and witness the slaughter of innocents.
Despite these disclaimers concerning the response to a specific context, at a
fundamental level moral vegetarianism recognizes that the propensity to
violence is a learned response, and only seems appropriate and even inevitable as a general response because we have been trained to respond violently to challenges.

The common tendency to dismiss vegetarianism as a kind of weak-
kneed retreat from the world misses the point that it is a strong affirmation
of participation in the world; it follows from a claimed power of self-definition in opposition to a dominant conceptual scheme. The distinction here
is not between strength and weakness, but between a hierarchical distinction in kind which treats nonhuman animals as objects ("others") to be
used for human ends without apology, and a relational power which recognizes difference.

I do not mean to imply by the examples given (the Ihalmiut, Tibetans)
that the choice to treat other animals as food is morally justifiable in exotic
cultures, or in the "Third World," or in extreme contexts.[18] The point is
that while the taking of life should be regarded as a morally serious matter
in any culture, response to violence needs to be understood within a particular cultural narrative. Just as an authentic presence to food is a response
in context, so moral vegetarianism is best understood as a response to a
particular context, to specific culturally embedded practices. While it is
possible to argue that vegetarianism follows from a recognition of universal rights held by all sentient beings regardless of context (see Regan
1983, 330–53), I am suggesting that authentic presence to food may express itself differently in different "worlds."

Some cultures, cultures that provide spiritual self-definition through
food, have cultural rituals that mediate the moral burden of killing and
inflicting pain for food. In western, industrialized countries flesh foods are
almost exclusively encountered in contexts that express alienation from
and dominance over other beings—a manner of relating to other beings
which treats them as objects and denies their difference.[19] If there is any
"world" in which contextual moral vegetarianism is compelling, therefore,
it is the world in which most of the readers of this book live, at least part of
the time.

In a "fast-food/food as high art" culture that lacks symbolic definition
through food, one good reason for becoming a vegetarian is that it can be

seen as a political act of self-empowerment that resists the externalizing pressures of society. To *choose* one's food and define oneself by that choice in opposition to a dominant conceptual scheme is empowering. Its empowerment may differ by gender.

Women, Carol Adams argues (1990, 39–62), have been oppressed in many ways by cultural attitudes linking women with meat. Historically, women have been expected to ensure men a supply of fresh meat while women were expected to subsist on nonmeat foods. Adams vividly connects attitudes toward women with attitudes toward animals, for example, through pornography in which women are depicted as animals ready to be butchered for consumption by men. Her feminist response to the linked oppression of women and animals is that women should choose vegetarianism. It might even be suggested that veganism (moral vegetarianism that excludes consumption of milk and dairy products as well as flesh) is compelling in these contexts because meat and dairy products are the result of exploitation of the reproductive capacities of females.[20]

A man in an industrialized culture is empowered by choosing vegetarianism because it constitutes a rejection of the disciplinary attempts of meat producers to decide what it means to be a "real man." It also marks a statement of solidarity with those who resist the oppression of women and nonhuman animals. Moral vegetarianism can be understood as a kind of protest.

Other reasons for committing to moral vegetarianism in the context in which most of us find ourselves is that most of the flesh foods available in supermarkets have been produced by factory farming methods, methods that vividly depict the fact that, as Heidegger said,[21] food is regarded in our culture as a standing-reserve. Books such as John Robbins's *Diet for a New America* and Peter Singer's *Animal Liberation* reveal the brutal facts about the way "food" is produced in this country. A visit to a "meat processing plant" would serve just as well.

Another contextual reason for committing to vegetarianism is that the diets of those in "developed" countries have devastating effects on those who live in countries that have become dependent on expensive food exports to countries like the United States. The destruction of rainforests to produce beef for the American market is well-publicized. Food economies that were once dedicated to produce low-cost food for local people have been changed to produce expensive food affordable only by the local economic elite and by those to whom it is exported. An increase in trade between so-called First and Third World countries is consistent with an increase in starvation in those countries (see Section Four, "Myths about Hunger").

To put the issue as concretely as possible, whereas vegetarianism for Plato (probably), and for the anorexic is seen as a way of dematerializing the self (thereby escaping our status as animals), the kind of vegetarianism I endorse is a response precisely to the recognition of ourselves as bodily sentient beings, as animals. This leads to a direct sense of action as participation among others. Healthy personhood understands the person's "home" to be inhabited as well by other animals, plants, rivers, and the air.

IV. THE ECO-POLITICAL SELF

A. Feminist Philosophy

Ecology is a feminist issue. Attending sympathetically to unspoken aspects of experience awakens a sense of self among others, and in bodily relation to others. The discovery of these deep relations to others awakens a sense of caring for them as beings whose lives are connected in defining ways to our own. The perspective I have been proposing here, which encourages the development of compassion or caring through mindfulness about food, suggests that there is no categorical way of distinguishing caring for persons from caring for nonhuman life. Whether or not nonhuman animals have moral rights independently of one's contextual relations to them, we certainly can and do care for them. This includes cases where we regularly experience care in return, as in a relationship to a "pet," as well as cases where there is no reciprocity, as in the case of working to preserve natural habitats for animals we will never see.

There seems to be no problem, furthermore, in saying that one can care for things like rocks. Karen Warren has written about two attitudes one can bring to mountain climbing. One seeks to dominate and conquer the mountain, the other seeks to "climb respectfully with the rock." One can care for the rock partly *because* it is "independent and seemingly indifferent to my presence" (Warren 1990, 135).

To consider another sort of example, one of the sources of the oppression of women in countries like India is that deforestation has a disproportionate effect on women, whose responsibility includes food preparation. A common sight in these countries is village women walking farther every year in search of safe water and fuel for food. In such contexts, the destruction of the environment *is* a source of women's oppression.[22] The point here is not that there is a single cause of women's oppression, or even that in countries like India, women's oppression is always ecologically based. Clearly, there are instances, like the euphemistically termed "kitchen accidents," in which women are burned to death by husbands who may be disappointed with the dowry. Yet, in the mosaic of problems that constitute women's oppression in a particular context, no complete account can be given that does not make reference to the connection between women and the environment.

As a feminist political program, caring for can encourage a sense of person-to-person and animal-to-animal connectedness that is absent in the abstract, universalizable Kantian model. Living "in awareness" increases the sense of bodily connectedness to others. As a sense of connectedness increases, it is marked by a transformation in the way we care from an abstract caring *about*, to a context-specific caring *for*. A generalized caring *about* is consistent with an interest in reading about issues relating to the old-growth forests, and even in joining a conservation organization. But care *for* specific trees, context-specific caring marked by "local knowledge," makes action a necessity; lack of action may be taken as reason to doubt one's sincerity in proclaiming care for old-growth forests.

Through extension of caring about to caring for, caring can be extended to contexts that are geographically removed from the care-giver and to beings (human and nonhuman) outside the normal circle of care. It could be argued that this is impossible. Since caring for is context-specific it could be argued that it is impossible to care for persons who are geographically remote. However, through a relational understanding of self and a budding political awareness of one's connectedness to others, one can commit to caring for. For example, when people of good will contribute to Oxfam or other relief organizations to relieve hunger in a country like Ethiopia, their actions are best understood as caring *about* the starving. This may lead to actions that result in caring for them by working to establish long-term bodily connections with specific others in awareness of local moral/aesthetic narratives.

Anticipating the dismissive treatment of nonviolence as a way of being in relation to others, it should be noted that there may be internal conflicts that arise through awakened caring *about* and a resultant desire to care *for*. It is notoriously the case that we cannot care *for* everyone and everything we care *about*. Through engaging in genuine caring for *some* starving people, through knowing their particular histories, a sense of anxiety may arise because we are only able to care about other people in similar situations in a generalized way. However, a contextualist ethic should not give in to the illusion that there is a universalizable program of caring that will magically alleviate all suffering. To the contrary, it should foster the idea that self-development comes only in small increments in contexts of genuine caring which are not easily (if at all) transferable to other contexts. What counts as human and ecological development is context-specific. Caring for must always maintain its contextual character.

As an antidote to the caricature of caring for as a moral utopia advocated only by the hopelessly naive, it is important to note that other conflicts will certainly arise on this model. There is nothing in this view to prevent conflict in principal. In fact, one might say that, in contrast to a morality based on the logic of identity where all conflicts are regarded as just temporary confusions on the way to final, absolute agreement, a morality of caring risks genuine disagreement. It grants that there are legitimate and divergent interests. What is distinctive about an attitude of caring for, however, is that it does not see others as threats to one's own autonomy. (Others may be threats, but they are not threats to one's autonomy.) In other words, it commits to nonviolence as a practical way of living in awareness of our existence as multiple selves. Whereas there is a structural connection between self-understanding as autonomous, and the propensity to objectify others as threats to autonomy (thereby making violence seem "natural" in a "dog-eat-dog" world), a relational self sees through this illusion and understands that violence causes violence. It therefore commits to mindful and peaceful mutual accommodation of divergent interests as a practical method of resolving the *causes* of violence.

I write these words mindful of the fact that marginalized persons, like nonhuman animals, often have violence committed against them. In fact, a dominant conceptual scheme may define them as "those against whom violence can be committed." For this reason, just as I cannot characterize moral vegetarianism as a position of absolute nonviolence, but, rather, a commitment to a moral direction, so I cannot, in good conscience, tell the wife who is beaten by her husband that she must respond nonviolently. I would, however, distinguish the issue of self-defense in dealing with the *effects* of violence (if she doesn't shoot him she will die), from the issue of what would really be effective in treating the *causes* of violence in the long term. Wife-beating is a desparate act of objectification of the woman. Surely, one of its causes is that a dominant conceptual scheme tells the man he *should* be powerful, yet he does not experience himself as powerful. So, he takes out this internal conflict on the one who "should" submit to his power. What appears to be an act of power is, in fact, a desparate act of weakness. To respond by objectifying one's oppressor as "the kind of person" who is violent is to turn an illness into a natural kind. If he is seen as the kind of person who must be that way, there is no hope of treating the causes of violence. A commitment to nonviolent action is a commitment to relieve the structural causes of violence; that requires seeing even our enemies or our oppressors as real persons who exist in relation to ourselves. We must come to see them relationally even if they do not see themselves that way.

The same can be said of seemingly intractable political events. Often, even in events that are covered by the western press, almost no attention is paid to those who seek peaceful resolutions to complex, violent situations. This leads to the impression that violence "works" as a means of resolving conflict. But consider Mubarak Awad, who is seeking a peaceful remedy to the treatment of Palestinians in the West Bank; A. T. Ariyaratne, leader of the Gandhian-inspired Buddhist social movement, Sarvodaya Shramadana, who is speaking out against Tamil/Sinhalese violence in Sri Lanka; the Indian women whose "tree-hugging" resistance to logging in the Himalayan foothills led to the nonviolent ecological and community development movement called Chipko; and the Dalai Lama, winner of the 1989 Nobel Peace Prize, who has offered a peace plan to the Chinese, which includes the provision that Tibet will become an ecological sanctuary, despite the genocide they have been committing against Tibet—all are examples that should be kept in mind when considering the practicability of nonviolence to resolve conflicts in a violent world.[23] Commitment to nonviolent resolution of conflict results from a sober analysis of the causes of violence, causes that connect to our deepest understanding of who we are as persons.

B. BUDDHIST PHILOSOPHY

Ecology is a Buddhist issue.[24] Buddhism is nothing if not the deliberate cultivation of the awareness of interrelatedness. Taken most broadly, this means an awareness of oneself as an ecological being.

Buddhist moral philosophy is positioned to draw out the connection between the participatory self and a way of ecologically mindful action. Whereas western[25] moral philosophy has usually assumed that a proper moral agent must be autonomous in order to apply moral rules to the world (an objectified understanding of this relationship that has caused no end of problems for western moral philosophers), early Buddhist moral philosophy was designed as a direct response to transcendentalizing ethics. If a person is understood as *Nāmarūpa*, a continuous process of experience, a person's moral life obeys the law of causality. Causality is not understood in the sense of strict determination of consequent events by antecedent events, but in the sense that one's past acts condition one's present and future acts.[26] The agent functions within a complex network of defining relations which condition future actions without determining them absolutely. Such an ethic is context-specific while being open to the contingency of the future. A causally based ethic accepts the fact that life is conditioned by perfect ordinariness; it is willing to be judged by our relations to food, and, more generally, by our relations to the environment.

From a Buddhist perspective, if our dispositions lead us to think we are a substance, our acts lead to suffering. When we misconceive ourselves, that is, we think of those things to which we are attached by our dispositions as having value because they are eternal. *Whether we intend to do good or evil*, therefore, we make the process unhealthy.

The crucial distinction in Buddhist ethics is between one who thinks of himself as a substance, and, therefore, does not understand this causal process as defining, and one who understands the causal process for what it is—a purely contingent process of experience. The former is determined by dispositions; the latter is released from them. Understanding that brings moral health results in "letting go" (an attitude Lugones calls playfulness? 94*) of the determination to think of ourselves as substances. Since we no longer cling to the delusion of ourselves beyond the ravages of time, we can live happily through reconciliation with ordinary, temporal existence.

Buddhist ethics is not based on an exclusive dualism between good and evil. Rather, it sees good and evil as co-dependent. It sees good and evil, nonviolence and violence, understanding and delusion, oppressor and oppressed, in everyone. When there is understanding of the causal process of one's life, one becomes, quite literally, "healthy" or "wholesome" as a result.[27] A mindful attitude toward food is productive of health because it reminds us that food is like all life: it comes and goes and exists only here and now. It allows us to understand life for what it is; it brings us into what Dōgen calls the " 'presence of things as they are' (*genjokoan*)" (Kasulis, 84). Mindfulness about food, in turn, is an entrée into ecological consciousness.

The Buddhist ethic of compassion is the result of the conception of personhood as *nāmarūpa*. For the nonsubstantial self the goal of the moral life is to make each moment of the causal process a healthy one so it does not poison later moments. One makes each moment healthy by acknowledging one's co-dependence, one's interrelatedness, to other beings as defining. By caring for oneself, one also cares for others, and this shows itself through compassionate action. Through learning to have compassion for oneself as multiply defined (as including understanding and ignorance, as being oppressor and oppressed), one also learns compassion for others. When one's oppressor is regarded only as "other," one can only relate to that person in the language of substance. One is either oppressed or oppressor. To experience an aspect of oneself as oppressor is to enable oneself to relate to others participatorily as neither (exclusively) oppressor or oppressed. This is a kind of healthy power.[28]

I understand ecological consiousness as consciousness for the ordinary. To value the environment, and to value oneself as a participant in the environment, require "bodily knowledge" that draws one into a sense of healthy participation among others.

V. LIVING PARTICIPATORILY

Early in this essay I said that an authentic presence to food leads us to value and participate in the world differently. Later, in describing the differences between Dōgen's attitude toward food and Revel's, I characterized Dōgen's as participatory and Revel's as critical. Whereas Dōgen's approach to food does not depend on a value hierarchy, and he allows his practice to be judged by its relation to food, Revel's does depend on a value hierarchy, and he understands his critical relationship to food as requiring him to stand apart from it so he can apply normative rules to it. I now want to conclude this section by summarizing concretely how daily experience can be transformed by an authentic presence to food understood as part of an ethic of care or compassion.

A critical stance toward the world describes our relation to the world in dualistic terms; it pictures value and epistemic inquiry as standing apart from what is valued or inquired about; it applies criteria to the world while standing "objectively" apart from it. A participatory involvement in the world regards the critical stance as an unhealthy story which masks our daily involvement in the ordinary affairs of life. Such a participatory stance is not monist, however, in contrast to the dualism of the critical approach.

Monism is itself an unhealthy abstraction. True participation accepts the world as a place buzzing with chaos as well as order, with multiple meanings as well as tracts of the opaquely meaningless, and of deep commonalities as well as real and important differences. Meaning is seen as a daily project which takes place from squarely within the hum of ordinary life. Coming to see ourselves as relational beings means we experience direct, daily, bodily connections to other beings.

Daily experience with other human beings can be transformed by a commitment to participatory living. Much of the anger we experience toward others is the direct result of thinking of ourselves as autonomous substances. We think of others as a potential threat. With such a self-conception, the understandable reaction in cases of food scarcity, for example, is to insist on our "rights," guarantees we grant only on the basis of reciprocity to creatures of like kind who can establish their autonomous spheres of influence. Judged by their exchange value, rights can only protect those who have their own sphere of autonomy to protect. One disastrous result of this adversarial way of thinking is that persons in developing countries are not fully "autonomous agents" capable of defending their interests. A participatory understanding, by contrast, sees questions of scarcity not as cases of "mine against yours," but in terms of respectful usage of what is limited and what we all have in common. In place of the assertion of rights, it recommends compassionate entrance into the worlds of others, world-travelling. It therefore tends to think in terms of economy. It thinks, "How little can we use?" instead of "How much can I have?" Its ethic is one of economy and compassion, not rights.

A compassionate concern for the affairs of other beings resolutely opposes the *identification* of one's interests with another's. That is not compassion, but slavery. The clearest example of this occurs in the home where a mother's compassionate concern for her family is often distorted into a complete identification of her interests with the interests of her family. This often happens through culturally enforced food practices. When her children leave, or her husband decides on divorce, the woman finds she has no "self" left. Living participatorily has as much to do with respect for difference as it has to do with affirmation of commonness.

Conflicts arise out of divergent interests. Participatory living commits to engaging in resolution of conflicts with a compassionate mind. It does not suffer from the delusion that conflicts are the result of a contest between autonomous agents, so that compromise must be viewed as at least a partial loss, if not complete identification with the other.

Another result of a commitment to participatory living is that an ethic of compassion, since it does not demand identity of interests or reciprocity between beings of the same kind, includes a direct, bodily commitment to the welfare of nonhuman beings. We should be committed to a sustainable ecology, including ourselves and nonhuman animals, neither because it egoistically benefits oneself, nor because it altruistically benefits others, but because the health of all beings requires it. Our human interests are directly related to the interests of nonhuman animals.[29]

Furthermore, participatory living is inherently political in its commitment to the public, relational definition of value. It is not political in the style of the Chicago ward boss, however, because it is committed to entering politics mindfully. People can differ legitimately over the wisdom of pacifism, but the least an authentic presence to food can teach is that violence unredeemed by exculpatory ritual is unhealthy. Participatory living means not only working toward peace, but working toward peace with a peaceful mind.

Finally, participatory living requires a healthy dose of sobriety about how much hold any ideas can ultimately have on the world (including the ideas just expressed). Just as physical conflict can be the direct result of thinking of ourselves as autonomous agents, so can intellectual conflict. One idea that should become bodily knowledge is that ideas are things held in common and in response to our connectedness with others (without which communication would not be possible). Ideas are, at best, reflective positionings in the blur of ordinary life.

N O T E S

Note: References to texts printed in this anthology are followed by an asterisk (*). Other page references refer to citations in the list of references.

1. See Warren for a feminist ecological ethic specified in terms of "boundary conditions." Boundary conditions "clarity some minimal conditions of a feminist ethic without suggesting that feminist ethics has an 'essence' " (Warren 1988, 148).

2. For the distinction between participatory and objectified, or defining and nondefining relations, see Section One, p. 11.*

3. See the distinctions in Section One between objectified and participatory ways of understanding relations (p. 11) and between the two claims I am making about these, the ontological and the epistemic (p. 12*). With those distinctions in mind, I am saying here that an authentic presence to food brings us into a healthy epistemic (including bodily) awareness of our ontological relatedness to food.

4. This characterization of typically male and female orientations is based on the psychological research of Carol Gilligan. See Gilligan 1982.

5. At the end of a year spent in Japan, one of the most treasured gifts I received from a student was a large tray of plastic food that had been displayed outside a department store restaurant. (Obviously, the gift was from a student who had gotten to know my "tastes" very well.) My favorites were the plastic sushi. I can never look at them without being reminded of the sushi shop in our neighborhood where my family and I often went for a snack. The contrast between plastic "food" and real sushi indicates what is taken for granted in Japan: that sushi must be made from fish caught on the same day.

6. See Kasulis 1981, chapter 6, for a philosophical interpretation of Dōgen, and Tanahashi 1985 and Yokoi 1976 for selections of his writings.

7. The reason we do not understand our proper relations to food, and resist such understanding, is that we misconceive what it means to be a person. We cling to the idea that, at least, an aspect of us is not affected by time. See Section One, "The Non-Substantial Self."

8. Attentiveness to food is not the only way to learn this. In a Buddhist temple, epigrammatic reminders of our temporality are just as likely to be found in the bathroom as in the kitchen. But Dōgen is saying a direct presence to food is one way of establishing a transformative experience which brings us into consciousness of what I have called "defining relations" throughout our lives.

9. See Kasulis for an explication of "the retrospective reconstruction of reality" (56–61).

10. See Bray 1986. She argues that a western misunderstanding of wet-rice economies in Asia is responsible for the misperception that these cultures are "backward," whereas, in fact, they are responsible for Japan's postwar economic miracle and China's medieval Green Revolution. The benefits of rice cultures extend far beyond the spiritual.

11. It is helpful to read the verse by Sen-No-Rikyu, the Japanese tea master, in this narrative context (164–66*; Sadler 1962). "The Way of Tea" is a way of life that is governed by a moral/aesthetic narrative. But the ritual serves merely to highlight, for Rikyu, the ordinariness of friends drinking tea together. Rikyu was not a gourmet. See Castile 1871 and Sadler 1962 for dependable explanations of the tea ceremony.

12. Some vegetarians eat only foods that naturally fall off plants, thus avoiding killing for food. While this is a view that commands respect, it seems to me that it regards vegetarianism as a kind of moral purism. As I warn below, this seems to me a mistake. See Sharma 1990 for an account the the Jain philosophy of absolute nonviolence which includes an extreme form of vegetarianism.

13. Buddhist vegetarianism is a commitment that comes from the idea of *ahimsa,* the non-harming of sentient beings. For a summary of the history of Buddhist vegetarianism and its contemporary relevance, see Kapleau 1986.

14. Also contrast this mindfulness about one's own body as possibly counting as food with Jonathan Swift's "suggestion" (354–55*) that the bodies of poor children be used for food. See Section Four.

15. Pacifism often receives the same kind of contemptuous response as moral vegetarianism, possibly for similar reasons. It is easy to dismiss it as hopelessly naive about the way life "really is." But this is a stereotype rather than an honest response. Gandhi, identified most often as the exemplar of principled nonviolence, never absolutely renounced the use of violence (Gandhi 1951). As Duane Cady has argued (1989), pacifism is better understood as one of a range of moral views along the spectrum from what he calls "warism" to pacifism rather than a stance of absolute nonviolence. For an important statement of the connection between mothering as a feminist practice and pacifism, see Ruddick 1989, chapter 7. Ruddick's view is criticized by Davion (1990).

16. A friend, Jeremy Iggers, has defended a gradualist approach to the justification of suffering inflicted on animals according to which it is worse to kill a cow than a lobster because lobsters have less complex nervous systems. According to what I have said, there may be merit to this argument. It certainly recognizes that there is a spectrum of available moral positions. My own view, however, is that this is not likely to be a stable moral position. As a direction, moral vegetarianism has the tendency (at least in my own case—so far) to move one gradually in the direction of less and less violence. Violence, even to lobsters, can be avoided. The death clattering of their shells against the pot is hard to forget. In fact, many people try

boiling lobsters alive only once. I would grant, however, that it is important to keep in mind that this movement toward less violence *cannot* terminate in a position of no violence.

17. It is instructive to survey an anthology such as Regan's (1989) with the issue of the logic of identity in mind. Almost without exception, the relevant question is taken to be whether there is some sense in which nonhuman animals are identical to human beings. This assumption is as common among contemporary writers as it was for Descartes or Kant. I argue (1991) that this emphasis on cross-species identity is a mistake, particularly if one's concern is to establish an eco-feminist ethic.

18. The term "Third World" is used with caution since it replicates the hierarchy of "worlds" being called into question here. For now, it can stand as a filler until these issues can be explored in Section Three.

19. I reject the claim that most hunters are more directly present to the food they eat than those who buy meat pre-packaged at the grocery store. If anything, most hunters are worse since they knowingly commit violence, whereas our culture shelters other consumers from acts of violence committed on their behalf. While I have acknowledged that some hunters need to hunt for food, I find highly doubtful the claim frequently made by well-fed hunters that they only hunt for food.

20. Colman McCarthy made this suggestion in conversation.

21. See Section One, Part VI, "The Objectification of Food," referring to Heidegger 1977, 296 and 300.

22. An excellent source is Shiva. See particularly her account of the Chipko movement which began when women in the Himalayan foothills literally hugged trees that were sacred to them to spare them from deforestation. The movement has grown into a full-scale human development project (Shiva 1988, 67–77).

23. See Ingram 1990 for interviews with both men. Also see Macy 1983 for an account of the Sarvodaya Shramadana movement. Holmes 1990 contains many of the classic, as well as little-known, writings on nonviolence, including Awad's "Nonviolent Resistance: A Strategy for the Occupied Territories" (1990).

24. See Badiner 1990 for a collection of Buddhist writings on ecology.

25. In speaking about assumptions generally made by western philosophy, I do not intend to indicate that there is something unique to either eastern or western philosophy. As I have noted, there have always been alternatives in western philosophy to those ideas that have dominated. The same can be said of eastern philosophy. In fact, as Kalupahana points out (101*), the Buddha was reacting against earlier ideas that are similar to Kantian philosophy. Buddhist philosophy and most western philosophy have, however, chosen to emphasize radically different ideas among those that were commonly available to them. The most that can be said is that different ideas have become central to their respective traditions.

26. The Buddha's account of causality is strikingly similar to Hume's in "On Liberty and Necessity" (Hume 1902).

27. See Kalupahana 1976, chapters 5 and 6.

28. This approach to moral philosophy is sympathetic to feminist moral philosophy. Carol Gilligan's research (1982) strongly indicates that there are differences in the ways male and female children tend to think about and experience moral development, and that the psychological and philosophical accounts of moral development generally depict only the typical goal of a (western?) man's moral development. In ordering the development into moral personhood as the movement from interdependence to independence, this model prioritizes men's typical development over women's. Men, for example, tend to resolve conflict by appeal to a formalistic hierarchy of impersonal rules. Women tend to resolve conflict contextually and interpersonally, referring not to rules, but to relationships. Gilligan argues that whereas the male model of moral development highlights autonomy and

rights, the female model values interdependence, personal relationships, and caring. She says, "The morality of rights differs from the morality of responsibility in its emphasis on separation rather than connection, in its consideration of the individual rather than the relationship as primary" (19).

Buddhist moral philosophy is sympathetic to what Gilligan characterizes as a female understanding of morality: both are nonhierarchial and tend to see morality in terms of relations in specific context to specific others. If both, too, can be seen as stressing the bodily way in which moral agents participate in a context and are therefore sympathetic to moral vegetarianism, it is possible to see ecological consequences drawn from them. See Sunstein 1990 and Kittay 1987 for helpful collections of papers illustrating the influence of Gilligan's research. Flanagan and Jackson (Flanagan 1990) give a helpful overview of the large body of literature on this subject. On a feminist ethic of care see Noddings 1984, 1989, 1990; Ruddick 1989. For feminist critiques of an ethic of care see Houston 1990; Card 1990; Hoagland 1990; Puka 1990.

29. These ideas are developed by Heldke in Section Four.

R E F E R E N C E S

Adams, Carol J. *The Sexual Politics of Meat: A Feminist-Vegetarian Critical Theory.* New York: The Continuum Publishing Company, 1990.

Awad, Mubarak E. "Nonviolent Resistance: A Strategy for the Occupied Territories." *Nonviolence in Theory and Practice.* Ed. Robert L. Holmes. Belmont, CA: Wadsworth Publishing Company, 1990.

Badiner, Allan Hunt, ed. *Dharma Gaia.* Berkeley: Parallax Press, 1990.

Bray, Francesca. *The Rice Economies: Technology and Development in Asian Societies.* Oxford: Basil Blackwell, 1986.

Cady, Duane. *From Warism to Pacifism: A Moral Continuum.* Philadelphia: Temple University Press, 1989.

Card, Claudia. "Caring and Evil." *Hypatia* 5, no. 1 (1990): 101–108.

Castile, Rand. *The Way of Tea.* Tokyo: Weatherhill, 1971.

Curtin, Deane. "Toward an Ecological Ethic of Care." *Hypatia* 6, no. 1 (1991): 60–74.

Davion, Victoria. "Pacifism and Care." *Hypatia* 5, no. 1 (1990): 90–100.

Dumoulin, Heinrich. *Zen Buddhism: A History.* Vol. 2. New York: Macmillan Publishing Company, 1990.

Flanagan, Owen, and Kathryn Jackson. "Justice, Care, and Gender: The Kohlberg-Gilligan Debate Revisited." *Feminism and Polticial Theory*, ed. Cass R. Sunstein. Chicago: University of Chicago Press, 1990: 37–52.

Gandhi, Mohandas K. "The Doctrine of the Sword." *Non-violent Resistance*, ed. Bharatan Kumarappa. New York: Schocken, 1951: 132–134.

Gilligan, Carol. *In a Different Voice: Psychological Theory and Women's Development.* Cambridge, MA: Harvard University Press, 1982.

Hanh, Thich Nhat. *Being Peace.* Berkeley: Parallax Press, 1987.

Heidegger, Martin. "The Question Concerning Technology." *Basic Writings*, ed. David Farrell Krell. San Francisco: Harper and Row, 1977: 284–317.

Hoagland, Sarah Lucia. "Some Concerns about Nel Noddings' Caring." *Hypatia* 5, no. 1 (1990): 108–114.

Holmes, Robert, L., ed. *Non-Violence in Theory and Practice*. Belmont, CA: Wadsworth Publishing Company, 1990.

Houston, Barbara. "Caring and Exploitation." *Hypatia* 5, no. 1 (1990): 115–119.

Hume, David. *Enquiries Concerning the Human Understanding and Concerning the Principles of Morals*. 2 ed. Ed. L. A. Selby-Bigge. Oxford: Oxford University Press, 1902.

Ingram, Catherine, ed. *In the Footsteps of Gandhi: Conversations with Spiritual Social Activists*. Berkeley: Parallax Press, 1990.

Kalupahana, David J. *Buddhist Philosophy: A Historical Analysis*. Honolulu: University of Hawaii Press, 1976.

Kant, Immanuel. "Foundations of the Metaphysics of Morals." *Kant Selections*, ed. Lewis White Beck. New York: Macmillan, 1988.

Kapleau, Philip. *To Cherish All Life: A Buddhist Case for Becoming Vegetarian*. Rochester, NY: The Zen Center, 1986.

Kasulis, T.P. *Zen Action Zen Person*. Honolulu: University of Hawaii Press, 1981.

Kittay, Eva Feder, and Diana T. Meyers, eds. *Women and Moral Theory*. Savage, MD: Rowman and Littlefield Publishers, Inc., 1987.

Macy, Joanna. *Dharma and Development: Religion as a Resource in the Sarvodaya Self-Help Movement*. West Hartford, CT: Kumarian Press, 1983.

Noddings, Nel. *Caring: A Feminine Approach to Ethics and Moral Education*. Berkeley: University of California Press, 1984.

———. *Women and Evil*. Berkeley: University of California Press, 1989.

———. "A Response." *Hypatia* 5, no. 1 (1990): 121–126.

Puka, Bill. "The Liberation of Caring: A Different Voice for Gilligan's 'Different Voice.' " *Hypatia* 5, no. 1 (1990): 59–82.

Regan, Tom. *The Case for Animal Rights*. Berkeley: University of California Press, 1983.

——— and Peter Singer, eds. *Animal Rights and Human Obligations*. 2 ed. Englewood Cliffs: Prentice Hall, 1989.

Robbins, John. *Diet for a New America*. Walpole, NH: Stillpoint Publishing, 1987.

Ruddick, Sara. *Maternal Thinking: Toward a Politics of Peace*. New York: Ballantine Books, 1989.

Sharma, I. C. "The Ethics of Jainism." In *Nonviolence in Theory and Practice*, ed. Robert L. Holmes. Belmont, CA: Wadsworth Publishing Company, 1990: 10–14.

Shiva, Vandana. *Staying Alive: Women, Ecology and Development*. London: Zed Books Ltd., 1988.

Singer, Peter. *Animal Liberation*. 2 ed. New York: New York Review, 1990.

Sunstein, Cass R., ed. *Feminism and Political Theory*. Chicago: University of Chicago Press, 1990.

Tanahashi, Kazuaki, ed. *Moon in a Dewdrop: Writings of Zen Master Dōgen*. San Francisco: North Point Press, 1985.

Warren, Karen J. "Toward an Ecofeminist Ethic." *Studies in the Humanities* 15 (1988): 140–156.

Yokoi, Yuho, ed. *Zen Master Dōgen: An Introduction with Selected Writings*. New York: Weatherhill, 1976.

from *Culture and Cuisine*

How to eat well without really taking nourishment? This might well be the question that gastronomy seeks to answer. Being hungry is not always a state favorable to the appreciation of food, because at such a time any dish seems delicious. Conversely, satiety, the permanent state of semirepletion in which people in prosperous countries live, may make them sensitive to the exploits of their chefs, but it also limits the extent and the frequency of the use that can be made of their chefs' talents and the legacy of tradition.

It is unfortunately a fact, however, that gastronomical pleasure can really be experienced to the fullest only if a variety, a contrast, and hence a multiplicity of dishes and wines is offered. Therefore the summits of this art are reached in precisely those periods when the refinement of recipes allies complexity of conception with lightness of touch in execution. This is a basic principle that should never be forgotten while reading these pages: expert cuisine is not a matter of accumulation alone; mixing is not the same as combining; the most barbarous dishes may be very heavy without being any more flavorful. Conversely, the most simple preparations may be *haute cuisine* when the association of two or three foods, which may be quite ordinary, results in an original flavor, a flavor that only the proper skill can produce.

Periodically in the course of this history we see a return to the natural product being preached as a reaction against an excessively heavy and complicated cuisine. But the real art lies neither in products in their natural state nor in heaviness and complexity: a great chef glorifies natural elements, uses them in ways that enhance their essence, knows how to extract their aromas and flavors and set off their consistencies—but he does so by transposing them into a new register, where they disappear only to be reborn as a whole that owes its existence to intelligence. In this respect, the knowledge of flavorful associations (what are the foodstuffs that can set each other off best and how should they be cooked?) is as important as the knowledge of the quantities, the proportions that must guide their marriage. There were entire centuries, for example, in which every dish was bombarded with spices and smelled only of cinnamon, nutmeg, saffron, or hot pepper. At other times and places, everything was drowned in cream or olive oil, two culinary adjuvants that have a particularly negative effect when used heavy-handedly. In tourist restaurants today, one sees the incorrect, theatrical use of herbs becoming the general rule: thyme for grilled meats, branches of fennel for sea perch (*loup*), that fish called sea bass (*bar*) in the North of France. Steaks are served smothered in thyme, an herb never meant to be eaten—does one eat the tea leaves that remain in the bottom of the teapot? The sole value of thyme is the aroma it gives a sauce, a stew, or possibly a grilled mutton chop, but only if one tosses a few bits of it *under* the grill to burn on the coals. As for branches of fennel, it is a veritable farce that we witness in the so-called "great fish restaurants" of Paris every time we see uniformed maîtres d'hôtel making desperate efforts to control a fire that they themselves have just lighted by putting a match to a heap of hay piled up under the wrinkled flanks of some hapless sea-creature whose skin thus chars to a cinder while its flesh remains ice-cold. No, Mr. Swallow-Tails! When one bakes a sea perch in the oven, in a white wine sauce or a lemon sauce, one delicately places two or three bits of fennel in the belly, so that the aroma will impregnate it, after which one puts them aside as one detaches the filets.

This leads us to note that only very rarely does good cuisine take place in the dining room. The little ballet round crêpes suzette, a flaming omelette, a pepper steak soaked with cognac, in the hollow of a silver platter beneath which a dangerous and evil-smelling alcohol lamp is burning, may be mindful of a traveling show and of the vigilance of a fire department, but not of gastronomy.

Let us say it once and for all: regional cuisine does not travel well. This is a basic truth that experience confirms, and before grouping it with certain principles that I shall set forth in the following pages, I shall here provide a few illustrative examples.

Let us take *bouillabaisse marseillaise*. In every seaside region there exists a fisherman's dish that consists of putting various kinds of fish into a pot and putting this pot on the fire, adding to the fish condiments that vary with the region and may be cream, hot pepper, saffron, white wine, onion, etc. . . . The result of this *pot-au-feu* made with fish (which need not necessarily be salt-water fish since there exists a *bouillabaisse* of fresh-water fish in white wine, called *pochouse* or *pauchouse*) is first of all a soup with bits of vegetables, bread, and fish (more or less softened by boiling) floating in it. In *cacciucco livornese,* mussels are added, and *moules marinières* (mussels fisherman-style), for which there are many recipes, depending on the region, are nothing but a *bouillabaisse* made exclusively of mussels. The *baudroie en bourride* (Provençal fish soup) of Sète is a *bouillabaisse* in which the sole ingredient is anglerfish (*baudroie*), the stock of which is particularly spicy and refined. Moreover, this anglerfish must come from the Mediterranean and not the Atlantic: the two are not the same. The anglerfish of the Atlantic, otherwise known as *lotte,* whose head has a different shape from that of the Mediterranean *baudroie,* is an excellent fish, but it is not the traditional ingredient of *bourride sétoise.* The *bourride* of Marseille in turn is a *bouillabaisse* consisting of only three species of fish—anglerfish, sea perch, and whiting (*merlan*)—and is characterized above all by the fact that one mixes garlic-flavored *aïoli* into the stock before serving. Aside from these variations, there are certain skillful touches to improve the dish that depend not on the recipe but on its execution: in particular knowing how to measure the cooking time so that one ends up with both a flavorful stock and edible fish; that is, fish not overcooked to the point that they fall apart. This is achieved in some instances by learning to put the fish with the most delicate flesh in the pot last. If *bouillabaisse marseillaise* has become famous all over the world, it is because the fish of the Golfe du Lion, called rockfish (*poisson de roche*), happens to be particularly tasty and firm. Into the making of a classic *bouillabaisse* go not only fish that are to be eaten but also fish included solely for their aroma, principally scorpion fish (*rascasse*). On the other hand, lobster in a *bouillabaisse marseillaise* is merely a tourist "frill": its flesh becomes flabby in the cooking and its flavor is lost, adding nothing to the dish. But this dish is indissolubly linked to local conditions, in the sense that its merits are due less to the recipe, which is actually quite ordinary, than to the nature and the origins of the products that go into it. Already very difficult to make well on the spot (since rockfish are rare and saffron that has not lost its flavor is hard to come by), and almost always adulterated even in Provençal restaurants (which use already-prepared stocks or, more precisely, *leftovers,* for real stocks are meat juices that are very costly to make and that have their role to play in Grand Cuisine) real *bouillabaisse* can be had only in private homes or on special order, that is to say, in the precise circumstances in which it came into being—after the day's fishing, at the water's edge—and it becomes tasteless when attempts are made to reconstitute it in the abstract, in Paris, for example.

In such cases, culinary genius is the genius of a particular place. Unfortunately, an immense majority of the clientele of restaurants around the world confuse gastronomy with exoticism. In their eyes, the dish that is special is an exotic dish. But it is precisely this sort of dish that has the least chance of being prepared successfully. That is why the restaurateur makes up for it by "flaming" his grilled sea perch, or, in the case of *bouillabaisse,* by serving it with a *rouille,* an overrated sauce made with hot peppers or mayonnaise with garlic whose link with classic *bouillabaisse* is as extrinsic as that of mustard with meat. As for grilled fish, I merely point out that of all fish sea perch is the least fit to be grilled, being one with very dry flesh. No Provençal cookbook prior to 1914 gives a recipe for grilled sea perch. When it is grilled, the flesh of sea perch loses its flavor and dries out. Only "fat" fish—sardines, mackerel—gain by such treatment. But ours is the era of "grilling"; this method of cooking is its predominant bias, just as other eras had a veritable obsession for boiling, and subjected every sort of meat to this treatment, even that destined to be subsequently fried or roasted.

I have here sought only to give a few examples of the misdeeds of the

picturesque in gastronomy; for usually, instead of making an effort to prepare what can be well prepared in their region, too many people imagine
that they are improving their menu by introducing into it supposed exotic
concoctions that for material reasons have no chance of success. It is not
true of course that all local traditions are incapable of being exported, but
Provençal cuisine is one of those that is the least capable of being repro-
duced elsewhere. I have chosen it as my example because of the current
fad for cuisine from the South of France. But I might well have chosen
examples from other parts of France: how, for instance, to make a successful *potée franc-comtoise* (a sort of *pot-au-feu* with bacon and Morteau sausages scented with cumin) without the marvelous, irreplaceable aroma of
bacon and sausages that have hung in the fireplace for months before
being placed in the stewpot? *Potée* is basically the same sort of sturdy
peasant dish that turns up in other slightly different versions as Flemish
hochepot, as *petit salé* with cabbage, or as the *pot-au-feu* of the Île de
France, with or without a marrow bone. The chef's art is precisely the art of
knowing what he can borrow from various traditions without betraying
them.

You have doubtless already wondered why the author of the present
book has adopted the tone of the critic, and why he has assumed from the
outset the role of the moralist rather than that of the historian. It is because—fortunately or unfortunately—cuisine is a normative art in which,
as with grammar, ethics, and medicine, description and prescription can
scarcely be separated. And, second, it is because the history of cuisine
cannot be properly understood unless the origin of various types of dishes
is understood.

Cuisine stems from two sources: a popular one and an erudite one, this
latter necessarily being the appanage of the well-off classes of every era. In
the course of history there has been a peasant (or seafarer's) cuisine and a
court cuisine; a plebeian cuisine and a family cuisine prepared by the
mother (or the humble family cook); and a cuisine of professionals that
only chefs fanatically devoted to their art have the time and the knowledge
to practice.

The first type of cuisine has the advantage of being linked to the soil, of
being able to exploit the products of various regions and different seasons,
in close accord with nature, of being based on age-old skills, transmitted
unconsciously by way of imitation and habit, of applying methods of cooking patiently tested and associated with certain cooking utensils and recipients prescribed by a long tradition. It is this cuisine that can be said to be
unexportable. The second cuisine, the erudite one, is based by contrast on
invention, renewal, experimentation. From antiquity to our own day, in
Europe and elsewhere, as we shall see, a number of such erudite gastronomic revolutions have taken place, the two most important of which, at
least insofar as European cuisine is concerned, occurred at the beginning

of the eighteenth century and at the beginning of the nineteenth. As we shall see, certain of these revolutions even represented an unwitting step backward: thus the alliance of sweet and salt, of meat and fruit (duck with peaches for instance), which today is regarded as an eccentric specialty of certain restaurants, was the rule in the Middle Ages and held sway down to the end of the seventeenth century: almost all recipes for meat up to that time contain sugar.[1] But if erudite cuisine for its part innovates, creates, imagines, it also sometimes risks falling into the sort of pointless complication that we spoke of earlier, into a dangerous form of the Baroque, thus impelling amateurs to return periodically to the cuisine whose roots lie in the products of the land. I shall add that a chef who loses all contact with popular cuisine rarely succeeds in putting something really exquisite together. Furthermore, it is a striking fact that truly great erudite cuisine has arisen principally in places where a tasty and varied traditional cuisine already existed, serving it as a sort of basis. Let us point out, finally, that the formation of urban middle classes, in the eighteenth and above all the nineteenth century, brought "marriages" of the two cuisines, the popular and the erudite, the cuisine unconsciously transmitted and the cuisine deliberately created. The result was what is called "bourgeois" cuisine, which was codified in numerous treatises and which retains the heartiness and the savor of peasant cuisine while at the same time introducing into it the subtlety and the "distinction" of *haute gastronomie,* in sauces for instance.

If regional, peasant cuisine has sturdy basic qualities that allow it to be compared to the draft horse or the plow horse, if *haute gastronomie* has the elegant virtues and the fragility of the thoroughbred, bourgeois cuisine is what breeders call a half-bred horse: it trots but it does not gallop. It nonetheless trots faster than its peasant mother, from which it has inherited staying power and resistance, and outlasts its galloping father the purebred, from which it has inherited finesse and the ability to sprint. What is more, bourgeois cuisine does not exclude invention, unlike strictly traditional cuisine which is transmitted with the invariability of a genotype. No "cordon bleu" hesitates to incorporate his own personal variations in a recipe, and all of us have seen family recipe books for bourgeois cuisine, stuffed full of yellowed handwritten pages that are precious witnesses to an oral teaching handed down by a forebear or to a little "extra secret" recently discovered.

The history of gastronomy is nothing more nor less than a succession of exchanges, conflicts, quarrels, and reconciliations between everyday cuisine and the high art of cuisine. Art is a personal creation, but this creation is impossible without a base in traditional craftsmanship.

An example will serve to demonstrate what I mean by collaboration between popular cuisine and erudite cuisine. In Tuscany there exists a certain peasant know-how with regard to the preparation of white beans (*fagioli*), which makes them particularly rich and tasty. The process consists of filling a bottle, or better still a flask from which the raffia wrappings have been removed, three quarters full of beans, of covering the beans with water, and then hanging the flask by a string at a slight angle above a continuous slow fire of charcoal and warm ashes. After eight to ten hours or more of very slow evaporation and cooking, the beans, though still whole, are tender enough to melt in one's mouth and can be eaten either *all'uccelletto*, that is to say with a ragout sauce, or with olive oil and raw onions (which in my opinion sets them off better). A painting by Annibale Carracci, "*Il Mangiafagioli*" ("*The Bean-eater*"), attests to how far back in time the fondness for this dish goes in Central Italy and in Tuscany.[2] This is a case of genuine popular cuisine, in which intelligence and experience find the best possible preparation for a foodstuff, which costs nothing outside of the basic ingredient. How could *haute cuisine* be grafted onto this gift from peasant tradition? By incorporating beans cooked in a flask within a master chef's recipe (I leave this task to the reader's imagination, since no such recipe exists in Tuscany).

Cuisine is a perfecting of nutrition. Gastronomy is a perfecting of cuisine itself. A chef who does not begin by cooking or seasoning the basic foodstuffs of cuisine, which for him should be the notes of a more complex symphony, at least as well as a peasant, is an impostor, as would be an orchestra leader who would endeavor to improve his art by gathering together a large number of musicians, each of whom played off-key individually. Such cooks ruin cuisine: they are the plague of modern gastronomy. I do not mean to say that culinary art is always the prolongation of popular cuisine, which is a refined way of preparing food but one that never aims at the unexpected and indeed steers clear of it. Often the reformers of gastronomy, on the contrary, must know how to react against family cuisine, which clings to its errors as to its qualities and can both drown in grease and boil to death things that ought to be grilled plain or barely poached. These remarks are intended to demonstrate, however, that great cuisine is not only the cuisine of the privileged. Rich people, the wealthy classes, are not necessarily those that eat the best. Since antiquity, a real connoisseur such as Horace has reacted by deliberately and judiciously embracing rusticity as an antidote to the pretentious mixtures of parvenu gastrophiles who, thanks to their heavy-handed combinations, worshiped their pride rather than their stomachs. It is scarcely my intention to contest the legitimacy of great art, but the sublime marriage of ingredients of an Antonin Carême is no more within the scope of the first kitchen bungler who comes along than the *terribilità* of Michelangelo is a model to assign to the first wielder of a hammer to happen by. There would be something immoral about treating the subject of cuisine as if money were all it takes to consume good food—it is among the poor peoples of the world that the author of the present book has on occasion eaten exquisite dishes: the *barbacoa* of the Indians of Mexico, a young goat cooked slowly beneath warm earth, or *mole poblano* in the same country, or, yet again, *caponata* in Sicily.[3] But it is unfortunately true that even though a high standard of living is not sufficient in and of itself to call forth great culinary art, a gastronomic tradition nonetheless tends to suffer if poverty is too extreme and too prolonged. Sicily is a good example of this: a country where gastronomy flourished in the classic era of Greece (since in Athens itself cookbooks written by Sicilians were used, and Plato, in the *Gorgias,* goes so far as to have Socrates specifically cite a certain "Mithraicos, the author of the treatise on Sicilian cuisine"),[4] Sicily would appear to have had a great deal of difficulty preserving this culinary patrimony in the course of its long dark age. A tradition cannot be perpetuated unless it is applied daily, and it cannot be applied without a modicum of general material well-being. If Mexican *tacos*[5] have a flavor and an aroma alongside which our general run of sandwiches, however numerous the layers, are mere blotting paper embellished with rubber, let us not underestimate the immensity of the cataclysm that engulfed pre-Columbian cuisines once the impoverishment of the Indians in the colonial era set in.

These are the two sources of gastronomic art, which is produced by their subtle and indispensable intermingling. Let us note, however, that the history of gastronomy is above all that of erudite gastronomy, for this is the tradition that has left the greatest number of written traces. The great cookbooks are obviously the fruit of study, of invention, or the reflection of a *change,* rather than the fruit of the everyday run of things. The meals which history has recorded are clearly memorable repasts, princely wedding banquets, the menus served on festive occasions. This is a drawback when one is attempting to trace the history of societies and of their everyday life. It is not a drawback, however, when one is attempting to write the history of gastronomy as art, as it is in exceptional circumstances that the great masters had the freedom and the material means to give full play to their creative imagination.

N O T E S

1. In Pierre de Lune's *Le Cuisinier* (*The Chef*) (1656) we find recipes mixing oranges with meat; preserved fruits and dates with salted fish; raspberry, melon, muscat grape soups. . . .

2. The recipe obviously does not antedate the sixteenth century, for white beans were imported then from America.

3. *Mole* is turkey served with a chocolate sauce. In its natural state chocolate is not sweet; it is pure cocoa flour. This is a pre-Columbian dish par excellence, since both turkey and chocolate originated in the New World and were unknown in Europe before Columbus. *Poblano* may come from the word *pueblo* (meaning *people* or *village*), thus indicating that *mole* is a popular dish (on feast days at

least), or from Puebla (a Mexican city), which would point to a regional origin of this dish. *Mole poblano* is brown, but there is also *mole verde,* with a green sauce whose principal ingredient is a local hot greet pepper (*chile verde*). *Mole* sauce made with chocolate is also very hot.

4. *Gorgias,* 518 B. There is also mention in the *Gorgias* of the existence of another gastronomical author, Archestratus of Gela, some of whose texts have come down to us.

5. Meat and hot peppers or black beans (*frijoles*), rolled in corn-flour pancakes (*tortillas*). As a cheap and tasty popular snack we might also mention *temales,* small cakes more or less the shape of a European roll made of hot cornmeal and flavored with ground hot peppers (*chiles*).

Fushuku-Hampō
(Meal-time Regulations)

"When one is identified with the food one eats one is identified with the whole universe; when we are one with the whole universe we are one with the food we eat,"—this comes from the *Vimalakirti Scripture.* The whole universe and a meal are identical in quality.

If the whole universe is the Dharma then food is also the Dharma: if the universe is Truth then food is Truth: if one is illusion then the other is illusion: if the whole universe is Buddha then food is Buddha also: all are equal in all their aspects. "Both concept and reality are equal as they are in the eye of the Buddhas, there being no difference between them whatsoever,"—this comes from the *Lankavatara Scripture.*

"If the universe is seen to be the realm of the spirit, there is nothing outside the realm of the spirit; if it is seen to be Truth then there is nothing other than Truth; if it is seen to be the equal essence then there is only essence; if it is seen as 'different appearance' then there is only 'different appearance;' "—these are the words of Basō.

Here "equal" is not relative but absolute, meaning the Buddha's Wisdom: there is no difference between the whole universe and the Truth when they are seen with this Wisdom eye for the very manifestation of Truth is the above mentioned equalness. We are, therefore, the personification of the universe when we eat—this is a fact that only the Buddhas fully understand—and the universe is the personification of Truth. When we eat, the universe is the whole Truth in its appearance, nature, substance, force, activity, cause, effect, relatedness, consequence and individuality. The Truth manifests itself when we eat and, when eating, we can realise the manifestation of Truth. The correct mind, when eating, has been Transmitted from one Buddha to another and creates ecstasy of both body and mind.

When the bell rings for the end of morning Zazen, breakfast is taken in the Meditation Hall, each trainee remaining in the same place that he occupied for meditation. The drum is struck thrice and the bell eighteen times to announce to all the trainees that it is time for breakast. In city temples the bell is rung first; in country ones the drum is beaten first. At the sound of the drum or the bell, those facing the wall turn around to face each other across the *tan* and those who work outside the Meditation Hall cease to do so, washing their hands and returning to the Meditation Hall with dignity. After hearing the three slow strokes on the wooden *han,* they enter the hall in silence and without looking about them. No speaking is permitted in the hall.

Whenever a trainee enters the hall, he must make gasshō; this means that the tips of the fingers must be just below the tip of the nose. If the bead is dropped, tilted or kept upright the finger tips must always be in alignment therewith and, when making gasshō, the arms must be kept away from the chest wall and the elbows away from the sides. When entering the hall through the front door, all except the Abbot must enter by the left side, irrespective of where his seat may be, using the left foot as he passes the left pillar of the door lintel. The Abbot enters the hall by the right side of the door or straight through the middle of the doorway. In either case he enters with the right foot first, which is the traditional manner, bows to the statue of Manjusri, turns right and sits in his chair. The Chief Junior trainee goes through the gaitan and enters to the left of the front entrance. If trainees enter by the rear door of the hall those in the right half thereof enter by the right side of the rear door, using their right foot first, and those in the left half enter at the left side using their left foot first. They bow to the east behind the statue of Manjusri and go to their seats.

Seats in the Meditation Hall are allotted according to the date of ordination, admittance to the temple or the work done by the trainee; however, during the training period of ninety days, the first of these three considerations is the one always taken into account.

When wishing to sit on the tan, a trainee must first bow to his own seat, which means that he bows to his neighbours' seats, turn round clockwise and bow to the trainee on the opposite side of the tan, push the left sleeve of his *koromo* under his left arm with his right hand, the right sleeve under the right arm with the left hand, lift the kesa in front with both hands, hold it with the left hand, put the feet together, sit down on the edge of the tan and remove the slippers. He next presses on the tan with his right hand, lifts first the left leg and then the right one, pushes the body backwards on the seat from the edge so that he is not sitting on the part used as a table, sits upright and places his left leg on his right one. The kesa is then spread over the knees so as to hide the inner robes from others' eyes. Robes must never be allowed to fall over the edge of the tan and enough space must be left between the seated trainee and the edge for the food bowls to be spread out, this space being regarded as pure. The three reasons for this are called the "Three Purities:—" a. the kesa is laid there, b. bowls are spread there, c. heads point there during sleep.

The Director, Disciplinarian, Cook, General Maintenance, and Abbot's Assistant priests sit on the right side of the gaitan and the Guest Master, Bathhouse, Sickroom, Librarian, Outdoor and Teacher priests sit on the left side of it at this time.

After the wooden fish has been struck three times all must be in their seats and no one may enter the hall thereafter. The *umpan,* which is hung outside the kitchen, is then struck several times, to tell the trainees to rise, collect their bowls from above their seats and carry them to the pure place in front of their seats; all do this at the same time. All stand up quietly, turn to the right, bow reverently to the name over their seats, make gasshō, hold up the bowl with both hands, taking care that it is neither too high nor too low, turn to the left with the bowl near the chest, sit down and put the bowl to the left behind them. All trainees must be careful not to disturb their neighbouring trainees by bumping against them with any part of the body or turning so fast that the holy kesa flies out and scrapes their faces or shaven heads.

After this the senior who is in charge of the statue of Manjusri offers boiled rice thereto, making gasshō, accompanied by a serving monk who carries the rice box. He then bows to the statue, goes behind it, removes the crêpe cover from the mallet found on the wooden block behind the altar, returns to the front of the statue with his hands in gasshō, bows again, turns to the right, leaves the hall and goes to his own seat, passing the tan of the officers in charge of the eastern half of the temple.

After three strokes on the drum, the bell is struck seven times in front of the Meditation Hall: the Abbot then enters and the trainees immediately leave their seats. The Abbot bows to Manjusri and the trainees and sits down in his chair: the trainees then take their seats again. When they are settled, the attendant priest who has followed the Abbot to the hall and is waiting outside it, bows immediately, enters, places a table in front of the Abbot's chair, bows and leaves the hall. The Abbot's bowl is placed upon this table: the trainees, sitting upright and in a straight line, place their bowls in front of them. The Disciplinarian enters, bows to Manjusri, offers incense, bows again and walks to the mallet making gasshō. After the wooden block has been struck once with the mallet, the trainees unfold their bowl covers.

In order to set out the bowls, one must first make gasshō, untie the knot on the bowl cover and fold the dishcloth to an unobtrusive size, twice crosswise and thrice lengthwise, placing it, together with the chop-stick bag, just in front of the knees. Spread the pure napkin over the knees and put the dishcloth, with the chop-stick bag on top of it, under the napkin. The cover is then unfolded and the farther end is allowed to fall over the edge of the tan, the other three corners being turned under to make a pad for the bowls to be placed upon. The lacquered-paper table-top is taken in both hands, the under fold being held in the right hand and the top one in the left, and is unfolded as if to cover the bowls. Whilst holding it in the right hand, take the bowls with the left and place them in the centre of the left end of this table-top, thereafter taking them out of the large one separately, in order, beginning with the smallest. Only the ball of the thumb of each hand is used for removing them so as to prevent any clattering: when the meal is a small one, only three bowls are used. The chop-sticks are then taken out of the bag followed by the spoon; when the meal is over they are put in again, in reverse order; the bowl-washing stick remains in the bag. The chop-sticks and the spoon are placed with their handles to the right on the table-top in front of the bowls. The bowl-washing stick is then removed from the bag and placed between the soup bowl and the pickle one, with its handle pointing to the edge of the tan. After this all trainees wait for the offering of rice to be made to the hungry ghosts. The empty chop-stick bag is folded in three and replaced under the napkin, on top of the lacquered divider, the latter being on top of the dishcloth.

When the meal has been offered by a donor, the Sickroom priest enters the hall carrying the incense-burner followed by the donor. After offering incense to Manjusri, he leads the donor all round the hall: at this time the donor holds his hands in gassho and keeps his head bowed. The trainees make gassho, without speaking, laughing, looking from side to side or moving their bodies, just sitting calmly and quietly.

The Disciplinarian then strikes the wooden block once and recites the following:—

> We take refuge in the Buddha,
> The completely Perfect Scriptures,
> The Saints and Bodhisattvas
> Whose merit is beyond all understanding:
> To-day a donor has offered food; I pray you all to
>   understand well his reasons for doing so which I am
>   about to read to you.

> (The statement of the donor is read.)

> I have read the donor's reasons for his offering and I call upon the Buddhas and Bodhisattvas to witness its sincerity for they are endowed with holy eyes which can see beyond both self and other. Now let us chant the names of the Ten Buddhas in chorus.

The Disciplinarian and the trainees make gassho, chanting as follows:—

> The completely pure Buddha, Vairocana Buddha, Dharma Itself;
> The complete Buddha Who has been rewarded for His previous
>   training;
> Shakyamuni Buddha, one of the many Buddhas Who has appeared
>   in the many worlds;
> Maitreya Buddha Who will appear in the future;
> All the Buddhas in all directions in the Three Worlds;
> The great and excellent *Dharma Lotus Scripture*;
> Holy Manjusri Bodhisattva;
> The great and wise Samantabhadra Bodhisattva;
> The great and kind Avalokitesvara;
> All the Bodhisattvas and Ancestors;
> The *Scripture of Great Wisdom.*

The Disciplinarian continues:—

In the beginning the mallet will strike the Buddha on the foot; later it will strike Him on the head.

If the meal is an ordinary breakfast or lunch, the Disciplinarian will again strike the wooden block, saying:—

Having taken refuge in the Three Treasures,
All will be able to grasp them perfectly.

When the names of the Ten Buddhas have been chanted, the Disciplinarian strikes the wooden block once. In order to show that a true trainee will be willing to offer food to all other creatures, the Chief Junior makes gasshō and chants the following verse loudly:—

(For breakfast)

The ten benefits bless the breakfast gruel
And all trainees profit greatly therefrom;
Since these wonderful results are limitless,
Pleasure is ours for eternity.

(For dinner)

Since I will give Three Merits and six tastes
To all the Buddhas and the members of the priesthood,
All sentient beings within the universe
Will enjoy this offering.

When the Chief Junior is not present, the priest next in rank chants the above verses. A trainee then enters and says in a loud voice, "Breakfast is served." This trainee must enter the hall to the left of the door, bow to Manjusri, bow to the Abbot, bow to the Chief Junior, stand near the left side of the front door, bow to Manjusri again and make gasshō. The words must be spoken clearly and no errors made in their announcement since, if these words are pronounced incorrectly, the meal cannot be taken: should this happen, the announcement must be made again. The Chief Junior bows to the food in front of him, meditates and then he and all trainees start to eat. If a donor has offered money or food, the Disciplinarian comes from behind the statue of Manjusri, bows to the Chief Junior and asks him to give thanks for the gift. The Disciplinarian strikes the wooden block once and the Chief Junior recites the thanksgiving verse loudly:—

The two kinds of alms, material and spiritual,
Have the endowment of boundless merit:
Now that they have been fulfilled in this act of charity
Both self and others gain pleasure therefrom.

The rice must be served carefully and never in a hurry for, if the serving is hurried, they who receive the food will be flustered; it must not be served slowly, however, for then the recipients will become tired. The rice must be served by those whose duty it is to act as waiters; no one who is sitting on the tan may serve himself. The first person to be served is always the Chief Junior, the Abbot being served last. During the serving, the hands of others and the brims of bowls must never be soiled with either soup or gruel. In order to indicate how much they wish to receive, those sitting on the tan must hold a spoon in their right hand, with the bowl towards the chest and the handle towards the serving trainee. The handle must be moved up and down gently two or three times, when enough has been placed in the bowl, and the body bowed slightly: the amount of gruel received depends entirely upon this. The spare hand must never hang down when a soup bowl, or other bowl, is being put down; it must be kept in a one-handed gasshō. Trainees may not sneeze or cough whilst receiving food; if, however, either is unavoidable, the trainee must turn his back to the others present before sneezing or coughing. The Precepts of Buddha must always be followed whenever one carries the rice box.

One must be respectful, when receiving gruel or rice, for the Buddha Himself said that we must receive food with respect; this fact must be carefully remembered. When receiving food, the bowl must be held up horizontally with both hands underneath it; only the correct amount of gruel or rice may be placed therein—there must never be so much that some is left uneaten and those who are doing the waiting must be notified when enough has been received by the lifting of two fingers of the right hand. When the food has been received, it must not be consumed greedily by seizing a spoon or chop-sticks from the trainee doing the waiting, nor may a trainee receive food from a waiting trainee to whom he has lent his own spoon or chop-sticks for the purpose of dishing it out. It was said by one of the Ancestors that one must have the correct mind when receiving food, holding the bowl horizontally. Both the rice and the soup bowls must be filled and the rice, soup and other food taken in regular sequence. Food may not be eaten with the knees drawn up. Should a waiting trainee be in so great a hurry that even a grain of rice, or a drop of soup, is spattered in another's bowl, the serving must be done again. The bowls may not be held up, nor may the trainees take food, until the Inō (Disciplinarian) has struck the wooden block to announce that the food has been served.

When the block is struck, the trainees make gasshō, bow to their food and recite the verse of the Five Thoughts:—

We will first share the merits of this food with the Three
   Treasures of the Dharma;
Second, we will share it with the Four Benefactors,—the Buddha,
   the President, our parents and all people;
Third, we will share it with the Six Lokas;

With all of these we share it and to all we make offering thereof.
The first bite is to discard all evil;
The second bite is so that we may train in perfection;
The third bite is to help all beings;
We pray that all may be enlightened.
We must think deeply of the ways and means by which this food
     has come:
We must consider our merit when accepting it.
We must protect ourselves from error by excluding greed from our
     minds.
We will eat lest we become lean and die.
We accept this food so that we may become enlightened.

Rice offerings for the hungry ghosts may not be made before this verse
is finished. To make this offering, seven grains of rice are placed on the
handle of the bowl-washing stick or the edge of the lacquered table: the
offering is always made with the thumb and middle fingers of the right
hand. If the food served is rice cakes, vermicelli or buckwheat, a ball, the
size of a dime, should be taken from the bowl and placed as above; if the
meal consists only of gruel, no offering is made, although there was a time
when this was actually done; no spoon or chop-sticks were used for the
purpose. After the offering, all trainees make gasshō and keep silent.
     The following is the correct way to eat breakfast. The gruel is received
in the largest of the set of bowls which is then replaced upon its holder.
After a few seconds wait, the second bowl is taken with the right hand,
placed on the left palm and held there by the top of the thumb which is
turned slightly inwards. The spoon is taken in the right hand and seven or
eight spoonfuls of gruel are transferred from the first bowl to the second
one, the latter being put on the left side of the former. The brim of the
second bowl is put to the lips and gruel may be taken with the spoon: all
the gruel is thus to be eaten up by repetitions of this sequence. Should
gruel be left in the first bowl, the second bowl must be replaced upon the
table, the first bowl taken and the gruel consumed with the spoon. The
bowl is then cleaned with the bowl-washing stick and replaced upon its
holder. The second bowl is picked up and any gruel left therein consumed; the trainee must wait for the water to be brought for washing-up
after cleaning the bowl with the bowl-washing stick.
     The following is the correct way to eat lunch. The first bowl is raised as
high as the mouth and rice is put therein: this bowl may not be left on the
table nor may it be put to the lips: the Buddha said that food must be eaten
with respect and never with arrogance for, should we have an arrogant
appearance, we are only equal to children or harlots: the upper part of the
bowl is regarded as pure and the lower part as defiled. The first bowl is
held with the fingers underneath and the thumbs in the brim, the second
and third fingers only being on the outside and the fourth and fifth being

kept away from the bowl entirely—this is the correct way to hold the bowls.

In far-off India, Shakyamuni Buddha and His disciples used neither chop-sticks nor spoons, simply making the rice into balls with their right hands—we present-day Buddhists must remember this fact; many heavenly deities, Cakravarti Raja and emperors did the same thing—we must understand that this was the ancient way. Only sick monks used spoons; all others ate their food with their hands. In India they have neither heard of, nor seen, chop-sticks: they may only be seen in use in China and certain other countries and it is only due to local customs that they are used in Zen monasteries. The Buddhist Precepts must be followed at all times; the custom of taking food with the hands has long died out. Since there are no teachers left whom we can question about the old traditional way, we use a spoon, chop-sticks and bowls.

When picking up, or replacing, bowls, spoons and chop-sticks, no noise may be made, nor may rice be stirred in the middle with the spoon. Only sick trainees may ask for extra food. The extra bowls may not be filled with rice, nor may a trainee look into a neighbor's bowl or disturb him. Lunch must be eaten carefully, large lumps of rice may not be crammed into the mouth nor may balls be made and thrown into the mouth. Not even a grain of rice that has fallen on the table may be eaten; the lips may not be smacked whilst chewing rice and it may not be chewed whilst drinking soup. The Buddha said that tongues must not be long nor lips be allowed to be licked whilst taking food: this must be studied well. The hands may not be waved whilst eating; the knees may not be held with the elbows nor the food stirred. The Buddha said that food may never be stirred as if by a cook, thus leaving the hands soiled, nor may it be consumed noisily: He also said that food may not be piled up, like the mound on a grave, or the bowl heaped full; soup may also not be poured upon food, as if to wash it within the bowl, other food may not be mixed with that in the bowl and other food may not be mixed with rice, and held in the mouth, after the manner of monkeys.

Meals may not be taken either too quickly or too slowly in the Meditation Hall: it is very impolite to eat everything up so fast that one sits and watches others eat with one's arms folded. Noise may not be made with bowls, or spittle swallowed, before the waiting trainee announces "Second helpings" in a loud voice. No rice may be left uneaten or anything else asked for. It is not permitted to scratch the head during a meal; dandruff may not be allowed to drop into the bowls and the hands must not be soiled. The body may not be shaken; the knees may not be raised or held; yawning is not permitted nor may the nose be blown loudly; if a fit of sneezing comes on, the nose must be carefully covered with the hand. If any food becomes jammed between the teeth, it must be removed with one hand covering the mouth from the sight of others. Fruit seeds and other similar waste must be put in a place where it will give no offence to others—a good place being on the lacquered table top in front of the bowl, slightly hidden by the bowl's rim—others must never be allowed to become disgusted by such a sight. If another tries to give food or cake that is left over in his bowls to another it may not be received. No waiting trainee may use a fan in the Meditation Hall during the heat of summer, especially if a neighbouring trainee feels a chill; if a trainee feels that he has a chill coming on he should tell the Disciplinarian and take his meal elsewhere. If a trainee wishes to ask for something he must do so quietly. If, at the end of the meal, any food remains in the bowl, it must be wrapped in the dishcloth. The mouth may not be opened wide nor may rice be eaten in large spoonfuls; rice may not be spilled into the first bowl nor the spoon soiled. The Buddha said that one may not wait with one's mouth open for food nor speak with one's mouth full: He also said that trainees must not try to get extra food by covering the food in their bowls with rice or by covering the rice with other food: careful notice must be taken of this advice. The Buddha also said that tongues must not be smacked at meal times, lips may not be licked or food blown up to warm or cool it; this must also be carefully remembered. After breakfast, all bowls must be cleaned with the bowl-washing stick. If each mouthful is ladled carefully three times before eating it will become of a suitable size. The Buddha said that, when eating, rice-balls must be made neither too large nor too small.

The whole of the bowl of the spoon must be put completely into the mouth when eating lest food be spilled; no food or rice may be spilled upon the napkin—if any food is found upon the napkin it must be given to the waiting trainee. If any unhusked rice is found in the rice in the bowl it must be husked and eaten; it may not be thrown away nor swallowed without being husked.

In the *Scripture of the Three Thousand Manners* it says that, if something unpleasant is found in the food, it may not be eaten and its presence may not be made known to any neighbouring trainee; also the food may not be spat out. If any rice should be left in the bowl it must not be kept in the presence of a Senior but given to a waiting trainee. When the meal is over, trainees must be satisfied with it and require nothing more. From both the rational and practical outlook, one should try never to waste a single grain of rice at mealtimes; the whole universe is completely identified with the meal. The bowls may not be struck with the chop-sticks or spoon, thus causing noise, nor may the lustre of the bowls be impaired. If the bowls lose their lustre they will become unuseable as a result of dirt and grease. When water is drunk from the bowls no sound may be made with the mouth in doing so and it may not be disgorged into the bowl or other utensils. The face and hands may not be wiped with the napkin.

In order to wash the bowls, the sleeves of the robe must be carefully arranged so that they do not touch anything; after this hot or cold water must be received in the first bowl. After receiving the water, the bowl must be carefully washed with the washing-up stick, the bowl being turned carefully from left to right. The used water is poured into the second bowl and the first bowl is washed carefully again, both inside and out, with the washing-up stick; the bowl is turned with the left hand whilst the washing-up stick is held in the right hand. The bowl is then held in the left hand whilst the dishcloth is unfolded with the right one and spread out as if to cover it. After this the bowl is taken in both hands and wiped with the unfolded dishcloth; it is turned from left to right in the wiping. The dish-cloth is put into the bowl so that it may not be seen from the outside and the bowl is replaced on its stand. The spoon and chop-sticks are washed next in the second bowl and wiped with the dishcloth. During this time, the dishcloth must remain in the first bowl to hide it from view, only a corner of it being used to wipe the spoon and chop-sticks. When the spoon and chop-sticks have been wiped, they must be put into the chop-stick bag and placed in front of the second bowl. The second bowl is then washed in the third bowl; it and the washing-up stick are held lightly with the left hand and the third bowl is taken in the right hand and put in the place that the second one occupied. The water is transferred from the second bowl to the third one, and the second bowl is washed in the third one in the same way as the first bowl was. The same sequence for washing is used for the third and fourth bowls. No spoon, chop-sticks or bowls may be washed in the first bowl. The sequence is:—the first bowl is washed and wiped, then the spoon, then the chop-sticks, and the second, third and fourth bowls. All the bowls are then put separately into the first one as each is washed; the bowl-washing stick is wiped and put into the chop-stick bag last. The nap-kin may not be folded before the dirty water has been discarded; this water may not be thrown upon the floor—also the Buddha said that left-over food may not be put into the water; this point must be studied carefully. When the dirty-water bowl is brought, trainees must make gasshō and empty their dirty water into it taking care to see that it does not soil the sleeves of the robe. Fingers may not be washed in the water and the water may not be thrown away in an unclean place. The second, third and fourth bowls are put into the first one, with the thumbs only, in the reverse order from when they were removed.

The first bowl, containing the other bowls, is then held up with the left hand and placed in the middle of the bowl cover, the lacquered table-top being taken out from underneath it with the right hand. This table-top is folded with both hands above the first bowl and placed on top of it. The bowls are covered with the cover, the nearer end of it being put over the bowls first and the far end then folded over them towards the trainee. The napkin is folded and placed on the cover and the chop-stick bag is placed on top of the napkin. Originally the washing-up stick was put on top of the napkin but now it is put into the bag. The dishcloth is put on top of the chop-stick bag and the two other corners of the cover are tied together over the bowls. Both ends of this tie should be on the right in order to tell the right way round of the bowls and to make their untying simple. When the bowls have been wrapped, the trainees make gasshō and sit quietly. The wooden block is struck once by the Manjusri statue attendant to signify that the trainees may leave the Meditation Hall.

The trainee sitting to the left of the Abbot's attendant on the gaitan rises, bows to the Manjusri statue, goes to the west side of the wooden block on the south side of the incense bowl, bows to the block, makes gasshō and waits for the Abbot and the trainees to wrap their bowls completely. When they have all finished, he hits the wooden block once, covers the mallet with the mallet cover, makes gasshō and again bows to the block. The Disciplinarian then recites the following:—

The universe is as the boundless sky,
As lotus blossoms above unclean water;
Pure and beyond the world is the mind of the trainee;
O Holy Buddha, we take refuge in Thee.

Abbot Eisai transmitted this traditional way of ending meals and so we continue to do it thus.

The Abbott leaves the hall: when he leaves his chair the Manjusri statue attendant must immediately leave the place where he has been standing beside the wooden block and hide behind the curtain of the Manjusri statue lest he should be seen by the Abbot.

The trainees rise and replace their bowls above their seats; the bowls must be held with both hands as the trainees stand up, turn to the right and place them above their seats with their right hands, hanging them, by the tied covers, on their hooks whilst supporting them with their left hands. The trainees then make gasshō, come back to the edge of the tan and descend slowly; they put on their slippers and bow to each other. When tea is taken in the Meditation Hall the trainee's behaviour is the same as the above and the method of sitting down on the tan and descending from it is always the same at all times.

The cushions are placed under the tan and the trainees leave the hall. When the Abbot has left the hall, the end of morning Zazen is announced by three strokes of the bell: if Zazen is to be continued no bell is sounded. If, however, a donor asks the trainees to go to the Meditation Hall, they must do so even if the bell has already been rung and, thereafter, the bell must be rung again to announce the end of morning Zazen. When tea is over in the afternoon and the Abbot has bowed to Manjusri and left the hall, the bell is struck three times to tell the trainees to leave the hall and they then descend from the tan: they leave the hall in the same way they entered it as described earlier. All walking in the Meditation Hall must be in the manner of kinhin—half a step to each breath—as in the manner of the kinhin periods during Zazen.

Verses of Sen-No-Rikyu

Though I sweep and sweep,
Everywhere my garden path,
Though invisible
On the slim pine needles still
Specks of dirt may yet be found.

When below the eaves,
The moon's flood of silver light
Chequers all the room,
There's no need to be abashed
If our heart is pure and clear.

When you hear the splash
Of the water drops that fall
Into the stone bowl
You will feel that all the dust
Of your mind is washed away.

In my little hut,
Whether people come or not
It is all the same.
In my heart there is no stir
Of attraction or disgust.

What have I to give?
To my guests for their repast
If I don't rely
On the monkeys of the vale
For the fruits they bring to me.

There is no fixed rule
As to when the window should
Closed or open be.
It depends on how the moon
Or the snow their shadows cast.

Flowers of hill or dale.
Put them in a simple vase
Full or brimming o'er.
But when you're arranging them
You must slip your heart in too.

Every morn and eve
When I sweep the Dewy Path
All is calm and still.

Though it seems a guest is there
No one comes to lift the latch.

Many though there be,
Who with words or even hands
Know the Way of Tea.
Few there are or none at all,
Who can serve it from the heart.

If I look upon,
The still mirror of my heart
What there do I see?
Is it the same mind it was
Yesterday, or is it changed?

Though invisible
There's a thing that should be swept
With our busy broom.
'Tis the dirt that ever clings
To the impure human heart.

Though you wipe your hands
And brush off the dust and dirt
From the tea vessels.
What's the use of all this fuss
If the heart is still impure?

Since the Dewy Path
Is a way that lies outside
This most impure world.
Shall we not on entering it
Cleanse our hearts from earthly mire?

When we leave behind
The Three Worlds' Abodes of Fire,
Storm and Passion tossed,
Entering the Dewy Path
Through the pines a pure breeze blows.

Just a little space
Cut off by surrounding screens
From the larger hall.
But within we are apart
From the common Fleeting World.

In the Dewy Path
And the Tea-room's calm retreat
Host and guests have met.
Not an inharmonious note
Should disturb their quiet zest.

On a Chinese stand
Vessels all of various shapes

Made of gourds are seen
'Tis a feast that we receive
Both from China and Japan.

Just a simple shelf
Hanging from the corner wall
By a plain bamboo.
All we need in such a world
Are these artless simple things.

Take a 'Go' bamboo
Split it up and from the joints
You can fabricate
All the things that you will need
For the use of Cha-no-yu.

When you take a sip
From the bowl of powder Tea
There within it lies
Clear reflected in its depths
Blue of sky and grey of sea.

What a lot of things
Just as though by sleight of hand
Can be done with you.
Everything you can include
In your maw O double shelf.

I am never tired
Of this simple straw-thatched hut.
Wrought of plain round wood
Does its middle pillar stand
Just exactly to my mind.

CALVIN TRILLIN

from *American Fried:*
Adventures of a Happy Eater

The best restaurants in the world are, of course, in Kansas City. Not all of them; only the top four or five. Anyone who has visited Kansas City and still doubts that statement has my sympathy: He never made it to the right places. Being in a traveling trade myself, I know the problem of asking someone in a strange city for the best restaurant in town and being led to some purple palace that serves "Continental cuisine" and has as its chief creative employee a menu-writer rather than a chef. I have sat in those places, an innocent wayfarer, reading a three-paragraph description of what the trout is wrapped in, how long it has been sautéed, what province its sauce comes from, and what it is likely to sound like sizzling on my platter—a description lacking only the information that before the poor trout went through that process it had been frozen for eight and a half months.

In American cities the size of Kansas City, a careful traveling man has to observe the rule that any restaurant the executive secretary of the chamber of commerce is particularly proud of is almost certainly not worth eating in. Its name will be something like La Maison de la Casa House, Continental cuisine; its food will sound European but taste as if the continent they had in mind was Australia. Lately, a loyal chamber man in practically any city is likely to recommend one of those restaurants that have sprouted in the past several years on the tops of bank buildings, all of them encased in glass and some of them revolving—offering the diner not only Continental cuisine and a twenty-thousand-word menu but a spectacular view of other restaurants spinning around on the top of other bank buildings. "No, thank you," I finally said to the twelfth gracious host who invited me to one of those. "I never eat in a restaurant that's over a hundred feet off the ground and won't stand still."

What is saddest about a visitor's sitting in the Continental cuisine palace chewing on what an honest menu would have identified as Frozen Duck à l'Orange Soda Pop is that he is likely to have passed a spectacular restaurant on the way over. Despite the best efforts of forward-looking bankers and mad-dog franchisers, there is still great food all over the country, but the struggle to wring information from the locals about where it is served can sometimes leave a traveler too exhausted to eat. I often manage to press on with a seemingly hopeless interrogation only because of my certain knowledge that the information is available—discussed openly by the residents in their own homes, the way that French villagers might have discussed what they really thought of the occupation troops they had been polite to in the shops. As it happens, I grew up in Kansas City and spent hours of my youth talking about where a person could find the best fried chicken in the world or the best barbecued ribs in the world or the best hamburgers in the world—all, by chance, available at that time within the city limits of Kansas City, Missouri. I grew up among the kind of people whose response some years later to a preposterous claim about Little Rock's having a place that served better spareribs than the ones served by Arthur Bryant's Barbecue at Eighteenth and Brooklyn was to fly to Little Rock, sample the ribs, sneer, and fly back to Kansas City.

Knowing that the information exists does make me impatient if some civic booster in, say, one of the middle-sized cities of the Southwest is keeping me from dinner by answering my simple questions about restaurants with a lot of talk about the wine cellar of some palace that has inlaid wallpaper chosen personally by a man who is supposed to be the third best interior decorator in San Francisco. As the booster goes on about the onion soup with croutons and the sophisticated headwaiter named Jean-Pierre, my mind sometimes wanders off into a fantasy in which my interrogation of the booster is taking place in the presence of one of those ominous blond Germans from the World War II films—the ones with the steel-blue eyes and the small scars who sit silently in the corner while the relatively civilized German line officer asked the downed Allied flyer for military information. "I do hope you will now agree to tell me if there's any Mexican food worth eating around here and quit talking about the glories to be found in La Maison de la Casa House, Continental cuisine," I tell the booster. "If not, I'm afraid Herr Mueller here has his methods."

It is common for an American city to be vaguely embarrassed about its true delights. In the fifties, a European visitor to New Orleans who insisted on hearing some jazz was routinely taken to hear a group of very respectable-looking white businessmen playing Dixieland. A few years ago, I suspect, an Eastern visitor to Nashville who asked a local banker if there was any interesting music in town might have been taken—by a circuitous route, in order to avoid overhearing any of the crude twanging coming out of the Grand Old Opry or the country recording studios—to the home of a prominent dermatologist who had some friends around every Friday night for chamber music. In most American cities, a booster is likely to insist on defending the place to outsiders in terms of what he thinks of as the sophisticated standards of New York—a city, he makes clear at the start, he would not consider living in even if the alternative were moving with his family and belongings to Yakutsk, Siberia, U.S.S.R. A visitor, particularly a visitor from the East, is invariably subjected to a thirty-minute commercial about the improvement in the local philharmonic, a list of Broadway plays (well, musicals) that have been through in the past year, and some comment like "We happen to have an *excellent* French restaurant here now." The short answer to that one, of course, would be "No you don't." An American city's supply of even competent French restaurants is limited by the number of residents willing to patronize them steadily, and, given the difficulty of finding or importing ingredients and capturing a serious chef and attracting a clientele sufficiently critical to keep the chef from spending most of his time playing the commodities market out of boredom, "an *excellent* French restaurant" will arrive in Tulsa or Omaha at about the time those places near the waterfront in Marseilles start turning out quality pan-fried chicken. In New York, where I live now, the few restaurants that even pretend to serve French food comparable to the food available in the best restaurants in France are maintained at a cost so high that dinner at any one of them seems bound, sooner or later, to face competition from the round-trip air fare to Paris or Lyon.

"I don't suppose your friends took you to Mary-Mac's on Ponce de Leon for a bowl of pot likker, did they?" I once said to a friend of mine who had just returned from her first visit to Atlanta. Naturally not. No civic-minded residents of Atlanta—which advertises itself as the World's Next Great City—would take an out-of-town guest to Mary-Mac's. Their idea of a regional eating attraction is more likely to be some place built to look like one of the charming antebellum houses that Atlanta once had practically none of—having been, before Sherman got there, an almost new railroad terminus that had all the antebellum charm of Parsons, Kansas. Pot likker, I told my friend, is the liquid left in the bottom of the greens pot, is eaten like a soup, after crumbling some corn bread into it, and is what a Great City would advertise instead of a lot of golf courses.

"They took me to a very nice French restaurant," she said, gamely claiming that it was almost as good as the one she can go to for lunch on days she doesn't feel like walking far enough to get to the decent places.

Since "No you don't" would be considered an impolite reply to the usual boast about a city's having a three-star French restaurant, I have, in the past, stooped to such responses as "French food makes me break out." I love French food. (In fairness, I should say that I can't think of a nation whose food I don't love, although in Ethiopia I was put off a bit by the appearance of the bread, which looks like a material that has dozens of practical uses, not including being eaten as food.) But who wants to hear a skin doctor saw away at the cello when Johnny Cash is right down the street? Lately, when the local booster informs me—as the city ordinance apparently requires him to do within ten minutes of meeting anyone who lives in New York—that he would never live in New York himself, I say something like, "Well, it's not easy of course. There's no barbecue to speak of. That's because of a shortage of hickory wood, I think, although I haven't checked out that theory with Arthur Bryant. We don't really have any Mexican restaurants—I mean the kind you find in Texas, say. Oh, we have Mexican restaurants run by maybe a guy from the East Side who picked up a few recipes while he was down in San Miguel de Allende thinking about becoming a painter, but no Mexican family restaurants. No señora in the kitchen. No Coors beer. No Lone Star. I wouldn't claim that you can live in New York and expect to drink Lone Star. There's a shortage of Chicago-style pizza south of Fourteenth Street. They don't know much about boiling crabs in New York. It's only since the soul-food places opened that we've been able to get any fried chicken, and we still don't have those family-style fried-chicken places with the fresh vegetables and the pickled watermelon rind on the table. Sure we've got problems. Grits are a problem. I'd be the last one to say living in New York is easy."

Somehow, people have listened to my entire speech and then suggested that I forget my troubles with some fine Continental cuisine at La Maison de la Casa House. I'm then forced into playing the restaurant section of the Yellow Pages—trying one system after another, like a thoroughly addicted horseplayer who would rather take his chances with a palpably bad system than give up the game altogether. I go with small listings for a while—no place that says anything like "See Advertisement Page 253 of this section." Then places called by someone's first name. Then places not called by someone's first name. For a while, I tried a complicated formula having to do with the number of specialties claimed in relation to the size of the entry, but I could never remember whether the formula called for me to multiply or divide. Constant traveling has provided me with some information on some cities, of course, but the discovery process remains a strain. Who would have ever guessed, for instance, that the old Mexican street near downtown Los Angeles that looks as if it was restored by the MGM set department and stocked by one of the less tasteful wholesalers in Tijuana would have one place that served delicious hand-patted soft tacos packed with *picadillo* or *chicharrón?* How can an innocent traveler be expected to guess that he going to be subjected to the old Hollywood mystery-film trick of hiding the real jewel in a case full of paste imitations?

There are some types of food that do lend themselves to sophisticated techniques of interrogation. When an Italian restaurant is suggested, for instance, I always say, "Who controls the city council here?" I suppose a good Italian restaurant could exist in a city that doesn't have enough Italians to constitute at least a powerful minority in city politics, but a man in town for only two or three meals has to go with the percentages. It is axiomatic that good barbecue is almost never served in an obviously redecorated restaurant—the reason being, according to my favorite theory on the subject, that walls covered with that slick precut paneling let the flavor slide away.

Some time ago, I found myself in Muskogee, Oklahoma, with dinnertime approaching, and I asked some people I was having a drink with if they knew of any good barbecue places. Through a system of what amounted to ethnic elimination, I had arrived at barbecue as the food most likely to see me through the evening. There is, I am relieved to say, no Continental cuisine in Muskogee, Oklahoma. The people I was having a drink with were trying to be helpful, perhaps because the liquor laws of Oklahoma see to it that citizens who are taking a Bourbon in public feel so much like criminals—having skulked in through an unmarked back door and flashed some patently phony membership cards—that we had developed the closeness of conspirators. (Even states that allow grown-ups to drink in public with comparative ease expect a traveler to observe some bizarre liquor laws, of course, including at least one I approve of— the Vermont statute that makes it illegal for a customer to carry a drink from one table to another. I have found that a man who picks up his drink and moves to your table is invariably a man who is going to talk at length about how many miles his car gets to the gallon.) One barbecue place was mentioned, but something about the way it was mentioned made me suspicious.

"They have plates there?" I asked.

"What do you mean 'plates'?" one of my fellow criminal-boozers asked me.

"You know—plates you eat off of," I said.

"Of course they have plates," he said.

"You have any other barbecue restaurants around here?" I asked. I have eaten fine barbecue on plates—Arthur Bryant, in fact, uses plates—but I would hesitate to eat barbecue in a place that has plates "of course" or "naturally" or "certainly." The next piece of information an outsider is likely to extract about such a place is that it also serves steaks and chicken and maybe even a stray lobster tail.

"Well," my partner in crime began, "there's an old colored fellow out on the highway who—"

"Tell me how to get there," I said.

It turned out to be a small diner, and if it had been a half-mile closer I might have been able to locate it unassisted by following the perfume of burning hickory logs. There were, as it happened, no plates. The proprietor's version of the formal restaurant custom of including a dinner plate on top of a larger plate at each setting was to put down a piece of butcher paper and then a piece of waxed paper and then the barbecue—first-class barbecue. It would have been a thoroughly satisfying meal except that my success in finding the place caused me to ponder all through dinner on how much happier traveling would be if only I could think of a workable formula for finding fried-chicken restaurants.

PETER SINGER

Becoming a Vegetarian . . .

or how to produce less suffering and
more food at a reduced cost to the
environment

Now that we have understood the nature of speciesism* and seen the
consequences it has for nonhuman animals it is time to ask: What can we
do about it? There are many things that we can and should do about
speciesism. We should, for instance, write to our political representatives
about the issues discussed in this book; we should make our friends aware
of these issues; we should educate our children to be concerned about the
welfare of all sentient beings; and we should protest publicly on behalf of
nonhuman animals whenever we have an effective opportunity to do so.

While we should do all these things, there is one other thing we can do
that is of supreme importance; it underpins, makes consistent, and gives
meaning to all our other activities on behalf of animals. This one thing is
that we take responsibility for our own lives, and make them as free of
cruelty as we can. The first step is that we cease to eat animals. Many
people who are opposed to cruelty to animals draw the line at becoming a
vegetarian. It was of such people that Oliver Goldsmith, the eighteenth-
century humanitarian essayist, wrote: "They pity, and they eat the objects
of their compassion."[1]

As a matter of strict logic, perhaps, there is no contradiction in taking an
interest in animals on both compassionate and gastronomic grounds. If
one is opposed to inflicting suffering on animals, but not to the painless
killing of animals, one could consistently eat animals who had lived free of
all suffering and been instantly, painlessly slaughtered. Yet practically and
psychologically it is impossible to be consistent in one's concern for nonhuman animals while continuing to dine on them. If we are prepared to
take the life of another being merely in order to satisfy our taste for a

*Singer defines speciesism as " . . . a prejudice or attitude of bias in favor of the interests of
members of one's own species and against those of members of others species" (*Animal
Liberation*, p. 6). —Ed.

particular type of food, then that being is no more than a means to our end. In time we will come to regard pigs, cattle, and chickens as things for us to use, no matter how strong our compassion may be; and when we find that to continue to obtain supplies of the bodies of these animals at a price we are able to pay it is necessary to change their living conditions a little, we will be unlikely to regard these changes too critically. The factory farm is nothing more than the application of technology to the idea that animals are means to our ends. Our eating habits are dear to us and not easily altered. We have a strong interest in convincing ourselves that our concern for other animals does not require us to stop eating them. No one in the habit of eating an animal can be completely without bias in judging whether the conditions in which that animal is reared cause suffering.

It is not practically possible to rear animals for food on a large scale without inflicting considerable suffering. Even if intensive methods are not used, traditional farming involves castration, separation of mother and young, breaking up social groups, branding, transportation to the slaughterhouse, and finally slaughter itself. It is difficult to imagine how animals could be reared for food without these forms of suffering. Possibly it could be done on a small scale, but we could never feed today's huge urban populations with meat raised in this manner. If it could be done at all, the animal flesh thus produced would be vastly more expensive than animal flesh is today—and rearing animals is already an expensive and inefficient way of producing protein. The flesh of animals reared and killed with equal consideration for the welfare of animals while they were alive would be a delicacy available only to the rich.

All this is, in any case, quite irrelevant to the immediate question of the ethics of our daily diet. Whatever the theoretical possibilities of rearing animals without suffering may be, the fact is that the meat available from butchers and supermarkets comes from animals who were not treated with any real consideration at all while being reared. So we must ask ourselves, not: Is it *ever* right to eat meat? but: Is it right to eat *this* meat? Here I think that those who are opposed to the needless killing of animals and those who oppose only the infliction of suffering must join together and give the same, negative answer.

Becoming a vegetarian is not merely a symbolic gesture. Nor is it an attempt to isolate oneself from the ugly realities of the world, to keep oneself pure and so without responsibility for the cruelty and carnage all around. Becoming a vegetarian is a highly practical and effective step one can take toward ending both the killing of nonhuman animals and the infliction of suffering upon them. Assume for the moment, that it is only the suffering that we disapprove of, not the killing. How can we stop the use of the intensive methods of animal rearing described in the previous chapter?

So long as people are prepared to buy the products of intensive farming, the usual forms of protest and political action will never bring about a major reform. Even in supposedly animal-loving Britain, although the wide controversy stirred by the publication of Ruth Harrison's *Animal Machines* forced the government to appoint a group of impartial experts (the Brambell committee) to investigate the issue of mistreatment of animals and make recommendations, when the committee reported the government refused to carry out its recommendations. In 1981 the House of Commons Agriculture Committee made yet another inquiry into intensive farming, and this inquiry also led to recommendations for eliminating the worst abuses. Once again, nothing was done.[2] If this was the fate of the movement for reform in Britain, nothing better can be expected in the United States, where the agribusiness lobby is still more powerful.

This is not to say that the normal channels of protest and political action are useless and should be abandoned. On the contrary, they are a necessary part of the overall struggle for effective change in the treatment of animals. In Britain, especially, organizations like Compassion in World Farming have kept the issue before the public, and even succeeded in bringing about an end to veal crates. More recently American groups have also started to arouse public concern over intensive farming. But in themselves, these methods are not enough.

The people who profit by exploiting large numbers of animals do not need our approval. They need our money. The purchase of the corpses of the animals they rear is the main support the factory farmers ask from the public (the other, in many countries, is big government subsidies). They will use intensive methods as long as they can sell what they produce by these methods; they will have the resources needed to fight reform politically; and they will be able to defend themselves against criticism with the reply that they are only providing the public with what it wants.

Hence the need for each one of us to stop buying the products of modern animal farming—even if we are not convinced that it would be wrong to eat animals who have lived pleasantly and died painlessly. Vegetarianism is a form of boycott. For most vegetarians, the boycott is a permanent one, since once they have broken away from flesh-eating habits they can no longer approve of slaughtering animals in order to satisfy the trivial desires of their palates. But the moral obligation to boycott the meat available in butcher shops and supermarkets today is just as inescapable for those who disapprove only of inflicting suffering, and not of killing. Until we boycott meat, and all other products of animal factories, we are, each one of us, contributing to the continued existence, prosperity, and growth of factory farming and all the other cruel practices used in rearing animals for food.

It is at this point that the consequences of speciesism intrude directly into our lives, and we are forced to attest personally to the sincerity of our concern for nonhuman animals. Here we have an opportunity to do something, instead of merely talking and wishing the politicians would do something. It is easy to take a stand about a remote issue, but speciesists, like racists, reveal their true nature when the issue comes nearer home. To protest about bullfighting in Spain, the eating of dogs in South Korea, or the slaughter of baby seals in Canada while continuing to eat eggs from hens who have spent their lives crammed into cages, or veal from calves who have been deprived of their mothers, their proper diet, and the freedom to lie down with their legs extended, is like denouncing apartheid in South Africa while asking your neighbors not to sell their houses to blacks.

To make the boycott aspect of vegetarianism more effective, we must not be shy about our refusal to eat flesh. Vegetarians in omnivorous societies are always being asked about the reasons for their strange diets. This can be irritating, or even embarrassing, but it also provides opportunities to tell people about cruelties of which they may be unaware. (I first learned of the existence of factory farming from a vegetarian who took the time to explain to me why he wasn't eating the same food I was.) If a boycott is the only way to stop cruelty, then we must encourage as many as possible to join the boycott. We can only be effective in this if we ourselves set the example.

People sometimes attempt to justify eating flesh by saying that the animal was already dead when they bought it. The weakness of this rationalization—which I have heard used, quite seriously, many times—should be obvious as soon as we consider vegetarianism as a form of boycott. The nonunion grapes available in stores during the grape boycott inspired by Cesar Chavez's efforts to improve the wages and conditions of the grape-pickers had already been produced by underpaid laborers, and we could no more raise the pay those laborers had received for picking those grapes than we could bring our steak back to life. In both cases the aim of the boycott is not to alter the past but to prevent the continuation of the conditions to which we object.

I have emphasized the boycott element of vegetarianism so much that the reader may ask whether, if the boycott does not spread and prove effective, anything has been achieved by becoming a vegetarian. But we must often venture when we cannot be certain of success, and it would be no argument against becoming a vegetarian if this were all that could be said against it, since none of the great movements against oppression and injustice would have existed if their leaders had made no efforts until they were assured of success. In the case of vegetarianism, however, I believe we do achieve something by our individual acts, even if the boycott as a whole should not succeed. George Bernard Shaw once said that he would be followed to his grave by numerous sheep, cattle, pigs, chickens, and a whole shoal of fish, all grateful at having been spared from slaughter because of his vegetarian diet. Although we cannot identify any individual animals whom we have benefited by becoming a vegetarian, we can assume that our diet, together with that of the many others who are already avoiding meat, will have some impact on the number of animals raised in factory farms and slaughtered for food. This assumption is reasonable because the number of animals raised and slaughtered depends on the profitability of this process, and this profit depends in part on the demand for the product. The smaller the demand, the lower the price and the lower the profit. The lower the profit, the fewer the animals that will be raised and slaughtered. This is elementary economics, and it can easily be observed in tables published by the poultry trade journals, for instance, that there is a direct correlation between the price of poultry and the number of chickens placed in broiler sheds to begin their joyless existence.

So vegetarianism is really on even stronger ground than most other boycotts or protests. The person who boycotts South African produce in order to bring down apartheid achieves nothing unless the boycott succeeds in forcing white South Africans to modify their policies (though the effort may have been well worth making, whatever the outcome); but vegetarians know that they do, by their actions, contribute to a reduction in the suffering and slaughter of animals, whether or not they live to see their efforts spark off a mass boycott of meat and an end to cruelty in farming.

In addition to all this, becoming a vegetarian has a special significance because the vegetarian is a practical, living refutation of a common, yet utterly false, defense of factory farming methods. It is sometimes said that these methods are needed to feed the world's soaring population. Because the truth here is so important—important enough, in fact, to amount to a convincing case for vegetarianism that is quite independent of the question of animal welfare that I have emphasized in this book—I shall digress briefly to discuss the fundamentals of food production.

At this moment, millions of people in many parts of the world do not get enough to eat. Millions more get a sufficient quantity, but they do not get the right kind of food; mostly, they do not get enough protein. The question is, does raising food by the methods practiced in the affluent nations make a contribution to the solution of the hunger problem?

Every animal has to eat in order to grow to the size and weight at which it is considered ready for human beings to eat. If a calf, say, grazes on rough pasture land that grows only grass and could not be planted with corn or any other crop that provides food edible by human beings, the result will be a net gain of protein for human beings, since the grown calf provides us with protein that we cannot—yet—extract economically from grass. But if we take that same calf and place him in a feedlot, or any other confinement system, the picture changes. The calf must now be fed. No matter how little space he and his companions are crowded into, land must be used to grow the corn, sorghum, soybeans, or whatever it is that the calf eats. Now we are feeding the calf food that we ourselves could eat. The calf needs most of this food for the ordinary physiological processes of day-to-day living. No matter how severely the calf is prevented from exercising, his body must still burn food merely to keep him alive. The food is also used to build inedible parts of the calf's body, like bones. Only the food left over after these needs are satisfied can be turned into flesh, and eventually be eaten by human beings.

How much of the protein in his food does the calf use up, and how much is available for human beings? The answer is surprising. It takes twenty-one pounds of protein fed to a calf to produce a single pound of animal protein for humans. We get back less than 5 percent of what we put in. No wonder that Frances Moore Lappé has called this kind of farming "a protein factory in reverse"![3]

We can put the matter another way. Assume we have one acre of fertile land. We can use this acre to grow a high-protein plant food, like peas or beans. If we do this, we will get between three hundred and five hundred pounds of protein from our acre. Alternatively we can use our acre to grow a crop that we feed to animals, and then kill and eat the animals. Then we will end up with between forty and fifty-five pounds of protein from our acre. Interestingly enough, although most animals convert plant protein into animal protein more efficiently than cattle do—a pig, for instance, needs "only" eight pounds of protein to produce one pound for humans—this advantage is almost eliminated when we consider how much protein we can produce per acre, because cattle can make use of sources of protein that are indigestible for pigs. So most estimates conclude that plant foods yield about ten times as much protein per acre as meat does, although estimates vary, and the ratio sometimes goes as high as twenty to one.[4]

If instead of killing the animals and eating their flesh we use them to provide us with milk or eggs we improve our return considerably. Nevertheless the animals must still use protein for their own purposes and the most efficient forms of egg and milk production do not yield more than a quarter of the protein per acre that can be provided by plant foods.

Protein is, of course, only one necessary nutrient. If we compare the total number of calories produced by plant foods with animal foods, the comparison is still all in favor of plants. A comparison of yields from an acre sown with oats or broccoli with yields from an acre used for feed to produce pork, milk, poultry, or beef shows that the acre of oats produces six times the calories yielded by pork, the most efficient of the animal products. The acre of broccoli yields nearly three times as many calories as pork. Oats produce more than twenty-five times as many calories per acre as beef. Looking at some other nutrients shatters other myths fostered by meat and dairy industries. For instance, an acre of broccoli produces twenty-four times the iron produced by an acre used for beef, and an acre of oats sixteen times the same amount of iron. Although milk production does yield more calcium per acre than oats, broccoli does better still, providing five times as much calcium as milk.[5]

The implications of all this for the world food situation are staggering. In 1974 Lester Brown of the Overseas Development Council estimated that if Americans were to reduce their meat consumption by only 10 percent for one year, it would free at least 12 million tons of grain for human consumption—or enough to feed 60 million people. Don Paarlberg, a former U.S. assistant secretary of agriculture, has said that merely reducing the U.S. livestock population by half would make available enough food to make up the calorie deficit of the nonsocialist underdeveloped nations nearly four times over.[6] Indeed, the food wasted by animal production in the affluent nations would be sufficient, if properly distributed, to end both hunger and malnutrition throughout the world. The simple answer to our question, then, is that raising animals for food by the methods used in the industrial nations does not contribute to the solution of the hunger problem.

Meat production also puts a strain on other resources. Alan Durning, a researcher at the Worldwatch Institute, an environmental thinktank based in Washington, D.C., has calculated that one pound of steak from steers raised in a feedlot costs five pounds of grain, 2,500 gallons of water, the energy equivalent of a gallon of gasoline, and about thirty-five pounds of eroded topsoil. More than a third of North America is taken up with grazing, more than half of U.S. croplands are planted with livestock feed, and more than half of all water consumed in the United States goes to livestock.[7] In all these respects plant foods are far less demanding of our resources and our environment.

Let us consider energy usage first. One might think that agriculture is a way of using the fertility of the soil and the energy provided by sunlight to increase the amount of energy available to us. Traditional agriculture does precisely that. Corn grown in Mexico, for instance, produces 83 calories of food for each calorie of fossil fuel energy input. Agriculture in developed countries, however, relies on a large input of fossil fuel. The most energy-efficient form of food production in the United States (oats, again) produces barely 2.5 food calories per calorie of fossil fuel energy, while potatoes yield just over 2, and wheat and soybeans around 1.5. Even these meager results, however, are a bonanza compared to United States animal production, every form of which costs more energy than it yields. The least inefficient—range-land beef—uses more than 3 calories of fossil fuel for every food calorie it yields; while the most inefficient—feedlot beef—takes 33 fuel calories for every food calorie. In energy efficiency, eggs, lamb, milk, and poultry come between the two forms of beef production. In other words, limiting ourselves to United States agriculture, growing crops is generally at least five times more energy-efficient than grazing cattle, about twenty times more energy-efficient than producing chickens, and more than fifty times as energy-efficient as feedlot cattle production.[8] United States animal production is workable only because it draws on millions of years of accumulated solar energy, stored in the ground as oil and coal. This makes economic sense to agribusiness corporations because meat is worth more than oil; but for a rational long-term use of our finite resources, it makes no sense at all.

Animal production also compares poorly with crop production as far as water use is concerned. A pound of meat requires fifty times as much water as an equivalent quantity of wheat.[9]*Newsweek* graphically described this volume of water when it said, "The water that goes into a 1000 pound steer would float a destroyer."[10] The demands of animal production are drying up the vast underground pools of water on which so many of the drier regions of America, Australia, and other countries rely. In the cattle country that stretches from western Texas to Nebraska, for example, water tables are falling and wells are going dry as the huge underground lake known as the Ogalalla Aquifer—another resource which, like oil and coal, took millions of years to create—continues to be used up to produce meat.[11]

Nor should we neglect what animal production does to the water that it does not use. Statistics from the British Water Authorities Association show that there were more than 3,500 incidents of water pollution from farms in 1985. Here is just one example from that year: a tank at a pig unit burst, sending a quarter-million liters of pig excrement into the River Perry and killing 110,000 fish. More than half of the prosecutions by water authorities for serious pollution of rivers are now against farmers.[12] This is not surprising, for a modest 60,000-bird egg factory produces eighty-two tons of manure every week, and in the same period two thousand pigs will excrete twenty-seven tons of manure and thirty-two tons of urine. Dutch farms produce 94 million tons of manure a year, but only 50 million can safely be absorbed by the land. The excess, it has been calculated, would fill a freight train stretching 16,000 kilometers from Amsterdam to the farthest shores of Canada. But the excess is not being carted away; it is dumped on the land where it pollutes water supplies and kills the remaining natural vegetation in the farming regions of the Netherlands.[13] In the United States, farm animals produce 2 billion tons of manure a year—about ten times that of the human population—and half of it comes from factory-reared animals, where the waste does not return naturally to the land.[14] As one pig farmer put it: "Until fertilizer gets more expensive than labor, the waste has very little value to me."[15] So the manure that should restore the fertility of our soils ends up polluting our streams and rivers.

It will, however, be the squandering of the forests that turns out to be the greatest of all the follies caused by the demand for meat. Historically, the desire to graze animals has been the dominant motive for clearing forests. It still is today. In Costa Rica, Colombia, and Brazil, in Malaysia, Thailand, and Indonesia, rainforests are being cleared to provide grazing land for cattle. But the meat produced from the cattle does not benefit the poor of those countries. Instead it is sold to the well-to-do in the big cities, or it is exported. Over the past twenty-five years, nearly half of Central America's tropical rainforests have been destroyed, largely to provide beef to North America.[16] Perhaps 90 percent of the plant and animal species on this planet live in the tropics, many of them still unrecorded by science.[17] If the clearing continues at its present rate, they will be pushed into extinction. In addition, clearing the land causes erosion, the increased runoff leads to flooding, peasants no longer have wood for fuel, and rainfall may be reduced.[18]

We are losing these forests just at the moment when we are starting to learn how truly vital they are. Since the North American drought of 1988, many people have heard of the threat posed to our planet by the greenhouse effect, caused mainly by increasing amounts of carbon dioxide in the atmosphere. Forests store immense amounts of carbon; it has been estimated that despite all the clearing that has taken place, the world's remaining forests still hold four hundred times the amount of carbon released into the atmosphere each year by human use of fossil fuels. Destroying a forest releases the carbon into the atmosphere in the form of carbon dioxide. Conversely, a new, growing forest absorbs carbon dioxide from the atmosphere and locks it up as living matter. The destruction of existing forests will intensify the greenhouse effect; in large-scale reforestation, combined with other measures to reduce the output of carbon dioxide, lies our only hope of mitigating it.[19] If we fail to do so, the warming of our planet will mean, within the next fifty years, widespread droughts, further destruction of forests from climatic change, the extinction of innumerable species unable to cope with the changes in their habitat, and a melting of the polar ice caps, which will in turn raise sea levels and flood coastal cities and plains. A rise of one meter in the level of the sea would flood 15 percent of Bangladesh, affecting 10 million people; and it would threaten the very existence of some low-lying Pacific island nations such as Maldives, Tuvalu, and Kiribati.[20]

Forests and meat animals compete for the same land. The prodigious appetite of the affluent nations for meat means that agribusiness can pay more than those who want to preserve or restore our forests. We are, quite literally, gambling with the future of our planet—for the sake of hamburgers.

How far should we go? The case for a radical break in our eating habits is clear; but should we eat nothing but plant foods? Where exactly do we draw the line?

Drawing precise lines is always difficult. I shall make some suggestions, but the reader might well find what I say here less convincing than what I have said before about the more clear-cut cases. You must decide for yourself where you are going to draw the line, and your decision may not coincide exactly with mine. This does not matter all that much. We can distinguish bald men from men who are not bald without deciding every borderline case. It is agreement on the fundamentals that is important.

I hope that anyone who has read this far will recognize the moral necessity of refusing to buy or eat the flesh or other products of animals who have been reared in modern factory farm conditions. This is the clearest case of all, the absolute minimum that anyone with the capacity to look beyond considerations of narrow self-interest should be able to accept.

Let us see what this minimum involves. It means that, unless we can be sure of the origin of the particular item we are buying, we must avoid chicken, turkey, rabbit, pork, veal, beef, and eggs. At the present time relatively little lamb is intensively produced; but some is, and more may be in future. The likelihood of your beef coming from a feedlot or some other form of confinement—or from grazing land created by clearing rainforest—will depend on the country in which you live. It is possible to obtain supplies of all these meats that do not come from factory farms, but unless you live in a rural area this takes a lot of effort. Most butchers have no idea how the animals whose bodies they are selling were raised. In some cases, such as that of chickens, traditional methods of rearing have disappeared so completely that it is almost impossible to buy a chicken that was free to roam outdoors; and veal is a meat that simply cannot be produced humanely. Even when meat is described as "organic" this may mean no more than that the animals were not fed the usual doses of antibiotics, hormones, or other drugs; small solace for an animal who was not free to walk around outdoors. As for eggs, in many countries "free range eggs" are widely available, though in most parts of the United States they are still very difficult to get.

Once you have stopped eating poultry, pork, veal, beef, and factory farm eggs the next step is to refuse to eat any slaughtered bird or mammal. This is only a very small additional step, since so few of the birds or mammals commonly eaten are not intensively reared. People who have no experience of how satisfying an imaginative vegetarian diet can be may think of it as a major sacrifice. To this I can only say: "Try it!" Buy a good vegetarian cookbook and you will find that being a vegetarian is no sacrifice at all. The reason for taking this extra step may be the belief that it is wrong to kill these creatures for the trivial purpose of pleasing our palates; or it may be the knowledge that even when these animals are not intensively raised they suffer in the various ways described in the previous chapter.

Now more difficult questions arise. How far down the evolutionary scale shall we go? Shall we eat fish? What about shrimps? Oysters? To answer these questions we must bear in mind the central principle on which our concern for other beings is based. As I said in the first chapter, the only legitimate boundary to our concern for the interests of other beings is the point at which it is no longer accurate to say that the other being has interests. To have interests, in a strict, nonmetaphorical sense, a being must be capable of suffering or experiencing pleasure. If a being suffers, there can be no moral justification for disregarding that suffering, or for refusing to count it equally with the like suffering of any other being. But the converse of this is also true. If a being is not capable of suffering, or of enjoyment, there is nothing to take into account.

So the problem of drawing the line is the problem of deciding when we are justified in assuming that a being is incapable of suffering. In my earlier discussion of the evidence that nonhuman animals are capable of suffering, I suggested two indicators of this capacity: the behavior of the being, whether it writhes, utters cries, attempts to escape from the source of pain, and so on; and the similarity of the nervous system of the being to our own. As we proceed down the evolutionary scale we find that on both these grounds the strength of the evidence for a capacity to feel pain diminishes. With birds and mammals the evidence is overwhelming. Reptiles and fish have nervous systems that differ from those of mammals in some important respects but share the basic structure of centrally organized nerve pathways. Fish and reptiles show most of the pain behavior that mammals do. In most species there is even vocalization, although it is not audible to our ears. Fish, for instance, make vibratory sounds, and different "calls" have been distinguished by researchers, including sounds indicating "alarm" and "aggravation."[21] Fish also show signs of distress when they are taken out of the water and allowed to flap around in a net or on dry land until they die. Surely it is only because fish do not yelp or whimper in a way that we can hear that otherwise decent people can think it a pleasant way of spending an afternoon to sit by the water dangling a hook while previously caught fish die slowly beside them.

In 1976 the British Royal Society for the Prevention of Cruelty to Animals set up an independent panel of inquiry into shooting and angling. The panel was chaired by Lord Medway, a noted zoologist, and made up of experts outside the RSPCA. The inquiry examined in detail evidence on whether fish can feel pain, and concluded unequivocally that the evidence for pain in fish is as strong as the evidence for pain in other vertebrate animals.[22] People more concerned about causing pain than about killing may ask: Assuming fish *can* suffer, how much *do* they actually suffer in the normal process of commercial fishing? It may seem that fish, unlike birds and mammals, are not made to suffer in the process of rearing them for our tables, since they are usually not reared at all: human beings interfere with them only to catch and kill them. Actually this is not always true: fish farming—which is as intensive a form of factory farming as raising feedlot beef—is a rapidly growing industry. It began with freshwater fish like trout, but the Norwegians developed a technique for producing salmon in cages in the sea, and other countries are now using this method for a variety of marine fish. The potential welfare problems of farmed fish, such as stocking densities, the denial of the migratory urge, stress during handling, and so on have not even been investigated. But even with fish who are not farmed, the death of a commercially caught fish is much more drawn out than the death of, say, a chicken, since fish are simply hauled up into the air and left to die. Since their gills can extract oxygen from water but not from air, fish out of the water cannot breathe. The fish on sale in your supermarket may have died slowly, from suffocation. If it was a deep-sea fish, dragged to the surface by the net of a trawler, it may have died painfully from decompression.

When fish are caught rather than farmed, the ecological argument against eating intensively reared animals does not apply to fish. We do not waste grain or soybeans by feeding them to fish in the ocean. Yet there is a different ecological argument that counts against the extensive commercial fishing of the oceans now practiced, and this is that we are rapidly fishing out the oceans. In recent years fish catches have declined dramatically. Several once-abundant species of fish, such as the herrings of Northern Europe, the California sardines, and the New England haddock, are now so scarce as to be, for commercial purposes, extinct. Modern fishing fleets trawl the fishing grounds systematically with fine-gauge nets that catch everything in their way. The nontarget species—known in the industry as "trash"—may make up as much as half the catch.[23] Their bodies are thrown overboard. Because trawling involves dragging a huge net along the previously undisturbed bottom of the ocean, it damages the fragile ecology of the seabed. Like other ways of producing animal food, such fishing is also wasteful of fossil fuels, consuming more energy than it produces.[24] The nets used by the tuna fishing industry, moreover, also catch thousands of dolphins every year, trapping them underwater and drowning them. In addition to the disruption of ocean ecology caused by all this overfishing there are bad consequences for humans too. Throughout the world, small coastal villages that live by fishing are finding their traditional source of food and income drying up. From the communities on Ireland's west coast to the Burmese and Malayan fishing villages the story is the same. The fishing industry of the developed nations has become one more form of redistribution from the poor to the rich.

So out of concern for both fish and human beings we should avoid eating fish. Certainly those who continue to eat fish while refusing to eat other animals have taken a major step away from speciesism; but those who eat neither have gone one step further.

When we go beyond fish to the other forms of marine life commonly eaten by humans, we can no longer be quite so confident about the existence of a capacity for pain. Crustacea—lobster, crabs, prawns, shrimps—have nervous systems very different from our own. Nevertheless, Dr. John Baker, a zoologist at the University of Oxford and a fellow of the Royal Society, has stated that their sensory organs are highly developed, their nervous systems complex, their nerve cells very similar to our own, and their responses to certain stimuli immediate and vigorous. Dr. Baker therefore believes that lobster, for example, can feel pain. He is also clear that the standard method of killing lobster—dropping them into boiling water—can cause pain for as long as two minutes. He experimented with other methods sometimes said to be more humane, such as putting them in cold water and heating them slowly, or leaving them in fresh water until they cease to move, but found that both of these led to more prolonged struggling and, apparently, suffering.[25] If crustacea can suffer, there must be a great deal of suffering involved, not only in the method by which they are killed, but also in the ways in which they are transported and kept alive at markets. To keep them fresh they are frequently simply packed, alive, on top of each other. So even if there is some room for doubt about the capacity of these animals to feel pain, the fact that they may be suffering a great deal, combined with the absence of any need to eat them on our part, makes the verdict plain; they should receive the benefit of the doubt.

Oysters, clams, mussels, scallops, and the like are mollusks, and mollusks are in general very simply organisms. (There is an exception: the octopus is a mollusk, but far more developed, and presumably more sentient, than its distant mollusk relatives.) With creatures like oysters, doubts about a capacity for pain are considerable; and in the first edition of this book I suggested that somewhere between a shrimp and an oyster seems as good a place to draw the line as any. Accordingly, I continued occasionally to eat oysters, scallops, and mussels for some time after I became, in every other respect, a vegetarian. But while one cannot with any confidence say that these creatures do feel pain, so one can equally have little confidence in saying that they do not feel pain. Moreover, if they do feel pain, a meal of oysters or mussels would inflict pain on a considerable number of creatures. Since it is so easy to avoid eating them, I now think it better to do so.[26]

This takes us to the end of the evolutionary scale, so far as creatures we normally eat are concerned; essentially, we are left with a vegetarian diet. The traditional vegetarian diet, however, includes animal products, such as eggs and milk. Some have tried to accuse vegetarians of inconsistency here. "Vegetarian," they say, is a word that has the same root as "vegetable" and a vegetarian should eat only food of vegetable origin. Taken as a verbal quibble, this criticism is historically inaccurate. The term "vegetarian" came into general use as a result of the formation of the Vegetarian Society in England in 1847. Since the rules of the society permit the use of eggs and milk, the term "vegetarian" is properly applied to those who use these animal products. Recognizing this linguistic *fait accompli,* those who eat neither animal flesh nor eggs nor milk nor foods made from milk call themselves "vegans." The verbal point, however, is not the important one. What we should ask is whether the use of these other animal products is morally justifiable. This question is a real one because it is possible to be adequately nourished without consuming any animal products at all—a fact that is not widely known, although most people now know that vegetarians can live long and healthy lives. I shall say more on the topic of nutrition later in this chapter; for the present it is enough to know that we can do without eggs and milk. But is there any reason why we should?

We have seen that the egg industry is one of the most ruthlessly intensive forms of modern factory farming, exploiting hens relentlessly to produce the most eggs at the least cost. Our obligation to boycott this type of farming is as strong as our obligation to boycott intensively produced pork or chicken. But what of free-range eggs, assuming you can get them? Here the ethical objections are very much less. Hens provided with both shelter and an outdoor run to walk and scratch around in live comfortably. They do not appear to mind the removal of their eggs. The main grounds for objection are that the male chicks of the egg-laying strain will have been killed on hatching, and the hens themselves will be killed when they cease to lay productively. The question is, therefore, whether the pleasant lives of the hens (plus the benefits to us of the eggs) are sufficient to outweigh the killing that is a part of the system. One's answer to that will depend on one's view about killing, as distinct from the infliction of suffering. There is some further discussion of the relevant philosophical issues in the final chapter of this book.[27] In keeping with the reasons given there, I do not, on balance, object to free-range egg production.

Milk and milk products like cheese and yogurt raise different issues. Dairy production can be distressing for the cows and their calves in several ways: the necessity of making the cow pregnant, and the subsequent separation of the cow and her calf; the increasing degree of confinement on many farms; the health and stress problems caused by feeding cows very rich diets and breeding them for ever-greater milk yields; and now the prospect of further stress from daily injections of bovine growth hormone.

In principle, there is no problem in doing without dairy products. Indeed, in many parts of Asia and Africa, the only milk ever consumed is human milk, for infants. Many adults from these parts of the world lack the ability to digest the lactose that milk contains, and they become ill if they drink milk. The Chinese and Japanese have long used soybeans to make many of the things we make from dairy products. Soy milks are now widely available in Western countries, and tofu ice cream is popular with those trying to reduce their intake of fat and cholesterol. There are even cheeses, spreads, and yogurts made from soybeans.

Vegans, then, are right to say that we ought not to use dairy products. They are living demonstrations of the practicality and nutritional soundness of a diet that is totally free from the exploitation of other animals. At the same time, it should be said that, in our present speciesist world, it is not easy to keep so strictly to what is morally right. A reasonable and defensible plan of action is to change your diet at a measured pace with which you can feel comfortable. Although in principle all dairy products are replaceable, in practice in Western societies it is much more difficult to cut out meat and dairy products than it is to eliminate meat alone. Until you start reading food labels with an eye to avoiding dairy products, you will never believe how many foods contain them. Even buying a tomato sandwich becomes a problem, since it will probably be spread either with butter, or with a margarine containing whey or nonfat milk. There is little gained for animals if you give up animal flesh and battery eggs, and simply replace them with an increased amount of cheese. On the other hand, the following is, if not ideal, a reasonable and practical strategy:

• replace animal flesh with plant foods;

- replace factory farm eggs with free-range eggs if you can get them; otherwise avoid eggs;
- replace the milk and cheese you buy with soymilk, tofu, or other plant foods, but do not feel obliged to go to great lengths to avoid all food containing milk products.

Eliminating speciesism from one's dietary habits is very difficult to do all at once. People who adopt the strategy I support here have made a clear public commitment to the movement against animal exploitation. The most urgent task of the Animal Liberation movement is to persuade as many people as possible to make this commitment, so that the boycott will spread and gain attention. If because of an admirable desire to stop all forms of exploitation of animals immediately we convey the impression that unless one gives up milk products one is no better than those who still eat animal flesh, the result may be that many people are deterred from doing anything at all, and the exploitation of animals will continue as before.

These, at least, are some of the answers to problems that are likely to face nonspeciesists who ask what they should and should not eat. As I said at the beginning of this section, my remarks are intended to be no more than suggestions. Sincere nonspeciesists may well disagree among themselves about the details. So long as there is agreement on the fundamentals this should not disrupt efforts toward a common goal.

Many people are willing to admit that the case for vegetarianism is strong. Too often, though, there is a gap between intellectual conviction and the action needed to break a lifetime habit. There is no way in which books can bridge this gap; ultimately it is up to each one of us to put our convictions into practice. But I can try, in the next few pages, to narrow the gap. My aim is to make the transition from an omnivorous diet to a vegetarian one much easier and more attractive, so that instead of seeing the change of diet as an unpleasant duty the reader looks forward to a new and interesting cuisine, full of fresh foods as well as unusual meatless dishes from Europe, China, and the Middle East, dishes so varied as to make the habitual meat, meat, and more meat of most Western diets stale and repetitive by comparison. The enjoyment of such a cuisine is enhanced by the knowledge that its good taste and nourishing qualities were provided directly by the earth, neither wasting what the earth produces, nor requiring the suffering and death of any sentient being.

Vegetarianism brings with it a new relationship to food, plants, and nature. Flesh taints our meals. Disguise it as we may, the fact remains that the centerpiece of our dinner has come to us from the slaughterhouse, dripping blood. Untreated and unrefrigerated, it soon begins to putrefy and stink. When we eat it, it sits heavily in our stomachs, blocking our digestive processes until, days later, we struggle to excrete it.[28] When we eat plants, food takes on a different quality. We take from the earth food that is ready for us and does not fight against us as we take it. Without meat to deaden the palate we experience an extra delight in fresh vegetables taken straight from the ground. Personally, I found the idea of picking my own dinner so satisfying that shortly after becoming a vegetarian I began digging up part of our backyard and growing some of my own vegetables—something that I had never thought of doing previously, but that several of my vegetarian friends were also doing. In this way dropping flesh-meat from my diet brought me into closer contact with plants, the soil, and the seasons.

Cooking, too, was something I became interested in only after I became a vegetarian. For those brought up on the usual Anglo-Saxon menus, in which the main dish consists of meat supplemented by two overcooked vegetables, the elimination of meat poses an interesting challenge to the imagination. When I speak in public about the issues discussed in this book, I am often asked about what one can eat instead of meat, and it is clear from the way the question is phrased that the questioner has mentally subtracted the chop or hamburger from his or her plate, leaving the mashed potatoes and boiled cabbage, and is wondering what to put in place of the meat. A heap of soybeans perhaps?

There may be those who would enjoy such a meal, but for most tastes the answer is to rethink the entire idea of the main course, so that it consists of a combination of ingredients, perhaps with a salad on the side, instead of detached items. Good Chinese dishes, for instance, are superb combinations of one or more high-protein ingredients—in vegetarian Chinese cooking, they may include tofu, nuts, bean sprouts, mushrooms, or wheat gluten, with fresh, lightly cooked vegetables and rice. An Indian curry using lentils for protein, served over brown rice with some fresh sliced cucumber for light relief, makes an equally satisfying meal, as does an Italian vegetarian lasagna with salad. You can even make "tofu meatballs" to put on top of your spaghetti. A simpler meal might consist of whole grains and vegetables. Most Westerners eat very little millet, whole wheat, or buckwheat, but these grains can form the basis of a dish that is a refreshing change. In the first edition of this book I provided some recipes and hints on vegetarian cooking to help readers make the transition to what was, then, still an unusual diet; but in the intervening years so many excellent vegetarian cookbooks have been published that the assistance I was able to provide seems quite unnecessary now. Some people find it hard, at first, to change their attitude to a meal. Getting used to meals without a central piece of animal flesh may take time, but once it has happened you will have so many interesting new dishes to choose from that you will wonder why you ever thought it would be difficult to do without flesh foods.

Apart from the tastiness of their meals, people contemplating vegetarianism are most likely to worry about whether they will be adequately nourished. These worries are entirely groundless. Many parts of the world have vegetarian cultures whose members have been as healthy, and often healthier, than nonvegetarians living in similar areas. Strict Hindus have been vegetarians for more than two thousand years. Gandhi, a lifelong vegetarian, was close to eighty when an assassin's bullet ended his active life. In Britain, where there has now been an official vegetarian movement for more than 140 years, there are third- and fourth-generation vegetarians. Many prominent vegetarians, such as Leonardo da Vinci, Leo Tolstoy, and George Bernard Shaw, have lived long, immensely creative lives. Indeed, most people who have reached exceptional old age have eaten little or no meat. The inhabitants of the Vilcabamba valley in Ecuador frequently live to be more than one hundred years old, and men as old as 123 and 142 years have been found by scientists; these people eat less than one ounce of meat a week. A study of all living centenarians in Hungary found that they were largely vegetarian.[29] That meat is unnecessary for physical endurance is shown by a long list of successful athletes who do not eat it, a list that includes Olympic long-distance swimming champion Murray Rose, the famous Finnish distance runner Paavo Nurmi, basketball star Bill Walton, the "ironman" triathlete Dave Scott, and 400-meter Olympic hurdle champion Edwin Moses.

Many vegetarians claim that they feel fitter, healthier, and more zestful than when they ate meat. A great deal of new evidence now supports them. The 1988 United States Surgeon General's Report on Nutrition and Health cites a major study indicating that the death rate for heart attacks of vegetarians between the ages of thirty-five and sixty-four is only 28 percent of the rate for Americans in general in that age group. For older vegetarians the rate of death from heart attacks was still less than half that of nonvegetarians. The same study showed that vegetarians who ate eggs and dairy products had cholesterol levels 16 percent lower than those of meat eaters, and vegans had cholesterol levels 29 percent lower. The report's main recommendations were to reduce consumption of cholesterol and fat (especially saturated fat), and increase consumption of whole grain foods and cereal products, vegetables (including dried beans and peas) and fruits. A recommendation to reduce cholesterol and saturated fat is, in effect, a recommendation to avoid meat (except perhaps chicken from which the skin has been removed), and cream, butter, and all except low-fat dairy products.[30] The report was widely criticized for failing to be more specific in saying this—a vagueness due, apparently, to successful lobbying by groups like the National Cattlemen's Association and the Dairy Board.[31] Whatever lobbying took place failed however, to prevent the section on cancer from reporting that studies have found an association between breast cancer and meat intake, and also between eating meat, especially beef, and cancer of the large bowel. The American Heart Association has also been recommending, for many years, that Americans reduce their meat intake.[32] Diets designed for health and longevity like the Pritikin plan and the McDougall plan are either largely or entirely vegetarian.[33]

Nutritional experts no longer dispute about whether animal flesh is essential; they now agree that it is not. If ordinary people still have misgivings about doing without it, these misgivings are based on ignorance. Most often this ignorance is about the nature of protein. We are frequently told that protein is an important element in a sound diet, and that meat is high in protein. Both these statements are true, but there are two other things that we are told less often. The first is that the average American eats too much protein. The protein intake of the average American exceeds the generous level recommended by the National Academy of Sciences by 45 percent. Other estimates say that most Americans consume between two and four times as much meat as the body can use. Excess protein cannot be stored. Some of it is excreted, and some may be converted by the body to carbohydrate, which is an expensive way to increase one's carbohydrate intake.[34]

The second thing to know about protein is that meat is only one among a great variety of foods containing protein, its chief distinction being that it is the most expensive. It was once thought that meat protein was of superior quality, but as long ago as 1950 the British Medical Association's Committee on Nutrition stated:

> It is generally accepted that it is immaterial whether the essential protein units are derived from plant or animal foods, provided that they supply an appropriate mixture of the units in assimilable form.[35]

More recent research has provided further confirmation of this conclusion. We now know that the nutritional value of protein consists in the essential amino acids it contains, since these determine how much of the protein the body can use. While it is true that animal foods, especially eggs and milk, have a very well-balanced amino acid composition, plant foods like soybeans and nuts also contain a broad range of these nutrients. Moreover by eating different kinds of plant proteins at the same time it is easy to put together a meal that provides protein entirely equivalent to that of animal protein. This principle is called "protein complementarity," but you do not need to know much about nutrition to apply it. The peasant who eats his beans or lentils with rice or corn is practicing protein complementarity. So is the mother who gives her child a peanut butter sandwich on whole wheat bread—a combination of peanuts and wheat, both of which contain protein. The different forms of protein in the different foods combine with each other in such a way that the body absorbs more protein if they are eaten together than if they were eaten separately. Even without the complementary effect of combining different proteins, however, most of the plant foods we eat—not just nuts, peas, and beans, but even wheat, rice, and potatoes—contain enough protein in themselves to provide our bodies with the protein we need. If we avoid junk foods that are high in sugar or fats and nothing else, about the only way we can fail to get enough protein is if we are on a diet that is insufficient in calories.[36]

Protein is not the only nutrient in meat, but the others can all easily be obtained from a vegetarian diet without special care. Only vegans, who take no animal products at all, need to be especially careful about their diet. There appears to be one, and only one, necessary nutrient that is not normally available from plant sources, and this is vitamin B12, which is present in eggs and milk, but not in readily assimilable form in plant foods. It can, however, be obtained from seaweeds such as kelp, from a soy sauce made by the traditional Japanese fermentation method, or from tempeh, a fermented soybean product eaten in parts of Asia, and often now available in health food stores in the West. It is also possible that it is produced by microorganisms in our own intestines. Studies of vegans who have not taken any apparent source of B12 for many years have shown their blood levels of this vitamin still to be within the normal range. Nevertheless to make sure of avoiding a deficiency, it is simple and inexpensive to take vitamin tablets containing B12. The B12 in these tablets is obtained from bacteria grown on plant foods. Studies of children in vegan families have shown that they develop normally on diets containing a B12 supplement but no animal food after weaning.[37]

I have tried in this chapter to answer the doubts about becoming a vegetarian that can easily be articulated and expressed. But some people have a deeper resistance that makes them hesitate. Perhaps the reason for hesitation is a fear of being thought a crank by one's friends. When my wife and I began to think about becoming vegetarians we talked about this. We worried that we would be cutting ourselves off from our nonvegetarian friends and at that time none of our long-established friends was vegetarian. The fact that we became vegetarians together certainly made the decision easier for both of us, but as things turned out we need not have worried. We explained our decision to our friends and they saw that we had good reasons for it. They did not all become vegetarians, but they did not cease to be our friends either; in fact I think they rather enjoyed inviting us to dinner and showing us how well they could cook without meat. Of course, it is possible that you will encounter people who consider you a crank. This is much less likely now than it was a few years ago, because there are so many more vegetarians. But if it should happen, remember that you are in good company. All the best reformers—those who first opposed the slave trade, nationalistic wars, and the exploitation of children working a fourteen-hour day in the factories of the Industrial Revolution—were at first derided as cranks by those who had an interest in the abuses they were opposing.

Notes

1. Oliver Goldsmith, *The Citizen of the World,* in *Collected Works,* ed. A. Friedman (Oxford: Clarendon Press, 1966), vol. 2, p. 60. Apparently Goldsmith himself

fell into this category, however, since according to Howard Williams in *The Ethics of Diet* (abridged edition, Manchester and London, 1907, p. 149), Goldsmith's sensibility was stronger than his self-control.

2. In attempting to rebut the argument for vegetarianism presented in this chapter of the first edition, R. G. Frey described the reforms proposed by the House of Commons Agriculture Committee in 1981, and wrote: "The House of Commons as a whole has yet to decide on this report, and it may well be in the end that it is diluted; but even so, there is no doubt that it represents a significant advance in combating the abuses of factory farming." Frey then argued that the report showed that these abuses could be overcome by tactics that stopped short of advocating a boycott of animal products. (R. G. Frey, *Rights, Killing and Suffering,* Oxford: Blackwell, 1983, p. 207.) This is one instance in which I sincerely wish my critic had been right; but the House of Commons did not bother to "dilute" the report of its Agriculture Committee—it simply ignored it. Eight years later nothing has changed for the vast majority of Britain's intensively produced animals. The exception is for veal calves, where a consumer boycott *did* play a significant role.

3. Frances Moore Lappé, *Diet for a Small Planet* (New York: Friends of the Earth/Ballantine, 1971), pp. 4–11. This book is the best brief introduction to the topic, and figures not otherwise attributed in this section have been taken from this book. (A revised edition was published in 1982.) The main original sources are *The World Food Problem,* a Report of the President's Science Advisory Committee (1967); *Feed Situation,* February 1970, U.S. Department of Agriculture; and *National and State Livestock-Feed Relationships,* U.S. Department of Agriculture, Economic Research Service, Statistical Bulletin No. 446, February 1970.

4. The higher ratio is from Folke Dovring, "Soybeans," *Scientific American,* February 1974. Keith Akers presents a different set of figures in *A Vegetarian Sourcebook* (New York: Putnam, 1983), chapter 10. His tables compare per-acre nutritional returns from oats, broccoli, pork, milk, poultry, and beef. Even though oats and broccoli are not high-protein foods, none of the animal foods produced even half as much protein as the plant foods. Akers's original sources are: United States Department of Agriculture, *Agricultural Statistics,* 1979; United States Department of Agriculture, *Nutritive Value of American Foods* (Washington, D.C., U.S. Government Printing Office, 1975); and C. W. Cook, "Use of Rangelands for Future Meat Production," *Journal of Animal Science* 45:1476 (1977).

5. Keith Akers, *A Vegetarian Sourcebook,* pp. 90–91, using the sources cited above.

6. Boyce Rensberger, "Curb on U.S. Waste Urged to Help World's Hungry," *The New York Times,* October 25, 1974.

7. *Science News,* March 5, 1988, p. 153, citing *Worldwatch,* January/February 1988.

8. Keith Akers, *A Vegetarian Sourcebook,* p. 100, based on D. Pimental and M. Pimental, *Food, Energy and Society* (New York: Wiley, 1979), pp. 56, 59, and U.S. Department of Agriculture, *Nutritive Value of American Foods* (Washington, D.C.: U.S. Government Printing Office, 1975).

9. G. Borgstrom, *Harvesting the Earth* (New York: Abelard-Schuman, 1973) pp. 64–65; cited by Keith Akers, *A Vegetarian Sourcebook.*

10. "The Browning of America," *Newsweek,* February 22, 1981, p. 26; quoted by John Robbins, *Diet for a New America* (Walpole, N.H.: Stillpoint, 1987), p. 367.

11. "The Browning of America," p. 26.

12. Fred Pearce, "A Green Unpleasant Land," *New Scientist,* July 24, 1986, p. 26.

13. Sue Armstrong, "Marooned in a Mountain of Manure," *New Scientist,* November 26, 1988.

14. J. Mason and P. Singer, *Animal Factories* (New York: Crown, 1980), p. 84, citing R. C. Loehr, *Pollution Implications of Animal Wastes—A Forward Oriented*

Review, Water Pollution Control Research Series (U.S. Environmental Protection Agency, Washington, D.C., 1968), pp. 26–27; H. A. Jasiorowski, "Intensive Systems of Animal Production," in R. L. Reid, ed., *Proceedings of the II World Conference on Animal Production* (Sydney: Sydney University Press, 1975), p. 384; and J. W. Robbins, *Environmental Impact Resulting from Unconfined Animal Production* (Cincinnati: Environmental Research Information Center, U.S. Environmental Protection Agency, 1978) p. 9.

15. "Handling Waste Disposal Problems," *Hog Farm Management,* April 1978, p. 17, quoted in J. Mason and P. Singer, *Animal Factories,* p. 88.

16. Information from the Rainforest Action Network, *The New York Times,* January 22, 1986, p. 7.

17. E. O. Williams, *Biophilia* (Cambridge: Harvard University Press, 1984), p. 137.

18. Keith Akers, *A Vegetarian Sourcebook,* pp. 99–100; based on H. W. Anderson, et al., *Forests and Water: Effects of Forest Management on Floods, Sedimentation and Water Supply,* U.S. Department of Agriculture Forest Service General Technical Report PSW-18/1976; and J. Kittridge, "The Influence of the Forest on the Weather and other Environmental Factors," in United Nations Food and Agriculture Organization, *Forest Influences* (Rome, 1962).

19. Fred Pearce, "Planting Trees for a Cooler World," *New Scientist,* October 15, 1988, p. 21.

20. David Dickson, "Poor Countries Need Help to Adapt to Rising Sea Level," *New Scientist,* October 7, 1989, p. 4; Sue Wells and Alasdair Edwards, "Gone with the Waves," *New Scientist,* November 11, 1989, pp. 29–32.

21. L. and M. Milne, *The Senses of Men and Animals* (Middlesex and Baltimore: Penguin Books, 1965), chapter 5.

22. *Report of the Panel of Enquiry into Shooting and Angling,* published by the panel in 1980 and available through the Royal Society for the Prevention of Cruelty to Animals (U.K.), paragraphs 15–57.

23. Geoff Maslen, "Bluefin, the Making of the Mariners," *The Age* (Melbourne), January 26, 1985.

24. D. Pimental and M. Pimental, *Food, Energy and Society* (New York: Wiley, 1979), chapter 9; I owe this reference to Keith Akers, *A Vegetarian Sourcebook,* p. 117.

25. See J. R. Baker: *The Humane Killing of Lobsters and Crabs,* The Humane Education Centre, London, no date; J. R. Baker and M. B. Dolan, "Experiments on the Humane Killing of Lobsters and Crabs," *Scientific Papers of the Humane Education Centre* 2: 1–24 (1977).

26. My change of mind about mollusks stems from conversations with R. I. Sikora.

27. See pages 230–231 below.

28. "Struggle" is not altogether a joke. According to a comparative study published in *The Lancet* (December 30, 1972), the "mean transit time" of food through the digestive system of a sample group of nonvegetarians on a Western type of diet was between seventy-six and eighty-three hours; for vegetarians, forty-two hours. The authors suggest a connection between the length of time the stool remains in the colon and the incidence of cancer of the colon and related diseases which have increased rapidly in nations whose consumption of meat has increased but are almost unknown among rural Africans who, like vegetarians, have a diet low in meat and high in roughage.

29. David Davies, "A Shangri-La in Ecuador," *New Scientist,* February 1, 1973. On the basis of other studies, Ralph Nelson of the Mayo Medical School has suggested that a high protein intake causes us to "idle our metabolic engine at a faster

rate" (*Medical World News,* November 8, 1974, p. 106). This could explain the correlation between longevity and little or no meat consumption.

30. *The Surgeon General's Report on Nutrition and Health* (Washington, D.C.: U.S. Government Printing Office, 1988).

31. According to a wire-service report cited in *Vegetarian Times,* November 1988.

32. *The New York Times,* October 25, 1974.

33. N. Pritikin and P. McGrady, *The Pritikin Program for Diet and Exercise* (New York: Bantam, 1980); J. J. McDougall, *The McDougall Plan* (Piscataway, N.J.: New Century, 1983).

34. Francis Moore Lappé, *Diet for a Small Planet,* pp. 28–29; see also *The New York Times,* October 25, 1974; *Medical World News,* November 8, 1974, p. 106.

35. Quoted in F. Wokes, "Proteins," *Plant Foods for Human Nutrition,* 1:38 (1968).

36. In the first edition of *Diet for a Small Planet* (1971), Frances Moore Lappé emphasized protein complementarity to show that a vegetarian diet can provide enough protein. In the revised edition (New York: Ballantine, 1982) this emphasis has disappeared, replaced by a demonstration that a healthy vegetarian diet is bound to contain enough protein even without complementarity. For another account of the adequacy of plant foods as far as protein is concerned, see Keith Akers, *A Vegetarian Sourcebook,* chapter 2.

37. F. R. Ellis and W. M. E. Montegriffo, "The Health of Vegans," *Plant Foods for Human Nutrition,* vol. 2, pp. 93–101 (1971). Some vegans claim that B12 supplements are not necessary, on the grounds that the human intestine can synthesize this vitamin from other B-group vitamins. The question is, however, whether this synthesis takes place sufficiently early in the digestive, process for the B12 to be absorbed rather than excreted. At present the nutritional adequacy of an all-plant diet without supplementation is an open scientific question; accordingly it seems safer to take supplementary B12. See also F. Wokes, "Proteins," *Plant Foods for Human Nutrition,* p. 37.

The Two Full of Butter

The two full of butter, beautiful masters of all creatures, broad and wide, milked of honey, beautifully adorned—sky and earth have been propped apart, by Varuna's law; unageing, they are rich in seed.

Inexhaustible, rich in streams, full of milk, the two whose vows are pure are milked of butter for the one who does good deeds. You two world-halves, rulers over this universe, pour out on us the seed that was the base for mankind.[1]

The mortal who makes an offering to you world-halves, sources of strength, so that he may walk on the right path, he succeeds: he is reborn through his progeny according to the law. Creatures with various forms but with a common vow have been poured out from you.

Enclosed in butter are sky and earth, beautiful in butter, gorged on butter, grown on butter. Broad and wide, they are the first priests[2] in the choice of the priest of the oblation. They are the ones that the priests invoke when they seek kindness.

Sky and earth that stream with honey, that are milked of honey, that have honey for their vow, let them soak us with honey, bringing sacrifice and wealth to the gods, great fame, the victory price, and virility to us.

Sky and earth, the all-knowing father and mother who achieve wondrous works—let them swell up with food to nourish us. Let the two world-halves, that work together to give benefits to all, together thrust toward us gain, and the victory prize, and wealth.

N O T E S

1. The seed from which mankind (or Manu) originally grew.
2. The Purohitas who cast the first vote in choosing the oblation priest to assist them.

Genesis 1–3

THE CREATION OF THE WORLD

In the beginning of creation, when God made heaven and earth, the earth was without form and void, with darkness over the face of the abyss, and a mighty wind that swept over the surface of the waters. God said, 'Let there be light', and there was light; and God saw that the light was good, and he separated the light from darkness. He called the light day, and the darkness night. So evening came, and morning came, the first day.

God said, 'Let there be a vault between the waters, to separate water from water.' So God made the vault, and separated the water under the vault from the water above it, and so it was; and God called the vault heaven. Evening came, and morning came, a second day.

God said, 'Let the waters under heaven be gathered into one place, so that dry land may appear'; and so it was. God called the dry land earth, and the gathering of the waters he called seas; and God saw that it was good. Then God said, 'Let the earth produce fresh growth, let there be on the earth plants bearing seed, fruit-trees bearing fruit each with seed according to its kind.' So it was; the earth yielded fresh growth, plants bearing seed according to their kind and trees bearing fruit each with seed according to its kind; and God saw that it was good. Evening came, and morning came, a third day.

God said, 'Let there be lights in the vault of heaven to separate day from night, and let them serve as signs both for festivals and for seasons and years. Let them also shine in the vault of heaven to give light on earth.' So it was; God made the two great lights, the greater to govern the day and the lesser to govern the night; and with them he made the stars. God put these lights in the vault of heaven to give light on earth, to govern day and night, and to separate light from darkness; and God saw that it was good. Evening came, and morning came, a fourth day.

God said, 'Let the waters teem with countless living creatures, and let birds fly above the earth across the vault of heaven.' God then created the great sea-monsters and all living creatures that move and swarm in the waters, according to their kind, and every kind of bird; and God saw that it was good. So he blessed them and said, 'Be fruitful and increase, fill the waters of the seas; and let the birds increase on land.' Evening came, and morning came, a fifth day.

God said, 'Let the earth bring forth living creatures, according to their kind: cattle, reptiles, and wild animals, all according to their kind.' So it was; God made wild animals, cattle, and all reptiles, each according to its kind; and he saw that it was good. Then God said, 'Let us make man in our image and likeness to rule the fish in the sea, the birds of heaven, the cattle, all wild animals on earth, and all reptiles that crawl upon the earth.' So God created man in his own image; in the image of God he created him; male and female he created them. God blessed them and said to them, 'Be fruitful and increase, fill the earth and subdue it, rule over the fish in the sea, the birds of heaven, and every living thing that moves upon the earth.' God also said, 'I give you all plants that bear seed everywhere on earth, and every tree bearing fruit which yields seed: they shall be yours for food. All green plants I give for food to the wild animals, to all the birds of heaven, and to all reptiles on earth, every living creature.' So it was; and God saw all that he had made, and it was very good. Evening came, and morning came, a sixth day.

Thus heaven and earth were completed with all their mighty throng. On the sixth day God completed all the work he had been doing, and on the seventh day he ceased from all his work. God blessed the seventh day and made it holy, because on that day he ceased from all the work he had set himself to do.

This is the story of the making of heaven and earth when they were created.

When the LORD God made earth and heaven, there was neither shrub nor plant growing wild upon the earth, because the LORD God had sent no rain on the earth; nor was there any man to till the ground. A flood used to rise out of the earth and water all the surface of the ground. Then the LORD God formed a man from the dust of the ground and breathed into his nostrils the breath of life. Thus the man became a living creature. Then the LORD God planted a garden in Eden away to the east, and there he put the man whom he had formed. The LORD God made trees spring from the ground, all trees pleasant to look at and good for food; and in the middle of the garden he set the tree of life and the tree of the knowledge of good and evil.

There was a river flowing from Eden to water the garden, and when it left the garden it branched into four streams. The name of the first is Pishon, that is the river which encircles all the land of Havilah, where the gold is. The gold of that land is good; bdellium and cornelians are also to be found there. The name of the second river is Gihon; this is the one which encircles all the land of Cush. The name of the third is Tigris; this is the river which runs east of Asshur. The fourth river is the Euphrates.

The LORD God took the man and put him in the garden of Eden to till it and care for it. He told the man, 'You may eat from every tree in the garden, but not from the tree of the knowledge of good and evil; for on the day that you eat from it, you will certainly die.' Then the LORD God said, 'It is not good for the man to be alone. I will provide a partner for him.' So

God formed out of the ground all the wild animals and all the birds of heaven. He brought them to the man to see what he would call them, and whatever the man called each living creature, that was its name. Thus the man gave names to all cattle, to the birds of heaven, and to every wild animal; but for the man himself no partner had yet been found. And so the LORD God put the man into a trance, and while he slept, he took one of his ribs and closed the flesh over the place. The LORD God then built up the rib, which he had taken out of the man, into a woman. He brought her to the man, and the man said:

'Now this, at last—
bone from my bones,
flesh from my flesh!—
this shall be called woman,
for from man was this taken.'

That is why a man leaves his father and mother and is united to his wife, and the two become one flesh. Now they were both naked, the man and his wife, but they had no feeling of shame towards one another.

The serpent was more crafty than any wild creature that the LORD God had made. He said to the woman, 'Is it true that God has forbidden you to eat from any tree in the garden?' The woman answered the serpent, 'We may eat the fruit of any tree in the garden, except for the tree in the middle of the garden; God has forbidden us either to eat or to touch the fruit of that; if we do, we shall die.' The serpent said, 'Of course you will not die. God knows that as soon as you eat it, your eyes will be opened and you will be like gods knowing both good and evil.' When the woman saw that the fruit of the tree was good to eat, and that it was pleasing to the eye and tempting to contemplate, she took some and ate it. She also gave her husband some and he ate it. Then the eyes of both of them were opened and they discovered that they were naked; so they stitched fig-leaves together and made themselves loincloths.

The man and his wife heard the sound of the LORD God walking in the garden at the time of the evening breeze and hid from the LORD God among the trees of the garden. But the LORD God called to the man and said to him, 'Where are you?' He replied, 'I heard the sound as you were walking in the garden, and I was afraid because I was naked, and I hid myself.' God answered, 'Who told you that you were naked? Have you eaten from the tree which I forbade you?' The man said, 'The woman you gave me for a companion, she gave me fruit from the tree and I ate it.' Then the LORD God said to the woman, 'What is this that you have done?' The woman said, 'The serpent tricked me, and I ate.' Then the LORD God said to the serpent:

'Because you have done this you are accursed
more than all cattle and all wild creatures.

On your belly you shall crawl, and dust you shall eat
all the days of your life.
I will put enmity between you and the woman,
between your brood and hers.
They shall strike at your head,
and you shall strike at their heel.'

To the woman he said:

'I will increase your labour and your groaning,
and in labour you shall bear children.
You shall be eager for your husband,
and he shall be your master.'

And to the man he said:

'Because you have listened to your wife
and have eaten from the tree which I forbade you,
accursed shall be the ground on your account.
With labour you shall win your food from it
all the days of your life.
It will grow thorns and thistles for you,
none but wild plants for you to eat.
You shall gain your bread by the sweat of your brow
until you return to the ground;
for from it you were taken.
Dust you are, to dust you shall return.'

The man called his wife Eve because she was the mother of all who
live. The LORD God made tunics of skins for Adam and his wife and clothed
them. He said, 'The man has become like one of us, knowing good and
evil; what if he now reaches out his hand and takes fruit from the tree of
life also, eats it and lives for ever?'' So the LORD God drove him out of the
garden of Eden to till the ground from which he had been taken. He cast
them out, and to the east of the garden of Eden he stationed the cherubim
and a sword whirling and flashing to guard the way to the tree of life.

Leviticus 11:1–47

LAWS OF PURIFICATION AND ATONEMENT

The LORD spoke to Moses and Aaron and said, Speak to the Israelites in these words: Of all animals on land these are the creatures you may eat: you may eat any animal which has a parted foot or a cloven hoof and also chews the cud; those which have only a cloven hoof or only chew the cud you may not eat. These are: the camel, because it chews the cud but has not a cloven hoof; you shall regard it as unclean; the rock-badger, because it chews the cud but has not a parted foot; you shall regard it as unclean; the hare, because it chews the cud but has not a parted hoof; you shall regard it as unclean; the pig, because it has a parted foot and a cloven hoof but does not chew the cud; you shall regard it as unclean. You shall not eat their flesh or even touch their dead bodies; you shall regard them as unclean.

Of creatures that live in water these you may eat: all those that have fins and scales, whether in salt water or fresh; but all that have neither fins nor scales, whether in salt or fresh water, including both small creatures in shoals and larger creatures, you shall regard as vermin. They shall be vermin to you; you shall not eat their flesh, and their dead bodies you shall treat as those of vermin. Every creature in the water that has neither fins nor scales shall be vermin to you.

These are the birds you shall regard as vermin, and for this reason they shall not be eaten: the griffon-vulture, the black vulture, and the bearded vulture; the kite and every kind of falcon; every kind of crow, the desert-owl, the short-eared owl, the long-eared owl, and every kind of hawk; the tawny owl, the fisher-owl, and the screech-owl; the little owl, the horned owl, the osprey, the stork, every kind of cormorant, the hoopoe, and the bat.

All teeming winged creatures that go on four legs shall be vermin to you, except those which have legs jointed above their feet for leaping on the ground. Of these you may eat every kind of great locust, every kind of long-headed locust, every kind of green locust, and every kind of desert locust. Every other teeming winged creature that has four legs you shall regard as vermin; you would make yourselves unclean with them: whoever touches their dead bodies shall be unclean till evening. Whoever picks up their dead bodies shall wash his clothes but remain unclean till evening.

You shall regard as unclean every animal which has a parted foot but has not a cloven hoof and does not chew the cud: whoever touches them shall be unclean. You shall regard as unclean all four-footed wild animals that go on flat paws; whoever touches their dead bodies shall be unclean till evening. Whoever takes up their dead bodies shall wash his clothes but remain unclean till evening. You shall regard them as unclean.

You shall regard these as unclean among creatures that teem on the ground: the mole-rat, the jerboa, and every kind of thorn-tailed lizard; the gecko, the sand-gecko, the wall-gecko, the great lizard, and the chameleon. You shall regard these as unclean among teeming creatures; whoever touches them when they are dead shall be unclean till evening. Anything on which any of them falls when they are dead shall be unclean, any article of wood or garment or skin or sacking, any article in regular use; it shall be plunged into water but shall remain unclean till evening, when it shall be clean. If any of these falls into an earthenware vessel, its contents shall be unclean and it shall be smashed. Any food on which water from such a vessel is poured shall be unclean, and any drink in such a vessel shall be unclean. Anything on which the dead body of such a creature falls shall be unclean; an oven or a stove shall be broken, for they are unclean and you shall treat them as such; but a spring or a cistern where water collects shall remain clean, though whatever touches the dead body shall be unclean. When any of their dead bodies falls on seed intended for sowing, it remains clean; but if the seed has been soaked in water and any dead body falls on it, you shall treat it as unclean.

When any animal allowed as food dies, all that touch the carcass shall be unclean till evening. Whoever eats any of the carcass shall wash his clothes but remain unclean till evening; whoever takes up the carcass shall wash his clothes and be unclean till evening. All creatures that teem on the ground are vermin; they shall not be eaten. All creatures that teem on the ground, crawl on their bellies, go on all fours or have many legs, you shall not eat, because they are vermin which contaminate. You shall not contaminate yourselves through any teeming creature. You shall not defile yourselves with them and make yourselves unclean by them. For I am the LORD your God; you shall make yourselves holy and keep yourselves holy, because I am holy. You shall not defile yourselves with any teeming creature that creeps on the ground. I am the LORD who brought you up from Egypt to become your God. You shall keep yourselves holy, because I am holy.

This, then, is the law concerning beast and bird, every living creature that swims in the water and every living creature that teems on the land. It is to make a distinction between the unclean and the clean, between living creatures that may be eaten and living creatures that may not be eaten.

SECTION THREE

LISA M. HELDKE

Foodmaking as a Thoughtful Practice

I. INTRODUCTION

What if Plato had regarded the preparation of food as a central source of philosophical insight? Would gardening have replaced the dialectic as the last stage in the education of the philosopher king? Would geometry have been regarded as a "mere knack," as compared to bread baking? Would those in the cave have climbed out to discover that the sun was the source of all heat, including the heat used to cook their food? Would the divided line culminate in eating?

It's extremely unlikely. Such impertinent speculation is based on the assumption that, had Plato considered foodmaking seriously, he simply would have inverted his philosophical system, placing those activities labeled crafts on the top, and relegating those he called arts to the basement.

Had he in fact taken foodmaking seriously (or more seriously than he did),[1] I think it is far more likely that Plato would not have developed that particular craft/art distinction in the first place—nor would he probably have distinguished as he does between knowledge and opinion, theory and practice. Furthermore, had subsequent philosophers continued to attend to such activities as growing and cooking food, it is likely that the theory/practice dichotomy, which threads its way through much of western philosophy, would not have developed as it did.

Foodmaking, rather than drawing us to mark a sharp distinction between mental and manual labor, or between theoretical and practical work, tends to invite us to see itself as a "mentally manual" activity, a "theoretically practical" activity—a "thoughtful practice." In this essay, I shall explore this suggestive if speculative claim.

In doing so, I first consider one formulation of the traditional theory/practice hierarchy, focusing on two of its features: (1) "knowing" retains separation between inquirer and inquired, while "doing" breaches this separation; and (2) "knowing" aims at producing timeless truths about unchanging reality, whereas "doing" is concerned with the transitory, the perishable, the changeable. How does this distinction between knowing and doing inform the way philosophers conceive of foodmaking and eating? It appears that those philosophers who *have* considered cooking have not thought it warranted detailed consideration, *precisely because* it is a manual activity, concerned with transitory, impermanent things.

I then consider one suggestive model for thinking about foodmaking processes which does not begin with a (hard-and-fast) separation between theory and practice, mental and manual, knowledge and knack. This model of "thoughtful practice" is derived from John Dewey, who suggests that the difference between theory and practice is a difference of degree, not kind; that theorizing is in fact a *kind* of practice. Dewey provides an account of human processes that displays greater respect for the integrity of growing, preparing, and eating food than does the account we can extract from, for example, Plato or Descartes.

Finally, I turn to the constructive task of developing understandings of foodmaking and eating as thoughtful processes. I do so by exploring some of the philosophical issues of foodmaking raised by the readings excerpted in this section. Attending foodmaking and eating directly, rather than pounding and squeezing them to make them fit "into" or "under" a theory, may make it possible to develop ways to think about, and *engage in,* activities which are more responsible and more respectful than the model which separates mental from manual tasks. The readings included here provide insights into a food-centered philosophy of thoughtful practice.

II. KNOWING VERSUS DOING: "HEAD WORK" AND "HAND WORK"

Philosophers in the western tradition have assigned value to human activities on the basis of two principles. First, activities have been considered valuable according to the degree to which they could be considered "knowing activities," "science," "theory," "art," or "head work."[2] Those activities not regarded as involving knowing—typically the "hand work" of practical, manual labor—have not generally merited philosophical attention.[3]

The division between "head" and "hand" work supports and is supported by a philosophical emphasis on maintaining separation between acting subject and acted-upon object.[4] This philosophical emphasis in turn supports and is supported by a class, gender, and race bias against those who engage in physical labor.[5] Biases embedded in philosophical theory thus find their way into the "nontheoretical" domain of everyday life, where they shape and are shaped by attitudes and structures that categorize and oppress people.

Second, western philosophers have traditionally valued activity aimed at producing timeless, unchanging results—known as genuine Knowledge. That which changes—the physical world in particular—has historically been regarded as in some sense unknowable. This philosophical assertion of the world's unknowability stems, in large part, from the fact that it does change.

Both knowing and its objects—timeless truths—are accorded value on a philosophical system which values changelessness. Thus, the philosophical predilection for the timeless and eternal also supports and is supported by social prejudices favoring those activities—mathematics, physics, literature, philosophy—aimed at the production of allegedly timeless knowledge as opposed to activities—cooking, farming, cleaning—that result in transitory products. (Given its preference for the eternal, western philosophy it seems would enjoin us to value the Twinkie, which has a shelf life of several years, more than the cheese soufflé, whose lifespan is about a minute, or the banana, which is ripe today, rotten tomorrow.)

In this first part of the essay, I provide an account of one conception of the theory/practice dichotomy, focusing on its conception of the relation between subject and object, and the importance it places upon atemporality. I look at one incarnation of this dichotomy which specifically addresses foodmaking—an account found in Plato's *Republic*. I offer several explanations why Plato's distinction between art and craft (theory and practice, knowing and opinion) disables him from acknowledging the importance of cooking. I conclude this first part by considering another treatment of foodmaking which still operates from a distinction between theory and practice, but which places foodmaking on the other side of the dichotomy. Revel and Suppes both treat cooking as a kind of theorizing. This alternative, while preferable to Plato's in some respects, is nonetheless still unsatisfactory. Attention to foodmaking, I conclude, reveals the inadequacy of the mental/manual split for understanding—or engaging in—growing, cooking, or eating food.

A. The Subject/Object Dichotomy

Inquiry has been regarded—by western philosophers and by non-philosophers influenced by western philosophical categories[6]—as an activity carried out by Subjects separated from the Objects of their inquiry. The separation is often described by using a metaphorical glass wall; subjects stand on one side of the wall, objects on the other. The wall prevents any actual physical contact between subject and object, but, being glass, it allows subjects to make all "necessary" observations of the objects. Controls are located on the subjects' side of the wall; it is they who set up the conditions for observation, determine the questions which will be posed, and decide what counts as an answer to them. Although objects may surprise subjects—with unexpected answers, or with a refusal to provide answers—it is the subjects who set the terms of the interchange. Thus, on the subject/object model for inquiry, not only are subjects separated from objects, but they also exercise autonomy and control over the objects of their inquiry. Objects, on the other hand, have comparatively little autonomy or control over subjects.[7]

Not surprisingly, vision—the sense that acts at a distance—has been the primary source for metaphors to describe inquiry.[8] One of the most famous of these metaphors, found in the *Republic,* is Plato's analogy of the cave, which charts the development of knowers as they journey from a world of darkness and illusory shadows to a world of light and objects genuinely seen. Descartes, attempting to arrive at something he can know for certain, similarly uses ocular metaphors, shining the "light of reason" upon each of the objects of his consciousness, to determine whether they can be seen/known "clearly and distinctly." Our everyday language is filled with similar visual metaphors that testify to the degree to which our thinking about thinking has been shaped by visual models.

There is no necessary causal connection between the fact that western philosophers have conceived of inquiry (mental work) in terms of vision and the fact that they have also tended to regard the self as a discrete and independent substance, radically separated from the object of its inquiry. But neither is it mere coincidence that these two conceptions have developed alongside each other. At least, the predominance of visual metaphors has served to bolster a separation between knower and known, subject and object. At most, it has actually helped to create that separation, and to shape conceptions of inquiry that presuppose it.

Once the distancing has been effected—once mental substance has been radically separated from physical substance, subject from object—a problem arises; how can we knowers ever *know* anything which is *that* separate/different from us?[9] Despite the persistence—and perniciousness—of this problem of knowledge, western epistemologists have continued to posit the necessity of maintaining a clear separation between subjects and objects, minds and bodies. As a result, the worth of an activity has tended to be judged—by philosophers and by those influenced by this philosophical distinction—in part by determining the degree to which the activity can be shown to preserve that separation, or can be described using the language of disembodied and noninvasive seeing.

In contrast to the mental activity of inquiry, traditional philosophy posits practice—practical activity in which the separation between subject and object is "violated." Practical activities are precisely those in which the external world of objects does not remain outside (and in which the inquirer often does not remain "inside"); one kneads the bread dough, picks the beans, feeds the baby. In all these activities, subject and object meet and touch, and that meeting is central to their nature as activities. Kneading bread dough is not a "subservient" physical activity which "supports" bread-making "theory," even while violating the separation between "bread theorizer" and bread dough. Rather, kneading is an essential part of the theoretical-and-practical process of making bread—a part in which subjects' and objects' boundaries necessarily meet, touch and overlap.

B. TEMPORALITY

The second feature of this conception of the theory/practice dichotomy that is significant for my account is temporality. On the schema inherited from Plato, knowledge can only be of that which does not change—and the only things which do not change are abstract, nonmaterial things. For Plato, the things most knowable are the Forms, and the highest activity is the contemplation of them. Descartes, although rejecting the notion of a separate realm of eternal Forms, retains the idea that what we know best about an object are not its transitory accidental properties, but its unchanging essential attributes.

Objects of genuine knowledge are not subject to the ravages of time; they exist today, tomorrow, and yesterday. It is precisely their imperviousness to time, in fact, which makes them knowable and valuable.[10] And, if we are able to come to know these essences, our contemplation of them will also become atemporal in a sense; true contemplation of the Forms is an activity that is always the same.

Practical activities, on the other hand, are carried out in a world of flux and change, a world where time is "inescapable"—and where its effects are unavoidable, and seen mostly as destructive (yes, there is growth, but there is also always decay). Food gives us striking examples of this: making and eating food are processes that take minutes, hours, or days. And these same processes must be repeated every day; unlike coming to know the Form of the Good, eating lunch doesn't produce anything that will stay with a person for good.

That which changes cannot be known; thus activities involving food can never bring us more than opinions, hunches, or good guesses. The reliability of our opinions may improve over time—next year we'll think twice before we plant radishes in April—but they can never, in principle, assume the status of knowledge. No amount of practice can overcome the capriciousness of time to give us certainty.

Because practical activities involve us directly in the physical, temporal world in ways we cannot ignore (try to remove yourself from the physical, temporal world when you are trying to get the hay in before it rains), and because that involvement is regarded as base, dirty, and inferior, in ordinary life physical processes become things we try to "hurry through" or from which we try to remove ourselves. Influenced by philosophical prejudices, our everyday response to being caught up in a world bounded by time is often to try to get the unpleasant tasks done quickly, so we can get to the pleasant ones—or escape to the eternal through "timeless literature," "contemplation of eternal truths," etc. Thus does Plato explain the length of the intestine in the *Timaeus;* it prevents us from having to eat frequently, and enables us to engage in contemplation for longer stretches of time.[11] And thus do food manufacturers seduce us into buying their products, with promises of split-second (but delicious!) foods, which allow us to "get on with our active life-styles."

In societies shaped by systems of exploitation and oppression, the most time-bound jobs—particularly those which are highly repetitive—are assigned the least value and are given to those members of the society who

are most oppressed and exploited within those systems; persons performing them are paid the least (or are not paid at all).[12] Many of the daily
chores of a domestic worker—shopping for food, cooking food, serving
food, cleaning the kitchen after cooking—are virtually invisible to those
who benefit from them, or are regarded by beneficiaries as beneath attention or comment. Food-factory workers are placed on assembly lines where
they perform the same action hundreds of times a day. The consequence
for workers is, at best, boredom; at worst, severe physical problems are
caused by their work environment.

Because food is temporal, food workers' jobs are often constructed
around its "times." Frequently it is not the temporality of food alone that
dictates the structure of workers' lives. Rather, farm owners, factory owners, husbands—those with power to dictate the actions of workers—may
determine the *ways* in which the temporality of food will dictate workers'
lives. Thus, migrant workers live in a world governed by the fruit or vegetable that is in season; they must be there, ready to work, when the crop is
ripe. And when it is ripe, they must be prepared to pick it all, no matter
how long the hours or how unbearable the working conditions. A homemaker is instructed by her husband to have dinner on the table when he
gets home—though that time may vary from day to day. She is responsible
for juggling the exigencies of her husband's schedule with those of the
foods she will prepare, for example, to ensure that the pork chops are done
but not dry by the time he gets home.

Those in a society who are privileged—by gender, class, or race—may
virtually avoid involvement with activities that remind of the temporality of
food. Middle- or upper-class people may buy all our foods—fresh, frozen
or canned—at one supermarket, where we may be assured of finding everything we want, regardless of the season. Husbands may find dinner
ready each evening as they come from work, and may retire to the living
room after dinner, unmindful of the mess that must now be cleaned up.
For many of us, the temporality of the physical world is mediated in various ways by maids, factory and farm workers, wives, servers, cooks; if we
are privileged enough, we may virtually forget the cycle of buy–cook–
serve–clean-up–put-away that governs the day of the homemaker or domestic worker.[13]

Few of us probably realize this degree of privilege. Those of us still
"trapped" by temporal aspects of our existence may thus seek to "escape"
them to the greatest degree possible. Present-day attitudes toward food
preparation (as displayed by advertising, by cookbooks, by conversations
at the coffee table) emphasize the value of ease, speed, and efficiency.
"Good" food for the two-career couple often means something which
takes very little time to prepare, doesn't use many dishes, contains the
necessary nutrients, and looks like the picture on the box (never mind the
taste). One assumption at work is that preparing food is not an activity that
has value in and of itself. Thus, if it can be eliminated, or speeded up, it

should be.[14] Al Sicherman's "investigative report" of the creation of a "perfect pie" (reprinted in this section) is a paradigm of one form taken by the modern obsession with speed; we wish to eat food that looks like (a computer-generated version of) what Grandma used to make, without being involved in the process of producing that food ourselves and without having to take the time such a process takes. It is the product, not the process, that matters.[15] (Consider the term "processed food.")

C. PLATO AND THE HEAD WORK/HAND WORK DICHOTOMY

One version of the philosophical dichotomy and hierarchy of head work and hand work is vividly illustrated in Plato's discussion of the three kinds of citizens/three parts of the soul in the *Republic*. Plato's account is particularly significant for the attention it pays to foodmaking; perhaps no other work of philosophy contains as many references to food and cooking. Emerging from the *Republic* is Plato's view that cooking, like all other crafts, is at best marginally relevant to the acquisition of wisdom.

In constructing his Republic, Plato divides its inhabitants into three groups; rulers, guardians, and "wage earners," the last being the bottom rank of people who provide the city with virtually all its goods and services (369ff.). Once we leave the city of pigs, Plato pays virtually no attention to the wage earners. Their education is not examined, and their actual roles in society are not addressed in any detail. Although these are the people who have the task of feeding everyone (and providing for all other basic needs), Plato dismisses them by observing that they are also the citizens whose souls are ruled by their appetitive parts. For him, this demonstrates the need for them to be subservient to the rulers, whose souls are governed by reason (431ff.).

Given the subject matter of the *Republic*—the nature of justice—Plato's neglect of the wage earners suggests that the particular nature of tasks like growing and cooking food is of little importance to the project of creating a just state. In Plato's just state, reason is the quality which must be developed, and reason is exhibited most fully not by those who cook, but by those who rule. If rulers are educated in the art of reason, everything else will follow. Residents' "mere bodily" needs will take care of themselves—or, more correctly, will be taken care of by the "appetitive" citizens, who will be well paid for their efforts. Their souls will be governed by their appetites—for money, food, and other pleasures—but in the just state they will also be reasonable enough to recognize the legitimacy of the rulers' rule.

Plato establishes a sharp separation and hierarchy both between the activities of reason and those of the appetites, *and* between those who do the work of reason and those whose work focuses on satisfying appetites. Plato recognizes that we cannot think if we are hungry, but on his schema, this fact gets translated into the notion that the bodily appetites must be satisfied but controlled. They must not be allowed to dictate their wishes, just as cooks should not be allowed to govern.

The relative unimportance of foodmaking is illustrated in a second way in the *Republic*. Cooking and other food preparation activities are absent from the roster of subjects the guardians must study. They learn music and geometry, but there is no need for them to learn how to cook; it is apparently not a subject the study of which will improve the guardians' souls.

It will, of course, be noted that the Greek system of education was not like the modern American land-grant university; Home Economics is a twentieth-century invention; it could not have occurred to Plato to include this subject in the guardians' education. This argument has considerable merit, but given that Plato was well aware of the need for education to attend to the body in other ways—as evidenced by his discussion of the role of physical exercise in the guardians' education—it becomes less convincing. In his discussion of the guardians' physical training, Plato even asserts that the guardians must pay careful attention to what they eat—they are restricted to a very simple diet—but we are told nothing about who will prepare that food (404c). Guardians should know *what* to eat, but need not know *how* to prepare it. Plato regards the role of food for sustaining the body a proper object of concern for the guardians. But, unlike abstract reasoning and physical training, he does not regard learning how to prepare that food to be a necessary element of the guardians' training. Education in cooking apparently would not improve either the soul or the body—the two aims of the guardians' education.

The subject of the cook raises another foodmaking issue in the *Republic*. Citizens of the Republic must adhere to the principle of "one soul, one job," which stipulates that everyone is well suited to just one occupation, which they must perform to the exclusion of every other occupation (443c). This principle emphasizes the unimportance of activities like cooking, even as it more generally sanctions the virtues of extreme specialization. In the ideal society, a ruler can rule well *only* by systematically ignoring everything except the carefully circumscribed tasks of ruling. For Plato, it is best for the city as a whole, and for everyone in it, if each person does only one thing. There is nothing to be gained—by either the city or the individual soul—by allowing people to do more than one task.

But how does this principle emphasize the insignificance of foodmaking? Plato worries a great deal about how the guardians shall live—forbidding them private property, requiring them to live collectively, etc. (416d). But he rejects by implication the possibility that their steadfastness as guardians might be promoted by a living environment in which they were required to provide for each others' basic needs—including the need for food. He does so by requiring that the guardians devote themselves single-mindedly to the tasks of guarding—and that they leave the cooking to the cooks.

Like each individual in the city, each part of the individual's soul must also have one and only one task. By carving the soul into reason, spirit, and appetite, Plato separates reason from all other faculties. And in elevating reason above the others, he makes it alone the proper governor of the soul. He terms bodily appetites unreasonable, and regards them as things to be controlled by reason (much as cooks must be controlled by rulers). It is unlikely that reason will benefit from the insight of the appetites, just as it is not likely that a ruler will receive good advice about ruling justly from a cook. Hunger can be rational only to the degree to which it realizes it must be held in control by reason.[16] Bodily knowledge in general, if such an expression is not simply a misnomer, can only be a lower, craft-like form of knowledge, subservient to the genuine knowledge of the rational soul.

Plato's hierarchy of kinds of humans/parts of the soul makes its way into present-day life in the way that certain kinds of "manual" labor are ranked below certain forms of "intellectual" labor. This ordering can be seen in the way that the work of farmers, homemakers, and other such "manual workers" is subordinate to the "knowing professions" like biochemistry, genetics, and other sciences.

Domestic and farm workers' places in the "chain of knowledge" prescribed by western philosophy, and encoded in popular thought, is that of consumers; they form the markets for the new technologies developed by "applied scientists" using the theories of the "pure scientists" (if indeed those divisions between pure and applied science can be set out so clearly). It is they who buy the new detergent, the new fertilizer, the new no-fat, high-fiber butter substitute. They are doers, not thinkers; users, not discoverers. And, like the artisans in Plato's *Republic,* they are presumed to be happy so long as they have enough to satisfy their various appetites.

Likewise, modern-day research scientists are conceived as being much like the guardians in Plato's *Republic* in their disconnection from the activities that "keep body and soul together.[17] Usually white and male, and frequently married, they tend to have wives who (whether *they* work outside the home or not) buy the groceries, prepare the meals, and clean up afterwards. The stereotypical absentminded professor often forgets to eat, and has to be reminded to come home from the lab. Traits such as being absentminded are considered admirable, for they show how serious the scientist is about science.

It apparently is not essential, or even important, for practitioners of the highest forms of knowing in our culture to participate in the activities that serve their day-to-day needs. Tasks like cooking and doing the dishes are necessary evils; they're evil for everyone, and if one can avoid doing them, so much the better. There is very little sympathy—either in Plato or in contemporary life—for the idea that foodmaking activities are valuable because of, not in spite of, the fact that they ground us in the concrete, embodied present.

John Dewey notes, "The depreciation of action, of doing and making, has been cultivated by philosophers. But while philosophers have perpetuated the derogation by formulating and justifying it, they did not originate it. . . . On account of the unpleasantness of practical activity, as much of it as possible has been put upon slaves and serfs. Thus the social dishonor in which this class was held was extended to the work they do" (1980, 4–5). Philosophy venerates and codifies a denigration of the practical which already exists in some form in social life.

Recently, many feminist philosophers have turned their attention to considerations of practical, embodied activities, examining both the way those activities have been ignored by Plato and other philosophers, and the philosophical significance such activities in fact have. These theorists' projects reveal the ways in which class, gender, and race hierarchies have helped to determine what counts as a philosophically interesting activity. Not surprisingly, they have found that philosophers have tended to valorize those activities in which it is the prerogative of educated and/or ruling-class men to engage.[18]

Such activities have tended to be those classed as theory or "head work." For example, contemplation—of the stars, of the Forms, of number and figure, of God—has been regarded as the philosophically most important human activity in part because it is one thing that leisure-class men did and continue to do. On the other hand, their wives, servants, slaves, and workers were more likely engaged in "hand work," work Dorothy Smith (1979, 168) describes as being in the "bodily mode."

> The place of women, then, . . . is where the work is done to facilitate man's occupation of the conceptual mode of action. Women keep house, bear and care for children, look after him when he is sick, and in general provide for the logistics of his bodily existence. . . . They do things which give concrete form to the conceptual activities. . . . At almost every point women mediate for men the relation between the conceptual mode of action and the actual concrete forms on which it depends.[19]

Accepting the knowing/doing model for classifying human processes leaves us with two ways to approach foodmaking, neither of which is particularly satisfactory. The first alternative—that chosen by Plato, and by the modern-day makers of the Burger King pie cutter of whom Sicherman writes—is simply to treat food preparation as hand work and give it the minimal attention and respect that such activities are "supposed" to receive.

The other, somewhat more promising, alternative is to treat foodmaking as a "knowing" activity. This is the choice of Patrick Suppes in his account (reprinted here) of recipes as "procedures" that can be "justified" the way a Euclidian geometrical construction is justified. While I do not suggest that such treatment of recipes is "wrong," I do think that Suppes's method cannot get at the interesting things about recipes and cooking precisely because it uses a framework—the knowing/doing framework—

which doesn't *allow for* the interesting things to emerge. He may strain at the limits of this framework, but he remains within it.

Suppes's account is a formalized analysis of the ways in which a step in a recipe can be justified. It accepts the legitimacy of a distinction between theoretical and practical activities, but shows that even an activity like cooking *can* be interpreted as theoretical. His explanation for using the example of cooking is that it is an activity involving "nontrivial procedures that almost everyone has some experience with" (236*). He doesn't include any analysis of why cooking is *not* generally treated by philosophers. (Because of this silence, I am left wondering if we are not to interpret this passage as slightly tongue-in-cheek.)

A similar sort of move—categorizing foodmaking as a theoretical activity—may lie behind such phenomena as middle- and upper-class cooks who invest enormous amounts of money in equipment and ingredients, to produce food that is "innovative" and "artistic." For these cooks, foodmaking is often not an everyday activity, but a special leisure activity. As such, it cannot be described as aimed at keeping body and soul together. Rather, it is often a highly intellectualized, highly theoretical enterprise. In certain respects, it seems to imitate sculpture—an activity that, although it involves the hands, certainly is not hand work.[20]

Jean-François Revel also can be said to move foodmaking into the realm of the theoretical, as is illustrated by his distinction between "international cuisine" and "regional cuisine," in the selection reprinted here. International cuisine is "not a corpus of recipes, but a body of *methods,* of *principles* amenable to *variations,* depending on different local and financial possibilities" (245*). This international Grand Cuisine he describes as an art, and contrasts it to regional cuisine, which "does not belong to the domain of art, but rather that of ethnology or a mixture of biology and ethnology" (246*). International cuisine transcends the (sometimes charming) parochialism of regional cuisine to establish general principles, methods, and techniques of cooking. "Gastronomical art is able, when necessary and possible, to find the equivalents of certain products or of certain ingredients and use them to replace other products and other ingredients that cannot be obtained in certain places" (246*). International cuisine is a scientific art, genuinely practiced only by "professionals" (248*), while regional cuisine is a knack, a set of skills, ingredients, etc., which may not be universalized, and therefore cannot be part of a genuine art. By separating international from regional cuisine, Revel sets up a distinction between head work and hand work *within* the domain of foodmaking. One form of cooking (the professional, method-governed form) he treats as a theoretical activity on a par with any other. The other he regards as a craft or knack, like whittling or fly tying.

Such accounts of foodmaking that redefine it as a kind of theoretical activity can only go so far toward creating a conception of foodmaking processes that treats them with integrity. Both Suppes and Revel stuff foodmaking into an existing framework, the theory/practice framework. I've been suggesting that this particular framework distorts foodmaking, whether it is treated as head work or as hand work. In the next part of this essay, I explore a reconceptualization of the theory/practice dichotomy that may provide a more promising way to address foodmaking on its own terms. The reconceptualization introduces a concept I call "thoughtful practice," a concept derived from the epistemological thought of John Dewey.

III. DEWEY AND THOUGHTFUL PRACTICE

Dewey's understanding of the traditional philosophical organization of human activities (and human "types")[21] is illustrated in the following passage from *Experience and Nature:*

> There is then an empirical truth in the common opposition between theory and practice, between the contemplative, reflective type and the executive type, the "go-getter," the kind that "gets things done." It is, however, a contrast between two modes of practice. One is the pushing, slam-bang, act-first and think- afterwards mode, to which events may yield as they give way to any strong force. The other mode is wary, observant, sensitive to slight hints and intimations. . . . [In the latter mode, one] lives on a conscious plane; thought guides activity, and perception is its reward. Action is not suppressed but is moderated. Like the scientific experimenter, one acts not just to act, nor rashly, nor automatically, but with a consciousness of purpose and for the sake of learning.[22]

Dewey describes the distinction between theory and practice as a difference in degree between two modes of practice. Contrary to the philosophical tradition, he suggests that there is no sharp distinction in kind between the two. Rather, they may most usefully be regarded as two forms of practice, one of which might be called "thoughtful practice" rather than "theory."

Dewey suggests that the dichotomization of theoretical and practical activity has not always been inaccurate in the particular way it is now, however. For the Greeks, it was a more "self-consistent position" (1958, 355), which distinguished between two separate spheres of reality, fixed and eternal Being, and changing uncertain Becoming.[23]

In contrast, modern philosophy presents a "curious mixture." It rejects the two-sphere model of the Greeks, but retains the distinction between theory and practice, "although formulating it in somewhat different language: to the effect that knowledge deals with objective reality as it is in itself, while in what is 'practical,' objective reality is altered and cognitively distorted by subjective factors of want, emotion and striving" (355). A "curious" inconsistency is displayed in the fact that modern philosophers introduce the new category of "fine arts"—manual activities that are nonetheless accorded the status of theoretical ones. Sculpture is revered along with mathematics.

Dewey suggests that one reason for the reshuffling of categories effected by modern philosophers is that, whereas the Greeks valued knowledge because of its contemplative nature, modern philosophers put "art and creation first" (357). But, as he points out, if they are justified in doing so,

> then the implications of this position should be avowed and carried through. It would then be seen that science is an art, that art is practice, and that the only distinction worth drawing is not between practice and theory, but between those modes of practice that are not intelligent, not inherently and immediately enjoyable, and those which are full of enjoyed meanings. (358)

It is worth noting in this context that Dewey himself does not carry through the implications of this position. In his own reworking of the theory/practice dichotomy he considers only practices with established philosophical legitimacy and respectability—experimental science being the most important for him. Dewey's understanding of the relation between "head work" and "hand work" prompts him to *reshape* the way science is categorized by philosophy, but in doing so he is only *reconsidering* an activity that philosophers have *traditionally* considered important. His redefinition of the nature of theory and practice does not impel him to attend to other human practices outside the traditional purview of philosophy. Except, perhaps, in his writings on philosophy of education (in which he acknowledges the usefulness of such activities as homemaking and carpentry for the education of children), Dewey's understanding of the centrality of practice and "the practical" does not bring him to undertake an examination of any activity typically dismissed as "practical" by philosophers. He does not seem to acknowledge the full significance of his own suggestion that the relevant distinction in human activities should be drawn between practices which are "full of enjoyed meanings" (1958, 358) and practices which are not. If Dewey had absorbed this observation fully, it seems likely that he would have been drawn to consider a variety of practical activities that are rich with enjoyed meaning. In particular, it seems he would have been led to a consideration of foodmaking.

For the most part, Dewey's reconceptualization of the relation between theory and practice leaves untouched the landscape of philosophically relevant human activity; nothing is let out and nothing is let in. In fact, Dewey is at great pains to insist that his use of terms like "practice," "practical," and "pragmatic" not be understood as committing or restricting him to a philosophy of ordinary everydayness. In "An Added Note as to the 'Practical,'" he insists that, although "practical" is generally "taken to signify some quite definite utilities of a material or bread and butter type" (330), in the case of his philosophy, this is a misconception: "the term 'pragmatic' means only the rule of referring all thinking, all reflective considerations, to *consequences* for final meaning and test" (330). Appearances to the contrary, Dewey insists that his philosophy is not a philosophy of ordinary practice.

It is understandable that Dewey would be sensitive to this issue; certainly pragmatism was denigrated as a crude philosophy of instant gratification because of the ways in which that term was misunderstood. Nonetheless, in his eagerness to assure other philosophers that pragmatism is not a philosophy of "immediately practical consequences"—that pragmatism does not have its eyes riveted on *immediate* results—Dewey too zealously and too willingly divorces himself from a consideration of everyday practical activities. He seems tacitly to assume that such activities are in fact concerned only with immediate consequences—an assumption he does not seem to examine.[24]

I suggest that Dewey's reconception of theory and practice as "kinds of practice" is a more profound and radical move than he acknowledges. In undermining the distinction between theory and practice, it becomes relevant to reexamine the reasons that "practical" foodmaking activities have been ignored by philosophers. Having removed the traditional, "official" justification for their being ignored—that they are not "theoretical" activities—Dewey must either replace it with another justification, or consider these activities. In effect, he does neither; his silence on the subject leaves us to assume either that he considers foodmaking to be concerned only with immediate gratification, or that he did not consider its possible philosophical significance at all. In the face of his silence, I propose taking Dewey's position in a radical—but obvious—direction; a philosophical consideration of foodmaking.

IV. FOODMAKING AS A THOUGHTFUL PRACTICE

From Dewey's analysis of the theory/practice distinction emerges a category of human activity I'll call "thoughtful practice." Thoughtful practices are those that are "intelligent," "inherently and immediately enjoyable," and "full of enjoyed meanings" (358). They are also "wary, observant, sensitive to slight hints and intimations. . . . [In them, a]ction is not suppressed but is moderated" (314–15). Growing, preparing, and eating foods are such activities. Although Dewey did not employ this concept to examine foodmaking, I suggest that the concept of thoughtful practice can be helpful for developing an understanding of the significance of foodmaking. Furthermore, an analysis of foodmaking can provide us with insight into ways of developing the notion of a thoughtful practice that are relevant for other activities.

In the last section of this essay, I will explore the notion of thoughtful practice by considering foodmaking from a variety of perspectives. The elements of thoughtful practice to be considered are: the relation between self and other; roles played by the community; bodily elements of thoughtful practice; and the significance of the emotional and the erotic. Each of these elements is useful for revealing the differences between activity conceived as a thoughtful practice and activity conceived of as theorizing. Whereas theorizing regarded in its "purest" form is abstract, disembodied, purely rational, and retains sharp boundaries between inquirer and the rest of the world, thoughtful practices turn out to focus on the concrete, embodied, emotional and erotic nature of activity, and to recognize the significant interconnections that exist between inquirers and their environments.

A. THE SELF-OTHER INTERCONNECTION

Considered on their own terms, foodmaking activities can challenge the sharp subject/object dichotomy that characterizes traditional inquiry, and that serves to separate such head work from hand work. Preparing food encourages us to blur the separation between ourselves and our food, even as we roll up our sleeves and stick our hands in the dough.

In "Recipes for Theory Making," reprinted here, I argue that thinking about bread-making as a kind of theorizing (or, as I would say now, as a kind of thoughtful practice) places me and bread dough in a relation with each other, a relation in which I assume neither total separateness from the ingredients I use, nor complete control over them.

Carol Adams suggests one concrete result that may emerge from rethinking the subject/object relation in terms of one aspect of food preparation, namely the creation of meat. In an excerpt from *The Sexual Politics of Meat* reprinted here, Adams suggests that if we start to speak clearly about the nature of our interconnections with other animals, this verbal clarity may transform our concrete relations with those others as well. Specifically, it may compel us to stop eating them. In the traditional "story of meat," the animal as a living, feeling creature is rendered invisible when it is killed for food. It becomes what she calls elsewhere in the book the "absent referent." "Animals in name and body are made absent *as animals* for meat to exist" (1989, 40). This story "ends when the male-defined consumer eats the female-defined body. The animals' role in meat eating is parallel to the women's role in narrative: we would have neither meat nor story without them. They are objects to others who act as subjects" (268*).

If we retell the story using words like "murder" to explain the processes by which a living pig is turned into a package of "pork," Adams suggests we may be moved and challenged to give the story an "alternative ending" (268*). Alternative endings might come from one of two sorts of perspectives—perspectives that she argues ought to be in more serious conversation with other—namely, vegetarianism and feminism. Understanding the relations between the systematic objectification of women and the objectification of animals, feminists may be drawn to see the theoretical importance of vegetarianism, and vegetarians may be compelled to embrace feminist principles.

Crucial to both projects is the necessity of undermining the subject/object dichotomy. By supporting the objectification of women and of other animals, the traditional dichotomy serves as a powerful tool used to construct and maintain systems that dominate, oppress, and exploit women and other animals.[25]

Replacing the subject/object dichotomy with a conception of relations between self and other that focuses on their interconnections is one necessary element in a conception of thoughtful practice. The traditional theory/practice dichotomy presumes that theoretical work involves no interconnections—or that any existent interconnections are irrelevant to the theory—and uses this presumption as one way of distinguishing theory from practice. By rejecting the dichotomy between theory and practice and replacing it with a view of all human activities as kinds of practice, we also begin to recognize the importance of interconnections between "self" and "other" in all activity. Attention to these interconnections may also compel us to reshape the ways they have been constructed under the influence of the theory/practice dichotomy.

B. Bodily Knowledge

By seeing ourselves as connected to the things we grow and cook—by transforming the subject/object dichotomy into a relationship which recognizes the interconnections between us and those foods—we are also called upon to recognize a mode of interaction that might be called "bodily knowledge." A conception of thoughtful practices should have as one of its foci a realization of the embodied nature of those activities.[26]

Theories like Descartes's conceive of my body as an external appendage to my mind, and see its role in inquiry as merely to provide a set of (fairly reliable) sensory data on which my reasoning faculty then operates to produce objects of knowledge. But growing and cooking food are important counterexamples to this view; they are activities in which bodily perceptions are more than meter readings which must be scrutinized by reason. The knowing involved in making a cake is "contained" not simply "in my head" but in my hands, my wrists, my eyes and nose as well. The phrase "bodily knowledge" is not a metaphor. It is an acknowledgment of the fact that I *know* things literally with my body, that I, "as" my hands, know when the bread dough is sufficiently kneaded, and I "as" my nose know when the pie is done.

In "The Demystification of Food," excerpted in this section, Verta Mae Smart-Grosvenor describes her cooking method as "vibration"; " . . . I never measure or weigh anything. I cook by vibration. I can tell by the look and smell of it" (294*). What is Grosvenor "demystifying" with this assertion? One thing she suggests is that "Cartesian" cooking methods—which presume a kind of separation and hierarchy between mind and body, which treat bodily activity as being in the service of mental activity, and which consequently require mathematical measurement and scientific technique—are inauthentic and pretentious. They attempt to make cooking a kind of science in the Cartesian sense. The results of such methods are sterile, flavorless foods—a fact which, for Grosvenor, confirms their inauthenticity.[27] In contrast, the kind of cooking she does shuns such pretentious mathematical precision and produces good food "by vibration"— by using her bodily understanding of (and connection with) the foods she's cooking.

To know food—to know how to cook food well—does not require an abstracted, measurement-conscious knowledge (a kind of knowledge which imitates the allegedly disembodied nature of scientific, theoretical knowledge), but rather a knowledge in the eyes and in the hands. You have to be able to "finger" a ball of pie dough to tell if it needs a bit more ice water. You must be able to smell when the garlic is just about to burn as it sautés in the oil. Grosvenor's recipes—brief and "imprecise," listing no measures or amounts—reflect her conception of the way cooking is done, and of the role that written instructions can play in cooking. If you don't know how you like it, what good is it for me to tell you how much rice to put in? And if you don't already know how to cook it, how is my writing it in a book going to help you learn? You need a teacher—a hands-on teacher—for that. Bodily knowledge is acquired through embodied experience.

Compare Grosvenor's recipes—and her accompanying account—to the recipes described and explained by Suppes. For Suppes, a recipe is a rational explanation, complete with justification, for how to do something. For Grosvenor, a recipe is more like a maxim, or a memory-jogger, or an inspiration. It cannot be a complete account. Nothing short of a day in the kitchen with Grosvenor could be such an account. Words can't explain what you must learn using your hands and nose and mouth.

On one level, such a claim states an obvious, seemingly trivial, fact; it is clear, after all, that one must be *shown* how to do all sorts of manual things. (Notably, the things about which we make this assertion are not things we call "knowledge" of the highest sort. They include pastry-making, but not mathematics.)

But on another level, this particular claim about the centrality of bodily experience in learning to cook has transformative potential. Recognizing it may press us toward an understanding of *all* human activities as bodily, in nontrivial, "unbracketable" ways. Even activities traditionally conceived as abstract, disembodied theorizing can be so understood. Such an understanding would transform Descartes's assertion that my essence is to be a disembodied thinking thing, and that knowing is fundamentally a mental activity in which my body plays only a supporting role—and would also transform Plato's assertion that manual activities are inferior to, and in the service of, theoretical activity.

Consider, for example, how Plato's explanation for our intestine might be transformed by a recognition of the bodily nature of knowledge. Plato, in explaining our intestine's length, acknowledges the importance of attending to bodily needs, as a means of enabling the soul to "get on" with its higher task—contemplation (1953, 72e–73a). That is, Plato (unlike Descartes) at least recognizes that our bodies cannot be ignored. However, Plato regards our embodied, appetitive nature as a rather unfortunate fact of human life; we must satisfy our base appetite for food, but beyond that, our desire for food is nothing to celebrate. Consider, on the other hand, how we might explain the relation between thinking and eating if we begin without presuming the subservience of body and bodily activity, and by acknowledging that we are indeed bodily beings. Rather than regarding time spent eating as an annoying necessity, it may come to be regarded as a resource—a source of physical strength, of enjoyment, of inspiration. Rather than something to be "gotten through," it becomes something to be anticipated and lived fully.

In describing this conception of embodiment as a transformation, I am not suggesting anything like the replacement of Descartes's essentialist conception of knowers and knowing with a new essentialist conception that includes bodies. I mean only to suggest that if we consider foodmaking seriously, having rejected presuppositions that label it an inferior form of interaction, we may be able to apply the understanding of it as an embodied activity to our investigation of other forms of human interaction in the world. These activities, too, may be seen as embodied, in significant, not subservient ways.

C. COMMUNITY MEMBERSHIP

In a variety of ways, foodmaking activities are community activities. Foodmaking processes may define membership in a community, and they may depend on the existence of a community in order to be practiced, or to be passed to the next generation of practitioners.

My account of recipe exchange in "Recipes for Theory Making" (reprinted here) discusses some of the senses in which creating, exchanging, and testing recipes are community activities. I do not mean to suggest anything idyllic in describing recipe exchange this way; indeed, as I point out, people are often unscrupulous, uncooperative, and even malicious members of the community of recipe exchangers. Clearly, the fact that creating food is an activity that often goes on in a community does not automatically mean that it is a positive one. When some members of the community hold disproportionate amounts of power over others (in the form of access to goods, share of the market, ability to dictate others' actions, etc.), they have the capacity to create an environment which exploits those others. Such a situation frequently obtains when one of the "members" of the community is a large food corporation; consumers are frequently disempowered in such relations, and consumers who are poor are particularly disempowered.

Buffalo Bird Woman, in a selection reprinted here, discusses one specific way in which food preparation is a community function when she describes guarding the corn crop in a Hidatsa village. Girls and women watched the corn from a "watchers' stage," built in the middle of the cornfield. The stage was a centerpiece in the field, a place where women of the community gathered for an activity that was a combination of our categories of "work" and "recreation"; resting from hoeing, scaring off birds, singing songs. Furthermore, because it was a gathering place for all women, from the very young to the old, it was also a place where young girls learned the ways of the garden, and where older women taught the younger ones the songs, the stories, and the planting, cultivating and harvesting techniques. Likewise, girls and younger women kept older women informed about goings-on in their lives and their circles of friends.

Watching the corn defined a community that was quite expressly a women's community; men and boys were not particularly welcome at the stage, and their presence was tolerated, at best. This strengthened the women's identification with each other and with the task of corn-growing. It explicitly was "women's work," though that term did not have for them the derogatory connotation it has in present American society—nor did it have the correspondingly low status in the community. Growing and harvesting the crops were clearly central to the life and livelihood of the entire community. Consider the account of justice that might emerge from this community, as compared to Plato's account of the just state.

In the excerpt from *Zami* reprinted here, Audre Lorde describes the entry of a young girl into adult membership in her community by giving an account of her first menstrual period, and of the preparation of her favorite food, souse. In a detailed description of the mortar and pestle she uses—explaining where it came from, how it differed from those used by people of other ethnicities—and of the method she had learned for pounding spice, we get a sense of that community, and of Lorde's uneasy relation to it.

In this account, Lorde reveals a tension between her growing-up self and her mother, a tension that is manifested in their different attitudes toward food preparation. For Lorde, the involved process of pounding spice for souse is a delight, while for her mother it is only a chore, and "she looked upon the advent of powdered everything as a cook's boon" (287*). As Lorde's account makes clear, becoming a full-fledged member of a community is not always a smooth transition—particularly not when you are a girl/young woman, and when you must overcome the resistance of a mother who rules her home with absolute authority: " . . . I realized that my old enjoyment of the bone-jarring way I had been taught to pound spice would feel different to me from now on, and also that in my mother's kitchen there was only one right way to do anything" (293*).

Verta Mae Smart-Grosvenor discusses another kind of food-centered tension that can arise in communities—in this case, a tension *between* communities—when she exposes the racism underlying white conceptions of food cultures and food traditions. "[W]ith the exception of black bottom pie and niggertoes, there is no reference to black people's contribution to the culinary arts. White folks act like they invented food" (294*). Elsewhere in her book she refers to terrapins, which "ain't nothing but swamp turtles. They used to be plentiful on the eastern seaboard. So plentiful that plantation owners gave them to their slaves. Now they are the rare discovery of so-called gore-mays. White folks are always discovering something . . . after we give it up" (44).

Grosvenor pointedly argues that dominant cultural attitudes toward soul food—that it's tasteless, that it's ordinary—reveal white presumptions about the "mystique" of food, about the difference between haute cuisine of the type prepared by "Julia and Jim" (294*) and the food that "brought my ancestors through four hundred years of oppression" (297*). By beginning with a racist presupposition about Blacks and Black culture, whites create a "high art/craft" distinction between "gore-may" cooking and soul-food cooking. But, as she points out, "there ain't but so many ways you can cook a sweet potato" (294*). Consider her discussion here in comparison to Revel's; his praise of "international cuisine" argues that its superiority lies precisely in the fact that it has transcended particular communities, with their specificity and idiosyncrasy. In fact, what Revel's analysis reveals is not a distinction between international cuisine and regional cooking, but a racist, Eurocentric conception of what counts as good food and knowledgeable foodmaking.

That attention to community is an important aspect of a conception of inquiry as a thoughtful practice is evidenced by the variety of ways in which communities are addressed. It might be said that attention to community is a natural consequence of the rejection of a subject/object model for human activity; once we recognize the importance of the relations between foodmaker and food, we are led to reconsider the importance of other kinds of relations as well—relations among foodmakers, and among foodmakers and eaters, etc.

D. EMOTIONAL AND EROTIC KNOWLEDGE

Growing and preparing food are activities which often require and generate emotional and erotic energy—and which see such emotion and eroticism as vital to the activity. In contrast to the received view of theory and practice, which tends to divorce reason from emotion and eroticism,[28] a transformed conception of foodmaking practices views them as thoughtful practices in which these forms of interaction are interrelated and mutually constitutive.

Grosvenor and Lorde, in particular, describe cooking in ways that highlight its emotional and erotic elements. Dispassionate objectivity, the standard for scientific inquiry, is not the ideal in cooking; good cooking is good in part because of the emotional attachment you have to the people for whom you're cooking, to the tools you're using, and to the foods you're making.

For Grosvenor, cooking is a form of love, one of the most powerful of all forms.[29] "So, if you cook with love and feed people, you got two forces cooled out already" (296*). Food is sustenance; for Grosvenor, this claim transcends nutrition in the narrow, scientific sense of that word: "Food changes into blood, blood into cells, cells change into energy which changes up into life and since your life style is imaginative, creative, loving, energetic, serious, food is life" (296*). For Grosvenor, the love and energy you put into your cooking come out in the form of love and energy in the person for whom you cook.

In Lorde's description of pounding spice—rich with details about the ingredients used and the mortar and pestle with which she pounded—food preparation becomes an erotic event. For Lorde, the concept of the erotic carries particular significance. In a suggestive if speculative essay entitled "Uses of the Erotic," Lorde reclaims the notion, rejecting the falsified, often misogynistic conceptions of eroticism that equate it with pornography. She defines the erotic as "an assertion of the lifeforce of women; of that creative energy empowered, the knowledge and use of which we are now reclaiming" (55). The erotic is a source of power that "comes from sharing deeply any pursuit with another person," and serves as an "open and fearless underlining of my capacity for joy" (56).

In an evocative metaphor, Lorde describes the erotic as a kernel, like the kernel of food coloring one used to get with a packet of uncolored margarine: "We would leave the margarine out for a while to soften, and then we would pinch the little pellet to break it inside the bag, releasing the rich yellowness into the soft pale mass of margarine. Then taking it carefully between our fingers, we would knead it gently back and forth, over and over, until the color had spread throughout the whole pound bag of margarine" (57).

Pounding spice—the rhythmic action, the fragrant spices, the feel of the mortar and pestle in her hands, the anticipation of tasting the souse—is an erotic activity for Lorde. And on the day she begins to menstruate, this normally erotic experience assumes new dimensions: it is being performed by a body which holds within it "a tiding ocean of blood beginning to be made real and available to me for strength and information" (292*). Eroticism and information, feeling and knowing are intertwined for Lorde.

In exploring the erotic and emotional potential of foodmaking—and in expanding our conception of the erotic—these texts reveal another layer of the inadequacies of the traditional theory/practice account. They invite us to transform our own perceptions of everyday activities like cooking, washing dishes, and eating. And they encourage us to participate in those activities in ways that leave us open to their emotional, erotic potential.

V. CONCLUSION

In this essay, I've suggested one way in which to transform the theory/ practice distinction into a framework for human activity that will enable us to understand foodmaking activities as philosophically significant. By conceiving of foodmaking as a thoughtful practice, I've suggested, we can begin to appreciate the deep significance of these activities. But thinking about foodmaking alone clearly will not remove (philosophical or cultural) biases against it or undermine the sharp theory/practice dichotomy on which such biases rest. Nor is thinking about food an activity uniquely valuable as an end in itself. Certainly we must also *make food* if we are serious about transforming conceptions of the significance of foodmaking, and of practice more generally. By becoming involved with others in making food in respectful ways, one can begin to transform philosophical ignorance of and disrespect for foodmaking into philosophical understanding of, and involvement in it.

Notes

1. Of course Plato does talk about food preparation far more than most subsequent western philosophers; his writing is filled with references to butchers and pastry chefs, etc. But although he mentions foodmaking frequently, he also makes it clear that such activities always play at most a supporting role in the quest for genuine wisdom.

2. Of course not all of these labels would be used by all philosophers. Plato, for example, would not describe activities which involve knowledge as "head" or "mental work" (because for him the modern mind/body dichotomy does not exist), but he would call them "arts," to distinguish them from "crafts" or "knacks." Descartes, on the other hand, would speak of "mental" as opposed to "manual" activity, but would not refer to mental activity as "art." However, despite the fact that there is no single, essential distinction between theoretical and practical activities, and although philosophers characterize the distinction in many different ways, it is a distinction that threads its way through much of western philosophy, and has, in its various historical forms, significantly influenced those of us who are its inheritors. Thus I refer to Plato and Descartes not as figures whose work captures some common "essence" of the theory/practice distinction, but as two central philosophical figures whose thoughts on human activity have continued profoundly to affect contemporary (philosophical and nonphilosophical) conceptions of human activity.

3. In considering the differences between theoretical and practical, mental and manual activity, it is important to keep in mind that the distinction is not a hard-and-fast distinction between activities using the hands and those involving only the mind. Rather, theoretical activities are those in which hand work is subservient to head work, the "truly theoretical" aspects of the activity. Activities defined as theoretical may have a practical component, but it plays a supporting role only.

Many, if not most, theoretical activities have such a physical component. One of the theoretical arts Plato often discusses is medicine, which clearly involves physical activity. And Descartes emphasizes the role of scientific experimentation—hand work—in achieving metaphysical certainty. Both philosophers, however, stress the primacy of the theoretical or mental aspect of these activities, and both also emphasize that the "purest" examples of knowing are those most completely removed from practice (mathematics, the dialectic)—therefore those in which our bodies are least involved.

4. The phrase "supports and is supported by" is intended to convey the notion that causality in effect runs in both directions here. That is, I am claiming that the philosophical distinction between head work and hand work is partly responsible for social hierarchies that privilege head workers, but I am also claiming that those social hierarchies are partly responsible for the philosophical distinction. In effect, the two systems have grown up alongside each other, each one serving as a support for the other. I shall use this notion of mutual causality at various points in my account.

5. That is, those who engage in work that is defined as manual labor are also those who generally are regarded as less than fully human by a society. Thus the slave woman working in the cotton fields of antebellum Mississippi, the Chicano migrant worker family picking fruit in Washington State today, and the white homemaker canning green beans in 1950s suburbia all are, to some degree, regarded as less than fully human because of the labor in which they engage. They are relegated to these kinds of labor, however, *because* they are regarded as less than fully human.

6. As we mentioned in the general introduction to the book, our treatment of the western philosophical tradition might be described as viewing philosophy as culture. That is, philosophical categories such as the subject/object dichotomy have seeped into other domains of western culture, and have even become "common sense" for some people. Thus in describing the way inquiry is regarded, my account here utilizes historical philosophical figures not primarily to summarize the history of philosophy's treatment of the nature of inquiry, but to provide a sketch of the way particular historical conceptions of the nature of inquiry function at the level of popular culture, common sense, etc.

7. Many feminists have written critiques of the subject/object model of inquiry from a variety of disciplinary and theoretical perspectives. See, for example, Anzaldúa 1987; Frye 1983; Griffin 1978; Harding 1977, 1978, 1981, 1982 and 1986; Keller 1983 and 1985; Jaggar 1983; and Smith 1979 and 1987.

8. Even in "emanation" theories of vision, such as the theory held by Plato, the subject and the object do not directly meet/touch each other; rather, their "emanations" meet at some intermediate point. Here, too, the separateness of substances is preserved.

9. In their essay "The Mind's Eye," Evelyn Fox Keller and Christine Grontkowski (1985) address this issue—and show how ocular imagery is used to explain both the separation between inquirer and inquired that is required for objectivity, and the connection between them that is required for knowledge.

10. As evidence of the degree to which this thinking has become "common sense" for at least some westerners, I mention the kind of conversation that frequently goes on in my introductory epistemology classes. When confronted with the possibility that nothing is unchanging, students often willingly conclude that then nothing is knowable either. For these students—most of whom have grown up on a diet of both "scientific laws" and mainstream Protestant theology—the connection between eternality and knowability is quite unambiguous.

11. "In order then that disease might not quickly destroy us, and lest our mortal race should perish without fulfilling its end—intending to provide against this, the gods made what is called the lower belly, to be a receptacle for the superfluous meat and drink, and formed the convolution of the bowels, so that the food might

be prevented from passing quickly through and compelling the body to require more food, thus producing insatiable gluttony and making the whole race an enemy to philosophy and culture, and rebellious against the distinct element within us" (1953, 72e–73a). Note that Plato suggests that a physiological makeup which required frequent eating would actually constitute *gluttony*—a moral state.

Earlier in that section, Plato also explains the location of the intestines—and of the appetitive part of the soul—thus:

> The part of the soul which desires meats and drinks and the other things of which it has need by reason of the bodily nature, they [the gods] placed between the midriff and the boundary of the navel. . . . They appointed this lower creature his place here in order that he might always be feeding at the manger, and have his dwelling as far as might be from the council chamber, making as little noise and disturbance as possible, and permitting the best part to advise quietly for the good of the whole and the individual. (70e)

12. Frequently, such jobs are made to be more horrible—more repetitive, boring, and often dangerous—than need be. One assumption that seems to operate is that such work is *intrinsically* uninteresting and therefore incapable of being made pleasant, safe, fulfilling—thus the assembly line poultry-processing plant, cannery, frozen-food factory. Such work is assigned to the most disempowered members of the society. Since those who do this work are those with the least access to legal counsel, the media, or others who might take their complaints seriously, factories often operate with little risk that their owners will be held responsible for having created monotonous, debilitating and dangerous jobs.

13. We may be *entirely* unmindful of the cycle of plant-cultivate-harvest-sell that governs the lives of farm workers. See "The Pleasures of Eating" in Section Four for a discussion of the ways in which American consumers are divorced from the agricultural aspects of food.

14. Of course my analysis of American eating habits here ignores the "yuppie" trend of buying expensive food preparation equipment and cooking "to relieve stress." While I don't condemn such practices, it seems to me that most of their practitioners have not made cooking anything like an ordinary, integral part of their lives. Rather, it is something they do as therapy, as a special treat, or for special occasions.

15. It might be more correct to say that only certain things about the product—namely physical appearances—matter. The apples in the pie can be tasteless, so long as they can be cut easily and cleanly, and so long as the pie is before us in the time it takes a food service worker to bag it.

16. One can see the connections between this notion of hunger—potentially dangerous if not held in check by reason—and the anorexic's conception of her hunger, as described by Bordo and Chernin in Section One.

17. Naomi Scheman reminded me of this phrase, and suggested its appropriateness to a philosophical context.

18. There are scores of works that undertake such projects. See, for a few examples, Aptheker 1989; Harding and Hintikka 1983; Hoagland 1988; Jaggar 1983; Jaggar and Bordo 1989; Smith 1979 and 1987; Young 1990. See also various issues of *Hypatia: A Journal of Feminist Philosophy,* and the *American Philosophical Association Newsletter on Feminism and Philosophy.*

19. In this passage, Smith speaks directly to the experiences of (some) women. Men who are servants, workers, etc., also can be said to occupy the bodily mode, and to mediate for ruling-class men, though the activities through which they do this would usually be different from those assigned to women.

20. It was for Plato. But after Renaissance Europe, it cannot be thought of as

such. See the following section on Dewey for more about the transformation of certain physical activities into head work.

21. Indeed, this passage really focuses on two "personality types" or "attitudes" as much as on theoretical and practical activity per se. In point of fact, the philosophical distinction between theory and practice does reside in the commonsense attitudes we hold about human personalities. That is, although the distinction carries tremendous philosophical baggage, it is also a distinction which colors our ordinary life to a tremendous degree.

22. 314–15. See *also The Quest for Certainty,* p. 245, for a similar discussion.

23. The fact that the position is self-consistent does not of course make it immune to criticism. We might still ask why chance and change—and the activities connected with them—are accorded inferior ontological and epistemological status in the first place for the Greeks.

24. This might be an appropriate moment to explain the spirit in which my criticism of Dewey is raised. I see myself as extending the scope of Dewey's project in ways that were perhaps unforeseen and unforeseeable by him. I do so in the spirit of Dewey himself, who, I believe, would approve of my questioning his unquestioned assumptions. Dewey did not regard his own philosophy as a set of inviolable tenets, and he would be suspicious of those who would treat it as such.

25. See the introductory essay to Section Four for a fuller discussion of the ways in which a subject/object dichotomy serves oppressive and exploitative social and political systems.

26. Another element of thoughtful practices that I do not investigate here, but which is also clearly important, is their temporality. I've already suggested that the traditional distinction between theoretical and practical activity is formed in part on the basis of a distinction between activities "caught in time," such as foodmaking, and activities which "transcend time," such as contemplation of eternal truths. A conception of thoughtful practice might begin from the assertion that this is a specious distinction, and go on to explore the ways in which foodmaking and eating situate us in temporal reality. Such a discussion would be particularly useful for augmenting and complementing the assertion that thoughtful practices are embodied.

27. For a hilarious account of the consequences of attempting to make cooking "scientific" see *Perfection Salad,* which documents the emergence of the "domestic science" movement in turn-of-the-century United States.

28. One important exception to this generalization is Plato, who in the *Phaedo* describes knowing using the metaphor of lover and beloved. For a full discussion of this, and other aspects of the historical relation between reason and emotions, see Jaggar 1989.

29. There are interesting connections, which cannot be explored here, between her account of cooking and the account Evelyn Fox Keller gives of the way Barbara McClintock does science; for McClintock, inquiry is a form of love. See *A Feeling for the Organism.*

REFERENCES

Anzaldúa, Gloria. *Borderlands/La Frontera: The New Mestiza.* San Francisco: Spinsters/Aunt Lute, 1987.

Aptheker, Bettina. *Tapestries of Life: Women's Work, Women's Consciousness, and the Meaning of Daily Experience*. Amherst: University of Massachusetts Press, 1989.

Descartes, René. *The Philosophical Writings of Descartes,* vol. II. Trans. John Cottingham, Robert Stoothoff, Dugald Murdoch. Cambridge: Cambridge University Press, 1984.

Dewey, John. "An Added Note as to the 'Practical.' " *Essays in Experimental Logic.* Chicago: University of Chicago Press, 1916.

_____. *Experience and Nature*. New York: Dover, 1958.

_____. *The Quest for Certainty*. New York: Perigee, 1980.

Frye, Marilyn. *The Politics of Reality: Essays in Feminist Theory.* Trumansburg, NY: Crossing Press, 1983.

Griffin, Susan. *Woman and Nature: The Roaring Inside Her.* New York: Harper and Row, 1978.

Harding, Sandra. "Does Objectivity in the Social Sciences Require Value Neutrality?" *Sounding* 60 (1977):351–366.

_____. "Four Contributions Values Can Make to a Conception of Rationality." *PSA* 1978, vol. 1. Ed. Peter Asquith and Ian Hacking. East Lansing: Philosophy of Science Association, 1981.

_____. "Is Gender a Variable in Conceptions of Rationality? A Survey of the Issues." *Dialectica* 36 (1982):225–241.

_____. "The Norms of Social Inquiry and Masculine Experience." *PSA* 1980. Ed Peter Asquith and Ronald Giere. East Lansing: Philosophy of Science Association, 1981.

_____. *The Science Question in Feminism.* Ithaca: Cornell University Press, 1986.

_____, and Merrill B. Hintikka, eds. *Discovering Reality: Feminist Perspectives on Epistemology, Metaphysics, Methodology, and Philosophy of Science.* Dordrecht: D. Reidel, 1983.

Hoagland, Sarah Lucia. *Lesbian Ethics: Toward New Value.* Palo Alto: Institute of Lesbian Studies, 1988.

Jacobus, Mary, Evelyn Fox Keller, and Sally Shuttleworth, eds. *Body/Politics: Women and the Discourses of Science.* New York: Routledge, 1990.

Jaggar, Alison. *Feminist Politics and Human Nature.* Totowa, NJ: Rowman and Allanheld, 1983.

_____. "Love and Knowledge: Emotion in Feminist Epistemology." *Gender/Body/Knowledge,* ed. Jaggar and Susan Bordo. New Brunswick: Rutgers University Press, 1989.

_____, and Susan Bordo, ed. *Gender/Body/Knowledge: Feminist Reconstructions of Being and Knowing.* New Brunswick: Rugters University Press, 1989.

Keller, Evelyn Fox. *A Feeling for the Organism: The Life and Work of Barbara McClintock.* New York: W.H. Freeman, 1983.

_____. *Reflections on Gender and Science.* New Haven: Yale University Press, 1985.

_____, and Christine Grontkowski. "The Mind's Eye." *Discovering Reality: Feminist Perspectives on Epistemology, Metaphysics, Methodology and Philosophy of Science.* Ed. Sandra Harding and Merrill B. Hintikka. Synthese Library, vol. 161. Dordrecht: D. Reidel, 1983.

Lorde, Audre. "Uses of the Erotic: The Erotic as Power." *Sister Outsider.* Trumansburg, NY: Crossing Press, 1984.

Plato. *Phaedo.* 1954. Trans. Hugh Tredennick. *The Collected Dialogues,* ed. Edith Hamilton and Huntington Cairns. Princeton: Princeton University Press, 1961.

_____. *Republic.* 1930. Trans. Paul Shorey. *The Collected Dialogues,* ed. Edith Hamilton and Huntington Cairns. Princeton: Princeton University Press, 1961.

_____. *Timaeus.* 1953. Trans. Benjamin Jowett. *The Collected Dialogues,* ed. Edith Hamilton and Huntington Cairns. Princeton: Princeton University Press, 1961.

Shapiro, Laura. *Perfection Salad: Women and Cooking at the Turn of the Century.* New York: Henry Holt, 1986.

Smith, Dorothy. "A Sociology for Women." *The Prism of Sex: Essays in the Sociology of Knowledge.* Ed. Julia A. Sherman and Evelyn T. Beck. Madison: University of Wisconsin Press, 1979.

————. *The Everyday World as Problematic.* Boston: Northeastern University Press, 1987.

Young, Iris Marion. *Throwing Like a Girl and Other Essays in Feminist Philosophy and Social Theory.* Bloomington: Indiana University Press, 1990.

from *Gorgias*

POLUS: Answer me, Socrates. Since Gorgias seems to you at a loss regarding the nature of rhetoric, what do you say it is?

SOCRATES: Are you asking what art I hold it to be?

POLUS: I am.

SOCRATES: To tell you the truth, Polus, no art at all.

POLUS: But what do you think rhetoric is?

SOCRATES: Something of which you claim to have made an art in your treatise which I recently read.

POLUS: What do you mean?

SOCRATES: I call it a kind of routine.

POLUS: Then you think rhetoric is a routine?

SOCRATES: Subject to your approval, I do.

POLUS: What kind of routine?

SOCRATES: One that produces gratification and pleasure.

POLUS: Then you do not think rhetoric a fine thing, if it can produce gratification among men?

SOCRATES: What, Polus? Have you already learned from me what I consider rhetoric to be, that you proceed to ask if I do not think it a fine thing?

POLUS: Have I not learned that you call it a kind of routine?

SOCRATES: Well, since you prize gratification so highly, will you gratify me to a small extent?

POLUS: I will.

SOCRATES: Then ask me what kind of art I consider cookery.

POLUS: I will. What art is cookery?

SOCRATES: No art, Polus.

POLUS: Then what is it? Tell me.

SOCRATES: In my opinion, a kind of routine.

POLUS: Tell me, what routine?

SOCRATES: One that produces gratification and pleasure, I claim, Polus.

POLUS: Then cookery and rhetoric are identical?

SOCRATES: By no means, but each is a part of the same activity.

POLUS: And what is that?

SOCRATES: I am afraid it may sound unmannerly to tell the truth, and I hesitate for fear that Gorgias may think I am caricaturing his profession. For my part, I do not know whether this is the rhetoric that Gorgias practices—for we reached no definite conclusion in our recent argument as to his opinion—but what I mean by rhetoric is part of an activity that is not very reputable.

GORGIAS: What is it, Socrates? Tell us and feel no scruples about me.

SOCRATES: Well then, Gorgias, the activity as a whole, it seems to me, is not an art, but the occupation of a shrewd and enterprising spirit, and of one naturally skilled in its dealing with men, and in sum and substance I call it 'flattery.' Now it seems to me that there are many other parts of this activity, one of which is cookery. This is considered an art, but in my judgment is no art, only a routine and a knack. And rhetoric I call another part of this general activity, and beautification, and sophistic—four parts with four distinct objects. Now if Polus wishes to question me, let him do so, for he has not yet ascertained what part of flattery I call rhetoric. He does not realize that I have not yet answered him, but proceeds to ask if I do not think it something fine. But I shall not answer whether I consider rhetoric a fine thing or a bad until I have first answered what it is. For that is not right, Polus. Then if you wish to question me, ask me what part of flattery I claim rhetoric to be.

POLUS: I will then; answer, what part?

SOCRATES: I wonder whether you will understand my answer. Rhetoric in my opinion is the semblance of a part of politics.

POLUS: Well then, do you call it good or bad?

SOCRATES: Bad—for evil things I call bad—if I must answer you as though you already understood what I mean.

GORGIAS: Why, Socrates, even I myself do not grasp your meaning.

SOCRATES: Naturally enough, Gorgias, for I have not yet clarified my statement. But Polus here, like a foal, is young and fighty.

GORGIAS: Well, let him alone, and tell me what you mean by saying that rhetoric is the semblance of a part of politics.

SOCRATES: I will try to explain to you my conception of rhetoric, and if it is wrong, Polus will refute me. You admit the existence of bodies and souls?

GORGIAS: Of course.

SOCRATES: And do you not consider that there is a healthy condition for each?

GORGIAS: I do.

SOCRATES: And a condition of apparent, but not real health? For example, many people appear to be healthy of body, and no one could perceive they are not so, except a doctor or some physical trainer.

GORGIAS: That is true.

SOCRATES: There exists, I maintain, both in body and in soul, a condition which creates an impression of good health in each case, although it is false.

GORGIAS: That is so.

SOCRATES: Let me see now if I can explain more clearly what I mean. To the pair, body and soul, there correspond two arts—that concerned with the soul I call the political art; to the single art that relates to the body I cannot give a name offhand. But this single art that cares for the body comprises two parts, gymnastics and medicine, and in the political art what corresponds to gymnastics is legislation, while the counterpart of medicine is justice. Now in each case the two arts encroach upon each other, since their fields are the same, medicine upon gymnastics, and justice upon legislation; nevertheless there is a difference between them. There are then these four arts which always minister to what is best, one pair for the body, the other for the soul. But flattery perceiving this—I do not say by knowledge but by conjecture—has divided herself also into four branches, and insinuating herself into the guise of each of these parts, pretends to be that which she impersonates. And having no thought for what is best, she regularly uses pleasure as a bait to catch folly and deceives it into believing that she is of supreme worth. Thus it is that cookery has impersonated medicine and pretends to know the best foods for the body, so that, if a cook and a doctor had to contend in the presence of children or of men as senseless as children, which of the two, doctor or cook, was an expert in wholesome and bad food, the doctor would starve to death. This then I call a form of flattery, and I claim that this kind of thing is bad—I am now addressing you, Polus—because it aims at what is pleasant, ignoring the good, and I insist that it is not an art but a routine, because it can produce no principle in virtue of which it offers what it does, nor explain the nature thereof, and consequently is unable to point to the cause of each thing it offers. And I refuse the name of art to anything irrational. But if you have any objections to lodge, I am willing to submit to further examination.

Cookery then, as I say, is a form of flattery that corresponds to medicine, and in the same way gymnastics is personated by beautification, a mischievous, deceitful, mean, and ignoble activity, which cheats us by shapes and colors, by smoothing and draping, thereby causing people to take on an alien charm to the neglect of the natural beauty produced by exercise.

To be brief, then, I will express myself in the language of geometricians—for by now perhaps you may follow me. Sophistic is to legislation what beautification is to gymnastics, and rhetoric to justice what cookery is to medicine. But, as I say, while there is this natural distinction between them, yet because they are closely related, Sophist and rhetorician, working in the same sphere and upon the same subject matter, tend to be confused with each other, and they know not what to make of each other, nor do others know what to make of them. For if the body was under the control, not of the soul, but of itself, and if cookery and medicine were not investigated and distinguished by the soul, but the body instead gave the verdict, weighing them by the bodily pleasures they offered, then the principle of Anaxagoras would everywhere hold good—that is something you know about, my dear Polus—and all things would be mingled in indiscriminate confusion, and medicine and health and cookery would be indistinguishable.

Well, now you have heard my conception of rhetoric. It is the counterpart in the soul of what cookery is to the body.

The Perfect Pie

Hi, it's Uncle Al again. I've been lying awake nights worrying about yet another of mankind's towering achievements: the piece of pie in a cardboard box.

Perhaps you are not familiar with this amazing phenomenon. Might I suggest a visit to a nearby Burger King? It is amazing enough to open a sealed box and find a nice, warm piece of apple pie in there, but in this sophisticated age we're used to minor miracles like that.

What is truly mind-boggling is the *condition* of that piece of pie. Think about this. What would you expect to happen if *you* tried to cut a piece of apple pie and drop it into a pie-shaped cardboard box hardly any larger than the piece of pie?

In fact, not to get too personal, what would you expect to happen if you tried to cut a piece of apple pie and just get it out of the pan? Let's be frank: Most pieces of pie served in this country—even by professional pie servers at professional pie shops—are at least a little uneven or dribbly around the edges. Some pieces of pie served at home have considerably less architectural integrity than that.

But look at *this* pie—especially the edges. Each is sliced absolutely evenly. The lattice crust comes up to that straight line, and each piece of the lattice stops as if it had hit a . . . an . . . I don't know what! And that's the point. The crust not only stops clean, it isn't even crumbled.

And the filling stops at the same perfect edge. Not a bit of apple, not a drop of goo sticks out to mar that perfect wall. And it's been inserted flawlessly into a box, to boot!

If I can't do that, and you (I assume) can't do that, and Sadie over at the cafe can't do that, then how does Burger King do that?

I must confess that I am often somewhat embarrassed to ask these silly questions of the truly important people who are movers and shakers at the powerful companies involved. I mean, who knows what moving and/or shaking I am interrupting.

I have never been condescended to in these quests for minor knowledge, but I am aware that could happen, so when I sought someone who could provide perspective to this pie puzzle, I was prepared to explain that I knew it wasn't important.

I was not at all prepared for the answer I ultimately received:

It's a trade secret.

When Jack Tidwell, an executive at Edwards Baking Co. in Atlanta, maker of those pies for Burger King, told me that, I giggled. *Really?*

"Would I lie to you?" Tidwell responded. Actually, since I hadn't met him, I didn't know. I was kind of hoping that he had, a little, maybe, and would then get to the answer. I pressed a bit.

"Well," he responded, "how about if I say, 'With a knife'?"

Cute, but not very helpful. "Then let's just say that it's a special pie-slicing machine that we developed."

Perhaps we can approach it another way. I assume that part of the reason the pie looks unscathed is that it goes into the carton before the carton is folded up, but. . . .

No, Tidwell said, although the cartons do arrive flat, a special machine forms the bottom of the carton; then the pie is inserted.

That's even more unbelievable. *I* might try to do it that way, once, but I would surely get pie all over and really mess things up. This pie looks as if it has been sliced with a laser.

"I *can* tell you this," Tidwell said. (Oh boy, I thought, here it comes—the sizzling secret of snazzy slicing.) "It's not a laser."

Amazing! This guy is willing to tell me less about how Burger King pie is cut than the Pentagon and NASA leaked about the supersecret spy satellite that was launched on the Atlantis space shuttle!

The $500 million imaging radar satellite, released in a 240-mile-high orbit that crosses the Equator at an angle of 57 degrees, is able to penetrate cloud cover and monitor military operations in Eastern Europe and approximately 80 percent of the Soviet Union.

The pie is cut using a special machine.

Only in America.

from *Probabilistic Metaphysics*

MODEL OF JUSTIFIED PROCEDURES

The Aristotelian model of rationality centers around the giving of good reasons for actions. The main texts about these matters are to be found in the *Nicomachean Ethics,* but important and significant remarks are to be found in *De Motu Animalium* and some other of Aristotle's writings as well. From a formal standpoint, Aristotle's concept of the practical syllogism is meant to provide for reasoning about actions the analogue of the theory of reasoning about knowledge embodied in the concept of the theoretical syllogism developed especially in the *Prior Analytics.* There is rather substantial literature on how the practical syllogism should be thought about in modern terms. For example, should the conclusion be thought of as being an action or a proposition? It is not my purpose here to review the ins and outs of this literature, which, in spite of its subtlety in the treatment of many points, does not get very far from a systematic standpoint.

There is, I think, a richer and better model in Greek thought that does not seem to have been much discussed but that I want to use, properly modernized of course, and that I think still catches much of the general spirit of the Aristotelian model. As already indicated, I have entitled the model that of justified procedures. The idea is that good reasons are given for the procedures we invoke. In the spirit of much recent philosophical literature, I could have used the phrase *model of justified actions,* but as will become clear I have deliberately chosen *procedure* to link the concept I have in mind both to ancient mathematical distinctions and the concept of a procedure in contemporary psychology and computer science.

The relevant Greek mathematical distinction corresponds only roughly to Aristotle's distinction between theoretical and practical syllogisms. It is the distinction in Euclid between problems and theorems. It is a distinction made by many other Greek mathematicians and commented upon extensively by Proclus. Although the Greek term is *problama* and there is therefore little excuse for not translating it as *problem,* the concept of what is intended is more easily understood in our terms if we think of the contrast between theorems and constructions. A theorem asserts something that is true of a given type of figure or combination of figures. A problem of construction, on the other hand, poses something that must be done, for example, to give a procedure "on a given finite straight line to construct an equilateral triangle," which is proposition 1, book 1, of Euclid. The solution of a problem naturally has two parts. One is to give the construction itself and the second is to prove that the construction is correct. Characteristically in Euclid, the proof that a construction is correct is concluded by saying "being what it was required to do." In such a proof the construction and the justification are given hand in hand. On the other hand, in the case of a theorem the characteristic closing of the proof is to say "being what it was required to prove."

One of the important features of Euclid's intertwining of problems and theorems as occurs throughout the *Elements* is that, although there is a sharp conceptual distinction between problems and theorems, the justification of each proceeds along very similar lines. There is no general distinction in the methods of proof that constructions are correct and theorems valid. Such a close intertwining of practice and theory, to use the implicit Aristotelian distinction, seems natural and straightforward in the case of a highly focused subject like geometry. The issue is complex and subtle, however, when we turn to more general questions of rational action. In the first place, it is a mistake to contrast the theoretical syllogism as dealing with theoretical scientific knowledge and the practical syllogism as dealing with practical actions, as the proper model, at least from the viewpoint I am advocating. But the question still remains for either facts or procedures in the case of a practical domain of action: can we give a proof of correctness? What is important here is that it is not the distinction between procedures or theoretical knowledge that is critical but whether the domain itself will support justification in the sense of proof for either knowledge or procedures.

On the other hand, the Euclidean example can itself be misleading in talking about most cases of justified procedures because the completeness of proof of correctness from a few basic axioms hardly ever obtains. In one sense, in comparing Aristotle and Euclid we seem to be faced with a dilemma. Aristotle's examples all seem trivial and rather uninteresting in terms of their content. The Euclidean examples, on the other hand, are interesting and nontrivial but far too restricted in character and use a methodology of proof that we scarcely believe possible to emulate in most domains of experience.

For these and other reasons it seems desirable to look at a number of different kinds of examples of procedures with and without intuitively adequate justification. I also want to emphasize that justified procedures are a matter of importance in every substantive area of experience.

Recipes as procedures.

One of the places where we can find nontrivial procedures that almost everyone has some experience with is in a subject of universal interest,

cooking. It is also possible to accept that we have a good intuitive understanding of the goal of the procedure, namely, the preparation of food of a
certain quality and taste, even if the standards of evaluation may not always
be completely and explicitly verbalized.

Let us begin with an example drawn from a book that is full of highly
codified recipes without any justification of the procedures given at all, *An
Encyclopedia of Chinese Food and Cooking,* by Winona W. and Irving B.
Chang and Helene W. and Austin H. Kutscher (1970). As a typical recipe, I
pick the one for stir-fried beef with broccoli (p. 358):

A. 2 tablespoons peanut oil.	H. 1 teaspoon cornstarch
B. 2 tablespoons salted black beans	I. teaspoon light soy sauce
C. ½ clove garlic, minced	J. 2 teaspoons sherry
D. 1 to 2 slices ginger, minced	K. ½ teaspoon sugar
E. ½ teaspooon salt	L. 1 bunch fresh broccoli
F. 1 lb flank steak	M. 2 teaspoons cornstarch
G. 1 teaspoon peanut oil	N. 2 tablespoons heavy soy sauce

Preparation
  I Slice F into ⅛-inch, bite-size pieces.
 II Mix G, H, I, J, K and marinate F in mixture 15 minutes.
III Mix B, C, D, E. Set aside.
 IV Slice stems of L diagonally into 1½ inch segments, splitting heavier
     stems. Parboil stems 2 minutes and set aside.
  V Mix M, N. Stir well before using.

Cooking
 1. Put A in very hot skillet and bring to high heat
 2. Add B–E mixture and stir-fry rapidly 15 seconds to brown garlic
    slightly.
 3. Add F and G–K and stir-fry until F is nearly done but remains rare on
    inside.
 4. Add L. Stir-fry 15 seconds.
 5. Add M–N mixture slowly. Stir-fry until sauce thickens and coats all
    ingredients well.

The hundreds of recipes in this book are admirably clear in terms of the
procedures to be followed. They are all written in this style, but there is no
justification of individual steps or of the choice of ingredients. On the
other hand, at the beginning of the volume there are brief sections on
Chinese cuisine, utensils for cooking, serving, and eating, a general discussion of cooking preparations and cooking techniques, and a guide to ingredients. What is totally missing is any attempt to justify individual steps in a
-recipe.

Staying with Chinese cuisine for the moment, a strong contrast is to be found in the book *How to Cook and Eat in Chinese* by Buwei Yang Chao (1963). Let me quote her recipe for redcooked whole pork shoulder (p. 52):

1 whole shoulder or fresh ham, 6–8 lbs with skin and bone on	1 cup soy sauce
2 cups cold water	1 tbsp. sugar
¼ cup sherry	2 or 3 slices fresh ginger (if you can get it)

Leave the whole fresh ham or shoulder with skin and bones on just as it is bought. After washing outside, cut a few long slashes on the sides where there is no skin (so that the sauce will seep in more easily when cooking). Place your shoulder in a heavy pot with the 2 cups water. Turn on big fire and cover pot. When it boils, add the sherry, soy sauce, and maybe ginger. Cover the pot tight again. Change to very low fire and cook for one hour. Then turn skin side down. Still with low fire cook for another hour. After this, add sugar and cook again for another ½ or 1 hour (2½ or 3 hours altogether, depending on the tenderness of the meat bought).

To test your cooking, stick a fork or chopstick through the meat. It is done when the stick goes through very easily. If not, cook over low fire a little longer. Make allowances of course that the prongs of a fork are sharper than most chopsticks.

On second serving, as must be done in a small family, it can be warmed over or eaten cold. Warm over low fire so you won't burn the bottom. When eating cold, it is stiffer and can be cut into more chewsome slices, with the jelly. (Save the fat on the top for making other dishes.)

Note the tendency to give justifications at various points, for example, in the parenthetical phrase "so that the sauce will seep in more easily when cooking" or, in the last paragraphs, the reason for warming over a low fire "so you won't burn the bottom" and in the last phrase one should save the fat "for making other dishes."

Note also another feature of this recipe. It is to provide tests that, if satisfied, show that a goal or a subgoal has been accomplished and, if not, how to proceed. The example here is in the passage: "To test your cooking, stick a fork or chopstick through the meat. It is done when the stick goes through very easily. If not, cook over low fire a little longer." Here it is understood that one of the goals of the recipe is to make the meat tender.

Finally, as a third example let me quote from an Italian cookbook by Marcella Hazan (1977) that my wife and I particularly like. I want to quote some passages from the recipe for *Ossobuco alla milanese*. Because of the length of the recipe I have only selected certain passages. In the first paragraph she says: "The hind shanks are better than the front ones for *ossobuco* because they are meatier and more tender." Notice this justification for selecting the hind shanks. She also suggests tests where appropriate, for example, "When the oil is quite hot (test it with the corner of one of the pieces of veal; a moderate sizzle means the heat is just right), brown the veal on all sides." As part of that same instruction about heating the oil, she also has the following, just after the sentence quoted above: "(Brown the veal as soon as it has been dipped in flour, otherwise the flour may dampen and the meat won't brown properly.)" The force of the *otherwise* is to justify the instruction for quickly browning the veal after it has been dipped in flour. A couple of paragraphs later, in talking about herbs and salt she says: "Hold off on salt until after cooking, if you are using canned beef broth. It is sometimes very salty." The last sentence provides the justification for the holding off. Finally, another implicit test procedure is found in the following two sentences: "The broth should come up to the top of the veal pieces. If it does not, add more." In our opinion, one of the great virtues of the Hazan book is the lucid justifications she gives for various recommended procedures.

Even in the cases of such excellent cookbooks as those of Chao and Hazan, we would not expect to find the kind of meticulous justification of each step found in Euclid. This is not a defect of these excellent cookbooks, but is appropriate to the procedures for preparing and cooking food. Of course it is not sufficient just to say that. We can also easily recognize that there is a profound difference in the two cases along the following important dimension. In the case of the geometry, each step is justified in a way that makes no further discussion or analysis of any kind appropriate, at least not within the confines of the subject matter as laid down by the axioms and postulates. (Fundamental investigations of the nature of space do properly challenge the Euclidean foundations, but these are very specialized enterprises that can be set aside in the present context.) In the case of cooking, on the other hand, the whole matter is very much more open-ended. There is not an intellectual regimentation of the subject. We do not have clearcut reasons to justify each step, and there would be a large amount of variation as well as debate about the proper formulation of each procedure. The variation here is not the kind to be found in Euclid. There are different ways of making the same construction, but here there are actually procedures that produce different results to obtain the same goal and there can be argument about the virtues of one procedure over another in terms of the outcome, quite apart from the question of which is more elegant or more efficient, an aspect of the geometrical constructions that could also be considered.

There will be a tendency on the part of many to make a separation between the problems of Euclid and the recipes I have cited along a traditional division between pure mathematics and practical art. I want to insist on the point that I think such a division is wrong. For purposes of administrative classification, the organization of universities, the awarding of degrees, etc., such divisions play a useful role, but I do not think they have any fundamental intellectual status. I think of the constructions of Euclid as being of the same sort as the recipes of Chao and Hazan. The subject is much better developed. We understand how to axiomatize geometrical constructions in a way that we do not understand how to axiomatize cooking, and it may very well be inappropriate even to seek for an axiomatization of cooking in the sense of axioms that lead to a justification of procedures. But in both cases we are being shown a procedure that we can use in the real world and that will lead to a specific concrete result when applied in a specific case. It is not to the point here to engage in a complicated argument about whether mathematics has a special a priori status. I think it does not. It seems to me especially true of the particular mathematical subject of plane geometry, which has so many practical applications, from carpentry to bridge-building.[1]

Rawls (1971, pp. 85–86) defines three kinds of procedural justice. Perfect procedural justice obtains when there is an independent criterion for judging the result and there is a procedure that in principle guarantees the just result. Imperfect procedural justice obtains when there is an independent criterion, but not necessarily a procedure to guarantee the desired result. Finally, pure procedural justice obtains when there is no independent criterion for judging the result, but there is a criterion for judging the fairness or correctness of the procedure itself.

It may be useful to see how well this tripartite division works with rational procedures as discussed here. Euclidean geometrical constructions exemplify perfect procedural rationality, for the fit between the desired result and the procedures used is exact. Practical geometry, e.g., surveying, cooking, and other practical arts, abound in examples of imperfect procedural rationality, because of the inevitable errors of measurement and variations in physical materials used. The Euclidean constructions are perfect only because of the high level of abstraction.

It is perhaps less clear what are the analogs of pure procedural justice. One reasonable candidate are recipes, not just for cooking, but in all the areas of activity for which how-to-do-it books are written. We may judge a recipe pure, but at the same time we can give no principled guarantee of the results obtained by using it. Experience validates the procedure but not the result. How probability comes into this picture is discussed in the next section.

Applications of procedures and probability.

When we look at geometry à la Euclid there seems to be no place for probability. There also seems to be no use of probabilistic concepts in the cooking recipes quoted, but there is a difference in the two cases. The recipes implicitly refer to *expected* results. Test procedures are also given for varying cooking times to get the desired tenderness, firmness, etc. The recipes are written at a more detailed level of application than is Euclid or similar geometry texts. Probability enters in terms of expectations when cooking, but where does it enter in geometry? At the level of abstraction of Euclid hardly at all, except in terms of mistakes in proofs. But when specific methods of application are considered, probabilities and expectations enter in a natural way, because the level of detail can be even more fine-grained than that of the recipes quoted. Here is an example of instructions for using dividers, which are compasses without a pen or pencil at the end of one leg. The passage is taken from a classic text on engineering drawing (French, 1941):

> The dividers are used for transferring measurements and for dividing lines into any number of equal parts. Facility in the use of this instrument is most essential, and quick and absolute control of its manipulation must be gained. It should be opened with one hand by pinching the chamfer with the thumb and second finger. This will throw it into correct position with the thumb and forefinger outside of the legs and the second and third fingers inside, with the head resting just above the second joint of the forefinger. . . . It is thus under perfect control, with the thumb and forefinger to close it and the other two to open it. This motion should be practiced until an adjustment to the smallest fraction can be made. In coming down to small divisions the second and third fingers must be gradually slipped out from between the legs while they are closed down upon them. Notice that the little finger is not used in manipulating the dividers. (p. 17)

Comparable detail in recipes would mean that they include directions for how to hold a skillet or a ladle, how to empty a pot, etc.

That the kind of manipulation of dividers described above is in practice never perfect is an obvious consequence of the continuous nature of the geometric quantities measured. In applications where it matters, a complicated and developed probabilistic theory of errors is used, e.g., in surveying. Instructions like those given above are intended to help reduce errors to a manageable level, but there is no illusion that errors can be eliminated.

I also emphasize that there are not two levels of geometry, the abstract and the concrete, or, in other familiar terms, the pure and the applied. There are many levels. An important feature of modern geometry has been to increase the level of abstraction found in Euclid. Perhaps the clearest and philosophically most satisfactory account of this view is the classic article of Tarski (1959). Clarity in the other direction is less standard. Geometrical procedures like other procedures can always be described by ever finer attention to detail. Probabilistic considerations enter more prominently as the level of detail increases. For example, we could expand upon the instruction for manipulating dividers given above by recommending how fast to move the dividers either in adjusting the radius or in moving from one fixed point to another. An actual path of motion that approximates the recommended one is most naturally viewed as a sample path of a certain continuous stochastic process. The refined study of important motor skills is properly conducted within such a stochastic framework.

Someone might claim that the execution of procedures by a computer constitutes an important class of counterexamples to what I am saying about how we execute procedures. The instructions are written, so it would be claimed, in a formal computer language, e.g., BASIC, FORTRAN or LISP, and their digital execution leaves no room for variation and thus no room for probability or error. But this claim is mistaken. As we enter into the details of the hardware, the digital view dissolves into a continuum of electromagnetic waves and pulses. Acceptable tolerance levels of variation are one of the most important features of hardware design, but the nature of the variation is no more described in any ultimate terms than is the variation of human motor skills. Expected hardware behavior is characterized carefully, along with less explicit tolerance bounds. Probabilistic variation within these limits is inevitable and accepted.

What I have said about the bottomless pit of detail raises at once a question about rationality. Is there an appropriate concept of rationality at every level of description and analysis? My answer should be apparent from what I have already said about procedures. In principle, there is a concept of rationality to match each level of detail. The explicit development of the concept, however, depends upon the demand or need for standards at the given level. The use of dividers by ordinary draftsmen is not monitored at a highly detailed level in order to obtain optimal results either in terms of accuracy or efficiency. Time-and-motion studies of assembly lines are often a different matter. Perhaps the best examples are in highly competitive sports where performance is measured on some simple quantitative dimension like time or distance. The best coaches study extraordinarily fine details of behavior in order to improve performance. Their constant recommendations for change always depend on an implicit criterion of rationality.

What I have just said also should make clear how I think the model of justified procedures can be joined without inconsistency to the model of expected utility, which I discuss at some considerable length later. The model of expected utility is formulated and analyzed at a high level of abstraction. The more detailed the level of analysis, the harder it is to apply in a genuine quantitative fashion. Justification of procedures in the sense of Aristotle and Euclid easily takes over. Then at some finer level still, verbal justification itself disappears, even though adjustments and improvements continue unceasingly. Adults, like children, are always in the process of learning and changing without knowing how or why. Verbal schemas of analysis and justification can rationally organize only the tip of the behavioral iceberg.

N O T E S

1. Practical geometry, closely associated with standard Euclidean geometry as its theoretical counterpart, has a long history going back to ancient times. A good

description of medieval treatises on practical geometry, their varying content, and their varying conceptions of rigor is to be found in Victor (1979).

R E F E R E N C E S

Archimedes. 1897. *On the Sphere and Cylinder.* Trans. T.L. Heath. Cambridge, England: Cambridge University Press.

———. 1897. *On the Equilibrium of Planes.* Trans. T.L. Heath. Cambridge, England: Cambridge University Press.

Aristotle. 1941. *Nichomachean Ethics.* New York: Random House.

———. 1966. *Posterior Analytics,* Loeb edition. Trans. H. Tredennick. Cambridge, MA: Harvard University Press.

———. 1967. *Prior Analytics,* Loeb edition. Trans. H. Tredennick. Cambridge, MA: Harvard University Press.

———. 1968. *Metaphysics,* Loeb edition. Translated by H. Tredennick. Cambridge, MA: Harvard University Press.

———. 1978. *De Motu Animalium.* Trans. P.H. Wickstead and F.M. Cornford. Cambridge, MA: Harvard University Press.

Chang, W.W. and I.B., and H.W. and A.H. Kutscher. 1970. *An Encyclopedia of Chinese Food and Cooking.* New York: Crown Publishers.

Chao, B.Y. 1963. *How to Cook and Eat in Chinese* (3d ed.). New York: Random House.

Euclid. 1926. *The Thirteen Books of Euclid's Elements.* Translated from the text of Heiberg with introduction and commentary by Sir Thomas L. Heath (2d ed.). Cambridge, England: Cambridge University Press.

———. 1945. *Optics.* Trans. H.E. Burton. *Journal of the Optical Society of America* 35, 357–372.

French, T.E. 1941. *A Manual of Engineering Drawing for Students and Draftsmen* (6th ed.). New York: McGraw-Hill.

Hazan, M. 1977. *The Classical Italian Cookbook.* New York: Alfred A. Knopf.

Hintikka, J., and U. Remes. 1974. *The Method of Analysis: Its Geometrical Origin and Its General Significance.* Dordrecht: Reidel.

Manin, Yu.I. 1979/1981. *Mathematics and Physics.* Trans. A. and N. Koblitz. Boston, MA: Birkhauser. (Originally published 1979.)

Nussbaum, M.C. 1978. *Aristotle's De Motu Animalium.* Princeton, NJ: Princeton University Press.

Ptolemy, C. 1952. *Almagest.* Trans. R.C. Taliaferro. Chicago, IL: Encyclopaedia Britannica.

Rawls, J. 1971. *A Theory of Justice.* Cambridge, MA: Harvard University Press.

Suppes, P. 1980. Procedural Semantics. In R. Haller and W. Grassl (eds.), *Pisa Conference Proceedings* (Vol. 1), pp. 197–213. Dordrecht: Reidel.

Tarski, A. 1959. What Is Elementary Geometry? In L. Henkin, P. Suppes, and A. Tarski (eds.), *The Axiomatic Method,* pp. 16–29. Amsterdam: North-Holland.

Victor, S.K. 1979. *Practical Geometry in the High Middle Ages. Artis Cuiuslibet consummatio and the Pratike de geometrie.* Philadelphia, PA: The American Philosophical Society.

JEAN-FRANCOIS   REVEL

from *Culture and Cuisine*

In gastronomy as in numerous other realms, history is indissociable from geography. The reader has doubtless been struck by the fact that beginning with the middle of the seventeenth century the author of the present book seems to have dealt exclusively with French cuisine, and doubtless he has attributed this predominance to the fact that the author is French.

But even though the last two chapters have been concerned almost entirely with French cuisine, the cause for this is not some sort of culinary nationalism. The author is, certainly, sensitive to the fact that gastronomy is one of the domains in which chauvinism and even parochialism make themselves felt in the most naïve and sometimes the most intolerant way. As Montaigne long ago pointed out, everyone is attached to the food habits of his childhood and finds himself inclined to consider foreign foods and ways of preparing them absurd and even disgusting. A Frenchman today is shocked by the mixture of the sweet and the salt to be found in certain present-day German dishes or in the classic mint sauce, made of mint added to unrefined sugar or white granulated sugar and diluted in vinegar, that sometimes accompanies lamb in English cuisine. This Frenchman has forgotten that barely two or three centuries ago, sugar, as we have seen, entered into numerous salted meat or fish dishes in French cuisine or, more precisely, in the medieval European tradition.[1] Similarly, a Frenchman today would consider it barbarous to be served watered wine in a carafe, and adding water to the wine in your glass is quite likely to make you the butt of gibes from the other guests at table. Yet—and here again it is Montaigne who tells us so—this was the usual practice in the sixteenth century, and doubtless remained so for a long time, indeed, until very recently among peasants. In Montaigne's day, drinking one's wine straight was considered to be, and in fact was, a German custom. The author of the *Essays* cites it as an exotic bit of behavior that the intelligent man should not laugh at when he travels abroad on the mere ground that it is different from his own habit. In point of fact, it could be said, to settle the debate, if a rational criterium can be said to apply in the realm of habit, which is by definition irrational, that today little local wines without a bouquet lend themselves to and even gain by being diluted with a little water, though obviously such a thing is out of the question in the case of great Burgundies, great Bourdeaux, and cooked wine.

To come back to what we were saying, if the two preceding chapters have been devoted to French cuisine, this is due to the fact that this cuisine was unquestionably the area in which a historic change took place in the eighteenth century. This change was to bear definite fruit at the beginning of the nineteenth century, after which revisions, reforms, improvements, and degenerescences were to take place within a given framework, but there was no longer to be any radical revolution.[2] In reality, this French cuisine whose historical development I have traced, is what I will refer to, following convention, as *international* cuisine. I in no way mean by that (happily!) that French cuisine as such invaded the entire world, for an equivalent movement in the opposite direction also took place and a certain number of recipes from all over the world have been incorporated into French cuisine.

To be more explicit, I shall say that there exists not so much an international cuisine as an international *culinary art*. I mean by "Venetian cuisine," "Irish cuisine," and so on, a *corpus* of fixed recipes, possessing essential ties to a given region and its resources. I mean by "international cuisine" not a corpus of recipes, but a body of *methods*, of *principles* amenable to *variations*, depending on different local and financial possibilities, just as this body of methods and principles is conducive to variations within a given country, depending on seasonal possibilities. The expression "international cuisine" takes on a pejorative connotation when it designates a certain false grand cuisine also known as "hotel cuisine," a cuisine that retains the outward features and, above all, the vocabulary of the Grand Cuisine of the nineteenth century, but that limits itself to drowning various foods in all-purpose sauces with pretentious names and to engaging in certain types of spectacular presentation for the mere sake of display.

Hence, the expression "international cuisine" has two precisely opposite meanings: on the one hand, it refers pejoratively to a rootless, anonymous cuisine, against which it is a healthy reaction to demand the return to local dishes with the tang of the soil, and, on the other hand, it designates Grand Cuisine, with the potentiality of becoming internationalized because the chefs who know it are men who understand its basic principles, and, since they are possessed of an inventive spirit, men who tirelessly seek to exploit these bases to create new dishes.[3] This cuisine is also international in the sense that it has the capacity to integrate, to adapt, to rethink, I will say almost to rewrite the recipes of all countries and all regions, or at least those that are amenable to such treatment.

The entire problem lies precisely therein. A certain number of recipes, reexamined in the light of the principles that they embody, can be internationalized. Indian curry, Valencian paella, sauerkraut, koulibiaka, red cabbage with chestnuts *à la limousine*, Italian *fritto misto* are capable of being internationalized, and they have proved it. Very often these preparations, once they are refined and improved, are better as dishes in international

Grand Cuisine than as regional dishes. In other instances, transposition is absolutely impossible. In these cases, the native tang of local products or techniques of cooking linked to a certain type of dwelling, or heat source, or fuel, or even odors in the air and climatic characteristics cause any attempt to "improve" a recipe, by making it obey the canons of gastronomic art, to end up merely depriving it of all personality. The more primitive a dish is, the more tasty it is. It does not belong to the domain of art, but rather that of ethnology or a mixture of biology and ethnology. Gastronomical art is able, when necessary and possible, to find the equivalents of certain products or of certain ingredients and use them to replace other products and other ingredients that cannot be obtained in certain places. It also knows the cases in which it is necessary to forbear to do so. Certain books on Chinese cuisine for the use of Westerners indicate equivalents of this sort.

To be still more precise, I will say that, in my opinion, there are no *national cuisines*: there is international cuisine, which must remain extremely flexible, and *regional* cuisine. The basic unit in gastronomy is the region, not the nation. A *pauchouse mâconnaise* is as difficult, if not impossible, to make in Marseille as in Sicily. *Cacciucco livornese* no longer has the same scent when it is made a hundred kilometers from the sea, in Florence, a region of inland and peasant cuisine, as when it is made right on the coast of Versilia, at Livorno or Viareggio. There is as much difference between Piedmontese cuisine and Calabrian cuisine as between this latter and Flemish cuisine. Certain regional dishes can travel, but others are refractory to any change of place. We must go to them; they cannot come to us.

In its attempt to assimilate the greatest number of regional dishes possible, international cuisine must be very attentive to the methods of cooking and the sources of the elements that give them their scent and flavor. If this condition is respected, it can absorb a very great number of ideas, because it alone is capable of comprehending the *creative principle* behind this or that local knack of preparing a dish and of applying consciously what was executed unconsciously and mechanically. For international cuisine has curiosity as its motivating force, unlike regional cuisine, which for its part is *obliged* to remain routine and exclusive, finding its salvation purely and simply in the refusal to take into consideration any other register of flavors than its own. But a good chef who wants to export North African couscous, for instance, will pay close attention not so much to the juxtaposition of the elements that make up the recipe—vegetables (including chick-peas), a hot sauce, wheat groats, etc.—as to two fundamental traits of this dish. Couscous is first and foremost the couscous itself, that is to say, the art of "rolling" the groats in such a way that it is as free from stickiness as possible and as free-flowing as sand. The grains of a proper couscous must scatter on the table when one blows on them, at least before they have been wet with bouillon. The second fundamental factor is the aroma of the meat. The only meat that must be used for it is the most tasty mutton; couscous with chicken must be avoided, because modern European chicken has no taste, and *méchoui* or roast mutton must also be avoided, for couscous is a stew, or, more precisely, a "soup," in the ancient meaning of the word. *Méchoui* makes no sense unless it is cooked whole in the open air, roasted above wood coals in which aromatic herbs are burned. This cooking in the open air is essential to give the surface of the roast the dryness responsible for its unique flavor. The couscous "with *méchoui*" offered on the menu of certain restaurants is therefore the perfect example of the sort of *bad* international cuisine that *transports the picturesqueness* of a regional dish without *transposing its principles*, because they have not been understood.

When such comprehension exists, on the other hand, real Grand Cuisine can sometimes give the diversity of local registers an interpretation that is at once faithful and new. Contrary to received opinion, erudite cuisine from its very inception introduced cosmopolitanism into the art of eating well. As early as the beginning of the nineteenth-century, Brillat-Savarin, speaking of Parisian cuisine, could write: "Among these diverse parts constituting the dinner of a gourmet, the principal parts, such as butchered meat, poultry, fruits, come from France; others, such as beefsteak, welch-rabbet [*sic*], punch, and so on, imitate English cuisine; and still other parts are from all over: from Germany come sauerkraut, hamburger, Black Forest filets; from Spain, *olla podrida*, chick-peas, dry raisins from Málaga, the peppered hams of Jerica, and cordials; from Italy, macaroni, Parmesan, Bologna sausages, polenta, ices, liqueurs; from Russia, dried meats, smoked eels, caviar; from Holland, cod, cheeses, peck herring, curaçao, anisette; from Asia, Indian rice, sago, *karrik*, soy sauce, the wine of Shiraz, coffee; from Africa, the wine of the Cape; finally, from America, potatoes, sweet potatoes, pineapple, chocolate, vanilla, sugar, etc. . . . which is sufficient proof of the statement that we have made elsewhere, namely, 'that a meal such as one can eat in Paris is a cosmopolitan whole in which every part of the world makes its appearance by way of its products.' "

Let us complete Brillat-Savarin's statement by declaring that it is obviously not only in Paris that gastronomical cosmopolitanism is practicable or practiced.

. . . . . .

In short, that cuisine that from the beginning of the nineteenth century came to be known as Grand Cuisine, the invariable expression after Carême, is international by vocation. It consists, certainly, of knowing how to make various dishes but even more of knowing *the conditions allowing them to be made*. It suffices to leaf through the great treatises on cuisine of the last hundred and fifty years to note that they have adapted the principal ideas, but not necessarily the exact *recipes*, of various regional cuisines. The fact, for example, that a master such as Escoffier worked in England for the greater part of his career resulted in the introduction of twenty-seven sauces of English origin into the list of those considered as forming part of Grand Cuisine, twenty-one of them hot, among them cranberry sauce, oyster sauce, reform sauce, and six cold sauces, among them Cambridge sauce, Cumberland sauce, mint sauce, and horseradish sauce. It is significant that none of these sauces, by reason notably of the unjust discredit into which English cuisine had fallen, had been adapted in England from traditional sources, that is to say, by direct and unconscious "osmosis." It had taken the conscious will of a professional chef.

An intelligent chef in the nineteenth century played on a worldwide keyboard, adopting methods from the cuisine of the Near East, so rich in original techniques, from the cuisine of central Europe, from Russian cuisine, from the Jewish cuisines of various countries of Europe or of various provinces of France (Alsace, in particular), from America, to which Brillat-Savarin claims he introduced scrambled eggs, that dish that was to have such a glorious destiny in that part of the world. Brillat-Savarin also recounts the adventure of another French political émigré who made a fortune in London during the French Revolution and the Empire by going into the richest households and making salad dressing, that thing that is so simple and yet so difficult, not to make but to explain how to make. Driving his tilbury himself, transporting all the ingredients in it, this émigré made the rounds of his customers at mealtime and turned out on the spot whatever salad dressing was desired.

Hence the difference between international cuisine and regional cuisines is not, as those who do not know are too often inclined to believe, the difference between the complicated and the simple. Certain phases of international cuisine, certain sauces, certain methods of cooking of Grand Cuisine are sometimes extremely simple, whereas certain regional dishes are neither simple nor complicated but merely impossible outside the local conditions of the land or the maritime region that make them what they are.

We must in all fairness recognize, however, that, on the whole, Grand Cuisine is a cuisine restricted to professionals. That is why, as we already have seen, it has developed and renewed itself in great restaurants down through the nineteenth and twentieth centuries. But it is capable of being adapted to a more modest and more simplified scale, as was the case in numerous cookbooks. At the end of the nineteenth century, for example, a book such as Reboul's *La Cuisinière provençale*, one which in fact goes beyond the framework indicated in the title, was a work intended for the housewife but one which nonetheless applied the fundamental methods of Grand Cuisine with regard to essential points. "Bourgeois" cuisine thus finds its place between the international cuisine of the professionals and the countless varieties of regional cuisine, benefiting from the know-how of the former while at the same time relying on the heritage of the latter.

This is not meant to suggest that "grand" cuisine and regional cuisine are diametrical opposites. Nor can it be said that there is absolutely no such thing as national cuisines, a "French cuisine," an "Italian cuisine," a "Spanish cuisine," and so on . . . Today's French cuisine, for example, has two separate and distinct sources: the various regional cuisines on the one hand and the cuisine practiced by professionals—the one born in the eighteenth century—on the other. The second naturally influenced the first, and today there are practical manuals, Ginette Mathiot's *La Cuisine pour tous*,[4] for example, in which we find both a simplified initiation into Grand Cuisine and a sampler of regional dishes ranging from *potage champenois* (soup from Champagne) to *poule à la comtoise* (hen, Franche-Comté style). The most humble family recipe, such as that for fricassee of chicken, benefits from the distant lessons of a Carême or an Escoffier. The minuteness of the various steps for making this dish that is nevertheless very simple, the spirit that inspires it are much further removed from the typical preparations, even characteristically peasant ones, of the nineteenth century, than they are from the preparations of any of the masters of the nineteenth century. It is not the time spent in preparation nor the amount of money that make the difference here, but rather the conception, and this is as true of simple recipes as it is of complex ones. We thus see how the cuisine of professionals influences popular cuisine, by way of details that are often apparently insignificant, such as the recommendation to sear the chicken parts in butter without browning them, and to mix bouillon with the white wine, or the indication of the precise moment at which the sauce should be thickened with egg yolks or the lemon juice added.

Conversely, certain recipes created directly in Grand Cuisine often evolve in the course of history under the pressure of a certain sort of popular good sense. Thus at the beginning of the nineteenth century the recipe for chicken Marengo (also used sometimes for veal) called for cooking these meats in hot oil till done. Chef Dunand, who had invented or was said to have invented the recipe for Napoleon I, added crayfish as well. Little by little the crayfish went by the board, for they really served no purpose in this dish. Later on, since cooking the chicken or veal in oil till done turned out to be too heavy, it came to be merely rapidly browned in the oil, then moistened with a little white wine. The recipe given by Pellaprat in the twentieth century has been even further improved, in that bouillon, which serves to moisten the meat, is added at the same time as the white wine. Little remains of Dunand's original conception, which was really nothing but a chicken *à la provençale* fried in oil with tomatoes and garlic; a "sauté" has been turned into a "stew," since instead of being cooked dry, the chicken or the veal are cooked in their sauce. In short "Marengo" was a fried dish in the beginning and it is today a stew. The popular talent for stews, which are lighter and more aromatic, has little by little—and rightly—pared away what was wrong with a "professional" recipe. (What I mean here by a "professional" recipe is not a refined one but a "creation," as contrasted with a traditionally transmitted recipe.)

Of the seven major types of cooking: boiling, deep frying, baking, grilling, braising, cooking in a sauce or stewing, and cooking in a frying pan or "sautéing," it is culinary art that often determines the one that is most appropriate for a given recipe and sets it off best, a recipe that cooks have stubbornly followed even though the method of cooking was inappropriate. How many times has it happened that someone has perceived that meats and vegetables that previously have been boiled before braising them, sautéing them, or roasting them could simply be braised, thus keeping all of their flavor intact?

In short, in keeping with the advice of Cussy, a gastronome of the nineteenth century: "Gourmets who read me, be content with the cuisine of Picardy, but educate it!"

N O T E S

1. Cookbooks dating from the end of the seventeenth century still contain recipes for fish with fruit preserves sprinkled with cinnamon.

2. Does the "New French Cuisine" that has appeared since 1970 deserve to be considered a revolution?

3. In the jet age, moreover, it is the great chefs themselves who have begun to travel, to open branches, and to train disciples all over the world.

4. Paris, Albin Michel, 1955, reprinted in a Livre de Poche edition. This work, while vastly simplified, nonetheless contains 1,243 recipes.

LISA M. HELDKE

Recipes for Theory Making

Could it ever make sense to think of cooking as a form of inquiry? Could thinking about cooking ever illuminate our thinking about philosophy? This paper is my attempt to show why "yes" is the appropriate answer to both these questions. Through an exploration of cooking—an exploration that focuses on the nature of recipes and recipe use—I'll develop my claim that cooking is a form of inquiry that is anti-essentialist, that successfully merges the theoretical and the practical, and that promotes a self-reflective and interactive model of an inquiry relationship.

My account of cooking grows out of a particular epistemological tradition, a tradition I label the Coresponsible Option. Members of this tradition are attempting to develop epistemological frameworks or attitudes that avoid the dichotomies of realism/antirealism and foundationalism/relativism. I contend that these dichotomies are not exhaustive, and that it is in fact important for feminists to find ways around them—to construct alternative attitudes in which to engage in epistemology. Before I turn to my account of cooking, I'll sketch out this epistemological tradition.

I. WHY SHOULD FEMINISTS WORRY ABOUT FOUNDATIONALISM AND RELATIVISM?

Philosophers working in a variety of traditions are trying to develop positions that avoid the sharp, pointy rocks of absolutism, realism and foundationalism, without falling into the murky swamps of relativism. Theorists engaged in these sorts of projects attempt (implicitly or explicitly) to undermine, dismantle, begin before, or otherwise avoid the metaphysical questions, "Is there something Out There that exists, unchanging and independent of us, or are we the creators of all that there is?" and the related epistemological question, "How can we ground our knowledge of the world—or *can* we?"

Sandra Harding, one important figure in the movement I'm describing/constructing, asks, "do we—should we—still believe that our representations can in principle reflect one uniquely accurate image of a world which is ready-made and out there for the reflecting? Should we really think a feminist philosophy or science can be the mirror of nature any more than non-feminist ones can?" (1985, 16). Philosophical claims are not " . . . 'approximations to the truth' which can be woven into a seamless web of representation of the world 'out there,' but permanently partial instigators of rupture . . . " 1985, 17–18). Philosophy is valuable not because it can uncover The Real, but because it can create alternative ways to think about whatever reality it is we've inherited/discovered/created.

Richard Bernstein, a theorist engaged in a related project, calls his an attempt to move "beyond objectivism and relativism." He suggests that we have to stop treating the epistemological terrain as necessarily bifurcated—as if there were a fundamental opposition between " . . . the basic conviction that there is or must be some permanent, ahistorical matrix or framework to which we can ultimately appeal in determining the nature of rationality, knowledge, truth, reality, goodness, or rightness," and the view " . . . that all such conceptions (taken to be fundamental) must be understood as relative to a specific conceptual scheme, theoretical framework, paradigm, form of life, society, or culture" (1983, 8). This opposition—accompanied, as it is, by the assumption that its two alternatives constitute our only available options—rests upon what Bernstein calls the "Cartesian Anxiety" (1983, 16), the conviction that either there is a firm foundation for our knowledge, or we are condemned to swirl endlessly in the morass of intellectual and moral indecision.

The assumption that our epistemological options are limited to two is unwarranted. Furthermore, neither option—foundationalism nor relativism—is particularly useful or desirable in its own right. My assessment of these options arises out of certain feminist concerns and aspirations; it is my contention that the epistemological "attitudes" that are foundationalism and relativism hobble efforts to inquire into, and theorize about, our experiences. In order to be able to do the kinds of inquiry I want to do, I feel the need to be free of the constraints these two attitudes place upon me.

Let me explain. I am interested in developing ways to do feminist inquiry that are respectful and illuminating of the differences in women's lives—that embody a respect for difference. At the same time, I do not want to interpret respect for difference as a blanket sanction of all and any differences. Specifically, I do not translate "respect for difference" into a demand that we respect or accept misogynist, racist, classist or otherwise oppressive views, simply because they are different from ours, or a demand that we always "resist the temptation" to try to convince others of our views. I think foundationalism and relativism are inadequate frameworks for doing this kind of inquiry.

Foundationalism treats difference as a "stage" or "phase" we pass through on our way to constructing adequate theory. Difference, for the foundationalist, reflects an inadequacy, a failure or incompleteness in our theorizing; if we had developed an adequate set of theories about subject X, the need for—and perhaps the possibility of—different approaches would be eliminated. On the other hand, relativism allows for and even encourages difference, but disables us from criticizing the theories of others for being incomplete, uninclusive or otherwise inadequate. The relativist is left to say "different is different; it's neither better nor worse."

In contrast, I would like to construct epistemologies that are respectful and representative of the differences in women's experiences, without being glib, unreflective or uncritical about those differences—that is, without defining all differences as necessarily good and desirable, or declaring a moratorium on convincing and persuading. In order to carry out this project, I find it necessary to develop attitudes toward inquiry that will allow such epistemologies to *exist.* That is, I want to develop epistemological options that are neither absolutist nor relativist.

My own approach to/avoidance of absolutism and relativism I label the "Coresponsible Option." The term "coresponsible" embodies the atmosphere of cooperation and interaction which characterizes inquiry activity.[1] Whether we acknowledge it or not, we enter into relationships when we engage in inquiry; relationships with other inquirers, and also with the things into which we inquire—the things labelled "objects" on a traditional account. The model of inquiry I'm suggesting rejects the strict subject/object dichotomy, with its emphasis on hierarchy and separation. In its place, I suggest we think of inquiry as a communal activity, that we emphasize the relationships that obtain between inquirers and inquired. In the words of John Dewey, inquiry is " . . . the correspondence of two people [or things] who 'correspond' in order to modify one's own ideas, intents and acts . . . " (1958, 283).

I label my approach an "option" to suggest that what I offer here is simply one way to think about the world and about inquiry, not *the* way. This is not simply a modest claim about the fallibility of my thought; it is an assertion of my view of the status of theories in general. They are tools we may choose to use, outlooks we may elect to assume. Some are more useful than others; none are universally reliable.

II. WHY SHOULD PHILOSOPHERS WORRY ABOUT COOKING?

I situate my examination of cooking within this context—a context in which the issue is not "Do we cast our lots with absolutism or with relativism?" but rather "How can we avoid both of these headaches?" I want to ask a question about inquiry and theorizing: If I do choose to resist the temptation to enter the absolutism/relativism debates, in what *spirit* might I set out to inquire and to develop theories? And how might I explain and justify doing theory?

(An aside. I speak here only partly facetiously of the "temptation" to enter these debates, for I have found them extremely seductive, for reasons

I can't quite diagnose. Choosing to throw them over has proven difficult psychologically—and *persevering* in avoiding them is sometimes even more so. Part of the difficulty for me stems from the fact that I just don't have good ways to talk that are both nonfoundationalist and nonrelativist. Furthermore, even when I *find* the ways, I don't always want to *use* them. There's something extremely comforting about believing that my alternatives are cut-and-dried, limited to two. This paper is my attempt to develop some useful and *attractive* ways to think about inquiry and theorizing, that break the seductive hold of this dichotomy.)

I'm motivated to ask questions about the "spirit" in which to inquire and to develop and promote theories, because doing theory is an activity whose legitimacy cannot be regarded as unimpeachable, once I reject the absolutist/relativist dichotomy. As I see it, I can no longer justify my theory-production-and-sale on "objectivist" grounds—that is, by asserting that "our" task as theory makers is to formulate true, faithful-to-Reality theories, which we then press upon "the public," on the assumption that they will of course want to adopt these truest-to-date theories (because true theories are epistemologically and morally superior to less true ones). By the same token, I cannot be satisfied with a relativist shrug of the shoulders, and the assertion that, of course we don't really have any "independent" reasons to promote or defend one theory over another, although, given our tradition, we'll of course prefer one over the other, and will be motivated to share that theory with others, the way we share a favorite story.

If I am going to do philosophy, I want to do it, think about it, and describe it in ways that are neither foundationalist nor relativist. This paper explores one possible way, a way entered through the kitchen.

Cooking is an activity that is somewhat foreign to the western epistemological tradition, especially in the 20th century, in which discussions of theory have come to be framed almost exclusively in terms of scientific models. I'm not a scientist, but I am a cook, and my familiarity with cooking methods and language allows me to speak with more knowledge and flexibility about this activity than about science.

That's one reason I've chosen to talk about cooking. Another reason is this: the activities that fall under the category of "cooking" manifest qualities that I want manifested in my philosophizing.

Simply put, I think cooking is a kind of inquiry. I take my cue in part from John Dewey, who defines inquiry as "the controlled or directed transformation of an indeterminate situation into one that is so determinate in its constituent distinctions and relations as to convert the elements of the original situation into a unified whole" (1938, 104–5). Such a definition certainly encompasses cooking.

Furthermore, I follow Dewey in eschewing the strict dichotomy between theory—the "knowledge gaining" activity—and practice—the "getting-things-done" activity. These are not two separate domains of human life, but two interrelated, interdependent domains. The difference is one of degree, not kind: "One is the pushing, slam-bang act-first-and-think-afterwards mode, to which events may yield as they give way to any strong force. The other mode is wary, observant, sensitive to slight hints and intimations" (1958, 314). For Dewey, the paradigm example of a discipline that had "completely surrendered the separation of knowing and doing" was science (1980, 79). I don't think this claim can still be made about the sciences, if indeed it ever could. For, whatever it may be that scientists do, the way in which most philosophers talk about science renders it a most abstract and theoretical activity, one in which "practice" is assigned a decidedly inferior role.

Cooking doesn't suffer from this problem—at least certain kinds of cooking don't.[2] In it, the theoretical and the practical work together in an activity that genuinely does justice to Dewey's definition of inquiry. I want to speak in praise of the practical. Cooking is a vehicle that allows me to do so.

I must stress here that I'm not using cooking and recipes simply as analogies to, or metaphors for, philosophical or scientific inquiry and theory. Certainly my account of recipes can be regarded as a metaphor. But it is something more and other than that. It is a philosophical investigation of the nature of cooking—cooking being an activity that has yet to be so investigated. I am considering cooking qua inquiry, if you will.

This suggests yet another reason I've chosen to discuss cooking. It has never really been the subject of philosophical consideration (Plato's discussion of pastry cooking notwithstanding). This is at least partly due to the fact that cooking is a "woman's activity," like child rearing. Traditionally, western philosophers have regarded such women's activities to be philosophically irrelevant; they have defined them out of existence, rendered them invisible, described them through their silence. They have done so by constructing categories that consider and account for only (certain) men's activities. Activities like cooking and child rearing turn out to look trivial on traditional philosophical accounts, because they don't fit into any philosophical categories. In exploring cooking, I want to begin to remove this curse of irrelevance under which it has lain, and to begin to illuminate its philosophical significance.

Even as my account is a philosophical investigation of cooking, it is also my intention that it enhance and expand the ways in which we do philosophical theory. To be succinct: I am using the tools and language of philosophy to investigate a particular set of human practices. In turn, I intend for my investigation of those practices to have an impact upon philosophy.

My exploration of cooking tends to focus on the construction and use of recipes. I'll look at five aspects of recipes and recipe-cook relationships, and shall show how each aspect can illuminate our thinking about theorizing. First, I briefly explore some of the ways cooks create recipes. I then consider the forms or systems under which people collect them. Next, I turn to the focus of my account: an explanation of how cooking, because of

the relationships that obtain between cook, recipe and ingredients, es-
capes both absolutism and relativism. In relation to this, I consider the
issue of flexibility: how do I-the-cook determine how flexible a recipe is? I
conclude with a discussion of flops in the kitchen.

A. Anti-Essentialism in the Kitchen: Creating Recipes

Cooks create new recipes and experiment with old familiar ones for all
sorts of reasons—to enter contests, to use up a bit of leftover something, to
experiment with tastes, to secure their job, to play. It's important, I think,
to recognize that there is *no one* reason people experiment in the kitchen.
I may be faced with economic necessity—I have only cornmeal and a little
dried up cheese in the house, and no money for groceries. I may be feeling
playful—I have an afternoon free, a full cupboard and the urge to make
something gorgeous and delicious. Or I may have a set of job demands to
meet—I have sixty people to serve on a limited budget, and am required
to meet certain stipulated dietary requirements.[3] Furthermore, any two
people respond to a particular demand in different ways; a fun, exciting
challenge to you may be a tedious exercise in battling miserliness to me.

Perhaps you might argue that although I might be motivated—or compelled—to come up with a new recipe for a variety of context-dependent
reasons, this does not deny that there is still a general, overarching, *aim* in
experimenting in the kitchen; namely, to produce some *food*. But in fact
this is not alway the case. Sometimes food is a sort of accidental byproduct
of the experiment, second in importance to some other aim. Sometimes,
for example, the experimenter herself may never actually *make* the food
for which she's created a recipe; I've heard of cases in which people won
contests with recipes they've never tried. And even in the many cases
where creating some food *is* the aim, a variety of not-necessarily-related
things may count as fulfilling that aim. Making a special surprise dish for
someone's birthday is quite a different thing from making a filling food
that can be prepared in ten minutes and will serve one hundred.

I stress the fact that cooks create recipes for a variety of reasons, because I think this observation is helpful for thinking about epistemological
inquiry and theorizing. It seems to me that there isn't one central reason,
or type of reason, people come up with new theories, or modify existing
ones. My sense is that theories, like recipes, are most usefully regarded as
tools we use to do things. The range of things that we may do with them is
at least as broad as the range of things one may do with recipes. I may
develop a theory to help myself tolerate a situation in which I find myself,
or to explain to myself and others a set of experiences I've had. I may take
up and modify a theory in order to help me develop a relationship with
another person or persons. I may create a theory in order to have something to write about in a paper for a class.

Granting my claim that people create theories for many reasons, you might still want to ask me, is a theory like a recipe in that, when it *is* implemented, a "product" results? In thinking about theories in relation to recipes, I was initially quite troubled by this question. I couldn't seem to come up with something that was the *theory* equivalent of *food*—that all theories *produced* when they were implemented. I toyed with the suggestion that all theory aims at improving our ability to get on in the world, or at establishing relationships in the world. But this seemed obviously false. It may be regarded as a good "product" of theory, but surely not the only good product, and definitely not the only product. But then I flipped the problem over; I realized that what I had taken to be an obvious general fact about the creation of recipes—namely that their creators are all *ultimately* interested in making food, in some unambiguously essential sense of the word—is simply not a fact, and that, as I said above, food doesn't always even result when someone creates a recipe.

My conclusion from all of this is that perhaps we might want to say that the "product" of theorizing is some sort of relationship or practice in the world, but that such a claim has no more value as an essentialist claim about theorizing than the claim that the "product" of creating a recipe is food.[4]

Some people "never use a recipe," by which they mean that they never look at a cookbook, and perhaps never do the same thing twice, while other people religiously follow a recipe no matter what they're cooking and how often they've made it. The way you treat written recipes often reflects your degree of skill and confidence as a cook, your spirit of adventure, your knack for imagining what foods might taste good together. Blending flavors in creative and artful ways requires you to be sensitive to those flavors, to know which ones "like" each other and which ones don't. It also requires a spirit of adventure, the derring-do to mix together two ingredients that normally aren't thought to go together. And it requires the expertise to know when enough is enough: when a rule cannot be broken or bent, or when adding another ingredient will upset the balance of flavors you've constructed.

The level of cooking at which dramatic-and-daring experimentation goes on is a level perhaps few of us reach. In order to be good at it, you must understand the foods with which you're experimenting; you need to know what temperatures they can withstand, how they react with other foods, how much of them is needed to produce a particular result. This kind of knowledge is difficult and time consuming to obtain. It's also extremely rewarding and useful, for it allows you to create wonderful foods, and it enables you to be flexible in the face of a nearly empty refrigerator.

So it is with theorizing. It's relatively easy to take up a theory, whole-cloth, and use it. But to do so is to run the heavy risk of being irrelevant, harmful, or destructive. To do useful theory, I think it is necessary to explore and experiment, to know extremely well the things with which you're inquiring. It's necessary in inquiry in a way that it may not be in cooking, for whereas in cooking a failure to experiment leaves you with a boring diet, in theorizing, it makes you into an arrogant, unperceptive inquirer.

B. A BROWSER'S GUIDE TO RECIPE COLLECTIONS

Recipes get collected into all sorts of books and files, organized under myriad systems and anti-systems, by people with any number of motives for collecting them, profit or personal use. Go to any large best-seller bookstore, and you'll find at least three rows of cookbooks. There are general cookbooks that will instruct you in the rudiments of preparing anything from a boiled egg to a roasted armadillo (*Joy of Cooking*, 516). Then there are cookbooks devoted to recipes for a single kind of food or for food of a single ethnicity. Others feature recipes for special diets—low sodium, gluten free, sugar-free, vegetarian. There are cookbooks put out by civic organizations and churches, containing their members' favorite recipes. And then there are the recipe files, recipe drawers, recipe boxes of individual cooks. These, if they are organized, are done so on the basis of the particular idiosyncracies of that cook, and the eaters for whom they normally cook. (My mom has separate bundles of recipes, housed in plastic strawberry boxes, for recipes containing either rhubarb or dried apricots, two of my family's favorite foods.)

Most recipe collectors have stacks of recipes—in cookbooks, copied out of magazines, clipped out of newspapers—that they've never tried. Collecting and exchanging recipes, and imagining what they might be like if I made them, is an activity that takes up as much of my time as actual cooking does.

I think of philosophical theorizing as collecting, trading, developing, using, adapting and discarding recipes/theories. I collect ideas from various sources. Some of them I try—and some of these I keep and modify for use again. Others I talk and think about, the way I talk about what a recipe might taste like and how long it might take to prepare. They don't become a part of my theoretical/practical life, but hover in the wings, waiting for a situation in which they might be useful.

Sometimes, when I'm thinking about theorizing, I see myself as trying to write an epistemological cookbook—not *the* epistemological cookbook, mind you, but a largish volume that attempts to provide ways to think about a wide variety of issues.

In developing and passing out epistemological cookbooks, I include recipes on which I'd stake my reputation—I'm not going to abdicate responsibility in the event of their failure, but will try to discover why it might have occurred, and to think of ways to fix it. Nonetheless, some of them might fail.

I connect the recipes in my cookbook in a systematic way, but I don't pretend that they are the only sorts of recipes one would ever need, or that this system is the only system under which they could be organized. There are at least as many varieties of philosophical systems as there are cookbook organizing schemes. And, as with cookbooks, it would be misguided to believe that one system only is sufficient or useful or reliable; that only one system could or should be used to organize theories.

You could use my epistemological cookbook exclusively—many cooks swear that all they need is a copy of Julie Child—but I would advise against such exclusivity. Better that my recipes be used as part of a larger collection, or that certain of them be selected and modified for use in your cookbook. They are my recipes, filled with the idiosyncrasies of my life. I cannot imagine that they would prove universally useful to anyone else. (They aren't even that for me.)

C. OUT OF THE FRYING PAN *AND* THE FIRE: AVOIDING ABSOLUTISM AND RELATIVISM

A recipe is a description or explanation of how to do something—specifically, how to prepare a particular kind of food. As such, it does not present itself as *the* way to make that food—the opinion of some cooks notwithstanding—nor does it suggest that this food is *the* food to eat—the opinion of some eaters notwithstanding. Consider theorizing in this light: imagine developing and exchanging theories the way you create a recipe and share it with a friend. What would such theorizing be like?

On the "recipe plan" of theory/recipe development and exchange I, as theorizer, do not (generally) assert that the project I take up must be taken up by others. On a "recipe plan" I-the-theorist don't set an absolutist agenda of things that you-the-other-theorist must work on. Rather, I present issues that I find important, and suggest reasons that you may also. Likewise, I cannot assert that anyone who does choose to take up this project must approach it using the same methods I use. All I can do is offer my approach, explaining why I found it useful.

I think of pieces of philosophical theory created on the recipe plan as if/then statements. If you find this project compelling, then you might find this approach useful. "Do you like asparagus? It's really inexpensive right now. You might like to try the recipe I have for asparagus soup."

This way of thinking about theorizing, and about how to offer theories to others, is not absolutist. But, while it avoids absolutism, doesn't it send me sliding into relativism? Nothing I've said so far seems to *prevent* it. After all, if anyone is free to select problems "at random," and if no one must proceed in any particular way using any particular strategy, then haven't I simply asserted (in the now-famous words of an infamous philosopher of science) that anything goes? I think this is not the case. Let me explain why.

Recipes allow cooks to vary their preparation techniques and to fiddle with the ingredient list. Some recipes permit considerably more fiddling than others, but virtually all of them have their breaking point. I can make equally wonderful chocolate chip cookies either by dumping all the ingredients in a bowl at the same time and stirring them together, or by first mixing butter and sugar together, and then adding eggs one at a time. Chocolate chip cookie dough is extremely resilient; when I mix the ingredients for it, almost anything *can* go and they'll still turn out. If I attempted the same sort of radical variation in technique when I was making puff pastry, I'd probably produce all sorts of interesting food products, but only some of them would resemble puff pastry.

Similarly, some recipes allow me to substitute, to add or delete items, while others "demand" rigid adherence to their ingredient list. You can toss in anything from nuts to cheese to herbs when making bread, but if you're making Scotch shortbread, you dare not change a single ingredient. (If you add raisins to shortbread, one cookbook warns, you may make something delicious. But it won't be shortbread.) I should point out here that many kinds of reasons may fuel a demand for adherence to a recipe. The example I've given is of a case in which the "historical integrity" of the product rests on the integrity of the ingredient list. In other cases, changing an ingredient might not only destroy the integrity, it might actually render the product inedible.

Here, then, is the basis for my assertion that the recipe plan is not relativist: once you decide to make a certain food—take on a certain philosophical problem—some methods of proceeding will be closed to you, because of the nature of the project. The number and nature of those limitations will vary according to the project you've chosen, but most any project will have its limits. Similarly, the ingredients (aspects of the world) you select will be restricted because of the project you've chosen—again, in degrees that vary with the project. In other words, while it may be true that there is no cherry pie that is more cherry pie than any other, it is also true that certain things just aren't cherry pies; recipes are not infinitely flexible.

I'd also suggest that the recipe plan avoids relativism at an earlier stage: my initial *choice* of recipes is not simply the result of personal whim combined with tradition. Certainly these factors come into play; I choose to make certain foods because I grew up eating them, and I'm very fond of them. But other concerns influence my choice as well; health/nutrition and environmental concerns restrict the range of foods I prepare. These concerns may well transcend the narrow limits of gastronomy, and enter the realm of morality; my decision about the foods I eat is shaped by my concern for the environment, and my concern about the labor and investment practices of the companies that produce my food. None of these concerns binds me, but once I choose (or am enjoined) to pay attention to them, my subsequent food choices are affected. If I decide to become a vegetarian, I will have to give up the chicken I now eat.

In describing recipes as nonrelativist, I've been drawing a picture of nested concerns-and-suggestions; I've suggested that selecting a particular moral stance might restrict the recipes I use, while selecting a particular recipe might restrict the ingredients and methods I use to execute it. At no level have I labelled something as "imperative," because in the strongest sense of that word, *nothing* is imperative. There are some rules that we might call absolute—such as the rule that you boil all water that comes from an untested source, or the rule that you not pour boiling water on yeast—but if you look back a step, you find that even these imperatives rest upon choices, choices so universally made in favor of one alternative rather than another that we almost stop thinking of them as choices. The demand that you boil water assumes that you are interested in preserving your life—that you don't want to get parasites or any other illness. And the demand that you not pour boiling water on yeast assumes that you want the yeast to live—that the reason you're using yeast in the first place is that you want your bread to rise.

D. Me and My Recipe: Understanding the Relationship

I've described recipes as flexible to varying degrees. One question that arises from this kind of description is, when faced with a new recipe, how do I go about determining how flexible it is? How do I determine what I can and can't do to it? Learning the limitations on a recipe is part of what is involved in learning to be a cook. It's a *self-reflective* process, because in order for me to determine the spirit in which I should receive a set of instructions, I must know what kind of an operator I am—how I tend to work with ingredients and so on. Ultimately, I must determine how I-and-the-recipe work together—how I am to interpret the instructions given by the writer of the recipe.

Let me be more specific. In assessing the flexibility of a recipe/theory, it's often important to consider its source—the person or institution from whom I received the recipe. Why has s/he given the instructions the way s/he has? Is it really necessary that I do step B before proceeding to step C? If my mom gave me a recipe, she's no doubt stripped the instructions to the bare minimum, even leaving out steps she knows I'll know to do. On the other hand, if I use a recipe from the 4-H cookbook that I got when I was nine, I know that I can eliminate about half the steps immediately ("Ask your mother if you can use the oven.").

On a related note, the tone in which a rule is issued need not be the tone in which you receive it. Sometimes the recipe writer tells you it's absolutely necessary to use this particular ingredient or method. The experienced cook will realize that this is the preference of the author speaking, or a marketing ploy being used by the Kraft corporation to get you to use Parkay margarine. The more I know about the recipe giver, the more able I'll be to assess the relevance of their instructions for me.

Pie crust makers are notorious for issuing *commands* when they give out recipes: they insist that only shortening X will produce a light, flaky piecrust. Sometimes shortening X is lard, sometimes it's Crisco, and sometimes it's Another Vegetable Shortening. Having made a lot of piecrusts in the last ten years, I can say quite confidently that it doesn't matter one whit what you use. Unless you're motivated by additional dietary concerns, lard and vegetable shortening work equally well. But recognizing this fact— and recognizing that what looked like imperatives were actually personal preferences—was something I was able to do only when I had enough experience to formulate my own judgment.

This propensity to command that you often find in recipe givers suggests that it's important to learn how to assess the motives of the recipe giver. In my Kraft example, it's obvious that the giver has something to gain by issuing a rule as if it were a command; they'll sell more Parkay margarine. In other instances, it may not be so obvious why someone tells you to do something a specific way—but it's important to try to figure out. (There's an old joke about a family in which two generations of women cut the end off their roasts before roasting them "because Mom did it that way." And why did the original Mom do it that way? Because her roasting pan was too small.)

In general, when I receive a recipe, the more I know about the recipe giver, the better the position I'll be in to assess the relevance *for me* of their instructions. And, when I'm in the position of giving out recipes, the more I take into account my recipient, the more I attempt to give information that is sensitive to their level of experience, the better off my recipient will be.

Let me reiterate this point specifically in terms of theories. In interpreting the theories of others, it is vitally important that I understand the motives driving those "others." How is it that they have come to pay attention to this issue? What do they stand to gain from issuing that rule as an absolute demand? Why do they leave out entirely any discussion of that concern in their theory? Developing such an understanding is important, and it can be very difficult. Sometimes it may well be that the person who created the theory wishes to conceal certain ulterior motives from me-the-recipient. Examples of this phenomenon include political theories through which those in positions of power mystify those whom they oppress, in order to ensure the continuance of their power.

In cases where such willful concealment is being employed, no easy access to the theorist's motives is available. But, although that theorist may not volunteer information about their motives, it may be possible to get that information through other means. In such a situation, I would suggest that it is of particular importance to investigate the other's motives, for it is precisely in such situations where ignorance can leave you disempowered.[5]

E. WHEN RECIPES FAIL (OR WHEN WE DO)

Recipes are usually tested by someone—your grandmother or the Betty Crocker test kitchen worker—and the tester often offers some sort of promise that the recipe will work for you. (This promise varies considerably in formality—and effusiveness—depending upon its source.) Despite this promise, the recipe may not work, for all sorts of reasons. Perhaps the food turns out just as the recipe "intended" it to, but you find out that in fact you don't like tripe. Or perhaps you live in a place where climatic or other conditions cause different dietary concerns to come into play, and this food doesn't fill the requirements.

On the other hand, maybe the recipe really doesn't turn out as it was intended to, because you haven't established a working relationship with the recipe; as I've suggested, learning how to read a recipe involves learning what kind of relationship obtains between you-the-cook and this recipe (and its author). In instances where the recipe doesn't work, perhaps you've used techniques or ingredients, or are working under conditions (like high altitude) that differ from those used by the recipe creator in ways that this recipe can't tolerate. So, the recipe/cook team fails. Or it succeeds in a totally unexpected way. (Lousy popovers, but great edible tennis balls.)

This kind of failure may be overcome by *thoughtful practice*; by following the recipe more literally, perhaps, and introducing variations only when you've achieved the results you desire; by asking the recipe creator for a more detailed explanation of how to do whatever it is they're telling you to do; or by asking someone else for suggestions about how they would proceed.

The recipe-cook team might also fail because of a poorly tested recipe, or a recipe that leaves out an ingredient or instruction. In such cases, fixing the problem might be extremely difficult, especially if you cannot consult the person who wrote the recipe, but are left to unravel the problem on your own. And again, the recipe creator might intentionally leave something out, or might deliberately obscure the instructions, in order to guarantee your failure, and ensure the "superiority" of their cooking skills.

To describe these *recipe* failures in *theory* terms, I'd suggest that it won't do to treat theorizing as an activity in which I, the disinterested, semi-omniscient theory creator unveil a set of universally-applicable laws about a bunch of mute, lifeless Stuff of the Universe. Nor is it useful to think that I, the theory recipient, can simply take up someone else's theory as is, follow its unambiguous, universally-applicable instructions, and unproblematically apply it to the "same" phenomena they were exploring.

With respect to the former assertion, that theorizing is not the one-sided activity of a detached subject, think about making bread. The dough responds to your warm hands' kneading action, and you learn to respond to it, to know when you've kneaded it long enough, and when to add more flour. It's an activity that depends upon a connection between bread maker and bread dough. This relationship takes time to develop; the first time you make bread, it may well turn out dry or holey because you haven't yet figured out how to read the messages the dough is giving. Reciprocal responses characterize things that exist in relation to each other, that can affect and be affected by each other. When I use a recipe, I enter into a kind of relation with the ingredients. I do not assume complete separateness from them, nor total power over them.

I think the same claim can be made, to some degree, about any kind of inquiry-activity. It's most obviously true of theorizing with ("about") other people. And, although it is yet to be shown, I'm willing to believe the same will be true of even the hardest of "hard sciences."[6]

With respect to the latter assertion about the way to approach someone else's theory, I'm suggesting that it is useful to ask the giver about the conditions that prompted the development of a particular theory. Trying to see how their experiences relate to mine, how they challenge and conflict with mine, and how their theory fits with or contrasts to mine enables me to create useful, successful, helpful theories. At the center of this activity stands always a relation between me and the other theorizer. The more developed this relation, the better equipped am I to modify and implement their theory.

What I've given in this paper is, I suggest, a little methodological cookbook. In it, I've offered a collection of some ways to go about doing philosophical theory. I offer them as tested products, and as parts of an integrated system. Further tests may prove them wrong or unhelpful or misleading, and I may have to throw out some recipes. But I issue them in good, provisionally-foundational faith.

NOTES

1. I say that this atmosphere does characterize inquiry, though sometimes it might be more appropriate to say that I *wish* it characterized inquiry. But I do wish to say that, whatever the attitude that prevails between inquirers, there is a sense in which their activity is at least interactive. What I mean is that, despite the stories that inquirers may tell themselves about being disinterested subjects, they are in fact in relations, both with the things into which they inquire, and with other inquirers.

2. I'm sure the sorts of cooking that go on in multi-star restaurants do or could manifest an element of abstracted theoreticity that would rival that of the sciences.

3. Thanks to Susan Heineman for this example.

4. There still may seem to be a troubling disparity between cooking and theorizing, however, because it seems that cooking produces food a lot more often than theories produce practical consequences in one's life in the world. Precisely. I think there is. And I think this is a failure of theorizing. I *am* willing to say that it would be very useful to try to make theories that matter to people in our lives, just as it's useful to create recipes that go on to get used. But again, I don't want to translate this into an essentialist assertion.

5. It is a brutal fact that this relationship of mystification is far more common than a cooperative one. In some respects, then, the recipe model is an idealistic

one; it works best when the participants in inquiry are willing participants, anxious to reveal motives and strategies.

6. Evelyn Fox Keller has already given us an example, in Barbara McClintock, of a biologist who thinks of her research as a loving *communication* with her corn plants. And the work of some theoretical physicists, who utilize the notion of a "participatory universe," also point toward this way of thinking about inquiry.

R E F E R E N C E S

Bernstein, Richard. 1983. *Beyond Objectivism and Relativism: Science, Herme-neutics and Praxis.* Philadelphia: University of Pennsylvania Press.
Dewey, John. 1938. *Logic: The Theory of Inquiry.* New York: Holt, Rinehart and Winston, Inc.
————. 1958. *Experience and Nature.* 2nd ed. New York: Dover.
————. 1929. *The Quest for Certainty.* New York: Perigee.
Harding, Sandra. December, 1985. Feminist Justificatory Strategies and the Episte-mology of Science. Unpublished paper, delivered to meeting of Eastern Division, American Philosophical Association.
Rombauer, Irma, and Marion Rombauer Becker. 1977. *Joy of Cooking.* Indianapolis: Bobbs-Merrill.

CAROL J. ADAMS

from *The Sexual Politics of Meat: A Feminist-Vegetarian Critical Theory*

THE STORY OF MEAT

> These pheasants of course, if one
> wanted to be legalistic about it,
> wouldn't be here at all if we hadn't put
> them here, got the eggs, hatched them
> out, reared the chicks—you might say
> we gave them life and then after a bit
> we take it away again—arrogating to
> ourselves somewhat God-like powers I
> must admit. But let's not bother with all
> that.
> —the host of a shooting party
> in Isabel Colegate's
> *The Shooting Party*[1]

The story of meat follows the narrative structure of story telling. Alice B.
Toklas implies this in her cookbook when, in a chapter entitled "Murder in
the Kitchen," she uses the style of a detective story to describe killing and
cooking animals.[2] Through recipes she provides the appropriate conclusion to the animals' death according to the texts of meat; the animal becomes delectable, edible.

There are some incontrovertible assumptions that determine our approach to life: Stories have endings, meals have meat. Let us explore
whether these statements are interchangeable—stories have meat, that is,
meaning, and meals have endings. When vegetarians take meat out of the
meal, they take the ending out of the story of meat. Vegetarians become
caught within a structure they attempt to eliminate. Our experience of
meat eating cannot be separated from our feelings about stories.

We are the species who tell stories. Through narrative we confer meaning upon life. Our histories are structured as stories that postulate beginnings, crises, resolutions; dramas and fictions animate our imagination with stories that obviously have a beginning and an end. Narrative, by definition, moves forward toward resolution. By the time the story is concluded we have achieved some resolution, whether comic or tragic, and we are given access to the meaning of the story as a whole. Often meaning can only be apprehended once the story is complete. Detective stories demonstrate the closure of narrative, because the act of discovering at the end of the story who really "done it" often causes a reordering of all that transpired before the end of the story. Closure accomplishes the revelation of meaning and reinscribes the idea that meaning is achieved through closure.

Meat eating is story applied to animals, it gives meaning to animals' existence. To say this is to take Roland Barthes's statement literally: "Narrative is first and foremost a prodigious variety of genres, themselves distributed amongst different substances—as though any material were fit to receive humans' stories."[3] Animals' lives and bodies become material fit to receive humans' stories: the word becomes flesh.

We can isolate determining points in which the creation of meat recalls the movement of narration. There is a beginning, a postulating of origins that positions the beginning of the story: we give animals life. There is the drama of conflict, in this case of death. And there is the closure, the final summing up, which provides resolution to the drama: the consumption of the animal.

The story of meat follows a sacred typology: the birth of a god, the dismemberment of the god's body, and the god's resurrection. This sacred story paves the way for a mundane enaction of the meaning of dismemberment and the resurrection—achieved through consumption of meat.

The story begins with the birth of the animal, who would not have existed if meat eating did not require the animal's body. As we saw, Holcroft confides to his journal that his argument against vegetarianism is that meat eating has given innumerable animals life and thus increased "the quantity of sensation." His is one of the most frequently reiterated defenses of meat eating in which benignity is conferred with the beginning of the story because life has been conferred upon an animal. Here we have the reassurance that accompanies the doubling of origins: the birth of an animal and the beginning of the story lock the story in a traditional movement of narrativity and a cultural one of reciprocity. We give them life and later we can take it, precisely because in the beginning we gave it. Based on our knowledge of how the story is going to end we interpret its beginning. The way in which the story of meat is conceptualized is with constant references to humans' will; we allow animals their existence and we begin to believe that animals cannot exist autonomously.

The subterfuge in the story of meat occurs in the absence of agency and the emphasis on personal choice. The phrase humane slaughter and the eliding of fragmentation contribute to an elaborate artifice in which the person consuming meat is not implicated, because no agency, that is, no responsibility, no complicity, is inscribed in the story. This allows for the subjectivity of meat eating. Though inculcated through social processes, meat eating is unambiguously experienced as personal.

Meat eaters must assume the role of literacy critic, attempting to impose a positive interpretation on what they know to be a tragedy (the tragedy of killing animals), but which they see as a necessary tragedy. They do so by manipulating language and meaning through a code that subjugates animals' lives to human needs. The story of meat involves re-naming, repositioning the object, and re-birth. Re-naming occurs continuously. We re-position the animal from subject to object by making ourselves the subjects in meat eating. The story ends not with death but re-birth, and assimilation into our lives. Thus meat gives life. We accept meat eating as consumers because this role is continuous with our role of consumers of completed stories. Only through closure is the story resolved; only through meat eating does meat achieve its meaning and provide the justification for the entire meat production process. The meat herself represents the closure that occurs at the end of any story.

The threat to this story arises from two sources: vegetarianism and feminism. The vegetarian perspective seeks to establish agency and implicate the consumer. It challenges the notion that animals' deaths can be redeemed by applying human meaning to it; thus it stops the story of meat. The feminist theorist has concluded that traditional narrative is determined by patriarchal culture. According to feminist theory, patriarchal narrative depicts male quests and female passivity. Teresa de Lauretis comments, "For there would be no myth without a princess to be wedded."[4] It suggests that it is in the gaps and silences of traditional narrative that feminist meaning can be found. Thus it questions the structure of stories. With the lens of feminist interpretation we can see that the animal's position in the story of meat is that of the woman's in traditional patriarchal narrative; she is the object to be possessed. The story ends when the Prince finds his Princess. Our story ends when the male-defined consumer eats the female-defined body. The animals' role in meat eating is parallel to the women's role in narrative: we would have neither meat nor story without them. They are objects to others who act as subjects.

Vegetarians see themselves as providing an alternative ending, veggie burgers instead of hamburgers, but they are actually eviscerating the entire narrative. From the dominant perspective, vegetarianism is not only about something that is inconsequential, which lacks "meat," and which fails to find closure through meat, but it is a story about the acceptance of passivity, of that which has no meaning, of endorsing a "vegetable" way of living. In this it appears to be a feminist story that goes nowhere and accepts nothingness.

If, through the story of meat, the word and the flesh are united, we might further argue that the body equals a text, a text is a body. From this perspective, changing an animal from her original state into food parallels changing a text from its original state into something more palatable. The result is dismembered texts and dismembered animals. Freeing Metis' voice from the sexual politics of meat involves re-membering both.

N O T E S

1. Isabel Colegate, *The Shooting Party* (New York: The Viking Press, 1980, Avon Books, 1982), p. 94.
2. Alice B. Toklas, *The Alice B. Toklas Cook Book* (1954, Garden City, NY: Anchor Books, 1960), pp. 37–57.
3. Roland Barthes, "Introduction to the Structural Analysis of Narratives," *Image-Music-Text*, trans. Stephen Heath (New York: Hill and Wang, 1977), p. 79. Sexist language changed.
4. Teresa de Lauretis, *Alice Doesn't: Feminism, Semiotics, Cinema* (Bloomington: Indiana University Press, 1984), p. 5.

from *Buffalo Bird Woman's Garden*

CORN

PLANTING

Corn planting began the second month after sunflower-seed was planted, that is in May; and it lasted about a month. It sometimes continued pretty well into June, but not later than that; for the sun then begins to go back into the south, and men began to tell eagle-hunting stories.

We knew when corn planting time came by observing the leaves of the wild gooseberry bushes. This bush is the first of the woods to leaf in the spring. Old women of the village were going to the woods daily to gather fire wood; and when they saw that the wild gooseberry bushes were almost in full leaf, they said, "It is time for you to begin planting corn!"

Corn was planted each year in the same hills.

Around each of the old and dead hills I loosened the soil with my hoe, first pulling up the old, dead roots of the previous year's plants; these dead roots, as they collected, were raked off with other refuse to one end of the field outside of the cultivated ground, to be burned.

This pulling up of the dead roots and working around the old hill with the hoe, left the soil soft and loose for the space of about eighteen inches in diameter; and in this soft soil I planted the corn in this manner:

I stooped over, and with fingers of both hands I raked away the loose soil for a bed for the seed; and with my fingers I even stirred the soil around with a circular motion to make the bed perfectly level so that the seeds would all lie at the same depth.

A small vessel, usually a wooden bowl, at my feet held the seed corn. With my right hand I took a small handful of the corn, quickly transferring half of it to my left hand; still stooping over, and plying both hands at the same time, I pressed the grains a half inch into the soil with my thumbs, planting two grains at a time, one with each hand.

I planted about six to eight grains in a hill[1] (figure 1). Then with my hands I raked the earth over the planted grains until the seed lay about the length of my fingers under the soil. Finally I patted the hill firm with my palms.

The space within the hill in which the seed kernels were planted

FIGURE 1

should be about nine inches in diameter; but the completed hill should nearly cover the space broken up by the hoe.

The corn hills I planted well apart, because later, in hilling up, I would need room to draw earth from all directions over the roots to protect them from the sun, that they might not dry out. Corn planted in hills too close together would have small ears and fewer of them; and the stalks of the plants would be weak, and often dried out.

If the corn hills were so close together that the plants when they grew up, touched each other, we called them "smell-each-other"; and we knew that the ears they bore would not be plump nor large.

A Morning's Planting

We Hidatsa women were early risers in the planting season; it was my habit to be up before sunrise, while the air was cool, for we thought this the best time for garden work.

Having arrived at the field I would begin one hill, preparing it, as I have said, with my hoe; and so for ten rows each as long as from this spot to yonder fence—about thirty yards; the rows were about four feet apart, and the hills stood about the same distance apart in the row.

The hills all prepared, I went back and planted them, patting down each with my palms, as described. Planting corn thus by hand was slow work; but by ten o'clock the morning's work was done, and I was tired and ready to go home for my breakfast and rest; we did not eat before going into the field. The ten rows making the morning's planting contained about two hundred and twenty-five hills.

I usually went to the field every morning in the planting season, if the weather was fine. Sometimes I went out again a little before sunset and planted; but this was not usual.

Soaking the Seed

The very last corn that we planted we sometimes put into a little tepid water, if the season was late. Seed used for replanting hills that had been destroyed by crows or magpies we also soaked. We left the seed in the water only a short time, when the water was poured off.

The water should be tepid only, so that when poured through the fingers it felt hardly warmed. Hot water would kill the seeds.

Seed corn thus soaked would have sprouts a third of an inch long within four or five days after planting, if the weather was warm. I know this, because we sometimes dug up some of the seeds to see. This soaked seed produced strong plants, but the first-planted, dry seeds still produced the first ripened ears.

If warm water was not convenient, I sometimes put these last planted corn seeds in my mouth; and when well wetted, planted them. But these mouth-wetted seeds produced, we thought, a great many wi'da-aka'ta, or goose-upper-roof-of-mouth, ears.

PLANTING FOR A SICK WOMAN

It was usual for the women of a household to do their own planting; but if a woman was sick, or for some reason was unable to attend to her planting, she sometimes cooked a feast, to which she invited the members of her age society and asked them to plant her field for her.

The members of her society would come upon an appointed day and plant her field in a short time; sometimes a half day was enough.

There were about thirty members in my age society when I was a young woman. If we were invited to plant a garden for some sick woman, each member would take a row to plant; and each would strive to complete her row first. A member having completed her row, might begin a second, and even a third row; or if, when each had completed one row, there was but a small part of the field yet unplanted, all pitched in miscellaneously and finished the planting.

SIZE OF OUR BIGGEST FIELD

When our corn was in, we began planting beans and squashes. Beans we commonly planted between corn rows, sometimes over the whole field, more often over a part of it. Our bean and squash planting I will describe later; and I speak of it now only because I wish to explain to you how a Hidatsa garden was laid out.

The largest field ever owned in my father's family was the one which I have said my grandmother Turtle helped clear, at Like-a-fishhook village, or Fort Berthold, as the whites called it. The field, begun small, was added to each year and did not reach its maximum size for some years.

The field was nearly rectangular in shape; at the time of its greatest size, its length was about equal to the distance from this spot to yonder fence—one hundred and eighty yards; and its width, to the distance from the corner of this cabin to yonder white post—ninety yards.

The size of a garden was determined chiefly by the industry of the family that owned it, and by the number of mouths that must be fed.

When I was six years old, there were, I think, ten in my father's family, of whom my two grandmothers, my mother and her three sisters, made six. I have said that my mother and her three sisters were wives of Small Ankle, my father. It was this year that my mother and Corn Sucker died, however.

My father's wives and my two grandmothers, all industrious women, added each year to the area of our field; for our family was growing. At the time our garden reached its maximum size, there were seven boys in the family; three of these died young, but four grew up and brought wives to live in our earth lodge.

NA'XU AND NU'CAMI

In our big garden at Like-a-fishhook village, nine rows of corn, running lengthwise with the field, made one na'xu, or Indian acre, as we usually translate it. There were ten of these na'xus, or Indian acres, in the garden.

Some families of our village counted eight rows of corn to one na'xu, others counted ten rows.

The rows of the na'xus always ran the length of the garden; and if the field curved, as it sometimes did around a bend of the river, or other irregularity, the rows curved with it.

In our garden a row of squashes separated each na'xu from its neighbor.

Four rows of corn running widthwise with the garden made one nu'cami; and as was the na'xu, each nu'cami was separated from its neighbor by a row of squashes, or beans, or in some families, even by sunflowers.

Like those of the na'xus, the rows of the nu'camis often curved to follow some irregularity in the shape of the garden plot. (See figure 2.)

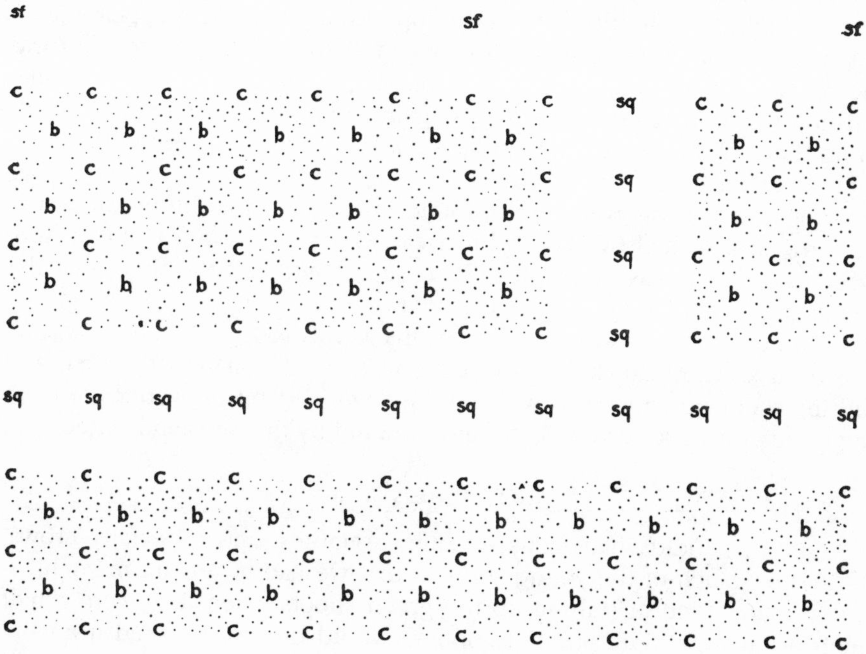

FIGURE 2

HOEING

Hoeing time began when the corn was about three inches high; but this varied somewhat with the season. Some seasons were warm, and the corn and weeds grew rapidly; other seasons were colder, and delayed the growth of the corn.

Corn plants about three inches high we called "young-bird's-feather-tail-corn," because the plants then had blunt ends, like the tail feathers of a very young bird.

Corn and weeds alike grew rapidly now, and we women of the household were out with our hoes daily, to keep ahead of the weeds. We worked as in planting season, in the early morning hours.

I cultivated each hill carefully with my hoe as I came to it; and if the plants were small, I would comb the soil of the hill lightly with my fingers, loosening the earth and tearing out young weeds.

We did not hoe the corn alone, but went right through the garden, corn, squashes, beans, and all. Weeds were let lie on the ground, as they were now young and harmless.

We hoed but once, not very many weeds coming up to bother us afterwards. In my girlhood we were not troubled with mustard and thistles; these weeds have come in with white men.

In many families hoeing ended, I think, when the corn was about seven or eight inches high: but I remember when my mothers finished hoeing their big field at Like-a-fishhook village, the corn was about eighteen inches high, and the blossoms at the top of the plants were appearing.

A second hoeing began, it is true, when the corn silk appeared, but was accompanied by hilling, so that we looked upon it rather as a hilling time. Hilling was done to firm the plants against the wind and cover the roots from the sun. We hilled with earth, about four inches up around the roots of the corn.

Not a great many weeds were found in the garden at hilling time, unless the season had been wet; but weeds at this season are apt to have seeds, so that it was my habit to bear such weeds off the field, that the seeds might not fall and sprout the next season.

With the corn, the squashes and beans were also hilled; but this was an easier task. The bean hills, especially, were made small at the first, and hilling them up afterwards was not hard work. If beans were hilled too high the vines got beaten down into the mud by the rains and rotted.

THE WATCHERS' STAGE

Our corn fields had many enemies. Magpies, and especially crows, pulled up much of the young corn, so that we had to replant many hills. Crows were fond of pulling up the green shoots when they were a half inch or an inch high. Spotted gophers would dig up the seed from the roots of young plants. When the corn had eared, and the grains were still soft, blackbirds and crows were destructive.

Any hills of young corn that the birds destroyed, I replanted if the season was not too late. If only a part of the plants in a hill had been destroyed, I did not disturb the living plants, but replanted only the destroyed ones. In the place of each missing plant, I dug a little hole with my hand, and dropped in a seed.

We made scarecrows[2] to frighten the crows. Two sticks were driven into the ground for legs; to these were bound two other sticks, like outstretched arms; on the top was fastened a ball of cast-away skins, or the like, for a head. An old buffalo robe was drawn over the figure and a belt tied around its middle, to make it look like a man. Such a scarecrow would keep the crows away for a few days but when they saw that the figure never moved from its place, they lost their fear and returned.

A platform, or stage, was often built in a garden, where the girls and young women of the household came to sit and sing as they watched that crows and other thieves did not destroy the ripening crop. We cared for our corn in those days as we would care for a child; for we Indian people loved our gardens, just as a mother loves her children; and we thought that our growing corn liked to hear us sing, just as children like to hear their mother sing to them.[3] Also, we did not want the birds to come and steal our corn. Horses, too, might break in and crop the plants, or boys might steal the green ears and go off and roast them.

Our Hidatsa name for such a stage was adukati′ i′kakĕ-ma′tsati, or field watchers' stage; from adukati′, field; i′kakĕ, watch; and ma′tsati, stage. These stages, while common, were not in every garden. I had one in my garden where I used to sit and sing.

A watchers' stage resembled a stage for drying grain, but it was built more simply. Four posts, forked at the top, supported two parallel beams, or stringers; on these beams was laid a floor of puncheons, or split small logs, at about the height of the full grown corn. This floor was about the length and breadth of Wolf Chief's table—forty-three by thirty-five inches—and was thus large enough to permit two persons to sit together. A ladder made of the trunk of a tree rested against the stage.

Such stages we did not value as we did our drying stages, nor did we use so much care in building them. If the posts were of green wood, we did not trouble to peel off the bark; at least, I never saw such posts with the bark peeled off. The beams in the forks of the posts often lay with the bark on. The puncheons that made the floor of the stage were free of bark, because they were commonly split from old, dead, floating logs, that we got down at the Missouri River; if the whole stage was built of these dead logs, as was often done, the bark would be wanting on every beam.

A watchers' stage, indeed, was usually of rather rough construction; wood was plentiful and easy to get, and the stage was rebuilt each year.

As I have said, it was our custom to locate our gardens on the timbered, bottom lands, and when we cleared off the timber and brush, we often left a tree, usually of cottonwood, standing in the field, to shade the watchers' stage. The stage stood on the north, or shady, side of the tree.

Cottonwood seedlings were apt to spring up in newly cleared ground. If there was no tree in the field, one of these seedlings might be let grow into a small tree. Cottonwoods grew very rapidly.

The tree that shaded the watchers' stage in our family field, and which I have indicated on the map, was about as high as my son Goodbird's cabin, and had a trunk about four inches in diameter. The cottonwood tree standing in Wolf Chief's corn field this present summer, is perhaps about the height of the trees that used to stand in our fields at Like-a-fishhook village.

. . . . .

The Watchers

The season for watching the fields began early in August when green corn began to come in; for this was the time when the ripening ears were apt to be stolen by horses, or birds, or boys. We did not watch the fields in the spring and early summer, to keep the crows from pulling up the newly sprouted grain; such damage we were content to repair by replanting.

Girls began to go on the watchers' stage to watch the corn and sing, when they were about ten or twelve years of age. They continued the custom even after they had grown up and married; and old women, working in the garden and stopping to rest, often went on the stage and sang.

Two girls usually watched and sang together. The village gardens were laid out close to one another; and a girl of one family would be joined by the girl of the family who owned the garden adjoining. Sometimes three, or even four, girls got on the stage and sang together; but never more than four. A drum was not used to accompany the singing.

The watchers sometimes rose and stood upon the stage as they looked to see if any boys or horses were in the field, stealing corn. Older girls and young married women, and even old women, often worked at porcupine embroidery as they watched. Very young girls did not embroider.

Boys of nine to eleven years of age were sometimes rather troublesome thieves. They were fond of stealing green ears to roast by a fire in the woods. Sometimes—not every day, however—we had to guard our corn alertly. A boy caught stealing was merely scolded. "You must not steal here again!" we would say to him. His parents were not asked to pay damage for the theft.

We went to the watchers' stage quite early in the day, before sunrise, or near it, and we came home at sunset.

The watching season continued until the corn was all gathered and harvested. My grandmother, Turtle, was a familiar figure in our family's field, in this season. I can remember her staying out in the field daily, picking out the ripening ears and braiding them in a string.

. . . . .

YOUTHS' AND MAIDENS' CUSTOMS

We always kept drinking water at the stage; and if relatives came out, we freely gave them to drink. But boys and young men who came were offered neither food nor drink, unless they were relatives.

Our tribe's custom in such things was well understood.

The youths of the village used to go about all the time seeking the girls; this indeed was almost all they did. Of course, when the girls were on the watchers' stage the boys were pretty sure to come around. Sometimes two youths came together, sometimes but one. If there were relatives at the watchers' stage the boys would stop and drink or eat; they did not try to talk to the girls, but would come around smiling and try to get the girls to smile back.

To illustrate our custom, if a boy came out to a watchers' stage, we girls that were sitting upon it did not say a word to him. It was our rule that we should work and should not say anything to him. So we sat, not looking at him, nor saying a word. He would smile and perhaps stop and get a drink of water.

Indeed, a girl that was not a youth's sweetheart, never talked to him. This rule was observed at all times. Even when a boy was a girl's sweetheart, or "love-boy" as we called him, if there were other persons around, she did not talk to him, unless these happened to be relatives.

Boys who came out to the watchers' stage, getting no encouragement from the girls there, soon went away.

A very young girl was not permitted to go the watchers' stage unless an old woman went along to take care of her. In olden days, mothers watched their daughters very carefully.

WATCHERS' SONGS

Most of the songs that were sung on the watchers' stage were love songs, but not all.

One that little girls were fond of singing—girls that is of about twelve years of age—was as follows:

> You bad boys, you are all alike!
> Your bow is like a bent basket hoop;
> You poor boys, you have to run on the prairie barefoot;
> Your arrows are fit for nothing but to shoot up into the sky!

This song was sung for the benefit of the boys who came to the near-by woods to hunt birds.

Here is another song; but that you may understand it I shall first have to explain to you what ikupa' means.

A girl whom another girl loves as her own sister, we call her ikupa'. I think your word chum, as you explain it, has about the same meaning. This is the song:

"My ikupa', what do you wish to see?" you said to me.
What I wish to see is the corn silk coming out on the growing ear;
But what *you* wish to see is that naughty young man coming!

Here is a song that we sang to tease young men that were going by:

You young man of the Dog society, you said to me,
"When I go to the east on a war party, you will hear news of me how brave I
am!"
I have heard news of you;
When the fight was on, you ran and hid!
And you think you are a brave young man!
Behold you have joined the Dog society;
Therefore, I call you just plain dog!

These songs from the watchers' stage we called mi'daxika, or garden-
ers' songs. The words of these I have just given you we called love-boy
words; and they were intended to tease.

NOTES

1. Buffalobird-woman says she planted six to eight kernels to a hill. Just what
pattern she used she could not tell until she went out with a handful of seed and
planted a few hills to revive her memory. The three patterns shown in figure 1 will
show how she laid the grains in the bottom of the several hills.—Gilbert L. Wilson
2. "Twice in the corn season were scarecrows used; first, when the corn was just
coming up; and again when the grain was forming on the ear and getting ripe."—
Edward Goodbird
3. In August, 1910, Buffalobird-woman related the story of "The Grandson," in
the course of which she said in explanation of reference to a watchers' stage:
"I will now stop a moment to explain something in the other form of this tale.
"According to this way of telling it, there was a garden and in the middle of the
garden was a tree. There was a platform under the tree made of trunks and slabs;
and there those two girls sat to watch the garden and sing watch-garden songs.
They did this to make the garden grow, just as people sing to a baby to make it be
quiet and feel good. In old times we sang to a garden for a like reason, to make the
garden feel good and grow. This custom was one used in every garden. Sometimes
one or two women sang.
"The singing was begun in the spring and continued until the corn was ripe.
We Indians loved our gardens and kept them clean; we did not let weeds grow in
them. Always in every garden during the growing season, there would be some one
working or singing.
"Now in old times, many of our gardens had resting stages, or watchers' stages,
such as I have just described. We always made our gardens down in the woods by
the river, because there is better ground there. When we cut off the timber we
would often leave one tree standing in the garden. Under this tree were erected

four forked posts, on which was laid a platform. This made the stage; in the tree overhead we often spread robes and blankets for shade.

"This resting stage was small. It was just big enough for two persons to sit on comfortably. Corn was never dried on it; it was used for a singing and resting place only. It was reached by a ladder. Its height was about four and a half feet high.

"This resting stage or watchers' stage was built on the north side of the tree so that the shade of the tree would fall upon it. Robes were laid on the floor of the stage to make a couch or bed. Sometimes people even slept on this platform—sometimes a man and his wife slept there.

"This resting stage we used to rest on after working in the garden; and to sing here the songs that we sang at this season of the year, and which I have called watch-garden songs. A place to cook in was not far away on the edge of the garden. It was a kind of booth, or bower. With a stake we made holes in the ground in a circle, and into the holes thrust willows. The tops of these willows we bent toward the center and joined together to make a bower. Over the top we threw a robe. We built a fire beneath to cook by.

"Our gardens I am describing were those at Like-a-fishhook village; and they were on the Missouri on either side of the village. They were strung along the river bank for a mile or more on either side of the village."

Tenzo Kyōkun[1]
(Instruction for the Tenzo)

1

Zen monasteries have traditionally had six officers who are all Buddha's disciples and all share buddha activities. Among them, the tenzo is responsible for preparing meals for the monks. *Regulations for Zen Monasteries* states, "In order to make reverential offerings to monks, there is a position called tenzo."

Since ancient times this position has been held by accomplished monks who have way-seeking mind, or by senior disciples with an aspiration for enlightenment. This is so because the position requires whole-hearted practice. Those without way-seeking mind will not have good results, in spite of their efforts. *Regulations for Zen Monasteries* states, "Use your way-seeking mind carefully to vary the menus from time to time, and offer the great assembly ease and comfort." Long ago, Guishan Lingyou, Dongshan Shouchu, and other great teachers held this position. A tenzo is not the same as an ordinary cook or waiter.

During my stay in Song China, in spare moments I questioned senior monks who had held various positions, and they spoke to me from their experience. Their words are the bones and marrow of the buddha ancestors who have attained the way and have been passed on since olden times. We need to read *Regulations for Zen Monasteries* carefully to understand the tenzo's responsibilities, and then consider carefully the words of these senior monks.

2

The cycle of the tenzo's work begins after the noon meal. First go to the director and assistant director to receive the ingredients for the next day's morning and noon meals—rice, vegetables, and so on. After you have received these materials, take care of them as your own eyes. Zen Master Baoning Renyong said, "Protect the property of the monastery; it is your eyeball." Respect the food as though it were for the emperor. Take the same care for all food, raw or cooked.

Next, in the kitchen, the officers carefully discuss the next day's meal, considering the tastes, the choice of vegetables, and the kinds of rice-gruel. *Regulations for Zen Monasteries* states, "The officers who oversee the kitchen should first discuss the menu-planning for the morning and noon meals." These officers are the director, assistant director, treasurer, ino, tenzo, and work leader. Soon after the menu is decided, post it on the board in front of the abbot's room and the study hall. Then prepare the gruel for the next morning.

When you wash rice and prepare vegetables, you must do it with your own hands, and with your own eyes, making sincere effort. Do not be idle even for a moment. Do not be careful about one thing and careless about another. Do not give away your opportunity even if it is merely a drop in the ocean of merit; do not fail to place even a single particle of earth at the summit of the mountain of wholesome deeds.

Regulations for Zen Monasteries states, "If the six tastes are not suitable and if the food lacks the three virtues, the tenzo's offering to the assembly is not complete." Watch for sand when you examine the rice. Watch for rice when you throw away the sand. If you look carefully with your mind undistracted, naturally the three virtues will be fulfilled and the six tastes will be complete.

Xuefeng was once tenzo at the monastery of Dongshan Liangjie. One day when Xuefeng was washing rice, master Dongshan asked him, "Do you wash the sand away from the rice or the rice away from the sand?"

Xuefeng replied, "I wash both sand and rice away at the same time."

"What will the assembly eat?" said Dongshan. Xuefeng covered the rice-washing bowl.

Dongshan said, "You will probably meet a true person some day."[2]

This is how senior disciples with way-seeking mind practiced in olden times. How can we of later generations neglect this practice? A teacher in the past said, "For a tenzo, working with the sleeves tied back is the activity of way-seeking mind."

Personally examine the rice and sand so that rice is not thrown away as sand. *Regulations for Zen Monasteries* states, "In preparing food, the tenzo should personally look at it to see that it is thoroughly clean." Do not waste rice when pouring away the rice water. Since olden times a bag has been used to strain the rice water. When the proper amount of rice and water is put into an iron pot, guard it with attention so that rats do not touch it or people who are curious do not look in at it.

After you cook the vegetables for the morning meal, before preparing the rice and soup for the noon meal, assemble the rice buckets and other utensils, and make sure they are thoroughly clean. Put what is suited to a high place in a high place, and what belongs in a low place in a low place. Those things that are in a high place will be settled there; those that are suited to be in a low place will be settled there.[3] Select chopsticks, spoons, and other utensils with equal care, examine them with sincerity, and handle them skillfully.

After that, work on the food for the next day's meals. If you find any grain weevils in the rice, remove them. Pick out lentils, bran, sand, and pebbles carefully. While you are preparing the rice and vegetables in this way, your assistant should chant a sūtra for the guardian spirit of the hearth.

When preparing the vegetables and the soup ingredients to be cooked, do not discuss the quantity or quality of these materials which have been obtained from the monastery officers; just prepare them with sincerity. Most of all you should avoid getting upset or complaining about the quantity of the food materials. You should practice in such a way that things come and abide in your mind, and your mind returns and abides in things, all through the day and night.

Organize the ingredients for the morning meal before midnight, and start cooking after midnight. After the morning meal, clean the pots for boiling rice and making soup for the next meal. As tenzo you should not be away from the sink when the rice for the noon meal is being washed. Watch closely with clear eyes; do not waste even one grain. Wash it in the proper way, put it in pots, make a fire, and boil it. An ancient master said, "When you boil rice, know that the water is your own life." Put the boiled rice into bamboo baskets or wooden buckets, and then set them onto trays. While the rice is boiling, cook the vegetables and soup. You should personally supervise the rice and soup being cooked. When you need utensils, ask the assistant, other helpers, or the oven attendant to get them. Recently in some large monasteries positions like the rice cook or soup cook have been created, but this should be the work of the tenzo. There was not a rice cook or a soup cook in olden days; the tenzo was completely responsible for all cooking.

3

When you prepare food, do not see with ordinary eyes and do not think with ordinary mind. Take up a blade of grass and construct a treasure king's land; enter into a particle of dust and turn the great dharma wheel. Do not arouse disdainful mind when you prepare a broth of wild grasses; do not arouse joyful mind when you prepare a fine cream soup. Where there is no discrimination, how can there be distaste? Thus, do not be careless even when you work with poor materials, and sustain your efforts even when you have excellent materials. Never change your attitude according to the materials. If you do, it is like varying your truth when speaking with different people; then you are not a practitioner of the way.

If you encourage yourself with complete sincerity, you will want to exceed monks of old in wholeheartedness and ancient practitioners in thoroughness. The way for you to attain this is by trying to make a fine cream soup for three cents in the same way that monks of old could make a broth of wild grasses for that little. It is difficult because the present and olden times differ as greatly as the distance between heaven and earth; no one now can be compared with those of ancient times. However, if you practice thoroughly there will be a way to surpass them. If this is not yet clear to you it is because your thoughts run around like a wild horse and your feelings jump about like a monkey in the forest. When the monkey and horse step back and reflect upon themselves, freedom from all discrimination is realized naturally.

This is the way to turn things while being turned by things. Keep yourself harmonious and wholehearted in this way and do not lose one eye, or two eyes. Taking up a green vegetable, turn it into a sixteen-foot golden body;[4] take a sixteen-foot golden body and turn it into a green vegetable leaf. This is a miraculous transformation—a work of buddha that benefits sentient beings.

4

When the food has been cooked, examine it, then carefully study the place where it should go and set it there. You should not miss even one activity from morning to evening. Each time the drum is hit or the bell struck, follow the assembly in the monastic schedule of morning zazen and evening practice instruction.

When you return to the kitchen, you should shut your eyes and count the number of monks who are present in the monks' hall. Also count the number of monks who are in their own quarters, in the infirmary, in the aged monks' quarters, in the entry hall, or out for the day, and then everyone else in the monastery. You must count them carefully. If you have the slightest question, ask the officers, the heads of the various halls or their assistants, or the head monk.

When this is settled, calculate the quantities of food you will need: for those who need one full serving of rice, plan for that much; for those who need half, plan for that much. In the same manner you can also plan for a serving of one-third, one-fourth, one-half, or two halves. In this way, serving a half portion to each of two people is the same as serving one average person. Or if you plan to serve nine-tenths of one portion, you should notice how much is not prepared; or if you keep nine-tenths, how much is prepared.

When the assembly eats even one grain of rice from Luling, they will feel the monk Guishan in the tenzo, and then the tenzo serves a grain of this delicious rice, he will see Guishan's water buffalo[5] in the heart of the assembly. The water buffalo swallows Guishan, and Guishan herds the water buffalo.

Have you measured correctly or not? Have the others you consulted counted correctly or not? You should review this closely and clarify it, directing the kitchen according to the situation. This kind of practice—effort after effort, day after day—should never be neglected.

When a donor visits the monastery and makes a contribution for the noon meal, discuss this donation with the other officers. This is the traditional way of Zen monasteries. In the same manner, you should discuss how to share all offerings. Do not assume another person's functions or neglect your own duties.

When you have cooked the noon meal or morning meal according to the regulations, put the food on trays, put on your kashāya, spread your bowing cloth, face the direction of the monks' hall, offer incense, and do nine full bows. When the bows are completed, begin sending out the food.

Prepare the meals day and night in this way without wasting time. If there is sincerity in your cooking and associated activities, whatever you do will be an act of nourishing the sacred body. This is also the way of ease and joy for the great assembly.

Although we have been studying Buddha's teaching in Japan for a long time, no one has yet recorded or taught about the regulations for preparing food for the monks' community, not to mention the nine bows facing the monks' hall, which people in this country have not even dreamed of. People in our country regard the cooking in monasteries as no more developed than the manners of animals and birds. If this were so it would be quite regrettable. How can this be?

NOTES

1. Written in Chinese as an independent work at Kōshō Hōrin Monastery in the spring of 1237, two years after the official completion of the monastery. Published in 1667 by Eihei-ji as part of the *Monastic Regulations of Zen Master Dōgen, the First Ancestor of the Sōtō School, Japan.*

Other translations: Kennett, pp. 175–90, "Instruction to the Chief Cook." Yokoi, *Regulations,* pp. 8–26. Dōgen and Uchiyama, pp. 3–19, "Instructions for the Zen Cook."

2. ALZSME, chap. 21. *Hongzhi's Capping Verses,* case 91.

3. When Yangshan was plowing a rice field with Guishan, Yangshan said, "One side is low and one side is high." Guishan said, "Water will even it out." Yangshan replied, "We don't need to depend on water. The high place is already even and high; the low place is already even and low." Guishan approved him. JRTL, chap. 11.

4. Because Dōgen is addressing a tenzo, he mentions a vegetable leaf instead of using a familiar expression in Zen: "a blade of grass."

5. *Guishan's water buffalo:* One day master Guishan taught the assembly, "After I have passed away I will become a water buffalo at the foot of the mountain. On the left side of the buffalo's chest the characters, "I am a monk of Guishan," will be written. When you call me the monk of Guishan, I will be a water buffalo. When you call me water buffalo, I will be a monk of Guishan. Then how are you going to call me?"

REFERENCES

Arrayed Lamps of the Zen School Merged in Essence [ALZSME]. A record of Zen tradition edited by Huiweng Wuming of the Linji School. Published in 1189.

Kennett, Roshi Jiyu. *Zen Is Eternal Life*. Emeryville, CA: Dharma Publishing, 1976.

Dōgen, Eihei. *Eihei-genzenji-shingi: Regulation for a Monastic Life by Eihei Dōgen*. Trans. Yuho Yokoi. Tokyo: Sankibo, 1973.

Dōgen, Zen Master, and Uchiyama Kosho. *Refining Your Life:. From Zen Kitchen to Enlightenment*. Trans. Thomas Wright. New York and Tokyo: Weatherhill, 1983.

Jingde Record of Transmission of Lamps [JRTL]. Compiled in the first year of the Jingde Era (1004, Song Dynasty), probably by Yongan Daoyuan of the Fayan School. A collection of words and deeds of 1701 masters.

AUDRE LORDE

from *Zami: A New Spelling of My Name*

When I was growing up in my mother's house, there were spices you grated and spices you pounded, and whenever you pounded spice and garlic or other herbs, you used a mortar. Every West Indian woman worth her salt had her own mortar. Now if you lost or broke your mortar, you could, of course, buy another one in the market over on Park Avenue, under the bridge, but those were usually Puerto Rican mortars, and even though they were made out of wood and worked exactly the same way, somehow they were never really as good as West Indian mortars. Now where the best mortars came from I was never really sure, but I knew it must be in the vicinity of that amorphous and mystically perfect place called "home." And whatever came from "home" was bound to be special.

My mother's mortar was an elaborate affair, quite at variance with most of her other possessions, and certainly with her projected public view of herself. It stood, solid and elegant, on a shelf in the kitchen cabinet for as long as I can remember, and I loved it dearly.

The mortar was of a foreign fragrant wood, too dark for cherry and too red for walnut. To my child eyes, the outside was carved in an intricate and most enticing manner. There were rounded plums and oval indeterminate fruit, some long and fluted like a banana, other ovular and end-swollen like a ripe alligator pear. In between these were smaller rounded shapes like cherries, lying in batches against and around each other.

I loved to finger the hard roundness of the carved fruit, and the always surprising termination of the shapes as the carvings stopped at the rim and the bowl sloped abruptly downward, smoothly oval but suddenly business-like. The heavy sturdiness of this useful wooden object always made me feel secure and somehow full; as if it conjured up from all the many different flavors pounded into the inside wall, visions of delicious feasts both once enjoyed and still to come.

The pestle was long and tapering, fashioned from the same mysterious rose-deep wood, and fitted into the hand almost casually, familiarly. The actual shape reminded me of a summer crook-necked squash uncurled and slightly twisted. It could also have been an avocado, with the neck of the alligator pear elongated and the whole made efficient for pounding, without ever losing the apparent soft firmness and the character of the fruit which the wood suggested. It was slightly bigger at the grinding end than most pestles, and the widened curved end fitted into the bowl of the mortar easily. Long use and years of impact and grinding within the bowl's worn hollow had softened the very surface of the wooden pestle, until a thin layer of split fibers coated the rounded end like a layer of velvet. A layer of the same velvety mashed wood lined the bottom inside the sloping bowl.

My mother did not particularly like to pound spice, and she looked upon the advent of powdered everything as a cook's boon. But there were some certain dishes that called for a particular savory blending of garlic, raw onion, and pepper, and souse was one of them.

For our mother's souse, it didn't matter what kind of meat was used. You could have hearts, or beefends, or even chicken backs and gizzards when we were really poor. It was the pounded-up saucy blend of herb and spice rubbed into the meat before it was left to stand so for a few hours before cooking that made that dish so special and unforgettable. But my mother had some very firm ideas about what she liked best to cook and about which were her favorite dishes, and souse was definitely not one of either.

On the very infrequent occasions that my mother would allow one of us three girls to choose a meal—as opposed to helping to prepare it, which was a daily routine—on those occasions my sisters would usually choose one of those proscribed dishes so dear to our hearts remembered from our relatives' tables, contraband, and so very rare in our house. They might ask for hot dogs, perhaps, smothered in ketchup sauce, or with crusty Boston-baked beans; or american chicken, breaded first and fried crispy the way the southern people did it; or creamed something-or-other that one of my sisters had tasted at school; what-have-you croquettes or anything fritters; or once even a daring outrageous request for slices of fresh watermelon, hawked from the back of a rickety wooden pickup truck with the southern road-dust still on her slatted sides, from which a young bony Black man with a turned-around baseball cap on his head would hang and half-yell, half-yodel—"Wahr-deeeeeee-mayyyyyyy-lawnnnnnnn."

There were many american dishes I longed for too, but on the one or two occasions a year that I got to choose a meal, I would always ask for souse. That way, I knew that I would get to use my mother's mortar, and this in itself was more treat for me than any of the forbidden foods. Besides, if I really wanted hot dogs or anything croquettes badly enough, I could steal some money from my father's pocket and buy them in the school lunch.

"Mother, let's have souse," I'd say, and never even stop to think about it. The anticipated taste of the soft spicy meat had become inseparable in my mind from the tactile pleasures of using my mother's mortar.

"But what makes you think anybody can find time to mash up all that stuff?" My mother would cut her hawk-grey eyes at me from beneath their heavy black brows. "Among-you children never stop to think," and she'd turn back to whatever it was she had been doing. If she had just come from the office with my father, she might be checking the day's receipts, or she might be washing the endless piles of dirty linen that always seemed to issue from rooming-houses.

"Oh, I'll pound the garlic, Mommy!" would be my next line in the script written by some ancient and secret hand, and off I'd go to the cabinet to get down the heavy wooden mortar and pestle.

I took a head of garlic out from the garlic bottle in the icebox, and breaking off ten or twelve cloves from the head, I carefully peeled away the tissue lavender skin, slicing each stripped peg in half lengthwise. I dropped them piece by piece into the capacious waiting bowl of the mortar. Taking a slice from a small onion, I put the rest aside to be used later over the meat, and cutting the slice into quarters, I tossed it into the mortar also. Next came the coarsely ground fresh black pepper, and then a lavish blanketing cover of salt over the whole. Last, if we had any, a few leaves from the top of a head of celery. My mother sometimes added a slice of green pepper, but I did not like the texture of the pepper-skin under the pestle, and preferred to add it along with the sliced onion later on, leaving it all to sit over the seasoned and resting meat.

After all the ingredients were in the bowl of the mortar, I fetched the pestle and placing it into the bowl, slowly rotated the shaft a few times, working it gently down through all the ingredients to mix them. Only then would I lift the pestle, and with one hand firmly pressed around the carved side of the mortar caressing the wooden fruit with my aromatic fingers, I thrust sharply downward, feeling the shifting salt and the hard little pellets of garlic right up through the shaft of the wooden pestle. Up again, down, around, and up—so the rhythm began.

The *thud push rub rotate up* repeated over and over. The muted thump of the pestle on the bed of grinding spice as the salt and pepper absorbed the slowly yielding juices of the garlic and celery leaves.

Thud push rub rotate up. The mingling fragrances rising from the bowl of the mortar.

Thud push rub rotate up. The feeling of the pestle held between my curving fingers, and the mortar's outside rounding like fruit into my palm as I steadied it against my body.

All these transported me into a world of scent and rhythm and movement and sound that grew more and more exciting as the ingredients liquefied.

Sometimes my mother would look over at me with the amused annoyance which passed for tenderness.

"What you think you making there, garlic soup? Enough, go get the meat now." And I would fetch the lamb hearts, for instance, from the icebox and begin to prepare them. Cutting away the hardened veins at the top of the smooth firm muscles, I divided each oval heart into four wedge-shaped pieces, and taking a bit of the spicy mash from the mortar with my fingertips, I rubbed each piece with the savory mix, the pungent smell of garlic and onion and celery enveloping the kitchen.

The last day I ever pounded seasoning for souse was in the summer of my fifteenth year. It had been a fairly unpleasant summer for me. I had just finished my first year in high school. Instead of being able to visit my newly found friends, all of whom lived in other parts of the city, I had had to accompany my mother on a round of doctors with whom she would have long whispered conversations. Only a matter of utmost importance could have kept her away from the office for so many mornings in a row. But my mother was concerned because I was fourteen and a half years old and had not yet menstruated. I had breasts but no period, and she was afraid there was something "wrong" with me. Yet, since she had never discussed this mysterious business of menstruation with me, I was certainly not supposed to know what all this whispering was about, even though it concerned my own body.

Of course, I knew as much as I could have possibly found out in those days from the hard-to-get books on the "closed shelf" behind the librarian's desk at the public library, where I had brought a forged note from home in order to be allowed to read them, sitting under the watchful eye of the librarian at a special desk reserved for that purpose.

Although not terribly informative, they were fascinating books, and used words like *menses* and *ovulation* and *vagina.*

But four years before, I had had to find out if I was going to become pregnant, because a boy from school much bigger than me had invited me up to the roof on my way home from the library and then threatened to break my glasses if I didn't let him stick his "thing" between my legs. And at that time I knew only that being pregnant had something to do with sex, and sex had something to do with that thin pencil-like "thing" and was in general nasty and not to be talked about by nice people, and I was afraid my mother might find out and what would she do to me then? I was not supposed to be looking at the mailboxes in the hallway of that house anyway, even though Doris was a girl in my class at St. Mark's who lived in that house and I was always so lonely in the summer, particularly that summer when I was ten.

So after I got home I washed myself and lied about why I was late getting home from the library and got a whipping for being late. That must have been a hard summer for my parents at the office too, because that was the summer that I got a whipping for something or other almost every day between Fourth of July and Labor Day.

When I wasn't getting whippings, I hid out at the library on 135th Street, and forged notes from my mother to get books from the "closed shelf," and read about sex and having babies, and waited to become pregnant. None of the books were very clear to me about the relationship between having your period and having a baby, but they were all very clear about the relationship between penises and getting pregnant. Or maybe the confusion was all in my own mind, because I had always been a very fast but not a very careful reader.

So four years later, in my fifteenth year, I was a very scared little girl, still half-afraid that one of that endless stream of doctors would look up into my body and discover my four-year-old shame and say to my mother, "Aha! So that's what's wrong! Your daughter is about to become pregnant!"

On the other hand, if I let Mother know that I knew what was happening and what these medical safaris were all about, I would have to answer her questions about how and wherefore I knew, since she hadn't told me, divulging in the process the whole horrible and self-incriminating story of forbidden books and forged library notes and rooftops and stairwell conversations.

It was a year after the rooftop incident, when we had moved farther uptown. The kids at St. Catherine's seemed to know a lot more about sex than at St. Mark's. In the eighth grade, I had stolen money and bought my classmate Adeline a pack of cigarettes and she had confirmed my bookish suspicions about how babies were made. My response to her graphic descriptions had been to think to myself, *there obviously must be another way that Adeline doesn't know about, because my parents have children and I know they never did anything like that!* But the basic principles were all there, and sure enough they were the same as I had gathered from *The Young People's Family Book.*

So in my fifteenth summer, on examining table after examining table, I kept my legs open and my mouth shut, and when I saw blood on my pants one hot July afternoon, I rinsed them out secretly in the bathroom and put them back on wet because I didn't know how to break the news to my mother that both her worries and mine were finally over. (All this time I had at least understood that having your period was a sign you were not pregnant.)

What then happened felt like a piece of an old and elaborate dance between my mother and me. She discovers finally, through a stain on the toilet seat left there on purpose by me as a mute announcement, what has taken place; she scolds, "Why didn't you tell me about all of this, now? It's nothing to get upset over, you are a woman, not a child anymore. Now you go over to the drugstore and ask the man for . . . "

I was just relieved the whole damn thing was over with. It's difficult to talk about double messages without having a twin tongue. Nightmarish evocations and restrictions were being verbalized by my mother:

"This means from now on you better watch your step and not be so friendly with every Tom, Dick, and Harry . . . " (which must have meant my staying late after school to talk with my girlfriends, because I did not even know any boys); and, "Now remember, too, after you wrap up your soiled napkins in newspaper, don't leave them hanging around on the bathroom floor where your father has to see them, not that it's anything shameful but all the same, remember . . . ''

Along with all of these admonitions, there was something else coming from my mother that I could not define. It was the lurking of that amused/ annoyed brow-furrowed half-smile of hers that made me feel—all her nagging words to the contrary—that something very good and satisfactory and pleasing to her had just happened, and that we were both pretending otherwise for some very wise and secret reasons. I would come to understand these reasons later, as a reward, if I handled myself properly. Then, at the end of it all, my mother thrust the box of Kotex at me (I had fetched it in its plain wrapper back from the drugstore, along with a sanitary belt), saying to me,

"But look now what time it is already. I wonder what we're going to eat for supper tonight?" She waited. At first I didn't understand, but I quickly picked up the cue. I had seen the beefends in the icebox that morning.

"Mommy, please let's have some souse—I'll pound the garlic." I dropped the box onto a kitchen chair and started to wash my hands in anticipation.

"Well, go put your business away first. What did I tell you about leaving that lying around?" She wiped her hands from the washtub where she had been working and handed the plain wrapped box of Kotex back to me.

"I have to go out, I forgot to pick up tea at the store. Now make sure you rub the meat good.''

When I came back into the kitchen, my mother had left. I moved toward the kitchen cabinet to fetch down the mortar and pestle. My body felt new and special and unfamiliar and suspect all at the same time.

I could feel bands of tension sweeping across my body back and forth, like lunar winds across the moon's face. I felt the slight rubbing bulge of the cotton pad between my legs, and I smelled the delicate breadfruit smell rising up from the front of my print blouse that was my own woman-smell, warm, shameful, but secretly utterly delicious.

Years afterward when I was grown, whenever I thought about the way I smelled that day, I would have a fantasy of my mother, her hands wiped dry from the washing, and her apron untied and laid neatly away, looking down upon me lying on the couch, and then slowly, thoroughly, our touching and caressing each other's most secret places.

I took the mortar down, and smashed the cloves of garlic with the edge of its underside, to loosen the thin papery skins in a hurry. I sliced them and flung them into the mortar's bowl along with some black pepper and celery leaves. The white salt poured in, covering the garlic and black pepper and pale chartreuse celery fronds like a snowfall. I tossed in the onion and some bits of green pepper and reached for the pestle.

It slipped through my fingers and clattered to the floor, rolling around in a semicircle back and forth, until I bent to retrieve it. I grabbed the head of the wooden stick and straightened up, my ears ringing faintly. Without even wiping it, I plunged the pestle into the bowl, feeling the blanket of salt give way, and the broken cloves of garlic just beneath. The downward thrust of the wooden pestle slowed upon contact, rotated back and forth slowly, and then gently altered its rhythm to include an up and down beat. Back and forth, round, up and down, back, forth, round, round, up and down. . . . There was a heavy fullness at the root of me that was exciting and dangerous.

As I continued to pound the spice, a vital connection seemed to establish itself between the muscles of my fingers curved tightly around the smooth pestle in its insistent downward motion, and the molten core of my body whose source emanated from a new ripe fullness just beneath the pit of my stomach. That invisible thread, taut and sensitive as a clitoris exposed, stretched through my curled fingers up my round brown arm into the moist reality of my armpits, whose warm sharp odor with a strange new overlay mixed with the ripe garlic smells from the mortar and the general sweat-heavy aromas of high summer.

The thread ran over my ribs and along my spine, tingling and singing, into a basin that was poised between my hips, now pressed against the low kitchen counter before which I stood, pounding spice. And within that basin was a tiding ocean of blood beginning to be made real and available to me for strength and information.

The jarring shocks of the velvet-lined pestle, striking the bed of spice, traveled up an invisible pathway along the thread into the center of me, and the harshness of the repeated impacts became increasingly more unbearable. The tidal basin suspended between my hips shuddered at each repetition of the strokes which now felt like assaults. Without my volition my downwards thrusts of the pestle grew gentler and gentler, until its velvety surface seemed almost to caress the liquefying mash at the bottom of the mortar.

The whole rhythm of my movements softened and elongated, until, dreamlike, I stood, one hand tightly curved around the carved mortar, steadying it against the middle of my body; while my other hand, around the pestle, rubbed and pressed the moistening spice into readiness with a sweeping circular movement.

I hummed tunelessly to myself as I worked in the warm kitchen, thinking with relief about how simple my life would be now that I had become a woman. The catalogue of dire menstruation-warnings from my mother passed out of my head. My body felt strong and full and open, yet captivated by the gentle motions of the pestle, and the rich smells filling the kitchen, and the fullness of the young summer heat.

I heard my mother's key in the lock.

She swept into the kitchen briskly, like a ship under full sail. There were tiny beads of sweat over her upper lip, and vertical creases between her brows.

"You mean to tell me no meat is ready?" My mother dropped her parcel of tea onto the table, and looking over my shoulder, sucked her teeth loudly in weary disgust. "What do you call yourself doing, now? You have all night to stand up there playing with the food? I go all the way to the store and back already and still you can't mash up a few pieces of garlic to season some meat? But you know how to do the thing better than this! Why you vex me so?"

She took the mortar and pestle out of my hands and started to grind vigorously. And there were still bits of garlic left at the bottom of the bowl.

"Now you do, so!" She brought the pestle down inside the bowl of the mortar with dispatch, crushing the last of the garlic. I heard the thump of wood brought down heavily upon wood, and I felt the harsh impact throughout my body, as if something had broken inside of me. Thump, thump, went the pestle, purposefully, up and down in the old familiar way.

"It was getting mashed, Mother," I dared to protest, turning away to the icebox. "I'll fetch the meat." I was surprised at my own brazenness in answering back.

But something in my voice interrupted my mother's efficient motions. She ignored my implied contradiction, itself an act of rebellion strictly forbidden in our house. The thumping stopped.

"What's wrong with you, now? Are you sick? You want to go to your bed?"

"No, I'm all right, Mother."

But I felt her strong fingers on my upper arm, turning me around, her other hand under my chin as she peered into my face. Her voice softened.

"Is it your period making you so slow-down today?" She gave my chin a little shake, as I looked up into her hooded grey eyes, now becoming almost gentle. The kitchen felt suddenly oppressively hot and still, and I felt myself beginning to shake all over.

Tears I did not understand started from my eyes, as I realized that my old enjoyment of the bone-jarring way I had been taught to pound spice would feel different to me from now on, and also that in my mother's kitchen there was only one right way to do anything. Perhaps my life had not become so simple, after all.

My mother stepped away from the counter and put her heavy arm around my shoulders. I could smell the warm herness rising from between her arm and her body, mixed with the smell of glycerine and rosewater, and the scent of her thick bun of hair.

"I'll finish up the food for supper." She smiled at me, and there was a tenderness in her voice and an absence of annoyance that was welcome, although unfamiliar.

"You come inside now and lie down on the couch and I'll make you a hot cup of tea."

Her arm across my shoulders was warm and slightly damp. I rested my head upon her shoulder, and realized with a shock of pleasure and surprise that I was almost as tall as my mother, as she led me into the cool darkened parlor.

from *Vibration Cooking: or The Travel Notes of a Geechee Girl*

In reading lots and lots of cookbooks written by white folks it occurred to me that people very casually say Spanish rice, French fries, Italian spaghetti, Chinese cabbage, Mexican beans, Swedish meatballs, Danish pastry, English muffins and Swiss cheese. And with the exception of black bottom pie and niggertoes, there is no reference to black people's contribution to the culinary arts. White folks act like they invented food and like there is some weird mystique surrounding it—something that only Julia and Jim can get to. There is no mystique. Food is food. Everybody eats!

And when I cook, I never measure or weigh anything. I cook by vibration. I can tell by the look and smell of it. Most of the ingredients in this book are approximate. Some of the recipes that people gave me list the amounts, but for my part, I just do it by vibration. Different strokes for different folks. Do your thing your way.

The amount of salt and pepper you want to use is your business. I don't like to get in people's business. I have made everything in here and found everything to be everything and everything came out very together. If you have any trouble, I would suggest that you check out your kitchen vibrations. *What kind of pots are you using?* Throw out all of them except the black ones. The cast-iron ones like your mother used to use. Can't no Teflon fry no fried chicken. I only use black pots and brown earthenware in the kitchen. White enamel is not what's happening.

I don't like fancy food. I like simple—plain—ordinary—call it what you choose. I like what is readily available. It is very easy to do special things. Like a cake you only make on your first cousin by your mother's second marriage's birthday. Or a ham you make for Sam's wedding anniversary every other February 29. I'm talking about being able to turn the daily ritual of cooking for your family into a beautiful everyday happening. Now, that's something else again.

The supermarket is full of exciting and interesting food. It don't really matter where you live. After a minute, there ain't but so many ways you can cook a sweet potato. I remember at a market on Rue Monge in Paris I saw some potatoes that looked very much in the sweet potato family. I asked and the lady said, *"C'est le pomme de terre douce."* She said that they came from Madagascar. Just then a sister from Senegal came by. I asked her how they cooked them where she came from and she said, "We make tarts . . . " (nothing but sweet potato pie); "We fry them in butter and sugar . . . " (nothing but candied sweet potatoes); "We roast them in the oven . . . " (nothing but baked sweet potatoes). It don't matter if it's Dakar or Savannah, you can cook exotic food any time you want. Just turn on the imagination, be willing to change your style and let a little soul food in. Ayischia says you are what you eat and that's what I believe, too.

An evening with good food and good vibrations from the people with whom you're eating—that's the kind of evening that turns me on. I like men who enjoy food. Cooking for a man is a very feminine thing, and I can't understand how a woman can feed her man TV dinners. Food is sexy and you can tell a lot about people and where they're at by their food habits. People who eat food with pleasure and get pleasure from the differ- ent stirring of the senses that a well-prepared food experience can bring are my kind of people.

Like Archie says, "Eating is a very personal thing; you can't eat with everybody." Some people got such bad vibrations that to eat with them would give you indigestion. I would rather give such a person money to go to Horn & Hardart than to eat with 'em. God knows, I've had some good times eating with my friends. What times! Times, oh, times! I often get nostalgia for the old days and old friends. Like those New Year's open houses I used to have and everyone I loved would come. Even Millie came from Germany one year. She arrived just in time for the black-eyes and rice. And that year I cooked the peas with beef neck bones instead of swine cause so many brothers and sisters have given up swine. I had ham hocks on the side for the others. You supposed to cook the whole hog head but I couldn't. I saw it hanging in the butcher store on Avenue D and I didn't dig it. I left the swine hanging right where he was.

If you eat black-eyed peas and rice (Hopping John) on New Year's Day, you supposed to have good luck for the coming year. Black people been eating that traditional New Year's Day dinner for years. That's why I'm not having no more open house on New Year's Day. I'm going to try some- thing new. Like Kali says,

> It's a New Kind of Day
> It's a New Kind of Day
> It's the love that make
> a New kind of day

HOPPING JOHN

Cook black-eyed peas.
When they are almost done add rice.

Mix rice and peas together.
Season and—*viola!*—you got it.

And speaking of rice. I was sixteen years old before I knew that everyone didn't eat rice everyday. Us being geechees, we had rice everyday. When you said what you were eating for dinner, you always assumed that rice was there. That was one of my jobs too. To cook the rice. A source of pride to me was that I cooked rice like a grown person. I could cook it till every grain stood by itself. What you do is to rub it together in the palms of your hands and make sure you get all grains washed. Then you put it in a pot with cold water.

Use 1 part rice to 2 parts water. Always use cold water. Let it come to a boil and cover it with a tight cover. Soon as it comes to a boil you turn it to simmer and you cover with a tight cover. Let it cook for exactly 13 minutes and then cut it off. Let it stand for 12 minutes before eating.

.   .   .   .   .

Stella,
You want to know why I say soul food is life? Well, first off, food ain't nothing but food. No matter who you are and where you live you got to eat. Cooking is a creative thing. Cooking is one of the highest of all the arts. It can make or break life. The word must be Gemini cause more manure has hit the fan over the twins' love and hunger than any other forces. So, if you cook with love and feed people, you got two forces cooled out already. Dig, food can cause happiness or unhappiness, health or sickness and make or break marriages.

I read the other day where this cat said that a lot of interracial marriages break up because of the cultural gap in cooking. Remember when you know who used to serve cottage cheese and frozen fish to you know who? Remember he used to come over to your house and cook pork chops?

Anyhow, soul food depends on what you put in it. I don't mean spices either.

If you have a serious, loving, creative energetic attitude towards life, when you cook, you cook with the same attitude.

Food changes into blood, blood into cells, cells change into energy which changes up into life and since your life style is imaginative, creative, loving, energetic, serious, food is life. You dig.

Vert

.   .   .   .   .

Dear Verta,
I have said it before but this time I mean it. Don't send me no more names and addresses. I am not interested in looking up any more of your

friends. With friends like you got you don't need enemies. I have started eating in more than ever now. I try to use all the spices and have developed a penchant for cumin. Here's my recipe.

Love,
Stella

EL COMINO REAL

Season (salt, pepper, garlic) a cut up chicken and marinate in a little lemon juice and peanut oil and onions for 1 hour. Then add cumin powder, tomatoes, zucchini and cook for ½ hour.

Dear Stella,
    Stop talking about my friends. I know they are crazy. But to tell it like it is, any nigger who ain't crazy in this society is out of his mind.

Verta Mae

P.S. Get the January 24 issue of *Time* magazine. Look under food.
    I had to write them a letter. Enclosed is a copy.

VM

January 24th
SIRS:
    You have the bad taste to say that soul food is tasteless. Your taste buds are so racist that they can't even deal with black food. Your comment that the "soul food fad" is going to be short-lived is dumb. But then your whole culture is made of short-lived fads. So you white folks just keep on eating that white foam rubber bread that sticks to the roof of your mouth, and keep on eating Minute Rice and instant potatoes, instant cereals and drinking instant milk and stick to your instant culture. And I will stick to the short-lived fad that brought my ancestors through four hundred years of oppression. *Time* magazine couldn't take any more and stopped here. Collard greens are thousands of years old and in the days of the Roman Empire were considered an epicurean delight. French restaurants too widely renowned even to depend on stars given by Guide Michelin serve chitlins sausages, only they call it *andouillette*. Soul food is more than chittlins and collard greens, ham hocks and black-eyed peas. Soul food is about a people who have a lot of heart and soul. Ask Doctor Christiaan Barnard about them black hearts.

Verta Mae

SECTION FOUR

LISA M. HELDKE

Food Politics, Political Food

I. INTRODUCTION

Frequently in the course of working on this book, I have been asked to explain what constitutes a "philosophy of food." In answering the question, I've met with considerable skepticism when I've suggested that thinking about food raises important epistemological and ontological questions about the nature of the relation between theory and practice, or about personhood. But I've experienced virtually none of that resistance when I've talked about the social and political significance of food. People have tended to be quite willing to accept the idea that philosophers might address food in this sense, because they've often seen food play a role in social movements and political debates. Whatever their personal experience, most people could draw upon something which made my claims about food and social issues seem legitimate, in a way that my other claims about the philosophical relevance of food did not.

Food often does play a central and highly visible role in social and political issues—whether they be high-level negotiations between the United States and the Soviet Union for wheat; grass roots organizing by consumers to exert pressure on multinational food manufacturers; or disaster relief collected by nongovernmental organizations for Ethiopia during a famine. Sometimes food is the source of a conflict, sometimes it's a goad or a weapon used to heighten the conflict, and sometimes it's a tool for resolution.

This essay will explore the construction of some social and political relations involving food, in order to suggest ways of engaging in practical, food-centered social action. For example, I am interested in considering how my ordinary, daily activities involving food—buying, preparing, and eating it—connect me with other workers in the world who grow the food we in the United States eat. How might I use my understanding of these connections to shape my actions? Despite the real interdependence that exists between U.S. consumers and farm workers—in the United States, Mexico, Costa Rica, and Kenya, for example—these connections are often conveniently obscure or invisible to middle-class American consumers, and thus do not inform our decision-making in the grocery store.[1]

I will also consider how activities connect me to large political and economic structures. Often when addressing issues involving corporations and governments, for example, one is overcome by the size and complexity of the issues, and by a sense of the futility and irrelevance of one's own actions. In the face of a corporation the size of Nestlé, for example, of what value can individual action be?[2] Here too, we often see little connection between our daily lives and the larger institutions. Frequently we are prevented from seeing these connections by those very institutions; it is in their interest for us to be ill-informed about their activity, and about the way individuals support that activity.

My emphasis, therefore, will be upon making clear some of the connections that exist between the small and the large, the proximate and the remote; upon exploring the theoretical connections between conceptions of personhood and conceptions of institutions; and the material connections between what I eat for dinner, the operations of U.S. multinational food companies, and the lives of food-industry workers. I will approach these issues by taking up the discussion of personhood begun in Section One. How might conceiving of the self as nonsubstantial and relational inform the way one conceives of social and political relations involving food—both relations *with* food/potential food, and with other beings *concerning* food?

In my attempt to be inclusive of both the range of issues involving food and the range of ways we may choose to involve ourselves, I will of necessity be somewhat general—but not so general as to render my ideas practically useless. I will consider primarily organizational efforts outside the governmental or corporate spheres; I will treat governments and corporations as institutions which must be influenced (forced) to do what more democratic and representative organizations desire them to do, rather than as organizations to which it is reasonable for me (singly) to provide suggestions. This strategy is in part due to my interest in connecting large structures to ordinary, daily activities of individuals. It is also due to my conviction that it is through such alternative organizing that genuine movement toward social change can come.

In addition to drawing upon themes in the first three sections of this book, my account relies heavily upon the work of certain progressive aid organizations from dominator[3] nations, such as Food First and Oxfam, and upon the writings of feminists from dominated countries, especially India. It is in these works that I find—sometimes explicitly, sometimes implicitly—the richest and most promising suggestions for understanding, challenging, and perhaps even transforming social relations and institutions through food and food-related issues. Such transformative changes are needed to shift the structure of relations away from political and economic systems which privilege white, western, wealthy men at the expense of women, "non-westerners," people of color, and the poor. How can individuals work to form coalitions which will be most effective in challenging oppressive structures, and in creating alternatives to those structures?

II. THE SUBSTANTIAL SELF AND MORAL MOTIVATION

In Section One, Curtin developed a relational, temporal, nonsubstantial conception of human personhood. He placed this conception in contrast to a substance-based conception of the self, a view that has predominated for much of the history of western philosophy. A substance view of the self is fundamentally dualistic, setting one's mental substance against one's physical substance, and maintaining a sharp separation between one's self and all other selves.

Curtin also explored the connections between a substance conception of human personhood and a view of human relations as objectified, rather than participatory. Given a view of the self as "self-contained," it follows that such a self will be related only externally, indirectly to others; a change in the nature of objectified relations need not result in any change to the self, since this relation is in no way constitutive of the self.

In developing an alternative, nonessentialist, relational conception of personhood, Curtin suggested conceiving of more relations—relations with food, in particular—as participatory. That discussion will be continued here through an exploration of food and social action. How is such action conceived under a substance view of the self? How does that view treat our motivation for engaging in action? And how might motivation be reconceived were we to adopt a relational, nonsubstantial view of the self?

A. EGOISM AND ALTRUISM

A substance-based view of the self, with its attendant focus on objectified relations, has engendered a dualistic account of humans' motivation for acting on behalf of others; on this view, we do things for others for either egoistic or altruistic motives. Either I am concerned, first and last, about benefiting my own (substantial) self, or I have entirely put aside all concern for myself and think only about the other. Our standard example of altruism is the mother who feeds her children first, leaving nothing for herself, while our example of egoism is the U.S. corporation which sells pesticides to the government of a dominated nation at a low cost—but only because they are illegal in this country.

As Curtin pointed out in Section One, we've inherited a conception of personhood which sees conflict at its heart. The struggle over whether one should fulfill one's own interests (egoism) or those of another (altruism) can be seen as yet one more species of that conflict. On the substance view, it is not possible truly to serve both oneself and others—at least not "purely." Self-interest and the interests of others are by nature at odds.

Furthermore, the substance view dictates that only humans' actions on behalf of other humans (as opposed to actions benefiting nonhuman others) can be described as moral in the fullest sense. According to the logic of identity,[4] we need only pay attention to those beings that are "like" ourselves in certain well-defined respects. The further removed other beings are from human life—the less intelligent, the less conscious they are—the less has western philosophy tended to describe our relations to them in moral terms. Though we may acknowledge that such relations have moral consequences, those consequences are thought to bear on other humans, not on the nonhuman others directly. Consider the fact that other mammals, particularly intelligent mammals such as the dolphin, are sometimes considered creatures with which we can have moral relations. Our relations with a plot of ground, on the other hand, would only be considered moral insofar as our damage to the plot of ground might affect other humans—or other intelligent mammals. Our relations with others lie on a spectrum, ranging from those which are *directly* egoistic or altruistic, to those which are only *indirectly* so.[5] The criteria determining the nature of the relation generally include intelligence, moral self-determination, self-consciousness and (as in the patch-of-ground example) consciousness.

I turn now to consider charity, a moral motivation that has been a particularly important outgrowth of the substance view of personhood. My discussion of charity here should not be regarded as praise of it; rather, I am trying to make clear the degree to which various kinds of charitable action do or don't "measure up" when placed against the standard of altruism.

B. The Particular Case of Charity

Actions done solely to benefit others are often described as being charitable. Charity is the quintessentially altruistic motivation,[6] considered to be at work in cases in which persons providing aid seem not to benefit in any way by their actions, or when their actions clearly come at considerable personal expense. Thus, Mother Theresa has been called a charitable worker, since her work has required considerable personal sacrifice. Likewise, low-profile, nonglamorous organizations, like urban soup kitchens or shelters for the homeless, are regarded as charitable in the "purest" sense, since they derive nothing, not even much publicity, from their action. Religious and other self-described "apolitical" institutions are those that have most often been described as charitable.

In other cases, it is less clear, from the perspective of the egoism/altruism dichotomy, that charity is the "genuine" motivation. In many cases, charity may be the ostensible aim, but those working on an issue may also derive considerable benefit from their actions—a fact which "dilutes" the legitimacy of their claim even as it blurs the distinction between one's own interests and others'. The cases of Live Aid and Band Aid—concerts and records produced by British and American musicians to raise money for the victims of Ethiopian famine—are examples of ambiguously charitable actions. Certainly those involved in the projects were motivated by compassion for the victims of famine, and the performers received no financial remuneration for their involvement in the projects. However, they did receive considerable positive publicity for participation; the projects were not without their rewards. Such side benefits certainly don't lead charity advocates to condemn the actions of the performers. It is more likely to make them remind each other that, after all, you have to look out for yourself. But such a realization itself diminishes the moral worth of such actions from the perspective of a charity model. One who realizes personal gain may have motives that are not purely charitable—that are, in fact, self-interested.[7]

Another sort of self-interest or egoism is thought to motivate the work of organizations that are clearly political, though nongovernmental. Organizations which have a stake not just in "helping the needy" with donations of food and expertise, but also with attempts to change government policy, cannot be "simply charitable."[8] This is because political conviction, within the framework of the egoism/altruism dichotomy, is generally treated as a form of self-interest. The claim that charity is at work is questioned once an organization provides aid which does not work within existing structures, but actually challenges those structures. Members of such organizations, of course, do not describe them as charitable either; rather, they speak of their aims as creating justice, eliminating exploitation and oppression, etc. Oxfam, Food First, and Bread for the World are food-focused examples of such organizations. Bread for the World, for example, is involved in lobbying activity aimed at shaping U.S. foreign and domestic policy.

To consider still another sort of case, charity may sometimes be thought to motivate government and corporate responses to the most extreme, most widespread food crises—the Ethiopian famine, for example.[9] But from the perspective of the egoism/altruism dichotomy, economic and political self-interest is more often believed to be behind any aid these institutions provide which is not intended to avert immediate crises. No one in the U.S. is particularly surprised to hear that most of this government's food aid to other nations is "tied"—given in the form of particular goods and services which the U.S. is especially interested in peddling, but which may not be at all useful to the recipient country.[10] American-developed hybrid seeds which require precisely controlled growing conditions, and American-made tractors and water purification equipment which cannot be repaired locally are among the well-worn examples of such aid. We suspected all along, after all, that government, hand-in-hand with industry, would only do things that are helpful to themselves in the end. It is hardly surprising—though it may be especially disturbing—that this policy extends to most food aid programs as well.

While these examples show that philosophers and others may debate whether someone's motives are actually charitable in any given situation (and while particular philosophers may not agree that actions must be altruistic in order to be considered morally worthy), for most of modern western philosophy's history, conceptions of human motivation for aiding others have been dominated by the egoism/altruism dichotomy, and charity has served as the textbook example of an altruistic motivation.

C. THE LIMITATIONS OF EGOISM AND ALTRUISM

Of course, there have always been critics of this dualistic account of human ethical motivation who take issue both with dualism in general, and with egoism and altruism in particular. The egoism/altruism dichotomy has most recently come under criticism from feminist philosophers. In particular, it has been argued that altruism, often stereotyped as the "feminine motivation" or even the "feminine virtue," is intimately connected with women's oppression in the family and elsewhere. Often, a wife and mother is expected to be "naturally" altruistic, to subordinate her desires to the desires of her husband and children, to make their wishes literally *become* hers. In the most extreme cases, she does just that—and is left literally with nothing to do when her children grow up and leave, or when her husband divorces her. Economically, emotionally, socially, she becomes her family. In the process, she loses any independent sense of herself.[11]

Such extreme cases of altruism may at first appear to be casebook examples of the dangers inherent in a relational view of personhood, and in a view of relations as participatory. It might seem that one whose self is constructed through her (participatory) relations with others, is precisely the one most susceptible to losing any *independent* sense of herself. Thus it might seem that the relational, not the substantial, self is indicted by such criticism.

I think, however, that this is not the case. Extreme altruism is not an example of the dangers of participatory relations; it is rather an instance of objectified relations that have taken over the individual, in which others' needs entirely replace those of the altruist. The altruistic individual is, in fact, a substantial self whose "substance" has been erased or subsumed by the other, leaving her with *only* her (objectified) relations.[12] Altruism is not an instance of participatory relations gone awry, but rather an example of objectified relations with no substantial self "behind" them.[13]

Egoism, not altruism, has generally been regarded as the more problematic motivation; as some of my earlier examples suggest, traditional western philosophy has seen it as morally reprehensible for one to have concern primarily for oneself. Those who benefit from their own so-called acts of kindness are regarded with great suspicion. (And, indeed, such suspicion may often be justified—recall the example of "tied aid.") Here, however, I would also call attention to another, more systemic problem with egoism.

The sharp dichotomy that has been drawn between my wishes and those of others creates a situation in which any attempt by me to link your interests with mine will be described as egoistic. And, since egoism is a position of dubious moral worth, we become suspicious of our motives whenever we find ourselves personally invested in, say, the happiness of another.[14] The egoism/altruism dichotomy produces interests in two varieties only; self-interest, and unselfish interest in another. There is no room on such an account for understanding another's interests as also being mine—unless we mean that our respective self-interests just happen to overlap in a particular case. Thus we look skeptically upon aid organizations that establish projects that benefit both their organization and the recipient. We may praise them for their shrewdness or their business savvy, but not for their charity. But such an attitude toward motivation is odd, at best. In the style of Kant, it leaves us as moral agents questioning our actions, and suspicious of our own pleasure. It establishes a boundary in principle which is rarely so clear-cut in fact.

This discussion of some shortcomings of egoism leads back to other serious problems with altruism. Because both motivations emerge from the same conception of human personhood, it is unsurprising that related concerns arise with respect to both. Charity, like self-interest, is predicated on a belief that I and my concerns are separate from you and your concerns. It describes my relations with you as external, objectified. Thinking of my "aid" to you in terms of charity encourages me to disconnect and bracket off my worries from yours, to ignore the (often deep and obvious) connections between us. Even as I immerse myself in your problems, I remain oddly separate from them. If I replace my interests with yours, rather than seeking ways in which our interests connect or are mutually constitutive or are at odds with each other, I preserve the separateness of those interests. Mine are hermetically sealed away. I may take them up again, at some later date, when I have finished with your projects, but for now, they must not motivate my actions.

Stated most dramatically, the separation which is presumed (by both altruism [charity] and egoism) renders as optional all relations between persons.[15] In consequence, all "charitable" actions are treated as actions which go above and beyond the call of duty, for they involve acting upon relations we needn't have established. There is no ontological or social necessity to these relations—they are forged out of the goodness of our hearts. That's part of what makes the resultant actions charitable. Choosing to give money to a famine relief organization, or to work for the Peace Corps, or to become a missionary in a dominated nation, bringing western farming technology, etc., to "the people," is a virtuous action in effect *because* I needn't have done it. I needn't have done it because my relations with those others are external to my self. Such a perception of one's engagement with others is a logical consequence of a substance view of personhood.

Not only does charity distance us, it also obviously places us in a hierarchical relation; I, because I am "granting" the aid, am in a superior, more powerful position. I can choose to set aside my own problems in order to aid you in solving yours. I have solutions; you have problems. You are comparatively powerless in the relation, and can offer me little in return for my aid. (Though charitable givers often talk about their rewards being greater than the value of anything they've given, such talk rings a bit hollow; yes, in one sense the warm feeling one gets more than repays one's efforts, but in another sense, it is clear that the person who can make such a claim occupies the position of power in the relation.)

One very concrete, common, and disastrous manifestation of the hierarchy and separation built into the structure of the charity motivation is that it enables those who offer aid to "forget" to involve recipients directly in the planning and implementation of aid projects. It is not only government- and corporate-sponsored (i.e., unsurprisingly self-interested) aid programs that ignore the interests of the recipients in their effort to further their own economic and strategic interests.[16] Charitable organizations too are often organized in ways that treat aid recipients as passive, their knowledge as irrelevant. Well-intentioned westerners may, for example, disregard poor Indians' farming methods as "primitive," in contrast to the "sophisticated" techniques which western science and technology make possible. Such an attitude reflects an inability to see the sophistication of, for example, low-technology farming techniques that have been carefully adapted to particular soil and climatic conditions, and to particular dietary needs.

Even if input from local recipients is sought, a charity-based model will tend to treat it as precisely that—input, participation, or "help" in a project already designed. The charity motivation, much like self-interest, tends to privilege exactly those resources—money, equipment, western scientific knowledge—the donor has, and to create projects which allow those resources most fully to be utilized, regardless of their appropriateness and desirability to the recipients. A charity model, then, tends to keep control of the situation very much in the hands of the donors. Oddly, but familiarly enough, this often means that well-intentioned, "charity-minded" projects turn out to do anything but benefit their recipients.[17]

That charitable organizations, not just government and for-profit organizations, are sites of paternalism and exploitation is unsurprising, given that they, too, exist in the racist, classist, and sexist systems which prevail in both dominator and dominated nations, and in a world in which colonial and neocolonial relationships prevail between dominator and dominated. Traditionally, most of what goes by the name of "aid" or "charity" has been delivered by privileged inhabitants of dominator nations to dominated nations and dominated inhabitants of their own nations. Such aid leaves oppressive structures intact, or even reinforces them. Socially and economically, as well as philosophically, charity retains the hierarchy between donor and recipient, while effecting certain (cosmetic) alterations in the distribution of wealth, knowledge, etc.[18]

It may seem that I am attacking an outdated model by criticizing charity as a motivation for aiding others; after all, the word "charity" is used infrequently today by any but the most conservative groups, and many nongovernmental organizations do not regard their mission as charitable. The problems inherent in charity-minded thinking, some of which I sketched above, are well recognized, and have already been well documented. Charity as a motivation is widely regarded as old-fashioned, and has been replaced—not only among progressive and radical organizations, but even in mainstream aid organizations.[19]While it is true that the rhetoric of aid organizations has moved away from charity and now is more likely to utilize notions like "empowerment" or "bottom-up organizing," whether the actual work of such organizations has likewise moved from charity is another matter.[20]

Certainly progressive organizations doing grass-roots organizing to demand land reform, for example, do not wish to preserve a model of change in which dominated people figure as "charity cases." The fact that such organizations may do so despite their intentions suggests not only the pervasiveness of systematic forms of domination, but also the tenacity and wide-ranging influence of western philosophical attitudes about the nature of humans and human relations.

If my analysis of the relations between charity and the substance view of the self is correct, it will follow that rooting out the charity motive would be a difficult undertaking—one that could not be accomplished simply through a change in language used to describe one's work. Following upon the issues explored in Section One, I suggest that to undermine the charity motivation requires rethinking the nature of ourselves as persons.

For people who have grown up with a view of the self as substantial, and who have lived in a dominator nation such as the United States, it is likely that we will formulate an understanding of aid which simply replicates the relationships of domination and subordination that shape our perceptions of the world. These include the relations of "first world" over "third world," "western" over "primitive," men over women, "educated" over "uneducated"—and also the more abstract philosophical relations of subject over object, mind over body, self over other. If we see ourselves as independent substances—subjects—with competing interests, we then see one person's gain as necessitating another's loss.[21] We necessarily see relationships as involving power struggles—or at least power inequalities. We see the aid we give to others as a personal sacrifice—quite literally bread from our own mouths.

Given that many of us live in a world in which oppressive structures shape the character of virtually all our relations, and given the ways in which structures of oppression support and are supported by an abstract conception of personhood that sees (some of) us as independent substances, what we require are alternative conceptions of human personhood and human relations, conceptions that are theoretical and practical, that provide other ways to think and act in this world. By transforming western conceptions of humans as independent substances into conceptions of humans as relational, we can in turn undermine the egoism/altruism dichotomy and the charity model, both of which depend upon a substance view of persons for their cogency.

Such transformed conceptions of persons and relations, if they are to be useful, must begin with a recognition of the situations in which we now find ourselves, situations in which dominance and subordination define our relations with others and in which the western philosophical conception of persons as substances prevails. Utopian models which deny these conditions are of little value; we require models which take account of the real, systemic inequalities shaping our lives at every level, from the personal to the international.[22] By taking seriously the project of reconceptualizing selves as relational, nonsubstantial beings, we can at the same time begin to create alternatives to charity, and to the egoism/altruism dichotomy.

III. CORESPONSIBILITY: AN ALTERNATIVE TO CHARITY AND EGOISM

The alternative I will develop here is a food-focused version of a position I call the Coresponsible Option, a position I developed elsewhere[23] as an epistemological framework, but which has considerable applicability to other kinds of relations, such as those I'm discussing here. The term "coresponsible" is meant to evoke, among other things, the fact that acting in the world is a communal, relational activity—that we are in corespondence with, and are also responsive and responsible to, others in the world. I describe the position as an option to emphasize its provisionality; it is one way, not *the* way to approach relations with others. The Coresponsible Option is a framework for action—moral, political, epistemological—that informs and is informed by a relational view of the self, for it regards relations as nonaccidental aspects of humans. To use the terminology Curtin introduced in Section One, the Coresponsible Option replaces the substance view of relations as objectified with a view of relations as participatory.

Furthermore, when it is used to address food, as I will use it here, the Coresponsible Option engenders an understanding of the web of human relations that transforms the way those relations are conceived on a substance view. The Option begins with a recognition of the constitutive role of relations in human personhood, and also redirects our attention toward those relations that are important for food. In this section, I will attempt to fill out the coresponsible conception of relations in a way that makes clear the ways in which our sense of ourselves as relational, combined with a recognition of the centrality of food in human lives, challenges us to render these relations more humane, more equitable, and healthier. Such an understanding, I suggest, has the potential to be genuinely transforma-tive—of our perceptions of ourselves and our relations, and of the ways in which we participate in and structure the social and political institutions which shape our lives.

Genuinely acting from an understanding of our relationality in order to develop a coresponsible alternative to charity requires unlearning lessons one learns well in a substance-based "upbringing." In the following sec-tion, I will examine several of these lessons, and will also suggest alterna-tive lessons/modes of action with which we might replace them. First, an understanding of selves as relational, not substantial, challenges us to re-ject the assumption that humans are fundamentally in conflict with each other, and that our needs must be either equated or compromised if we are to work with or for others. Second, it is important for the development of a coresponsible alternative to recognize that relations exist among all sorts of beings, and it is not only humans' relations with (particular) other humans that are relevant. Furthermore, a relational conception of selves requires the recognition that relations are asymmetrical; my connections to you may be stronger and of a different character than your connections to me. The final element of a coresponsible alternative I'll discuss is the understanding that we may—and indeed often must—choose the way we live out our relations with others.

A. Neither "Natural Enemies" nor "Natural Friends"

As Curtin suggested in Section One, the price for having a substantial conception of the self has been high; such a conception "implies an un-derstanding of human life pervaded by conflict"—in particular, conflict between my moral rights and the rights of another. A relational under-standing of persons challenges the notion that conflict is somehow funda-mental to the very nature of "the human condition." At the same time, a relational view avoids the opposite extreme, a utopian vision of the har-mony of all things, a vision on which conflict is viewed as an artificial consequence of our "unnatural" lives. Conflicts are neither essential fea-tures of human relationships, nor unnatural aberrations of them, but sim-ply the unsurprising outcomes of living in complex webs of relations.

A relational replacement for charity must move beyond enlightened self-interest. Enlightened self-interest represents perhaps the most pro-gressive motivation that can emerge from the egoism/altruism dichotomy. Nonetheless, I shall suggest that it falls short of being a motivation that springs from an understanding of relations as participatory.

Enlightened self-interest is sometimes pointed to as a kind of egoistic alternative to charity, one that leaves the dichotomy between egoism and altruism intact. Enlightened self-interest operates by arguing that others' interests actually *are* my own, and that in aiding these others, I am actually aiding myself as well. This motivation is often used to explain why those of us in "developed" nations should concern ourselves with the plight of people in "developing" nations. Appeals to (more or less) enlightened self-interest might range from showing our dependence upon people in dominated nations for our food supply, to showing the effects on our lives of the deforestation and pollution of air and water in dominated countries, to suggesting that in some general sense, we all suffer when anyone suffers.

There is certainly merit in this motivation, particularly when it is compared to charity or "unenlightened" egoism. Its advantage is that it provides a way to connect up interests that are seen as inherently disconnected—rather than requiring one set of interests to be suppressed (as is the case with charity, and also, for that matter, with unenlightened egoism). However, it is a position that still rests on the substance-based belief that my interests are intrinsically separate from those of others, that my self is *ontologically* prior to and separate from its relations with others. It may be true that I can equate my interests with others; the shortcoming of enlightened self-interest is that it still presumes the separateness of interests which must *be* equated. The model conceives of relations as external and objectified, and accepts the notion that conflict between my interests and yours is the driving force behind human relations.

With respect to my relations to dominated peoples, this conception of human motivation seems to suggest that unless and until I, as a member of a dominator society, can find some place in which my interests may be equated with those in a dominated culture, I have no reason to participate in their struggle. While it may always be possible to perform the equation—while I may always find ways in which my interests could be equated to those of another person or group—it is relevant to ask whether this should be necessary. Must another's struggle be "mine" before it is "worth my while" to take it on? Can I only find reason to act when I can "see myself in the other?" Enlightened self-interest would suggest that this is the case; it simply widens the field of things that are my interest by showing how many other lives affect my own.

As a move on the way to developing motivations for action that spring from relational selves, enlightened self-interest is important. It should not be mistaken for such a motivation, however. If we begin with an understanding of humans as participatorily relational, then it becomes impossible to define "selves" as substances ontologically prior to our relations. The relational view of self goes beyond the view that your interests can be shown to be the *same* as mine, to suggest that your interests and mine are (often) *connected* to each other, grow out of each other.[24] This is an ontological point, a consequence of defining human personhood as nonsubstantial and relational.

In spelling out the limitations of enlightened self-interest, a view that assumes the existence of a conflict between my interests and those of another, I do not suggest moving to the opposite extreme—asserting that conflict is somehow "unnatural"—either. To conceive of human persons as relational does not mean to conceive of our relations as without conflicts.

This point is more of a practical observation. From the claim that humans are relational, not substantial, selves, it does not follow that conflicts are foreign, any more than the claim that humans eat grains leads to the conclusion that no humans ever have any trouble digesting bread. Conflicts, challenges, and differences which resist reconciliation arise at least in part because of the complexity of our interconnectedness. Relational selves are the intersections of hosts of relations, some of which are likely to be incompatible. Coresponsibility begins with the understanding that humans and our interests are neither essentially at odds with others (human and nonhuman), nor essentially in harmony with them. This is true whether those in relation to each other are acting to preserve and strengthen relations, or are acting to preserve their own narrowly defined interests; even in a coresponsible utopia, conflicts would arise due to different perceptions of what is best overall.

Consider the interesting example of the ecology of Isle Royale, the largest island in Lake Superior, which has been relatively undisturbed by humans. This unusual island has resident populations of moose and wolves, both of which are thought to have floated over on ice floes from the Minnesota mainland. For several decades, the two populations have maintained an uneasy equilibrium, which ensured the continuation of other life on the island. (In part, this means that the wolves kept the population of moose down, thus preventing overbrowsing.) Even when equilibrium is maintained, it is clear that conflict is present; while some interests of both moose and wolf population are dependent on each other for their maintenance (both populations need each other literally to survive), both populations also obviously have other relations which are not compatible with their relations with each other.

Furthermore, this equilibrium is now being threatened due to the dwindling of the wolf population, a result of interbreeding in the tiny pack. The result, if the wolves become extinct on the island, will be a moose population explosion, a result which will dramatically threaten the fragile plant population of the island, and also, ultimately, the moose population. As such a system suggests, relations are neither static, nor always mutually beneficial.

Just as a coresponsible alternative to charity cannot begin with the view that conflict is aberrant, neither can it begin with the assumption that there is only one possible way to describe and act out our relationality and its resultant conflicts. Diane Di Prima's "Revolutionary Letter #42," reprinted in this section, challenges one popular western perception of the conflict over the earth's resources—namely the assumption that there is a "population problem" in the dominated world.

what is this
"overpopulation" problem, have you
looked at it, clearly, do you know

ten times as much land needed if we eat
hamburger, instead of grain; we can
all fit, not hungry, if we minimize
our needs. . . .

Di Prima changes the context of the problem by reperceiving the relevant relations. She challenges the perspective that sees American meat-eating and other forms of conspicuous food consumption as inalienable rights, and questions the line of thinking which locates the population problem squarely within the third world. If the conflict is conceived in terms of resource consumption, rather than in terms of how many (nonwhite) people live on an acre of land in dominated nations, middle-class, meat-eating Americans' roles in food/resource/population problems are revealed—as are ways for us to stop exacerbating those situations. "Revolutionary Letter #55," also reprinted here, suggests that we say no—no to a host of foods which are not only dangerous to producer and consumer, but are also likely wrapped in at least two layers of "disposable" (meaning nonrecyclable) plastic, metal, coated cardboard, etc. When one says "no" to these foods, one is also saying "no" to the processes used to produce them—processes harmful to people and things, and processes which accumulate mountains of nondisposable trash. Saying "no" also means refusing to accept the received view of relations between inhabitants of dominator and dominated nations and their respective roles in the "population problem," and turning that refusal into concrete action.

B. RELATIONALITY: IT'S NOT JUST WITH HUMANS ANYMORE

Another outgrowth of a relational sense of self that is important for the creation of a coresponsible alternative is charity and egoism is the recognition that relations exist among all sorts of beings, and that it is not only our relations with other humans that are significant in shaping our motives or determining our actions. Perhaps nowhere is this so apparent as with food, which involves humans in connections with other humans and human institutions (farms, corporations, governments, markets, cooperatives), but also with other animals, plants, soil, air, and water. Ideally, these relations would be organized so as to be mutually beneficial; however, our tendencies to focus only on relations involving a certain dominant world, masculine subset of the human population have created many relations that are beneficial only to humans, and then only in the short run.

As noted earlier, the western philosophical tradition has tended to treat human relations with other self-conscious and rational beings (that is, relations with other humans) as different in kind from humans' relations with all other beings. In particular, these relations have been set off as morally valuable. Humans' relations with animals, with inanimate objects, etc., have been seen, at best, as only indirectly or derivatively moral.[25]

This attitude has shaped relations between human and nonhuman worlds, and also between certain humans and those other humans who have been defined by westerners as *less* than fully human. This latter category has included, variously, those who are denied full humanity because of some combination of their race, sex, occupation, social class, etc.

As documented by both Wes Jackson and Vandana Shiva in their selections, the western emphasis on rationality—manifested, perhaps since Descartes, in an obsession with technological development—has resulted in farming practices which erode and deplete topsoil and pollute groundwater. This emphasis on rationality has also been instrumental in the shaping of "development" policies which destroy the local economies and ecologies of people in dominated nations. Soil, plants, other animals, and also "nonmale, nonwhite, non-European" peoples are perceived as being at some remove from the western ideal of humanness. Thus, "full humans" dealing with these "others" have often not found it necessary to treat them as full participants in their own futures. They have been and continue to be colonized and exploited by those who serve "human interests."

By beginning with a recognition of the vital importance of our relations to the soil, to water, to plant and animal species, as well as to all other humans, a food-centered philosophy would readily ascribe importance to qualities other than rationality, self-consciousness, and consciousness. Among the qualities which emerge from attention to food-based relations might be temporality, authenticity, diversity, integrity, relationality, and "thoughtful practicality."

Attention to food reveals complicated sets of connections that exist between us and the soil (ab)used to grow crops, fruits and vegetables; the animals grown to be slaughtered and to produce milk and eggs; and all those who participate in the growing and processing of the foods we ultimately eat. Food production in the United States, and at U.S.-owned facilities abroad, is characterized at virtually every level by abuse and exploitation.[26] Attention to the host of relationships in which food involves us can draw our attention to this abuse and exploitation, render visible relations that are invisible to the eye focused only on relations with other narrowly defined rational beings, and challenge us to see the interconnections between abuse of land and abuse of people that are carried out for the sake of producing the foods many North Americans have come to expect in our grocery stores: off-season produce, inexpensive meat, and "exotic" foods which cannot be grown on this continent.

To put it in the negative, attention to food and food-based relations "desanctifies" our relations with other humans. Recognizing the degree to which humans and the soil, for example, are interdependent brings me to resist a system which sees this relation as only derivatively significant, derivatively moral, because it involves a nonrational agent. Jackson provides a rich, suggestive account of the directions in which our recognition of the importance of our relation to the soil might take us.

Jackson discusses the destructive practices currently employed by U.S. farmers—practices which are fossil-fuel dependent and result in dramatic losses of topsoil—in terms of their connection to a subject-object conception of humans' relation to our environment. He traces this conception—which pervades farmers' everyday relations to the soil—through the thought of Bacon, Descartes, and others. In its place, Jackson proposes recognizing that "there is an interplay between organism and environment, and each is changed due to the presence of the other" (365*); that "interpenetration is the right definition of our relationship to the earth . . ." (368*).

This recognition of interplay and interpenetration, he suggests, should cause us to reinterpret the current crisis in farming. It is not an economic crisis: "it is a crisis *reflected* by economic problems which derive from a larger, cultural crisis" (368*). Jackson further states,

> Were we to act on the basis of ecological understanding, it would be possible to place the base of the pyramid firmly on the land. Society would then become a manifestation of what the land can support in a healthful and productive way. Only by meeting the land's expectations first can society be sustained. (369*)

For Jackson, the knowledge-based, subject/object paradigm for relations with our environment must be replaced by one which sees our relation to the earth as a kind of interdependence, an interdependence in which the land's needs and "expectations" (things usually only attributed to *conscious* beings) must be met at the outset, not after (some) humans' own (short-term) needs are filled.

An analysis similar to Jackson's can be made of western conceptions of relations between humans and other animals. As I have noted, the western philosophical tradition has tended to regard it as necessary that beings "possess" self-consciousness and rationality if we are to treat them as capable of morally relevant relations with us. Of course, this criterion excludes humans' relations with most—or perhaps all—animals from the class of morally relevant ones. Given this view, respectful treatment of animals by humans becomes a gift we give them—but not a right to which they are entitled.

Carol Adams, in the selection in Section Three, provides an account of one way this philosophical view has shaped the concrete nature of relations between humans and animals when she describes the literary and physical processes we go through in order to turn animals into things we eat. "Meat eating," she suggests, "is a story applied to animals, it gives meaning to animals' existence" (267*). In this story, "[a]nimals' lives and bodies become material fit to receive human's stories: the word becomes flesh" (267*). Rethinking our relations to animals—particularly rethinking the relations between animals' exploitation and oppression and the exploitation and oppression of women—can, she suggests, challenge us to tell alternative stories in which animals are not dismembered.

Finally, Jackson's analysis of the relations between humans and the soil can also serve as a model for examining the ways in which western philosophical thought has shaped relations between humans in dominator and dominated nations, or between those persons within a given culture who exploit and dominate, and those who are exploited and dominated.

Jonathan Swift's satiric work "A Modest Proposal," reprinted in this section, can be read as presenting the dark extreme to which the subject/object view of dominant peoples' relations to the rest of the world might be carried. In suggesting that the poor sell their children as food for the rich, Swift is not moving all that far beyond the situation that prevails in many of the places where our food is produced. While farm workers do not literally become my food—I do not eat their actual flesh—such workers around the world weaken, age prematurely, contract diseases, and die young because of the work they do, the conditions under which they work, and the wages they receive to grow food for consumption by well-off Americans. Swift challenges us to see that such activities (or seventeenth-century equivalents) result in the death of humans just as surely as would buying and eating babies. A system which encourages us to fix our gaze on relations among a narrow subset of human beings prevents us from seeing the consequences of our relations with other humans.

This theme is reiterated in Bernice Johnson Reagon's song "Are My Hands Clean?" Though its subject is the garment industry, it addresses conditions that also prevail in the food industry; instead of a blouse, Reagon could have written about canned pineapple. Reagon explains, in a flat and unadorned style, the work women do to make her/my clothing, and the reason that clothing is so relatively inexpensive. In stark language, it reveals the power relations that prevail in the world of international industry, relations that mean profit for corporate executives and short lives for their employees. With this song, Reagon urges me to look with her at my relations to sisters here and abroad, and then, ironically, invites me to contemplate whether my hands are "clean."

ASYMMETRY OF RELATIONS

Another aspect of relationality that is important for the development of a coresponsible alternative to charity is that relations are often asymmetrical. That is, my relations to you, and my understanding of them, may be stronger and of a different character than your relations to me. This may seem most obvious and least surprising in cases in which relations are not between two humans, but between humans and nonhumans. For example, because I am a human, connections between me and a patch of ground are not symmetrical. One of the most obvious differences between us, which has historically been taken to be definitive, is that I am self-conscious while the patch of ground is not. A less frequently discussed difference is that a patch of ground, under the right conditions, can support plants that I can eat, while I cannot in the same sense provide food for it.

My relations with other humans are also often not symmetrical. I depend upon you for, and provide you with, things different from that for which you depend upon me and with which you provide me. (The asymmetry of the relations is often part of what makes them valuable; if I didn't have what you need and need what you have, and vice versa, we would not benefit as we do from the relation.) Sometimes the "currency" exchanged in a relation may not be the same in both directions; I may depend upon you for something material, while you depend upon me for something spiritual or emotional.

Such differences are not in principle problematic. However, the asymmetry of relations often is problematic, for it enables powerful members of relations to exploit and oppress others. This happens when the asymmetry of the relations is a consequence of, or is exacerbated by, the fact that the relations are invisible to those who benefit from them. For example, while it may seem that private donations and governmental aid from the United States far outstrip the monetary value of goods received by the United States from dominated nations, in fact the debt often runs the other way. When American-owned "interests" pay rock-bottom market prices to desperately poor countries for their agricultural products, in the end U.S. consumers often come out ahead. Furthermore, since much aid is tied to the purchase of U.S.-made goods, U.S. corporations often see the largest benefits from aid projects.[27]

Often relations may be dramatically unbalanced, with one member of the relation possessing significantly more power than the other, and having the capacity to control both the relationship and the other. By viewing ourselves as substantial selves who have various external and objectified relations with others for the purpose of getting our food, those of us who (at least in some circumstances) occupy positions of privilege create relations which are pathologically asymmetrical. These relations bring disproportionate harm to dominated people, and disproportionate (if often short-term) benefit to dominators. The substance view supports this way of acting by enabling us to treat our relations with others as accidental—not constitutive—aspects of ourselves; as things to which we may choose to attend, but which it is not essential that we do.

Explaining "Are My Hands Clean?" at a Sweet Honey in the Rock concert, Reagon discussed the fact that people are often disturbed by it, because they would prefer not to know about their relations to others. Given that they cannot always "do something about it"—given that they cannot entirely remove themselves from the cycle of violence and exploitation that is sewn into their clothing, canned with their pineapple, etc.—these people prefer not to know about that violence and exploitation. Her response to this desire for ignorance/innocence was to point out that, whether we know about it or not, this is the reality of many women's and men's lives. We are only protecting a privilege we haven't earned by preserving our "right" to be ignorant of such things. Put another way, the connections between me and women all over the world are already in existence, whether I choose to recognize them or not. Choosing to ignore them means choosing to preserve my illegitimate privilege, and to preserve my view of myself as a substance only externally related to other beings.

Consider charity again. Charity places the charitable giver in a position of power; they can choose to give or not give aid, for example. This power lies in their hands because of the way relations among people have been constituted on a subject/object model. Because I ignore[28] my interdependence with the women who grow and process my food around the world, and because I have the privileges of wealth, color, education, etc., I have the power to define the nature of my relations with those women; I may choose to place importance upon certain aspects of those relations, and to disregard other aspects of them. My illegitimate privilege in a racist, classist, colonialist society, supported by a conception of humans as independent subjects whose relations to others are external, affords me this power. In other words, the relation is pathologically asymmetrical, for it locates power disproportionately with the charitable giver.

However, by beginning with a recognition of the relational nature of human personhood, the Coresponsible Option provides us with a framework in which to transform asymmetrical relations like charity into relations whose asymmetry is mutually beneficial. It does so by enabling us to recognize that relations are not things we may choose to have or not have with others, or things to which we may choose to attend or ignore, but are ordinary features of every life. (Certain particular relations may be avoidable—I may never eat bananas, for example—but entire classes of relations cannot be eliminated—I can't stop eating food.)

The very act of acknowledging my relatedness to all sorts of "others" places me in a different framework for acting than does the substance view of persons. Specifically, it rejects the presumption of the charity view that our relations with others are merely accidental, and that therefore our involvement in the problems of others is optional, a "favor" we do for them. On the Coresponsible Option, I instead begin with an acknowledgment of the constitutive nature of my relations to others. From here, it is not a matter of *deciding* to become involved with others' lives, but of recognizing the ways in which I am inevitably a part of them—and of understanding how their problems are also my own. With this understanding, I must recognize that I cannot choose to become involved or not, but can only choose (to some extent) the nature of my involvement. Having relations with others is not an option; it's a given.

By removing the sense that my connections with others are optional, a coresponsible understanding of my motivations for action undermines the element of moral superiority/inferiority built into the substance view. The charity model insists that I am acting out of the goodness of my heart, "helping" others *whom I have no particular reason to help.* (This is one source of pathological asymmetry in my relations.) By focusing instead on the very real connections between me and these others, and on the degree to which I am what I am because of those connections, I can no longer regard my involvement with them as optional, as a morally good act for which I deserve praise. Thus can we undermine the pathological asymmetry by eliminating the delusion that the powerful are choosing to forge connections to "help" the oppressed where no connections currently exist. Connections exist; choice lies in our determining the ways we participate in those relations.

We who are privileged by virtue of race, class, education, and/or sex cannot escape the fact that, in choosing to invest our energies in certain relations rather than others, we are in that very action exercising privilege. The question we must ask is not "how can I avoid privilege?" but "how can my actions work to undermine the structures that give me privilege?"[29] The first question speaks of a longing for moral purity, for blamelessness; it is predicated on a substance view of human personhood: "If I can just get myself in order, if I can just stop doing bad things and having relations with others who are bad, then I am a good person." Of course, we cannot simply stop being in relations with others, which means that we cannot simply "give up" our illegitimate power over them and become "good." But, as the second question suggests, even if it were possible for me to do so, working to eliminate my individual guilt would be beside the point; a relational conception of personhood directs me to work with those who would transform the oppressive nature of our relations. Arriving at this understanding by way of a transformation of the nature of personhood gives another dimension to the progressivist slogan that "we're none of us free until we're all free."

The interrelations in which food involves us provide powerful examples of the fact that our relations with others are not optional. They also reveal the difficulty of deciding upon a course of action in light of those relations. In a very real sense, I cannot even choose a diet in which I am not complicit in the oppression of others. I can, however, choose to withdraw support from systems that oppress and exploit workers, animals, and the soil—by growing my own food, by buying from worker-owned cooperatives, by not eating animals, etc.—and by talking with others in order to come to clearer understandings of how our actions support or undermine systems of oppression. A coresponsible replacement for charity aims not at giving me clean hands and a clean conscience, but at enabling me to live out my relations with others honestly, recognizing that I can never be "good" all alone—that in fact "being good" may be an inappropriate goal toward which to aim.[30]

D. Choosing Your Own Utensil

The final aspect of a coresponsible alternative to charity I note is that recognizing that we are relational, and that therefore our only choice is to act on those relations, does not dictate the form such action must take. Specifically, it must not be read as a command to "love unconditionally," or to "be nice to everyone." Action may be in solidarity with others with whom we have relations, or it may take the form of a challenge to those others. Recognizing a relation that had been invisible to us may move us to work in coalition with those we had been working against, or it may move us to remove support from those we had been unwittingly supporting. Perhaps hate is never an appropriate motivation for our actions, but at times it is nevertheless necessary to be self-loving enough to challenge those who wield power, and to work to undermine the illegitimate sources of that power.[31] Furthermore, given the realization that I am relationally connected to countless others, it is quite evident that I can and must make choices about those relations on which I will work. I cannot act on all connections at once, and it is in fact an egotistical holdover from a substance view of my self to think that I "must" or "should" do so.

I may engage in such action on many levels and in many venues, beginning with weekly grocery shopping. On what do I base decisions about which foods to buy? Are taste, convenience, and cost the only factors influencing me? If so, chances are that I am purchasing food produced by large multinational firms, with all that this entails—including supporting the exploitative and oppressive labor and land-use practices of such firms. On the other hand, purchasing from worker-organized collectives, whether locally or by mail, means supporting—both economically and symbolically—efforts of exploited and oppressed people to achieve independence and maintain integrity, while simultaneously withdrawing my support from multinationals.

I may further withdraw support by organizing or participating in boycotts or demonstrations, or by refusing to pay taxes. I may act in support of oppressed peoples, other animals, and the soil by eating more simply—choosing foods lower on the food chain, deemphasizing "exotic" foods, including only foods that are grown in my own bioregion—or by working with local collectives on projects collectively planned. I may commit money and labor to development projects designed by those who will use them, addressing needs they have assessed.

Wendell Berry suggests some ways we may choose to live out our relations—specifically with the earth and its resources—in "The Pleasures of Eating," reprinted here. Berry suggests trying to "eat responsibly," but as the title of the essay suggests, living out this responsibility, far from being a burden, is actually a source of pleasure. Understanding eating as an agricultural act—rather than an industrial act, which it has become for most

urban consumers—calls upon us to recognize that "how we eat determines, to a considerable extent, how the world is used. This is a simple
way of describing a relationship that is inexpressibly complex. To eat responsibly is to understand and enact, so far as one can, this complex relationship" (377*). Some ways to live out this relationship, he suggests,
include growing and preparing our own food, buying food from local
growers, and learning the origins of the rest of it. A companion essay to
Berry's could be written, detailing the ways in which eating is a *social* act,
one which puts us in connection not only with the people sitting at table
with us, but also with all those whose labor has helped produce the food
we are now eating. In addition to the suggestions he makes for eating
responsibly (suggestions which also manifest the social nature of eating),
such an essay would also advocate learning the living and working conditions of those who prepare this food, and learning how and why they come
to be growing food for sale.

   In whatever actions I take, I am making choices about how to act upon
my relationality. To be healthy, such choices must be intelligent, must be
based on an understanding of the specificity of my relations with particular
others (individuals, groups, companies). It is my responsibility to learn
about those with whom I will work, and those from whom I will withdraw
support. Making intelligent choices is a time-consuming project; there is
also always the danger that, in my desire to make intelligent choices, I will
lose perspective.[32] By making choices, I cannot deny the complexity of
relations, or behave as if the projects on which I work are the only "important" ones. Rather, I ought to work to understand the relations between the
actions I choose to take and actions taken by others; I must explore the
connections between issues: local and "remote" issues; environmental
and labor issues; issues for women of color and for white women.

   Whatever actions I choose, at whatever risk, and with whatever level of
intensity, a food-focused coresponsible model for action challenges me to
act in ways that will illuminate rather than mystify my relationality, that will
highlight the many ways in which those relations involve food, and that
will work toward the elimination of the pathological asymmetry that characterizes many of those relations.

N O T E S

1. Or, more recently, they inform those decisions, but in a temporary, often
superficial way. There has been a flurry of "earth-minded" activity among certain
sectors of the American population in the aftermath of Earth Day 1990. While on
one level such activity is heartening, on another level it is not. For frequently we

engage only in activities that are convenient to us, for as long as they are convenient. Furthermore, such activity often tends to focus on the "trees" while missing the "forest"—buying recycled paper from a company that is a major polluter of the Great Lakes, for example. Finally, as I will attempt to show, such activity frequently remains at the level of charity—a very unhelpful level from which to engage in political action.

2. I chose the example of Nestlé quite intentionally, of course. The boycott of Nestlé products spearheaded by the Infant Formula Action Coalition (INFACT) was a grassroots movement aimed at stopping the unethical selling practices Nestlé used to peddle its infant formula in dominated nations. Miraculously, this campaign actually achieved success when the World Health Organization (WHO) passed a code governing the promotion of baby formulas. Unfortunately, in 1988 it was found that Nestlé had failed to live up to the code, which prompted a renewal of the boycott.

3. I use the designations "dominator nation" and "dominated nation" because these terms make explicit the (colonial and neocolonial) economic and political relations that exist between nations of the world, relations that are masked by designations such as "first world/third world" or "developed/underdeveloped." The latter terms also establish the United States and other dominator nations as the standards toward which other nations are or should be evolving, whereas the terms "dominator" and "dominated" implicitly advocate nondominant relations as the standard.

4. See Curtin's essay "Food, Body, Person" in Section One.

5. One way to see this spectrum is to consider the various ways vegetarians eliminate foods from their diet: some self-described vegetarians eliminate only so-called red meats (which tend to come from large, relatively intelligent animals). Others also eliminate chicken, then fish, then finally even eggs and milk. On one view of vegetarianism, each elimination can be seen as extending the boundaries of what is considered "worthy" of treatment as another moral being. See Section Two for an extended discussion of the shortcomings of this motivation for vegetarianism, and also for an alternative—"contextual moral vegetarianism."

6. This is not to say that criticism of charity has not always existed. Criticism has often come from charity's recipients, but has tended to be ignored or minimized by the charity-minded. Charitable givers assume that their recipients are simply criticizing the particular form charity has taken—how one doled out the food, for example. It has often not been recognized by advocates of charity that a much deeper criticism is often actually being suggested by its critics.

7. Kant's moral philosophy is the western philosophical position that is perhaps most suspicious of actions that may be compelled by personal gain. For Kant, an action does not have clear moral content unless it is done from duty. Actions done in accordance with duty, but to which one is also inclined for other reasons (such as pleasure, or fear of consequences) are not unambiguously moral—we cannot know that duty, rather than pleasure, is what compels us to act in such cases. In the case of individuals who are kind to others because they derive joy from being kind, Kant says, "But I say that, however dutiful and however amiable it may be, that kind of action has no true moral worth" (1988, 252–53).

8. To put it another way, charity is regarded as "apolitical," meaning it accepts existing political institutions. Once one challenges a political structure, one's actions are no longer charitable. Charity is not political, and political action is not charitable.

9. In fact, it can be shown that economic self-interest, not charity, was at work here. Discussions of the politics of food aid may be found in Clark 1986; Lappe and Collins 1978, 1986; Lappe, Collins, and Kinley 1980; George 1977, 1979, and 1984; and Byron 1983.

10. See, for example, Clark 1986, particularly the chapter entitled "Aid," for a fuller discussion of this practice.

11. See, for example, Blum, Homiak, Housman, and Scheman 1973; and Scheman 1983.

12. It is not difficult to understand why such a woman is held in low regard by modern western culture; one who has no independent substance is one who does not exist (an assertion which is only partly metaphorical).

13. Another account of behavior which may seem to represent a loss of the self suggests that in fact it is the extreme of self-interest. Marilyn Frye, in her analysis of female sexual slavery, suggests that a woman who is kidnapped and forced into prostitution is placed in a position in which her pimp's interests quite literally *become* her interests (1983, 61–66). She becomes taken up with pleasing him, with anticipating his needs, not for his sake but for her own. She reaches a point at which she realizes that only by paying obsessive attention to his needs can she preserve her own life. What appears to be a loss of self-interest can, from another angle, be seen as a struggle for self-survival.

14. Consider, on this head, the fact that the stereotypical altruistic mother is sometimes described as actually being egoistic, since she recognizes that her own happiness would be destroyed if her child were to die. The fact that her happiness is involved is raised as a reason to reconsider the purity of her altruism. Of course, it is for reasons such as these that some have denied that a genuinely altruistic act is possible.

15. As Curtin suggests in Section One, on a substance view of personhood, such relations are not defining.

16. The "tied aid" of which I spoke earlier is one form this phenomenon may take. Particular examples of ignoring and failing to involve the recipients in the design and implementation of aid programs include the much-vaunted Green Revolution, which was to increase agricultural yields in India exponentially, thus eliminating hunger. The story of its failure is now very familiar.

17. The damage which can be done by poorly designed, if well-intentioned, projects, has been thoroughly documented by a number of writers. See, for example, Clark 1986; Shiva 1988; Sen and Grown 1987; Mies, Bennholdt-Thomsen, and von Werlhof 1988. It is especially painful to note, as Clark does, that when aid projects go wrong, their ill effects tend to be experienced disproportionately by the very poorest members of society, who are often women—i.e., by those already most heavily oppressed.

18. The economic and political point—that charity represents a very minor, cosmetic shift in the distribution of wealth from dominant to dominated peoples—is of course not a new one. By raising it again, I wish to contribute a philosophical understanding of the ways in which structures of oppression support and are supported by a conception of persons and their relations, which make hierarchy and separation seem inevitable.

19. Note that even the World Bank is now using a conception of the problems facing third-world nations which recognizes that they are the result of systematic oppression. See World Bank 1986.

20. One of my favorite examples of the use of what might be called "social justice" rhetoric is a conversation Curtin and I had with an Indian development worker in South India. He noted, with considerable pride but little specificity, that his organization employed a "bottom-up" development philosophy. He then pulled out a sheaf of papers that detailed the elaborate, extensive, and byzantine leadership structure of the organization. He went on to explain how directors were chosen, how often the full board of directors met, etc. We never returned to a

discussion of the specific bottom-up organizing efforts in which this group was involved. It is, of course, open to speculation why he chose to tell us, two Americans, the information he chose. But, whatever his motivation, it was clear both that he was well aware of the cachet of social justice rhetoric, and that his organization operated under anything *but* a bottom-up philosophy.

21. See Mary Beth Averill and Michael Gross 1984, for an interesting discussion of the way this competitive thinking has shaped biological understandings of the natural world.

22. In her book *Lesbian Ethics,* Sarah Hoagland describes her project as an attempt to develop

> a notion of moral agency under oppression. This includes developing ability within a situation without claiming responsibility for the situation. It involves resisting demoralization under oppression. And it involves resisting the belief that if we can't control a situation, our actions make no difference and we are powerless. Moral agency involves the ability to go on under oppression: to continue to make choices, to act within the oppressive structures of our society and challenge oppression, to create meaning through our living. (13)

It is in this spirit that I undertake the present project.

23. See Heldke 1987a, 1987b, 1988, and 1989 for other discussions of the Coresponsible Option. See also "Recipes for Theory Making," in the present volume.

24. Suzanne LaGrande explains this clearly by contrasting a relational self to an arrogated shelf, a term she derives from Marilyn Frye.

> In distinguishing a relational self from an arrogated self, it is helpful to distinguish between experiencing another person's needs, beliefs, etc., as being continuous with one's own, and experiencing another's needs, desires, etc., *as* one's own. To experience a property as continuous with one's own is to have a non-inferential awareness of it. To experience another's property *as* one's own is to be prevented, by coercion, from having any desires, needs, etc. which are not the arrogator's. (14)

The arrogated self may be seen to be the result of altruism taken to its logical limit: the complete erasure of one's own self-interests, and their replacement with the interests of another. The relational self of which LaGrande speaks is very similar to the conception of a participatorily relational self.

25. In this context it is relevant to recall another sort of relation, discussed in Section Three. The western tradition has tended to view the inquiry relation as a hierarchical one between inquiring subject and inquired-into object. Recall that this relation was characterized by its sharp separation between subject and object; it, too, is predicated on a substance-based conception of beings.

26. Certainly this is not true only of the United States, or even only of dominator nations. However, my familiarity with the United States will lead me to confine my discussion to it.

27. In contrast, the poorest inhabitants of a country being aided generally see the least benefit from the project. The development projects most often funded by western governmental and nongovernmental agencies tend to be costly, large-scale, highly technological projects that offer opportunities only to those in a society who are already the wealthiest.

28. This active verb is more appropriate than the passive construction "am ignorant" to which it is related.

29. To extend Reagon's metaphor, the *real* question is not "are my hands clean?" or even "how can I wash them?" but "where ought my particular pair of dirty hands scrub?"

30. In a conversation about this passage, Curtin suggested that if we take the relational view of self seriously, it in fact transforms the "I" in this sentence. He asked: "if we go beyond egoism and altruism, are we not going beyond the moral *motivation* of the substance project: performance *of* actions for which I deserve credit? If my involvement with others is not optional, why do I deserve praise?"

31. This idea is reminiscent of Paolo Freire's assertion that the violent responses of the oppressed to their oppressors ought in fact be understood as a form of love, specifically of self-love. See *Pedagogy of the Oppressed,* 41–42.

32. Loss of perspective, for example, is displayed when I spend ten minutes in a supermarket, trying to decide which brand of tomato sauce I should buy, when I know that one company has many women of color in management positions, but a poor environmental record, while the other company rates high for environmental consciousness, but has no women executives. To allow oneself to get caught up in such false choices is to become immobilized.

R E F E R E N C E S

Averill, Mary Beth, and Michael Gross. "Evolution and Patriarchal Myths of Scarcity and Competition." *Discovering Reality.* Ed. Sandra Harding and Merrill Hintikka. Dordrecht: D. Reidel, 1984.

Benjamin, Medea, and Andrea Freedman. *Bridging the Global Gap: A Handbook to Linking Citizens of the First and Third Worlds.* Cabin John, MD: Seven Locks Press, 1989.

Blum, Larry, Marcia Homiak, Judy Housman, and Naomi Scheman. "Altruism and Women's Oppression." *Philosophical Forum* 5 (Fall–Winter 1973), 222–247.

Byron, William, ed. *The Causes of World Hunger.* New York: Paulist Press, 1983.

Clark, John. *For Richer, For Poorer.* Oxford: Oxfam, 1986.

Friere, Paolo. *Pedagogy of the Oppressed.* New York: Continuum, 1970.

Frye, Marilyn. *The Politics of Reality.* Trumansburg: Crossing Press, 1983.

George, Susan. *Feeding the Few: Corporate Control of Food.* Amsterdam: Institute for Policy Studies, 1979.

———. *How the Other Half Dies: The Real Reasons for World Hunger.* Montclair: Allanheld, Osmun, 1977.

———. *Ill Fares the Land: Essays on Food, Hunger, and Power.* Washington: Institute for Policy Studies, 1984.

Heldke, Lisa. *Coresponsible Inquiry: Objectivity from Dewey to Feminist Epistemology.* Diss. Northwestern, 1987. Cited as 1987a.

———. "Foundationalism and Relativism: The Issue for Feminism." APA *Newsletter on Feminism and Philosophy* 88, no. 2 (1989): 39–42.

———. "John Dewey and Evelyn Fox Keller: A Shared Epistemological Tradition," *Hypatia* 2, no. 3 (1987): 129–140. Cited as 1987b.

———. "Recipes for Theory Making." *Hypatia* 3, no. 2 (1988): 15–30. Reprinted in this volume.

Hoagland, Sarah Lucia. *Lesbian Ethics: Toward New Value.* Palo Alto: Institute of Lesbian Studies, 1988.

Kant, Immanuel. *Selections.* Ed. Lewis White Beck. New York: Macmillan, 1988.

LaGrande, Suzanne. "Relational and Arrogated Senses of Self." Senior Thesis, Carleton College, 1988.

Lappe, Frances Moore, and Joseph Collins. *Food First: Beyond the Myth of Scarcity.* New York: Ballantine, 1978.

————. *World Hunger. Twelve Myths.* New York: Grove Weidenfeld, 1986.

———— and David Kinley. *Aid as Obstacle: Twenty Questions about Our Foreign Aid and the Hungry.* San Francisco: Institute for Food and Development Policy, 1980.

Mies, Maria, Veronika Bennholdt-Thomsen, and Claudia von Werlhof. *Women: The Last Colony.* Delhi: Kali for Women, 1988.

Reagon, Bernice Johnson. Sweet Honey in the Rock concert. St. Olaf College, Northfield, MN. 12 October 1990.

Scheman, Naomi. "Individualism and the Objects of Psychology." *Discovering Reality.* Eds. Sandra Harding and Merrill Hintikka, Boston: D. Reidel, 1983.

Sen, Gita, and Caren Grown. *Development, Crises, and Alternative Visions: Third World Women's Perspectives.* New York: Monthly Review, 1987.

Shiva, Vandana. *Staying Alive: Women, Ecology and Development.* London: Zed, 1988.

World Bank. *Poverty and Hunger: Issues and Options for Food Security in Developing Countries.* March 1986.

ANNE   BUCHANAN

Myths About Hunger

TOO MANY PEOPLE? TOO LITTLE LAND?

Among people in the developed countries the most widespread and simple explanation of hunger is that in the hungry countries there are just too many people for the amount of agricultural land available.[1] The solution is then seen as birth control.

There are about 4 billion people living in the world today. If a successful birth control programme (whereby each couple had only two children) could be put into effect immediately the world's population would still not stop growing until next century. This is because of the number of children already born who will reach child-bearing age in the next thirty years. Birth control programmes can thus be effective only in the long term. If the elimination of hunger is seen as a rather more urgent problem then a solution must be found *despite* population increases. Two other points are also important. The first is that people stop having babies when *they decide* they do not want any more, not because of access to techniques of birth control (although such techniques obviously help them implement their decision). And such decisions are made only when hunger is eliminated, when you no longer need six children to ensure a son will be living to look after you in your old age (daughters usually having left home at marriage). In other words, birth rates dropping are the *result* of improvements in living conditions rather than the *cause of* such improvements, which means hunger, not population increase, is the problem to be tackled first. The second point to consider is that the effect of population growth is very different in different parts of the world. If we measure the results by the drain on the world's resources (including food) when each new child is born, then North America's population growth is far more serious than is India's. For the average person in a developed country like the United States of America consumes about forty times the resources used by the average Asian. Thus the problem is not people as such but the drain on resources caused by the excessive demands of a rich minority.

The other half of the equation is that there is too little land for the world's population. That this is not in reality an overriding problem is shown by a U.S. Government study which confirms that only 44% of the world's potentially arable land is actually being cultivated (Lappé & Collins 1977: 16). More importantly, the world's farming area could be increased by about 50% without any serious ecological implications such as depletion of forests (George 1976: 299).

Orient!
The soil on which
   naked slaves
      die of hunger.
The common property of everyone
except those born on it.
The land where hunger itself
   perishes with famine!
But the silos are full to the brim,
full of grain—
      only for Europe.

             Nazim Hikmet in *Selected Poems*
                 (Cape, London 1967)

We had ourselves witnessed the famine in Northern Annam in the autumn of 1931 and seen the unsold consignments of rice piling up on the wharves at Saigon while the authorities refused to succour the famished, thus sowing the seeds of the recent conflict. As early as February 1934 we were unable to pass without comment a proposal put forward by the Association of Wheat Producers in France, which suggested that the "surplus" rice in Cochin-China should be bought up, like Brazilian coffee, and dropped into the sea. This noble grain, all too scarce in the bowl of the Tonkinese peasant, hindered the marketing of coarse grains at a 'fair' price when it was poured into our pig troughs and fed to our calves and our poultry.

                           Dumont 1957: vii

What a bewildering world!
While the fish are drinking coffee in Brazil
babies go without milk here . . .
They feed people with words,
the pigs with choice potatoes.

             Nazim Hikmet *op. cit.*

And if we look at what is actually being produced right now on the land already cultivated and for the existing world population we might wonder why there is a problem at all. For the world already produces 2 lbs of grain (3000 calories and 65 grams of protein—which is more than the highest estimates of average daily requirements) each day for every man, woman and child on earth (World Bank 1980: 61). 3000 calories a day before we start to count the other staples such as potatoes, cassava or protein-high beans, let alone fruit, vegetables or meat. Furthermore, it has been estimated that we could produce enough on the potentially cultivable area of the globe to support 38–48 billion people: 10–12 times the present world population (Robbins & Ansari 1976: 4) and 3–4 times more than the 12 billion at which it is estimated world population will stabilise within the next century (OECD 1979). In fact, as we know from the various EEC "mountains" one of the big problems today is how to get rid of surpluses! Even though there is enough land for the number of people overall it could be argued that, because people are very unevenly distributed over the earth's surface, some areas are overpopulated. Yet if we look at where people are most concentrated in relation to crop area we see that they are not necessarily the hungry areas. The UK has twice as many people per cultivated acre as has India; Taiwan, which has no serious hunger problem, has twice as many as Bangladesh—the country most people would cite as a clear example of hunger caused by "overpopulation." By contrast, much of Africa and Latin America with a low population/land ratio gives us examples of extreme poverty and hunger. But perhaps the best example is that of China; in 1948 William Vogt (in *Road to Survival,* N.Y.) concluded: "There is little hope that the world will escape the horror of extensive famine in China within the next few years"; many other experts agreed. Yet in the 'fifties and 'sixties, with a very much larger population, China not only fed its people but regarded them as its most important resource for, rather than hindrance to, development. The problem is not so much the number of people or the amount of arable land but rather whether the people have the opportunity to grow (and eat) the food they need.

A HOSTILE ENVIRONMENT?

Environmental difficulties are also blamed for hunger: poor soils, erratic climates which cause drought or flood, diseases and pests which ravage the crops. Obviously these are problems. Yet the impact of such factors varies widely between different societies according to the types of technology used and, perhaps more important, the social organization. People starve in Northeast Brazil despite a favourable agricultural environment because of the social organisation which denies access to land for the vast majority. The climate of China did not change yet the catastrophic famine foreseen by Vogt was averted because of social changes which gave land to the peasants and reorganised production and distribution of crops.

Extreme environmental difficulties—drought or crop failure for example—and the deaths associated with them are termed "natural" disasters. Yet the "naturalness" of such disaster is questionable. We will look at two such disasters, the Irish famine and the Sahel drought, to see just how far hunger *can* be blamed on environment.

"NATURAL" DISASTER? 1. IRELAND

From 1845 to 1848 in Ireland, the potato crops, on which the Irish peasants depended for food, failed because they were infested by a fungus called potato blight which caused them to rot, the whole effect being worsened by wet weather which helped the fungus spread. By December 1846 a Cork magistrate touring the country was writing:

"The scenes which presented themselves were such as no tongue or pen can convey the slightest idea of. In the first [hovel], six famished and ghastly skeletons, to all appearance dead, were huddled in a corner on some filthy straw, their sole covering what seemed a ragged horsecloth, their wretched legs hanging about, naked above the knees. I approached with horror, and found by a low moaning they were alive—they were in fever, four children, a woman and what had once been a man. It is impossible to go through the detail. Suffice to say, that in a few minutes I was surrounded by at least 200 such phantoms, such frightful spectres as no words can describe, either from famine or fever. Their demoniac yells are still ringing in my ears, and their horrible images are fixed upon my brain. My heart sickens at the recital, but I must go on. . . . " (quoted in Woodham-Smith 1964: 162)

One and a half million people died during the famine and a further million were forced to emigrate, thousands of whom died of disease and starvation in the overcrowded ships; thus Ireland lost two and a half million of its 8 million population in just 4 years.

The underlying causes of this famine are complex but a central factor was the system of landownership in Ireland. Under the tenure laws landlords had complete power to evict tenants and pull down their houses. To pay their rents the peasants grew grain for sale and relied almost exclusively on a diet of potatoes to support their families. Effectively they could not eat their cash crop any more than if it had been the cocoa or tobacco which today puts many peasants in tropical countries in just as precarious a position (see Pyke 1970: ch. 8). And when the peasants, weakened by hunger, due to the failure of their food crop, were unable to grow their cash crops, and thus could not pay their rents, they were evicted in their thousands in Ireland, adding homelessness to hunger. In short, they died, not because of one crop's failure but because, neither owning their land nor having secure tenure of it, they could not make the improvements or grow the range of crops which would have established a healthy farming community able to withstand what should have been a setback but not a disaster.

And that there was nothing, "natural" about the disaster which followed on the potato crop failures is indicated by the fact that through the worst years of the famine food in the form of cereals and cattle was being exported from Ireland. But the head of the British Treasury, Charles Trevelyan, a stubborn believer in the government's laissez-faire policies, refused to order cereals to be used for relief because he did not wish to "disturb the market." He and his government, like many governments today, were captive to a rigid economic philosophy which puts profit before people; a philosophy in which people are, perhaps, the most easily expendable item. Indeed the government's actions (and inaction) prompted Frank O'Connor to observe: " 'Famine' is a useful word when you do not wish to use words like 'genocide' or 'extermination' " (*The Backward Look* London, 1967: 133).

"Natural" disaster? 2. The Sahel

Other examples are numerous but let us take just one recent one: the much publicised Sahel[2] famine of the early 1970s, usually seen as a classic example of a natural disaster caused, in this case, by drought.

As one might expect, the peasants of the region were well aware of the possibility of drought. Meillassoux (1974) tells us that traditionally millet granaries in the Sahel region were constructed to hold four years' consumption and grain was not eaten until it was three years old. Agricultural techniques and cultural traditions were designed to meet possible shortages resulting from unpredictable rainfall. But colonial and modern exploitation (including that by agribusiness) changed this situation. Taxes made cash crops necessary; having less land available then for subsistence crops made the peasants dependent in part at least on the market for their food; and having to buy food in turn meant the necessity for more cash crops. Thus when drought struck the peasants had no reserves. Yet the food was there. Lappé and Collins, using FAO statistics, tell us that many food exports from the Sahel actually increased during the drought: "Cattle exports from the Sahel during 1971, the first year of full drought, totalled over 200 million pounds, up 41 per cent compared to 1968. The annual export of chilled or frozen beef tripled compared with a typical year before the drought. In addition 56 million pounds of fish and 32 million pounds of vegetables were exported from the famine-stricken Sahel in 1971 alone" (1977: 102), most going to consumers in Europe and North America. (Indeed the World Bank sees the region's future as a major vegetable producer for the North American and European markets.) The impact of the big cash crops can be seen in the figures for Mali: between 1967 and 1973 food crop production fell from 60,000 tonnes to 15,000 tonnes while, over the same period, groundnut exports rose from 8,000 to 11,000 tonnes and cotton exports increased from 3,165 to 22,000 tonnes. Yet even with this distortion of the agricultural economy, "every Sahelian country, with the possible exception of mineral rich Mauritania, actually produced enough grain to feed its total population even during the worst drought year" (Lappé & Collins, 1977: 104). Thus the famine was not caused by any overall shortage of food; rather was it caused by powerful indigenous elites and outside business groups who were able to manipulate the food situation to their own profit (see Meillassoux).

The ordinary people starved as the following sequence of events worked its way through. The taxes which fall immediately after the harvest (and repayment of debts) force the peasants to sell much of the food which they should store for the lean time before the next harvest. Profiteers who pay low prices at this time of plenty then sell back at high prices at the later time of demand, often forcing the farmer to obtain credit at usurious rates of interest. Even if not actually forced from their land the farmers certainly are unable to improve their land (for example, by irriga-

---

Famine is not always the result of an insufficient harvest, but rather of an insufficiency remaining to the farmer after the tax collector, the landlord, and the usurer have taken their share.

André Philip (quoted in De Castro 1952: 156)

The year before the drought they had sold their grain as was usual to the native store . . . [He] sent his men around the native villages, coaxing them to sell everything they had. He offered a little more money than they had been used to get. He was buying at half of what he could get in the city. And all would have been well if there had not been that season of drought. For the mealies wilted in the fields, the cobs struggled towards fullness, but remained as small as a fist. There was panic in the villages and the people came streaming towards the Greek store and to all the other native stores all over the country. The Greek said, Yes, yes, he had the maize, he always had the maize, but of course at the new price laid down by the Government. And of course the people did not have the money to buy this newly expensive maize.

Doris Lessing *Hunger in Five Short Novels* (Panther, St Albans 1969)

The poor do not necessarily starve because there is no food around, but because they simply do not have the buying power to acquire it. So, hunger and poverty cannot ipso facto be eliminated by producing more. What needs greater attention is how to empower the poor so that they may get their due share; for when the chips are down those who have power (land and other assets) survive, those who are powerless perish.

Malik 1980

---

tion, for which, with its major river systems, the Sahel has a great potential) and gradually exhaust their soils. Then, with drought, the profits increase for the few and the small farmers and labourers, poverty stricken and unable to buy the very food which they have produced, starve.

A similar story could be told about Bangladesh. But the reality is clear enough: "Natural calamities may point up the weaknesses of underlying social structures, but they do not *cause* them" (George 1976: 44). As a group of researchers from the University of Bradford's Disaster Research Unit conclude: "The time is ripe for some form of precautionary planning which considers vulnerability of the population as the real cause of disaster—vulnerability that is induced by socio-economic conditions that can be modified by man, and is not just an act of God" (O'Keefe *et al* 1976: 567).

THE EARTH IS A MOON SATELLITE

Apollo 2 cost more than Apollo 1
Apollo 1 cost plenty.

Apollo 3 cost more than Apollo 2
Apollo 2 cost more than Apollo 1
Apollo 1 cost plenty.

Apollo 4 cost more than Apollo 3
Apollo 3 cost more than Apollo 2
Apollo 2 cost more than Apollo 1
Apollo 1 cost plenty.

Apollo 8 cost a fortune but nobody minded
because the astronauts were Protestants
and from the moon they read the Bible
to the delight and edification of all Christians
and on their return Pope Paul gave them his blessing.

Apollo 9 cost more than all of them together
and that includes Apollo 1 which cost plenty.

The great-grandparents of the Acahualinca people
were less hungry than the grandparents.

The great-grandparents died of hunger.

The grandparents of the Acahualinca people
were less hungry than the parents.

The grandparents died of hunger.

The parents of the Acahualinca people
were less hungry than the people are today.

The parents died of hunger.

The people who live today in Acahualinca
are less hungry than their children.

The children of the Acahualinca people
are not born because of hunger
and they hunger to be born
so they can die of hunger.

And that is what the Acahualinca people do
they die of hunger.

Blessed are the poor
for they shall possess the moon.

Leonel Rugama (Nicaragua)
Published in *Spes,* Montevideo, Jan 1970
Translation by Gary MacEoin

N O T E S

1. This idea derives from the 19th century theories of the Rev. Thomas Malthus, theories rejected by all except those who fear the social change necessary for a more just distribution of the fruits of the earth.
2. The Sahel is a broad belt of land on the southern edge of the Sahara stretching across Mauritania, Senegal, Mali, Upper Volta, Niger, Chad and the Sudan.

R E F E R E N C E S

Dumont, René. 1957. *Types of Rural Economy* (English translation Methuen, London).
———. 1965. *Lands Alive* (English translation, Monthly Review, London).
——— and Cohen, N. 1980. *The Growth of Hunger* (Marion Boyars, London).
——— and Mottin, M. F. 1980. *L'Afrique entranglée* (Seuil, Paris).
George, Susan 1976. *How the Other Half Dies: The Real Reasons for World Hunger* (Penguin, Harmondsworth).
———. 1979. *Feeding the Few: Corporate Control of Food* (Institute for Policy Studies, Washington DC & Amsterdam).
Lappé, F. M., and Collins, J. 1977. *Food First: Beyond the Myth of Scarcity* (Houghton, Mifflin, Boston).
———. 1977. "The Eight Myths of Hunger," in *Ceres* July–August.
——— and Kinley, D. 1980. *Aid as Obstacle* (IFPD, San Francisco).
Malik, Baljit. 1980. "An Asian Panorama of Peasant Oppression," in *IFDA Dossier* 19, Sept./Oct.
Meillassoux, C. 1974. "Development or Exploration: Is the Sahel Famine Good for Business," in *Review of African Political Economy* (London) No. 1.
OECD. 1979. *Interfutures: Facing the Future: Mastering the Probable & Managing the Unpredictable* (Paris).
O'Keefe, P., Westgate, K., and Wisner, B. 1976. "Taking the Naturalness Out of Natural Disasters," in *Nature* Vol. 260, April 15.
Pyke, M. 1970. *Man and Food* (Weidenfeld & Nicolson, London).
Robbins, C. and Ansari, J. 1976. *The Profits of Doom* (War on Want, London).
Woodham-Smith, C. 1964. *The Great Hunger* (Readers Union/Hamish Hamilton, London).
World Bank, 1980. *World Development Report 1980* (OUP, Oxford & NY).

VANDANA SHIVA

Development, Ecology and Women

DEVELOPMENT AS A NEW PROJECT OF WESTERN PATRIARCHY

"Development" was to have been a post-colonial project, a choice for accepting a model of progress in which the entire world remade itself on the model of the colonising modern west, without having to undergo the subjugation and exploitation that colonialism entailed. The assumption was that western style progress was possible for all. Development, as the improved well-being of all, was thus equated with the westernisation of economic categories—of needs, of productivity, of growth. Concepts and categories about economic development and natural resource utilisation that had emerged in the specific context of industrialisation and capitalist growth in the centre of colonial power, were raised to the level of universal assumptions and applicability in the entirely different context of basic needs satisfaction for the people of the newly independent Third World countries. Yet, as Rosa Luxemberg has pointed out, early industrial development in western Europe necessitated the permanent occupation of the colonies by the colonial powers and the destruction of the local "natural economy."[1] According to her, colonialism is a constant necessary condition for capitalist growth: without colonies, capital accumulation would grind to a halt. "Development" as capital accumulation and the commercialisation of the economy for the generation of "surplus" and profits thus involved the reproduction not merely of a particular form of creation of wealth, but also of the associated creation of poverty and dispossession. A replication of economic development based on commercialisation of resource use for commodity production in the newly independent countries created the internal colonies.[2] Development was thus reduced to a continuation of the process of colonisation; it became an extension of the project of wealth creation in modern western patriarchy's economic vision, which was based on the exploitation or exclusion of women (of the west and non-west), on the exploitation and degradation of nature, and on the exploitation and erosion of other cultures. "Development" could not but entail destruction for women, nature and subjugated cultures, which is why, throughout the Third World, women, peasants and tribals are struggling for liberation from "development" just as they earlier struggled for liberation from colonialism.

The UN Decade for Women was based on the assumption that the improvement of women's economic position would automatically flow from an expansion and diffusion of the development process. Yet, by the end of the Decade, it was becoming clear that development itself was the problem. Insufficient and inadequate "participation" in "development" was not the cause for women's increasing under-development; it was rather, their enforced but asymmetric participation in it, by which they bore the costs but were excluded from the benefits, that was responsible. Development exclusivity and dispossession aggravated and deepened the colonial processes of ecological degradation and the loss of political control over nature's sustenance base. Economic growth was a new colonialism, draining resources away from those who needed them most. The discontinuity lay in the fact that it was now new national elites, not colonial powers, that masterminded the exploitation on grounds of "national interest" and growing GNPs, and it was accomplished with more powerful technologies of appropriation and destruction.

Ester Boserup[3] has documented how women's impoverishment increased during colonial rule; those rulers who had spent a few centuries in subjugating and crippling their own women into de-skilled, de-intellectualised appendages, disfavoured the women of the colonies on matters of access to land, technology and employment. The economic and political processes of colonial under-development bore the clear mark of modern western patriarchy, and while large numbers of women and men were impoverished by these processes, women tended to lose more. The privatisation of land for revenue generation displaced women more critically, eroding their traditional land use rights. The expansion of cash crops undermined food production, and women were often left with meagre resources to feed and care for children, the aged and the infirm, when men migrated or were conscripted into forced labour by the colonisers. As a collective document by women activists, organisers and researchers stated at the end of the UN Decade for Women, "The almost uniform conclusion of the Decade's research is that with a few exceptions, women's relative access to economic resources, incomes and employment has worsened, their burden of work has increased, and their relative and even absolute health, nutritional and educational status has declined.[4]

The displacement of women from productive activity by the expansion of development was rooted largely in the manner in which development projects appropriated or destroyed the natural resource base for the production of sustenance and survival. It destroyed women's productivity both by removing land, water and forests from their management and control, as well as through the ecological destruction of soil, water and vegetation systems so that nature's productivity and renewability were impaired. While gender subordination and patriarchy are the oldest of oppressions, they have taken on new and more violent forms through the project of development. Patriarchal categories which understand destruction as "production" and regeneration of life as "passivity" have generated a crisis of survival. Passivity, as an assumed category of the "nature" of nature and of women, denies the activity of nature and life. Fragmentation and uniformity as assumed categories of progress and development destroy the living forces which arise from relationships within the "web of life" and the diversity in the elements and patterns of these relationships.

The economic biases and values against nature, women and indigenous peoples are captured in this typical analysis of the "unproductiveness" of traditional natural societies:

> Production is achieved through human and animal, rather than mechanical, power. Most agriculture is unproductive; human or animal manure may be used but chemical fertilisers and pesticides are unknown. . . . For the masses, these conditions mean poverty.[5]

The assumptions are evident: nature is unproductive; organic agriculture based on nature's cycles of renewability spells poverty; women and tribal and peasant societies embedded in nature are similarly unproductive, not because it has been demonstrated that in cooperation they produce *less* goods and services for needs, but because it is assumed that "production" takes place only when mediated by technologies for commodity production, even when such technologies destroy life. A stable and clean river is not a productive resource in this view: it needs to be "developed" with dams in order to become so. Women, sharing the river as a commons to satisfy the water needs of their families and society are not involved in productive labour: when substituted by the engineering man, water management and water use become productive activities. Natural forests remain unproductive till they are developed into monoculture plantations of commercial species. Development thus, is equivalent to maldevelopment, a development bereft of the feminine, the conservation, the ecological principle. The neglect of nature's work in renewing herself, and women's work in producing sustenance in the form of basic, vital needs is an essential part of the paradigm of maldevelopment, which sees all work that does not produce profits and capital as non or unproductive work. As Maria Mies[6] has pointed out, this concept of surplus has a patriarchal bias because, from the point of view of nature and women, it is not based on material surplus produced *over and above* the requirements of the community: it is stolen and appropriated through violent modes from nature (who needs a share of her produce to reproduce herself) and from women (who need a share of nature's produce to produce sustenance and ensure survival).

From the perspective of Third World women, productivity is a measure of producing life and sustenance; that this kind of productivity has been rendered invisible does not reduce its centrality to survival—it merely reflects the domination of modern patriarchal economic categories which see only profits, not life.

MALDEVELOPMENT AS THE DEATH OF THE FEMININE PRINCIPLE

In this analysis, maldevelopment becomes a new source of male-female inequality. 'Modernisation' has been associated with the introduction of new forms of dominance. Alice Schlegel[7] has shown that under conditions of subsistence, the interdependence and complementarity of the separate male and female domains of work is the characteristic mode, based on diversity, not inequality. Maldevelopment militates against this equality in diversity, and superimposes the ideologically constructed category of western technological man as a uniform measure of the worth of classes, cultures and genders. Dominant modes of perception based on reductionism, duality and linearity are unable to cope with equality in diversity, with forms and activities that are significant and valid, even though different. The reductionist mind superimposes the roles and forms of power of western male-oriented concepts on women, all non-western peoples and even on nature, rendering all three "deficient," and in need of "development." Diversity, and unity and harmony in diversity, become epistemologically unattainable in the context of maldevelopment, which then becomes synonymous with women's underdevelopment (increasing sexist domination), and nature's depletion (deepening ecological crises). Commodities have grown, but nature has shrunk. The poverty crisis of the South arises from the growing scarcity of water, food, fodder and fuel, associated with increasing maldevelopment and ecological destruction. This poverty crisis touches women most severely, first because they are the poorest among the poor, and then because, with nature, they are the primary sustainers of society.

Maldevelopment is the violation of the integrity of organic, interconnected and interdependent systems, that sets in motion a process of exploitation, inequality, injustice and violence. It is blind to the fact that a recognition of nature's harmony and action to maintain it are preconditions for distributive justice. This is why Mahatma Gandhi said, "There is enough in the world for everyone's need, but not for some people's greed."

Maldevelopment is maldevelopment in thought and action. In practice, this fragmented, reductionist, dualist perspective violates the integrity and harmony of man in nature, and the harmony between men and women. It ruptures the co-operative unity of masculine and feminine, and places man, shorn of the feminine principle, above nature and women, and separated from both. The violence to nature as symptomatised by the ecological crisis, and the violence to women, as symptomatised by their subjugation and exploitation arise from this subjugation of the feminine principle. I want to argue that what is currently called development is essentially maldevelopment, based on the introduction or accentuation of the domination of man over nature and women. In it, both are viewed as the "other," the passive non-self. Activity, productivity, creativity which were associated with the feminine principle are expropriated as qualities of nature and women, and transformed into the exclusive qualities of man. Nature and women are turned into passive objects, to be used and exploited for the uncontrolled and uncontrollable desires of alienated man. From being the creators and sustainers of life, nature and women are reduced to being "resources" in the fragmented, anti-life model of maldevelopment.

TWO KINDS OF GROWTH, TWO KINDS OF PRODUCTIVITY

Maldevelopment is usually called "economic growth," measured by the Gross National Product. Porritt, a leading ecologist has this to say of GNP:

> *Gross* National Product—for once a word is being used correctly. Even conventional economists admit that the hey-day of GNP is over, for the simple reason that as a measure of progress, it's more or less useless. GNP measures the lot, all the goods and services produced in the money economy. Many of these goods and services are not beneficial to people, but rather a measure of just how much is going wrong; increased spending on crime, on pollution, on the many human casualties of our society, increased spending because of waste or planned obsolescence, increased spending because of growing bureaucracies: it's all counted.[8]

The problem with GNP is that it measures some costs as benefits (eg. pollution control) and fails to measure other costs completely. Among these hidden costs are the new burdens created by ecological devastation, costs that are invariably heavier for women, both in the North and South. It is hardly surprising, therefore, that as GNP rises, it does not necessarily mean that either wealth or welfare increase proportionately. I would argue that GNP is becoming, increasingly, a measure of how real wealth—the wealth of nature and that produced by women for sustaining life—is rapidly decreasing. When commodity production as the prime economic activity is introduced as development, it destroys the potential of nature and women to produce life and goods and services for basic needs. More commodities and more cash mean less life—in nature (through ecological destruction) and in society (through denial of basic needs). Women are devalued first, because their work cooperates with nature's processes, and second, because work which satisfies needs and ensures sustenance is devalued in general. Precisely because more growth in maldevelopment has meant less sustenance of life and life-support systems, it is now imperative to recover the feminine principle as the basis for development which conserves and is ecological. Feminism as ecology, and ecology as the revival of Prakriti, the source of all life, become the decentred powers of political and economic transformation and restructuring.

This involves, first, a recognition that categories of "productivity" and growth which have been taken to be positive, progressive and universal are, in reality, restricted patriarchal categories. When viewed from the point of view of nature's productivity and growth, and women's production of sustenance, they are found to be ecologically destructive and a source of gender inequality. It is no accident that the modern, efficient and productive technologies created within the context of growth in market economic terms are associated with heavy ecological costs, borne largely by women. The resource and energy intensive production processes they give rise to demand ever increasing resource withdrawals from the ecosystem. These withdrawals disrupt essential ecological processes and convert renewable resources into non-renewable ones. A forest, for example, provides inexhaustible supplies of diverse biomass over time if its capital stock is maintained and it is harvested on a sustained yield basis. The heavy and uncontrolled demand for industrial and commercial wood, however, requires the continuous overfelling of trees which exceeds the regenerative capacity of the forest ecosystem, and eventually converts the forests into non-renewable resources. Women's work in the collection of water, fodder and fuel is thus rendered more energy and time-consuming. (In Garhwal, for example, I have seen women who originally collected fodder and fuel in a few hours, now travelling long distances by truck to collect grass and leaves in a task that might take up to two days.) Sometimes the damage to nature's intrinsic regenerative capacity is impaired not by over-exploitation of a particular resource but, indirectly, by damage caused to other related natural resources through ecological processes. Thus the excessive overfelling of trees in the catchment areas of streams and rivers destroys not only forest resources, but also renewable supplies of water, through hydrological destabilisation. Resource intensive industries disrupt essential ecological processes not only by their excessive demands for raw material, but by their pollution of air and water and soil. Often such destruction is caused by the resource demands of non-vital industrial products. In spite of severe ecological crises, this paradigm continues to operate because for the North and for the elites of the South, resources continue to be available, even now. The lack of recognition of nature's processes for survival *as factors in the process of economic development* shrouds the political issues arising from resource transfer and resource destruction, and creates an ideological weapon for increased control over natural resources in the conventionally employed notion of productivity. All other costs of the economic process consequently become invisible. The forces which contribute to the increased "productivity" of a modern farmer or factory worker for instance, come from the increased use of natural resources. Lovins has described this as the amount of 'slave' labour presently at work in the world.[9] According to him each person on earth, on an average, possesses the equivalent of about 50 slaves, each working a 40 hour week. Man's global energy conversion from all sources (wood, fossil fuel, hydroelectric power, nuclear) is currently approximately 8×10^{12} watts. This is more than 20 times the energy content of the food necessary to feed the present world population at the FAO standard diet of 3,600 cal/day. The "productivity" of the western male compared to women or Third World peasants is not intrinsically superior; it is based on inequalities in the distribution of this "slave" labour. The average inhabitant of the USA, for example, has 250 times more "slaves" than the average Nigerian. "If Americans were short of 249 of those 250 'slaves,' one wonders how efficient they would prove themselves to be?"

It is these resource and energy intensive processes of production which divert resources way from survival, and hence from women. What patriarchy sees as productive work, is, in ecological terms highly destructive production. The second law of thermodynamics predicts that resource intensive and resource wasteful economic development must become a threat to the survival of the human species in the long run. Political struggles based on ecology in industrially advanced countries are rooted in this conflict between *long term survival options* and *short term over-production and over-consumption*. Political struggles of women, peasants and tribals based on ecology in countries like India are far more acute and urgent since they are rooted in the *immediate threat to the options for survival* for the vast majority of the people, *posed by resource intensive and resource wasteful economic growth* for the benefit of a minority.

In the market economy, the organising principle for natural resource use is the maximisation of profits and capital accumulation. Nature and human needs are managed through market mechanisms. Demands for natural resources are restricted to those demands registering on the market; the ideology of development is in large part based on a vision of bringing all natural resources into the market economy for commodity production. When these resources are already being used by nature to maintain her production of renewable resources and by women for sustenance and livelihood, their diversion to the market economy generates a scarcity condition for ecological stability and creates new forms of poverty for women.

TWO KINDS OF POVERTY

In a book entitled *Poverty: The Wealth of the People*[10] an African writer draws a distinction between poverty as subsistence, and misery as deprivation. It is useful to separate a cultural conception of subsistence living as poverty from the material experience of poverty that is a result of dispossession and deprivation. Culturally perceived poverty need not be real material poverty: subsistence economies which satisfy basic needs through self-provisioning are not poor in the sense of being deprived. Yet the ideology of development declares them so because they do not participate overwhelmingly in the market economy, and do not consume commodities produced for and distributed through the market *even though they might be satisfying those needs through self-provisioning mechanisms.* People are perceived as poor if they eat millets (grown by women) rather than commercially produced and distributed processed foods sold by global agri-business. They are seen as poor if they live in self-built housing made from natural material like bamboo and mud rather than in cement houses. They are seen as poor if they wear handmade garments of natural fibre rather than synthetics. Subsistence, as culturally perceived poverty, does not necessarily imply a low physical quality of life. On the contrary, millets are nutritionally far superior to processed foods, houses built with local materials are far superior, being better adapted to the local climate and ecology, natural fibres are preferable to man-made fibres in most cases, and certainly more affordable. This cultural perception of prudent subsistence living as poverty has provided the legitimisation for the development process as a poverty removal project. As a culturally biased project it destroys wholesome and sustainable lifestyles and creates real material poverty, or misery, by the denial of survival needs themselves, through the diversion of resources to resource intensive commodity production. Cash crop production and food processing take land and water resources away from sustenance needs, and exclude increasingly large numbers of people from their entitlements to food. "The inexorable processes of agriculture-industrialisation and internationalisation are probably responsible for more hungry people than either cruel or unusual whims of nature. There are several reasons why the high-technology-export-crop model increases hunger. Scarce land, credit, water and technology are pre-empted for the export market. Most hungry people are not affected by the market at all. . . . The profits flow to corporations that have no interest in feeding hungry people without money."[11]

The Ethiopian famine is in part an example of the creation of real poverty by development aimed at removing culturally perceived poverty. The displacement of nomadic Afars from their traditional pastureland in Awash Valley by commercial agriculture (financed by foreign companies) led to their struggle for survival in the fragile uplands which degraded the ecosystem and led to the starvation of cattle and the nomads.[12] The market economy conflicted with the survival economy in the Valley, thus creating a conflict between the survival economy and nature's economy in the uplands. At no point has the global marketing of agricultural commodities been assessed against the background of the new conditions of scarcity and poverty that it has induced. This new poverty moreover, is no longer cultural and relative: it is absolute, threatening the very survival of millions on this planet.

The economic system based on the patriarchal concept of productivity was created for the very specific historical and political phenomenon of colonialism. In it, the input for which efficiency of use had to be maximised in the production centres of Europe, was industrial labour. For colonial interest therefore, it was rational to improve the labour resource *even at the cost of wasteful use of nature's wealth.* This rationalisation has, however, been illegitimately universalised to all contexts and interest groups and, on the plea of increasing productivity, labour reducing technologies have been introduced in situations where labour is abundant and cheap, and resource demanding technologies have been introduced where resources are scarce and already fully utilised for the production of sustenance. Traditional economies with a stable ecology have shared with industrially advanced affluent economies the ability to use natural resources to satisfy basic vital needs. The former differ from the latter in two essential ways: first, the same needs are satisfied in industrial societies through longer technological chains requiring higher energy and resource inputs and excluding large numbers without purchasing power; and second, affluence generates new and artificial needs requiring the increased production of industrial goods and services. Traditional economies are not advanced in the matter of non-vital needs satisfaction, but as far as the satisfaction of basic and vital needs is concerned, they are often what Marshall Sahlins has called "the original affluent society." The needs of the Amazonian tribes are more than satisfied by the rich rainforest; their poverty begins with its destruction. The story is the same for the Gonds of Bastar in India or the Penans of Sarawak in Malaysia.

Thus are economies based on indigenous technologies viewed as "backward" and "unproductive." Poverty, as the denial of basic needs, is not necessarily associated with the existence of traditional technologies, and its removal is not necessarily an outcome of the growth of modern ones. On the contrary, the destruction of ecologically sound traditional technologies, often created and used by women, along with the destruction of their material base is generally believed to be responsible for the "feminisation" of poverty in societies which have had to bear the costs of resource destruction.

The contemporary poverty of the Afar nomad is not rooted in the inadequacies of traditional nomadic life, but in the *diversion of the productive pastureland of the Awash Valley.* The erosion of the resource base for survival is increasingly being caused by the demand for resources by the market economy, dominated by global forces. The creation of inequality through economic activity which is ecologically disruptive arises in two ways: first, inequalities in the distribution of privileges make for unequal access to natural resources—these include privileges of both a political and economic nature. Second, resource intensive production processes have access to subsidised raw material on which a substantial number of people, especially from the less privileged economic groups, depend for their survival. The consumption of such industrial raw material is determined purely by market forces, and not by considerations of the social or ecological requirements placed on them. The costs of resource destruction are externalised and unequally divided among various economic groups in society, but are borne largely by women and those who satisfy their basic material needs directly from nature, simply because they have no purchasing power to register their demands on the goods and services provided by the modern production system. Gustavo Esteva has called development a permanent war waged by its promoters and suffered by its victims.[13]

The paradox and crisis of development arises from the mistaken identification of culturally perceived poverty with real material poverty, and the mistaken identification of the growth of commodity production as better satisfaction of basic needs. In actual fact, there is less water, less fertile soil, less genetic wealth as a result of the development process. Since these natural resources are the basis of nature's economy and women's survival economy, their scarcity is impoverishing women and marginalised peoples in an unprecedented manner. Their new impoverishment lies in the fact that resources which supported their survival were absorbed into the market economy while they themselves were excluded and displaced by it.

The old assumption that with the development process the availability of goods and services will automatically be increased and poverty will be removed, is now under serious challenge from women's ecology movements in the Third World, even while it continues to guide development thinking in centres of patriarchal power. Survival is based on the assumption of the sanctity of life; maldevelopment is based on the assumption of the sacredness of "development." Gustavo Esteva asserts that the sacredness of development has to be refuted because it threatens survival itself. "My people are tired of development," he said, "they just want to live."[14]

The recovery of the feminine principle allows a transcendance and transformation of these patriarchal foundations of maldevelopment. It allows a redefinition of growth and productivity as categories linked to the production, not the destruction, of life. It is thus simultaneously an ecological and a feminist political project which legitimises the way of knowing and being that create wealth by enhancing life and diversity, and which deligitimises the knowledge and practise of a culture of death as the basis for capital accumulation.

N O T E S

1. Rosa Luxemberg, *The Accumulation of Capital,* London: Routledge and Kegan Paul, 1951.

2. An elaboration of how "development" transfers resources from the poor to the well-endowed is contained in J. Bandyopadhyay and V. Shiva, "Political Economy of Technological Polarisations" in *Economic and Political Weekly,* Vol. XVIII, 1982, pp. 1827–32; and J. Bandyopadhyay and V. Shiva, "Political Economy of Ecology Movements," in *Economic and Political Weekly,* forthcoming.

3. Ester Boserup, *Women's Role in Economic Development,* London: Allen and Unwin, 1970.

4. DAWN, *Development Crisis and Alternative Visions: Third World Women's Perspectives,* Bergen: Christian Michelsen Institute, 1985, p. 21.

5. M. George Foster, *Traditional Societies and Technological Change,* Delhi: Allied Publishers, 1973.

6. Maria Mies, *Patriarchy and Accumulation on a World Scale,* London: Zed Books, 1986.

7. Alice Schlegel (ed.), *Sexual Stratification: A Cross-Cultural Study,* New York: Columbia University Press. 1977.

8. Jonathan Porritt, *Seeing Green,* Oxford: Blackwell, 1984.

9. A. Lovins, cited in S. R. Eyre, *The Real Wealth of Nations,* London: Edward Arnold, 1978.

10. R. Bahro, *From Red to Green,* London: Verso, 1984, p. 211.

11. R. J. Barnet, *The Lean Years,* London: Abacus, 1981, p. 171.

12. U. P. Koehn, "African Approaches to Environmental Stress: A Focus on Ethiopia and Nigeria" in R. N. Barrett (ed.), *International Dimensions of the Environmental Crisis,* Colorado: Westview, 1982, pp. 253–89.

13. Gustavo Esteva, "Regenerating People's Space" in S. N. Mendlowitz and R. B. J. Walker, *Towards a Just World Peace: Perspectives from Social Movements,* London: Butterworths and Committee for a Just World Peace, 1987.

14. G. Esteva, Remarks made at a Conference of the Society for International Development, Rome, 1985.

Are My Hands Clean?

I wear garments touched by hands from all over the
    world
35% cotton, 65% polyester, the journey begins in
    Central America
In the cotton fields of El Salvador
In a province soaked in blood, pesticide-sprayed
    workers toil in a broiling sun
Pulling cotton for two dollars a day

Then we move on up to another rung—Cargill
A top forty trading conglomerate, takes the cotton thru
    the Panama Canal
Up the Eastern seaboard, coming to the U.S. of A. for
    the first time

In South Carolina
At the Burlington mills
Joins a shipment of polyester filament courtesy of the
    New Jersey petro-chemical mills of Dupont

Dupont strands of filament begin in the South
    American country of Venezuela
Where oil riggers bring up oil from the earth for six
    dollars a day
Then Exxon, largest oil company in the world
Upgrades the product in the country of Trinidad and
    Tobago
Then back into the Caribbean and Atlantic Seas
To the factories of Dupont
On the way to the Burlington mills

In South Carolina
To meet the cotton from the blood-soaked fields of El Salvador

In South Carolina
Burlington factories hum with the business of weaving
    oil and cotton into miles of fabric for Sears
Who takes this bounty back into the Caribbean Sea
Headed for Haiti this time
May she be one day soon free

Far from the Port-au-Prince palace
Third world women toil doing piece work to Sears
    specifications

For three dollars a day my sisters make my blouse
It leaves the third world for the last time
Coming back into the sea to be sealed in plastic for me

This third world sister
And I go to the Sears department store where I buy my
   blouse
On sale for 20% discount

Are my hands clean?

Composed for Winterfest, Institute for Policy Studies.
The lyrics are based on an article by Institute fellow
John Cavanagh, "The Journey of the Blouse: A Global Assembly."

Women Whose Lives Are Food, Men Whose Lives Are Money

Mid-morning Monday she is staring
peaceful as the rain in that shallow back yard
she wears flannel bedroom slippers
she is sipping coffee
she is thinking—
                    —gazing at the weedy bumpy yard
at the faces beginning to take shape
in the wavy mud
in the linoleum
where floorboards assert themselves

Women whose lives are food
breaking eggs with care
scraping garbage from the plates
unpacking groceries hand over hand

Wednesday evening: he takes the cans out front
tough plastic with detachable lids
Thursday morning: the garbage truck whining at 7
Friday the shopping mall open till 9
bags of groceries unpacked
hand over certain hand

Men whose lives are money
time-and-a-half Saturdays
the lunchbag folded with care and brought back home
unfolded Monday morning

Women whose lives are food
because they are not punch-carded
because they are unclocked
sighing glad to be alone
staring into the yard, mid-morning
mid-week
by mid-afternoon everything is forgotten
There are long evenings
panel discussions on abortions, fashions, meaningful work
there are love scenes where people mouth passions

sprightly, handsome, silly, manic
in close-ups revealed ageless
the women whose lives are food
the men whose lives are money

fidget as these strangers embrace and weep and mis-
   understand and forgive and die and weep and embrace
and the viewers stare and fidget and sigh and
begin yawning around 10:30
never made it past midnight, even on Saturdays,
watching their brazen selves perform

Where are the promised revelations?
Why have they been shown so many times?
Long-limbed children a thousand miles to the west
hitch-hiking in spring, burnt bronze in summer
thumbs nagging
eyes pleading
Give us a ride, huh? Give us a ride?

and when they return nothing is changed
the linoleum looks older
the Hawaiian Chicken is new
the girls wash their hair more often
the boys skip over the puddles
in the GM parking lot
no one eyes them with envy

their mothers stoop
the oven doors settle with a thump
the dishes are rinsed and stacked and
by mid-morning the house is quiet
it is raining out back
or not raining
the relief of emptiness rains
simple, terrible, routine
at peace

American Independence

Our balloon bodies float above the harbor
our fingers continue to pick at the empty red shells
grease-flecked, our large lips move
we are singing in near-unison
our thighs are enormous whitely-soft loaves of bread

"Why has this happened"
"What evil has been perpetrated upon us"
"Will no one have mercy"

Our skin is waffle-pocked
our fingers plump as breakfast sausage
our small eyes blink rapidly in our great faces
we carry souvenir lobster traps
one of us is vomiting into a Colonel Sanders bucket
"Why has this happened"
"Who is responsible"
we are waiting now for dinner

Patiently we turn the postcard racks
there are scoops of ice cream everywhere
gigantic yawns distort our faces
it is only 5:15
the day has been long
pistachio butternut raspberry coffee
New York strip steaks the red-boiled shells of dead creatures
tiny seals made of seal fur torn from living baby seals
"It is not our fault"

American flags float above the procession of cars
gulls dip and soar among us
doughy arms protrude from windows
fat knees are jammed up tight beneath chins
"Why is it so difficult to remain human"
we proclaim the American Independence
pancake batter clinging to our jowls
our stomachs test the resiliency of yellow stretch pants
oysters pulse a final spasm on our tongues
small curly dogs fret and yap and wet in our arms
"Let everything be ground down fine by our enormous jaws
by the heat of our tongues

let everything be transformed to human heat, human flesh,
human waste"

Immense with appetite we hurry to dinner
cockleshells and periwinkles and tiny moons are shattered
beneath our urgent shoes

A Modest Proposal

It is a melancholly Object to those, who walk through this great Town or travel in the Country, when they see the Streets, the Roads and Cabbin-doors crowded with Beggers of the Female Sex, followed by three, four, or six Children, all in Rags, and importuning every Passenger for an Alms. These Mothers instead of being able to work for their honest livelyhood, are forced to employ all their time in Stroling to beg Sustenance for their helpless Infants, who, as they grow up, either turn Thieves for want of Work, or leave their dear Native Country, to fight for the Pretender in Spain, or sell themselves to the Barbadoes.

I think it is agreed by all Parties, that this prodigious number of Children in the Arms, or on the Backs, or at the Heels of their Mothers, and frequently of their Fathers, is in the present deplorable state of the Kingdom, a very great additional grievance; and therefore whoever could find out a fair, cheap and easy method of making these Children sound and useful Members of the Common-wealth, would deserve so well of the publick, as to have his Statue set up for a Preserver of the Nation.

But my Intention is very far from being confined to provide only for the Children of professed Beggers, it is of a much greater Extent, and shall take in the whole Number of Infants at a certain Age, who are born of Parents in effect as little able to support them, as those who demand our Charity in the Streets.

As to my own part, having turned my Thoughts, for many Years, upon this important Subject, and maturely weighed the several Schemes of other Projectors, I have always found them grossly mistaken in their computation. It is true, a Child just dropt from its Dam, may be supported by her Milk, for a Solar Year with little other Nourishment, at most not above the Value of two Shillings, which the Mother may certainly get, or the Value in Scraps, by her lawful Occupation of Begging; and it is exactly at one Year Old that I propose to provide for them in such a manner, as, instead of being a Charge upon their Parents, or the Parish, or wanting Food and Raiment, for the rest of their Lives, they shall, on the Contrary, contribute to the Feeding and partly to the Cloathing of many Thousands.

There is likewise another great Advantage in my Scheme, that it will prevent those voluntary Abortions, and that horrid practice of Women murdering their Bastard Children, alas! too frequent among us, Sacrificing the poor innocent Babes, I doubt, more to avoid the Expence than the Shame, which would move Tears and Pity in the most Savage and inhuman breast.

The number of Souls in this Kingdom being usually reckoned one Million and a half, Of these I calculate there may be about two hundred thousand Couple whose Wives are Breeders; from which number I subtract thirty Thousand Couples, who are able to maintain their own Children, although I apprehend there cannot be so many, under the present Distresses of the Kingdom; but this being granted, there will remain an hundred and seventy thousand Breeders. I again Subtract fifty Thousand, for those Women who miscarry, or whose Children die by accident, or disease within the Year. There only remain an hundred and twenty thousand Children of poor Parents annually born: The question therefore is, How this number shall be reared, and provided for? which, as I have already said, under the present Situation of Affairs, is utterly impossible by all the Methods hitherto proposed; for we can neither employ them in Handicraft or Agriculture; we neither build Houses, (I mean in the Country) nor cultivate Land: They can very seldom pick up a Livelihood by Stealing till they arrive at six years Old; except where they are of towardly parts; although, I confess, they learn the Rudiments much earlier; during which time they can however be properly looked upon only as Probationers; as I have been informed by a principal Gentleman in the County of Cavan, who protested to me, that he never knew above one or two Instances under the Age of six, even in a part of the Kingdom so renowned for the quickest proficiency in that Art.

I am assured by our Merchants, that a Boy or a Girl before twelve years Old, is no saleable Commodity, and even when they come to this Age, they will not yield above three Pounds, or three Pounds and half a Crown at most, on the Exchange; which cannot turn to Account either to the Parents or Kingdom, the Charge of Nutriment and Rags having been at least four times that Value.

I shall now therefore humbly propose my own Thoughts, which I hope will not be liable to the least Objection.

I have been assured by a very knowing American of my acquaintance in London, that a young healthy Child well Nursed is at a year Old a most delicious nourishing and wholesome Food, whether Stewed, Roasted, Baked, or Boiled; and I make no doubt that it will equally serve in a Fricasie, or a Ragoust.

I do therefore humbly offer it to publick consideration, that of the Hundred and twenty thousand Children, already computed, twenty thousand may be reserved for Breed, whereof only one fourth part to be Males; which is more than we allow to Sheep, black Cattle, or Swine, and my Reason is, that these Children are seldom the Fruits of Marriage, a Circumstance not much regarded by our Savages, therefore, one Male will be sufficient to serve four Females. That the remaining Hundred thousand may at a year Old be offered in Sale to the Persons of Quality and Fortune, through the Kingdom, always advising the Mother to let them Suck plentifully in the last Month, so as to render them Plump, and Fat for a good Table. A Child will make two Dishes at an Entertainment for Friends, and when the Family dines alone, the fore or hind Quarter will make a reasonable Dish, and seasoned with a little Pepper or Salt will be very good Boiled on the fourth Day, especially in Winter.

I have reckoned upon a medium, that a Child just born will weigh 12 pounds, and in a solar Year, if tolerably nursed, encreaseth to 28 Pounds.

I grant this food will be somewhat dear, and therefore very proper for the Landlords, who, as they have already devoured most of the Parents seems to have the best Title to the Children.

Infant's flesh will be in Season throughout the Year, but more plentiful in March, and a little before and after; for we are told by a grave Author an eminent French physician, that Fish being a prolifick Dyet, there are more Children born in Roman Catholick Countries about nine Months after Lent, than at any other Season; therefore reckoning a Year after Lent, the Markets will be more glutted than usually, because the number of Popish Infants, is at least three to one in this Kingdom, and therefore it will have one other Collateral advantage, by lessening the Number of papists among us.

I have already computed the Charge of nursing a Begger's Child (in which List I reckon all Cottagers, Labourers, and four fifths of the Farmers) to be about two Shillings per Annum, Rags included; and I believe no Gentleman would repine to give Ten Shillings for the Carcass of a good fat Child, which as I have said will make four Dishes of excellent Nutritive Meat, when he hath only some particular Friend, or his own Family to dine with him. Thus the Squire will learn to be a good Landlord, and grow popular among his Tenants, the Mother will have Eight Shillings neat Profit, and be fit for Work till she produces another Child.

Those who are more thrifty (as I must confess the Times require) may flay the Carcass; the Skin of which, Artificially dressed, will make admirable Gloves for Ladies, and Summer Boots for fine Gentlemen.

As to our City of Dublin, Shambles may be appointed for this purpose, in the most convenient parts of it, and Butchers we may be assured will not be wanting; although I rather recommend buying the Children alive, and dressing them hot from the Knife, as we do roasting Pigs.

A very worthy Person, a true Lover of his Country, and whose Virtues I highly esteem, was lately pleased, in discoursing on this matter, to offer a refinement upon my Scheme. He said, that many Gentlemen of this Kingdom, having of late destroyed their Deer, he conceived that the Want of Venison might be well supply'd by the Bodies of young Lads and Maidens, not exceeding fourteen Years of Age, nor under twelve; so great a Number of both Sexes in every Country being now ready to Starve, for want of Work and Service: And these to be disposed of by their Parents if alive, or otherwise by their nearest Relations. But with due deference to so excellent a Friend, and so deserving a Patriot, I cannot be altogether in his Sentiments;

for as to the Males, my American acquaintance assured me from frequent Experience, that their Flesh was generally Tough and Lean, like that of our Schoolboys, by continual exercise, and their Taste disagreeable, and to fatten them would not answer the Charge. Then as to the Females, it would, I think with humble Submission, be a Loss to the Publick, because they soon would become Breeders themselves: And besides it is not improbable that some scrupulous People might be apt to Censure such a Practice, (although indeed very unjustly) as a little bordering upon Cruelty, which I confess, hath always been with me the strongest Objection against any Project, how well soever intended.

But in order to justify my Friend, he confessed, that this expedient was put into his Head by the famous Sallmanaazor, a Native of the Island Formosa, who came from thence to London, above twenty Years ago, and in Conversation told my Friend, that in his Country when any young Person happened to be put to Death, the Executioner sold the Carcass to Persons of quality, as a prime Dainty, and that, in his Time, the Body of a plump Girl of fifteen, who was crucified for an attempt to poison the Emperor, was sold to his Imperial Majesty's prime Minister of State, and other great Mandarins of the Court, in Joints from the Gibbet, at four hundred Crowns. Neither indeed can I deny, that if the same Use were made of several plump young Girls in this Town, who, without one single Groat to their Fortunes, cannot stir abroad with a Chair, and appear at a Play-house, and Assemblies in Foreign fineries, which they never will pay for; the Kingdom would not be the worse.

Some Persons of a desponding Spirit are in great concern about that vast Number of poor People, who are Aged, Diseased, or Maimed, and I have been desired to imploy my Thoughts what Course may be taken, to ease the Nation of so grevious an Incumbrance. But I am not in the least Pain upon that matter, because it is very well known, that they are every Day dying, and rotting, by cold and famine, and filth, and vermin, as fast as can be reasonably expected. And as to the younger Labourers, they are now in almost as hopeful a Condition. They cannot get Work, and consequently pine away for want of Nourishment, to a degree, that if at any Time they are accidentally hired to common Labour, they have not Strength to perform it, and thus the Country and themselves are happily delivered from the Evils to come.

I have too long digressed, and therefore shall return to my Subject. I think the Advantages by the Proposal which I have made are obvious and many, as well as of the highest Importance.

For *First*, as I have already observed, it would greatly lessen the Number of Papists, with whom we are Yearly over-run, being the principal Breeders of the Nation, as well as our most dangerous Enemies, and who stay at home on purpose with a Design to deliver the Kingdom to the Pretender, hoping to take their Advantage by the Absence of so many good

Protestants, who have chosen rather to leave their Country, than stay at home, and pay Tithes against their Conscience, to an Episcopal Curate.

Secondly, The poorer Tenants will have something valuable of their own which by Law may be made lyable to Distress, and help to pay their Landlord's Rent, their Corn and Cattle being already seized, and Money a Thing unknown.

Thirdly, Whereas the Maintenance of an hundred thousand Children, from two Years old, and upwards, cannot be computed at less than Ten Shillings a Piece per Annum, the Nation's Stock will be thereby increased fifty thousand Pounds per Annum, besides the Profit of a new Dish, introduced to the Tables of all Gentlemen of Fortune in the Kingdom, who have any Refinement in Taste, and the Money will circulate among our Selves, the Goods being entirely of our own Growth and Manufacture.

Fourthly, The constant Breeders, besides the gain of eight Shillings Sterling per Annum, by the Sale of their Children, will be rid of the Charge of maintaining them after the first Year.

Fifthly, This Food would likewise bring great Custom to Taverns, where the Vintners will certainly be so prudent as to procure the best Receipts for dressing it to Perfection; and consequently have their Houses frequented by all the fine Gentlemen, who justly value themselves upon their Knowledge in good Eating; and a skilful Cook, who understands how to oblige his Guests, will contrive to make it as expensive as they please.

Sixthly, This would be a great Inducement to Marriage, which all wise Nations have either encouraged by Rewards, or enforced by Laws and Penalties. It would encrease the Care and Tenderness of Mothers towards their Children, when they were sure of a Settlement for Life, to the poor Babes, provided in some Sort by the Publick, to their annual Profit instead of Expence; we should soon see an honest Emulation among the married Women, which of them could bring the fattest Child to the Market. Men would become as fond of their Wives, during the Time of their Pregnancy, as they are now of their Mares in Foal, their Cows in Calf, or Sows when they are ready to farrow, nor offer to beat or kick them (as is too frequent a Practice) for fear of a Miscarriage.

Many other Advantages might be enumerated. For Instance, the Addition of some thousand Carcasses in our Exportation of Barrel'd Beef: The Propagation of Swine's Flesh, and Improvement in the Art of making good Bacon, so much wanted among us by the great Destruction of Pigs, too frequent at our Tables, which are no way comparable in Taste, or Magnificence to a well grown, fat yearling Child, which roasted whole will make a considerable Figure at a Lord Mayor's Feast, or any other Publick Entertainment. But this, and many others, I omit, being studious of Brevity.

Supposing that one thousand Families in this City, would be constant Customers for Infant's Flesh, besides others who might have it at merry Meetings, particularly at Weddings and Christenings, I compute that Dublin would take off Annually about twenty thousand Carcasses, and the rest of the Kingdom (where probably they will be sold somewhat cheaper) the remaining eighty Thousand.

I can think of no one Objection, that will possibly be raised against this Proposal, unless it should be urged, that the Number of People will be thereby much lessened in the Kingdom. This I freely own, and 'twas indeed one principal Design in offering it to the World. I desire the Reader will observe, that I calculate my Remedy for this one individual Kingdom of Ireland, and for no Other that ever was, is, or, I think, ever can be upon Earth. Therefore let no man talk to me of other Expedients: Of taxing our Absentees at five Shillings a Pound: Of using neither Cloaths, nor Household Furniture, except what is of our own Growth and Manufacture: Of utterly rejecting the Materials and Instruments that promote Foreign Luxury: Of curing the Expensiveness of Pride, Vanity, Idleness, and Gaming in our Women: Of introducing a Vein of Parcimony, Prudence and Temperance; Of learning to love our Country, wherein we differ even from Laplanders, and the Inhabitants of Topinamboo: Of quitting our Animosities, and Factions, nor act any longer like the Jews, who were murdering one another at the very Moment their City was taken: Of being a little cautious not to sell our Country and Consciences for nothing: Of teaching Landlords to have at least one Degree of Mercy towards their Tenants. Lastly, Of putting a Spirit of Honesty, Industry, and Skill into our Shopkeepers, who, if a Resolution could now be taken to buy only our Native Goods, would immediately unite to cheat and exact upon us in the Price, the Measure, and the Goodness, nor could ever yet be brought to make one fair Proposal of just Dealing, though often and earnestly invited to it.

Therefore I repeat, let no Man talk to me of these and the like Expedients, till he hath at least some Glimpse of Hope, that there will ever be some hearty and sincere Attempt to put them in Practice.

But as to my self, having been wearied out for many Years with offering vain, idle, visionary Thoughts, and at length utterly despairing of Success, I fortunately fell upon this Proposal, which as it is wholly new, so it hath something Solid and Real, of no Expence and little Trouble, full in our own Power, and whereby we can incur no Danger in disobliging England. For this kind of Commodity will not bear Exportation, the Flesh being of too tender a Consistence, to admit a long Continuance in Salt, although perhaps I cou'd name a Country, which wou'd be glad to eat up our whole Nation without it.

After all, I am not so violently bent upon my own Opinion, as to reject any Offer, proposed by wise Men, which shall be found equally Innocent, Cheap, Easy, and Effectual. But before something of that Kind shall be advanced in Contradiction to my Scheme, and offering a better, I desire the Author or Authors, will be pleased maturely to consider two Points. *First*, As Things now stand, how they will be able to find Food and Raiment for a hundred Thousand useless Mouths and Backs. And *Secondly*, There

being a round Million of Creatures in Human Figure, throughout this Kingdom, whose whole Subsistence put into a common Stock, would leave
them in Debt two Millions of Pounds Sterling, adding those, who are Beggers by Profession, to the Bulk of Farmers, Cottagers and Labourers, with
their Wives and Children, who are Beggers in Effect; I desire those Politicians, who dislike my Overture, and may perhaps be so bold to attempt an
Answer, that they will first ask the Parents of these Mortals, Whether they
would not at this Day think it a great Happiness to have been sold for Food
at a Year Old, in the manner I prescribe, and thereby having avoided such a
perpetual Scene of Misfortunes, as they have since gone through, by the
Oppression of Landlords, the Impossibility of paying Rent without Money
or Trade, the Want of common Sustenance, with neither House nor Cloaths
to cover them from the Inclemencies of the Weather, and the most inevitable Prospect of intailing the like, or greater Miseries, upon their Breed for
ever.

I profess in the Sincerity of my Heart, that I have not the least Personal
Interest in endeavouring to promote this necessary Work, having no other
Motive than the Publick Good of my Country, by advancing our Trade,
providing for Infants, relieving the Poor, and giving some Pleasure to the
Rich. I have no Children, by which I can propose to get a single Penny; the
youngest being nine Years Old, and my Wife past Child-bearing.

Meeting the Expectations of the Land

Part of the modern problem in agriculture is that our policymakers, if not the population at large, treat agriculture as an isolated part of the society—a segment in which something has gone wrong. Expensive salvage operations are designed, therefore, around the notion that agriculture is a problem that needs fixing. The phrases that come tumbling out of many of the deeply troubled and the superficial are pretty much the same. We hear statements such as: "Pure and simple, it is strictly an economic problem." "Agriculture is in trouble." "Something needs to be done about the farm problem."

Sure, scarcely three percent of us in the United States are on farms. Farmers are a dispersed minority and have little political clout anymore. Were they a dispersed majority, the farm vote would still make a difference. Were they a concentrated minority, they would be close enough together to hammer out their differences and speak with one voice. But of course they are neither.

While most of the phrases about problems on the farm are true, at least in a limited sense, none suggests that problems on the farm are more the failure of culture than of economics and public policy. Economics can define the problem, but only in part. It won't provide a solution, yet nearly all our public policy decisions are based on economic pressures.

What I hope to offer here is the consideration that some of the problems *in* agriculture are mere derivatives of the problem *of* agriculture, which in turn is part of a systemic problem for the culture at large. This has scarcely been understood in the United States, or for that matter, I suspect, in any other country. We seem to keep hoping for a breakthrough. Note that several of our nation's music stars organized two huge fundraising concerts last year: one for the starving in Ethiopia, and one for the nation's farmers, who have produced too much and so have gone broke.

I see three tiers of problems embedded in the problem of agriculture. And though I want to deal mostly with the middle tier, I'll begin by considering the first. In an absolute sense, the problem of agriculture will probably never be solved. In my view, it is part of the Fall. I suspect that agriculture is at the core of the Fall. We can imagine that the Fall came when the gatherers and hunters *expanded their scale* from patches into fields. This decreased our reliance on nature's wisdom while increasing our dependence on human cleverness. We came to depend more on human knowledge. There are too many people now for us to become gatherers and hunters again and so, after the fossil fuels are gone, we will, with most of the world's people, once again earn our sustenance and health by the "sweat of our brow." (Our work at The Land Institute in Salina, Kansas, is for the purpose of establishing a relationship with the landscape that is a bit closer to the relationship we had with ecosystems before we changed the face of the earth with extensive till agriculture. I do think we can make some inroads for coping with the Fall but mostly I want to deal with the second tier of problems.)

In considering the second tier of problems, let us accept till agriculture as a given. Even though it has been around only about five percent of our total evolutionary history, it has become so all pervasive that we now have no choice but to figure out how to manage it wisely. Let us look at the major problems in this middle or second tier.

1. Soil loss is greater now than it was fifty years ago, when President Franklin Roosevelt appointed Hugh Hammond Bennett to be the founding chief of what was to become the Soil Conservation Service (SCS). It is not widely known that the loss of soil carbon is more serious than the loss of fossil fuel carbon through burning. The erosion loss of soil carbon and other soil nutrients to our offshore deltas and other places inaccessible to agriculture is more serious than the exhaustion of the metals and fossil minerals of our globe.

2. Soil loss lies at the core of the problem of agriculture. When the extractive economy of industry moved into the potentially renewable economy of agriculture—took it over, in fact—not only were the traditional problems of agriculture worsened, new problems were added. With the industrialization of agriculture the chemical industry made it possible to introduce chemicals into our fields with which our tissues had no evolutionary experience.

3. We now are almost totally reliant on finite fossil fuels for traction in our fields. It is in these second tier problems that we need to peel away the various masks, to assess the problems at a more fundamental level, and offer prescriptions for the culture at large. We will come back to this later.

The third tier of problems has to do with the work of numerous concerned people to make the best of a serious problem in the present. This involves the day-to-day struggle of helping farmers cope, helping them do the best they can. In a way, this work is like caring for a terminal cancer patient. We pour out our love and concern and help. We are with them through the period of chemotherapy or maybe surgery. We hope for immediate cures. We sit up at night. We suffer with them. We bury them. This is noble work, but it is more for the purpose of helping someone cope than it is to change the patient's fate. Sometimes to cope is to change, but we would be naive if we believed that we would cure the patient by easing the pain.

And so I return to the middle tier, with the hope that meaningful work in this tier can work to alleviate the first and third tier problems. If we are effective here, we might be able to soften the problem of the Fall. If we are effective here, many of the problems in the third tier may dry up entirely. Effective work in the middle tier, however, will involve a different way of thinking about our relationship to the earth. Some have called such a radical departure a paradigm shift. Whatever we call it, I think it is useful to understand, at least in a general sense, some of the history that has brought us to where we are.

I would like to begin with some Biblical history that pertains to the sin of idolatry—idol worship. As I understand that history, Hebrews were able to keep their monotheism alive because they were able to keep competing ideas of religious authority from corrupting their own loyalties. In the promised land of Canaan, the Hebrews confronted the baal worshipers, people who worshiped farm gods, gods responsible for every square foot of fertility. Every little village had its own baal. The old Hebrew god of the "mountain and the storm," the god that had brought them out of Egypt to Mount Sinai and finally into Canaan, had trouble competing with the baal gods of the Hebrews' Canaanite neighbors. The single, Hebrew tribe of goat and sheep herders in the rocky country to the south were better able to carry the notion of the god of the "mountain and storm" than those Hebrews who found themselves thrown into agriculture. These Hebrews' daily pattern was more like the pattern from their days of wandering in the desert. As farmers they had a terrible time resisting baal worship. Defeating baal worship meant defeating the idols that were made of the earth, in order to give emphasis to the more "correct" view of God, which is that He is a spirit. Clay and gold are materials; according to the Hebrew view, to pray to such "things of the earth" is to pray to the wrong stuff.

Such a worldview may have been essential for preserving the Hebrew people, whose lives were centered around the covenant with God, a covenant that was struck at Mt. Sinai where they "answered in one voice." But it created problems for European pantheists when the early Christians brought the legacy of their Hebrew tradition into Europe. Our pantheist forebears saw spirits in rocks, in waterfalls, in the deer of the forest, in the bear. By definition, Pan was everywhere. The early Christians who came into the wilds of Europe insisted that all of nature was "nothing but." To worship rocks and streams, bears and bees was to participate in the sin of idolatry. To lift our eyes up from the earth was culturally encouraged in another way, for even the most casual student of the stars could see there was order in heaven. On earth were uncertainties and constant problems with which we had to cope. The earth was an unlikely residence for God. Because the heavens were so orderly, any decent sort of god must be parked *there*. It was not that God couldn't and didn't roam around, but that heaven was, more or less, his permanent address.

For the Christian world, those who believed in a hereafter, the presence of God in heaven translated into an interpretation of heaven as their place of residence after death. These Christians viewed the earth as a launchpad, a place long on material and short on spirit. With the eventual extirpation of pantheism over vast stretches of the globe, the de-sacralization of nature was inevitable. The consequence is that science as we know it today was made possible. It is doubtful that the dissection of living animals and plants could be done by those who believe them to be holy. A pantheist would not view trees as so many board feet in the manner a Christian would. A pantheist would be less likely to measure the number of acre feet coming over a waterfall than his Christian descendent, centuries later, who had become a scientist. That which is sacred would be handled with a certain reverence.

I don't mean to pick on Christianity any more than any of the other major religions. Buddhists have often cut their sacred groves to build temples. Much of the Orient, where such religions flourish, has ruined environments. That is another subject, one that Yu-Fu Tuan has dealt with rather extensively. But our task is to understand our history a bit better.

Francis Bacon told us that knowledge is power, that the methodology of science would free us to organize the world sufficiently enough to give us a higher measure of comfort and security. More and more of us now know that comfort and security are not the solutions to the human condition, but few people knew it then. The experiment hadn't been run.

Long before the time of Bacon, people wanted power over nature. I don't doubt that there were some who believed that more power over nature would enable them to control their own lives. As far back as the thirteenth century there were sporadic pockets of individuals who *were* breaking from the dominant circumstance in which individuals' social positions determined their fates. Imagine, a person's actions, indeed his very quality, were dictated mostly by social position. This is hard for us to appreciate, since we own our own labor power for sale in a competitive market. Nevertheless, we are no more than sixteen generations away from a world that was completely different. This change, which began in the thirteenth century, did not culminate until the seventeenth and eighteenth centuries. The fossil fuel epoch and the opening of the New World coincided with the end of this era and the beginning of the Age of Enlightenment and the scientific revolution. Power over nature, much of it fossil fuel dependent, created lots of opportunity.

The question now becomes "So what?" The "sin of idolatry" with its accompanying de-sacralization of nature paved the way for the scientific revolution. After pantheism the world was more material than spiritual. Bacon was right. We see that knowledge is power. We are in the fossil fuel epoch. In four or five hundred years, we have inverted the structure of society from defining individuals by social position to individual determining their own social relationships. So we have had a bourgeois revolution. So what?

In their thoughtful book *The Dialectical Biologist* (Harvard University Press, 1985), Richard Levins and Richard Lewontin point out that the social ideology of the bourgeois society, this recent invention, assumes that the individual is "ontologically prior to the social." By this they mean that individuals are free-moving social atoms with their own intrinsic properties. Society is a collection of such individuals. In other words, society as a phenomenon consists of the outcome of the individual activities of individual human beings. This supports the view of Descartes, a view that became a central notion of modern science. This view, this Cartesian view, says that the part *has priority* over the whole. Cartesianism is not just a tool or a method of investigation. It is a *commitment* to how things really are. As Levins and Lewontin say, "The method is used because it is regarded as isomorphic with the *actual structure* of causation. The world is like the method." To say that knowledge is power, on the surface, may not sound all that bad. What was not perceived, I suspect, at the time of Bacon, is that the quantity of knowledge obtained by future scientific investigators would reward *them*, the investigators themselves, with power. "The success of the Cartesian method and the Cartesian view of Nature," Levins and Lewontin say, "is in part the result of a historical path of least resistance. Scientists work on the problems that yield to the attack." Investigators will not advance their careers, or should we say, they will not achieve power, by working on problems that they are unlikely to be able to solve. As Levins and Lewontin say, "brilliant careers are not built on persistent failure."

We can see readily how the path of least resistance *has* been employed in agricultural research. Practically no research has been devoted to the development of agricultural systems that will conserve soil, sponsor nitrogen fertility, manage water effectively, and control insects, pathogens, and weeds through biological, as opposed to industrial, means. Such research would require us to study whole systems and would violate the Cartesian view that places priority on parts over the whole.

So the question now becomes, "How do we break the stranglehold of Cartesianism?" Levins and Lewontin say that we should "look again at the concepts of part and whole." We used to justify holism or holistic thinking with the simple argument that the whole is greater than the sum of its parts. I know that I, at least, would nod knowingly and rest comfortably with such a simple justification. But Levins and Lewontin point out that "the parts acquire new properties . . . [and] as the parts acquire properties by being together, they impart to the whole new properties, which are reflected in changes in the parts, and so on. Parts and wholes evolve in consequence of their relationship, and the relationship itself evolves."

The purpose of the argument of Levins and Lewontin is to show that this relationship between parts and wholes, which is non-Cartesian, this relationship that has subject and object in constant interchange, this relationship of parts that can cause new properties to emerge in the parts themselves as the context changes, entails "properties of things that we call dialectical." That is to say, there is a thesis, an antithesis and a new synthesis or thesis. The Cartesian view believed that the world is like the method, that method was used because it is like the "actual structure of causation."

The authors point out how the Darwinian theory of evolution is a "quintessential product of the bourgeois intellectual revolution." First, it is a materialist theory in that it posits existing forces acting on real, existing objects, and so rejects the Platonic ideals. Second, evolution is a theory of change, as opposed to stasis. The nineteenth century was devoted to the idea of change, and biological evolution was simply a late example. Third, Darwin's idea of the adaptation of living things to the environment is, according to Levins and Lewontin, "pure Cartesian." The Darwinian assumption is that organisms change in response to an alien environment. The dialectical view accepts the first two premises of Darwin—the materialist theory and the theory of change—but rejects the third premise of Darwin—that organisms are *alienated* objects of external forces. The dialectical view holds that organism and environment interpenetrate so completely that both are at the same time subjects and objects of the historical process.

What is the utility of this history for those of us interested in achieving a proper relationship with the earth?

I have tried to show how the rejection of idol worship was rooted in the insistence that the material world is short on spirit, and that idols made from materials of this world, to the Hebrew and Christian mind, were not to be worshiped. This de-sacralization of nature helped set up the subject-object dualism. Darwin was a product of this culture, and though his theory of evolution involved real forces working on materials promoting change, he saw the environment, which is mostly physical, as consisting of objects that organisms had to adapt themselves to in order to live. Levins and Lewontin point out what numerous biologists and soil scientists have known for a long time: there is an interplay between organism and environment, and each is changed due to the presence of the other. Soil scientists are probably the most aware of this for they can readily see how the living world works to help form soil. Most biologists are less sophisticated.

Civilized people know that to objectify a person is dehumanizing, not only to the person but to the dehumanizer. Racism is a form of objectifying. Language that deals with the sexual parts of a person's body that does not carry a sense of reverence for the whole, we call obscene. Language that calls attention to skin color or ethnic background, elevating those factors above the whole person, we call racist.

366 COOKING, EATING, THINKING

We understand this very well when we talk about the human body but not when we think of nature. To talk about "the environment" as something apart from us is to separate us from the environment. We were, after all, made from the environment. We are maintained by it. The subject-object dualism has given us the notion that it is possible to isolate parts of the environment we don't like.

But there is more to consider before we turn this discussion back to agriculture and meeting the expectations of the land. Levins and Lewontin point out that many people will admit that social and economic factors strongly influence science. Newly graduated plant breeders with Ph.D.'s can command a starting salary one-third greater than newly graduated ecologists with Ph.D.'s. Why? Plant breeders can produce useable results faster than ecologists. Science is clearly influenced by the structure of social rewards and incentives. Look at the defense industry and its impact on science. But, as Levins and Lewontin point out, "nothing evokes as much hostility among intellectuals as the suggestion that *social forces influence or even dictate either the scientific method or the facts and theories of science.*" They believe that "science in all its senses, is a social process that both causes and is caused by social organization." Whether we like it or not, to be a scientist is "to be a social actor engaged in political activity." The speed of light may be the same under socialism or capitalism, but "is the cause of tuberculosis a bacillus or the capitalist exploitation of workers?" Would the death rate from cancer best be reduced "by studying oncogenes or by seizing control of the factories?" When Monsanto produces seeds resistant to a Monsanto-marketed herbicide, "the environment" receives an increased herbicide load because the crop is "protected." Here is a clear example of placing priority on part over whole, and producing a social problem in the process. Denying the interpenetration of the scientific and the social is *itself* a political act. It allows scientists to hide behind scientific objectivity and, however unwittingly, to perpetuate elitism, dependency, and exploitation.

I think we are beginning to see some small measure of polarization in our universities on this subject. The professors and scientists who are most threatened by this little bit of consciousness-raising are the ones who, in the short run, can gain position and power in the universities by sweeping the problems resulting from Cartesian thinking under the rug. I see this as the source of the rise of that new caste of progressive fundamentalists, which includes the new geneticists. They may be highly trained but too many of them are poorly educated. The neural firings and intellectual pathways of the progressive fundamentalists are like those of religious fundamentalists. Most biotechnologists don't like the suggestion that molecular biology should be in a subordinate role; they are apparently uninterested in working as fellow scientists alongside ecologists. Fundamentalism is the product of a mind bent on power and uneasy with ambiguity. Fundamentalism begins where thought ends.

What does all of this mean for those of us who want to see the life sustaining resources available for the unborn, who have a sense of intergenerational justice, who have extended their love beyond the here and now? What does it mean for those of us who believe that farming is our most basic work? I think it means that we have to look at the interpenetration of part and whole and acknowledge that how we look at the world is how it becomes. I believe, for example, that there is a law of human ecology that, bluntly stated, is: "Values dictate genotoype." I think we can safely say that our major crops, for example corn, soybeans, and wheat, have genes that we might call "Chicago Board of Trade genes." There are also wellhead genes and computer genes. In other words, there are ensembles of genes in our major crops that would not exist in their particular constellation were there not a Chicago Board of Trade (where a major share of the agricultural transactions occurs), or fossil fuel wellheads, or computers. Our values arrange even the molecules of heredity. That is interpenetration.

Gary Nabhan tells a story about a Native American woman in Mexico who had several ears of corn from her corn crop arranged before her as she shelled grain from each ear. There were ears that were tiny nubbins, and ears that were long; all had seeds of various colors. As she shelled grain from each ear to save for the next planting, Gary asked her why she saved seed for planting from the small ears. Her reply was that corn was a gift of the gods and to discriminate against the small in favor of the large would be to show a lack of appreciation for the gift. What she was doing, of course, was maintaining genetic diversity. Values dictate genotype. James B. Kendrick at the University of California at Berkeley says that if we had to rely on the genetic resources now available in the United States to minimize genetic vulnerability in the future, we would soon experience significant crop losses that would accelerate as time went by. Roughly one-third of our current crop comes from four inbred lines, which is roughly the same as the amount of variation that could be found in as few as two individuals.

I don't think that it is proper to say that the earth is an organism. An atom is an atom. A molecule is a molecule. A cell is a cell. A tissue is a tissue. An organ is an organ and an organism is an organism. Going up the hierarchy, we can say an ecosystem is an ecosystem and the earth is the earth. I believe that those who insist on calling the earth an organism are doing so because *they* happen to be organisms. We don't really know what the earth is, but we do know a little about it. We know that it is dynamic, the the inside is hot with heat left over from the earth's early days. And we have evidence that the hot core of our earth is responsible for life as we know it.

The old assumption was that the biota itself was self-renewing. Even in organic agriculture we assume that we can simply plant legumes, practice crop rotation, and thus renew a piece of land. This is true, but true in a sense that is more limited than we once believed. Within a very long time frame, a more accurate assumption is that the biota alone cannot rejuvenate an area; there must be some nonliving capital (i.e., inorganic nutrients) that will accommodate life. In geological time, this capital is made available by large changes in the earth's surface, changes that are largely abiotic caused by glaciers, shifts of the tectonic plates, volcanoes. We know for example, that before the Andean uplift the Amazon flowed toward the west. Nutrients that were once headed one way are now headed another. In the pygmy forest of Mendocino County, California, there are terraces where each step represents about one hundred thousand years. We have evidence that the once verdant growth there has gone into decline, as nutrients have become unavailable over time. Land that once supported a lush redwood forest now supports a pygmy forest, vegetation that now appears to be greatly stressed. Yet life has been constant in this area. If life alone were enough, living forms—in this case, the trees of the pygmy forest—could bootstrap themselves to a level of greater diversity and larger biomass turnover, but apparently the necessary nutrients have leached from the soil and are no longer available for plant growth.

Life working alone on this earth is not enough. Reverence for life alone is incomplete. The pantheists were more right than they probably knew, for the very inner heat of our earth may be essential to make the geological moves necessary to sustain the biota as we know it. So are the gases, heated by the sun, that we call wind. Controlled by the moon, the tides provide a nutrient wash on our coasts to support an abundance of life. The interpenetration of moon and earth, of sun and earth, of soil and organism are all essential for our livelihood.

With the understanding that interpenetration is the right definition of our relationship to the earth, I come back to the crisis on the farm, which clearly is not an economic crisis. As I mentioned earlier, it is a crisis *reflected* by economic problems which derive from a larger, cultural crisis. It is not a crisis that can be cured by economics.

What is happening to the farmer and the farm is a faint foreshadowing of what is to come to the culture at large. The farmer is not an atomistic unit or satellite, sitting off to one side, needing repair. Neither is the farm. Agriculture in the largest sense cannot be repaired independently of culture and society. Vulnerability and helplessness begin with the fields, which are subject to erosion and pollution. Next most vulnerable and helpless are the people who work those fields. Next are the suppliers of inputs: the farm machinery companies, the companies that provide inputs, and the rural bankers. This is an inverted pyramid of vulnerability that begins with the farmer, and widens as we move upward to include the larger society.

The Cartesian worldview allows us to talk about trade-offs as though for each gain there must be only one loss. The ecological worldview, on the other hand, will tell us that one thing done wrong can create numerous problems throughout a system. Or stated positively, if something is done right, if something is done that fits, several problems are taken care of at once. The ecological worldview involves a profound awareness of the total interpenetration of parts.

Were we to act on the basis of ecological understanding, it would be possible to place the base of the pyramid firmly on the land. Society would then become a manifestation of what the land can support in a healthful and productive way. Only by meeting the land's expectations first can society be sustained. However, when we impose the industrial or extractive economy on the land, the base of the pyramid—representing society's wishes—is at the top. The point of the pyramid is stuck into the land like a hypodermic needle, injecting into the soil all the chemicals necessary to meet the demands of society.

The ecological pyramid illustrated in the basic ecology texts surely stands as a rough model for an alternative economic order. It has been billions of years in the making. In such an ecological economy the producers would be many and the mere consumers are few, exactly as Confucius prescribed for a healthy human society tens of centuries ago. Why have we inverted the pyramid? Cheap oil? Human nature? The oil, at any rate, is about gone; and never in the history of our country have we been more up against human nature than we are today. In 1776, this continent could absorb lots of bad human nature. The frontier was before us. Now, though our outward frontier has come to an end, instead of facing our problems squarely we keep looking to expand our frontiers inwardly, always for the purpose of exploitation. We have gone into the inner recesses of the atom and the nucleus of the cell. The exploitation of both atom and cell is not at all unlike ripping open the prairies, the very heart of our continent, or going into Third World countries like Brazil, where skilled welders are paid a dollar an hour to make farm machinery for America's fields. It is all of the same greed.

Frederick Jackson Turner developed the thesis that the American's self-definition is derived from the early frontier days, a time, we might say, of horizontal colonization. About the time we were fresh out of longitude and latitude we funded a space program and went for altitude. But colonization is not discovery. The quintessential aspect of colonization is exploitation and violence. Astronauts headed for orbit may be given more status than a farmer protecting a hillside from erosion, but a farmer who is successful in discovering ways to arrest nutrient loss on his sloping farm has made a more significant discovery than all the colonizers of space combined. So has the farmer who is gradually weaning himself from costly input farming, who is becoming less a consumer and more a producer.

Revolutionary Letter #42

what is this
'overpopulation' problem, have you
looked at it, clearly, do you know

ten times as much land needed if we eat
hamburger, instead of grain; we can
all fit, not hungry, if we minimize
our needs, RIP OFF LARGE, EMPTY RANCHES, make the
                                                    food

nutritious: chemical fertilizers
have to go, nitrates
poison the water; large scale machine farming
has to go, the soil
is blowing away (300 years
to make one inch of topsoil), do you know

40% of the women of Puerto Rico
already sterilized, transistor radios
the 'sterilization bonus' in India; all propaganda
aimed at the 'non-white' and 'poor white' populations

something like 90% of the land of USA
belongs to 5% of the population:
how can they hold on
when the hordes of the infants of the very poor
grow up, grow strong

Revolutionary Letter #55

It takes courage to say no

No to canned corn & instant
mashed potatoes. No to rice krispies.
No to special K. No to margarine
mono- & di-glycerides, NSDA
for coloring, causing cancer. No to
white bread, bleached w/nerve gas (wonder
bread). No to everything fried
in hardened oil w/silicates. No to
once-so-delicious salami, now red
w/sodium nitrate.

No to processed cheeses. No
no again to irradiated bacon, pink
phosphorescent ham, dead plastic
pasteurized milk. No to chocolate pudding
like grandma never made. No thanx
to coca-cola. No to freshness preservers,
dough conditioners, no
potassium sorbate, no
aluminum silicate, NO
BHA, BHT, NO
di-ethyl-propyl-glycerate.

No more ice cream? not w/embalming fluid.
Goodbye potato chips. peanut butter, jelly, jolly
white sugar! No more DES
all-American steaks or hamburgers either!
Goodbye, frozen fish! (dipped & coated w/
aureomycin) Fried eggs over easy w/
hormones, penicillin & speed.
Carnation Instant Breakfast, Nestle's Quik.
Fritos, goodbye! your labels are very confusing.

All I can say
is what my daughter age six once said to me:
*"if I can't pronounce it
maybe I shouldn't eat it."*

               or, Dick Gregory
               coming out of a 20-day fast:
               *"the people of American are controlled
               by the food they eat"*

Thanksgiving Dinner
During Pelting Season (1957)

I.

Two years to maturity. A needle injected into the thigh.
A quick death for the animal with no visible sign of
damage to the skin of the mink.

> After two days of thawing the turkey, she begins
> preparing it. As she removes the soggy wrapping
> of giblets, she wonders if these parts belonged
> to this bird.

An incision in one foot, up the inside of the leg,
round the groin, and down the other leg to the foot.
His hand enters the opening and removes the carcass.

> Rice, chopped apples, spices. She puts the stuffing
> in the hollowed bird and sews it shut. She's grateful
> she didn't have to pluck and gut this one.

The skin is turned inside out and slipped onto a cone-
shaped hanger for cleaning. The hind feet attached at
the top with tacks. The scraping begins. Carefully
the fat is separated from the hide.

> She dips the cotton swab in a small bowl of oil,
> basting the turkey carefully as it turns on the
> rotisserie. The oil burns, the skin browns. Fat
> drips into the pan below.

In the drying room above the feed house, he wipes the hide
with soft cloth. The skins must be bone dry for market.
No oil, no odor.

> Her skin is dark like the brown parts of the cooked
> turkey. And dry, she says, from the time when her
> gas stove exploded when she tried to light it.
> The extra fat carried on her small frame came with
> marriage and babies.

He smells of mink, of the odor sacs broken. A survival
fluid passed from one species to another. His skin swells

into a softness from another season of mink oil soaked in.
His hair sports the shine of his best pelts.

ii.

Our skin scrubbed clean, my brothers and I sit
at the dinner table with our parents. We're quiet
and still as the mink pelts that hang in the drying
room above the feed house.

"Bless us, oh Lord, for these Thy gifts
which we are about to receive from Thy
bounty, through Christ our Lord. Amen."
She tells us these are the right words,
so we say them. He never says them. He's
not Catholic.

She is French-Canadian and Indian. She denies
the Indian part, so we're not sure whether
our people are Abanaki, Ojibwe, Algonquin, or
Mohawk. When we drive through Shawano on our way
to Escanaba, she tells us the Indians are worse
than the niggers. Worthless drunks, she calls
them and points out the shacks they live in.
You're not Indian, you're Irish Catholic.

The Catholic Church tells us stories about
their early missionaries in Canada. They say
the Iroquois made savage attacks on the clergy.
They say the Indians captured Antony Daniel and
flayed him. They say the Iroquois strung a necklace
of red-hot tomahawks around Jean de Breboeuf's neck,
then "baptised" him in boiling water. They claim
the tribal members drank his blood and that
the chief ate de Breboeuf's heart.

He eats the giblets and the neck first, then the dark
meat. She prefers the white meat. My brothers want
the drumsticks. I don't want any, but take a wing
and try to fill my plate with potatoes, vegetables,
salad, and bread. She offers us both pumpkin and
mincemeat pies for dessert.

The Pleasures of Eating

Many times, after I have finished a lecture on the decline of American farming and rural life, someone in the audience has asked, "What can city people do?"

"Eat responsibly," I have usually answered. Of course, I have tried to explain what I meant by that, but afterwards I have invariably felt that there was more to be said than I had been able to say. Now I would like to attempt a better explanation.

I begin with the proposition that eating is an agricultural act. Eating ends the annual drama of the food economy that begins with planting and birth. Most eaters, however, are no longer aware that this is true. They think of food as an agricultural product, perhaps, but they do not think of themselves as participants in agriculture. They think of themselves as "consumers." If they think beyond that, they recognize that they are passive consumers. They buy what they want—or what they have been persuaded to want—within the limits of what they can get. They pay, mostly without protest, what they are charged. And they mostly ignore certain critical questions about the quality and the cost of what they are sold: How fresh is it? How pure or clean is it, how free of dangerous chemicals? How far was it transported, and what did transportation add to the cost? How much did manufacturing or packaging or advertising add to the cost? When the food product has been manufactured or "processed" or "precooked," how has that affected its quality or price or nutritional value?

Most urban shoppers would tell you that food is produced on farms. But most of them do not know what farms, or what kinds of farms, or where the farms are, or what knowledge or skills are involved in farming. They apparently have little doubt that farms will continue to produce, but they do not know how or over what obstacles. For them, then, food is pretty much an abstract idea—something they do not know or imagine—until it appears on the grocery shelf or on the table.

The specialization of production induces specialization of consumption. Patrons of the entertainment industry, for example, entertain themselves less and less and have become more and more passively dependent on commercial suppliers. This is certainly true also of patrons of the food industry, who have tended more and more to be *mere* consumers—passive, uncritical, and dependent, Indeed, this sort of consumption may be said to be one of the chief goals of industrial production. The food indus-trialists have by now persuaded millions of consumers to prefer food that is already prepared. They will grow, deliver, and cook your food for you and (just like your mother) beg you to eat it. That they do not yet offer to insert it, prechewed, into your mouth is only because they have found no profit-able way to do so. We may rest assured that they would be glad to find such a way. The ideal industrial food consumer would be strapped to a table with a tube running from the food factory directly into his or her stomach.

Perhaps I exaggerate, but not by much. The industrial eater is, in fact, one who does not know that eating is an agricultural act, who no longer knows or imagines the connections between eating and the land, and who is therefore necessarily passive and uncritical—in short, a victim. When food, in the minds of eaters, is no longer associated with farming and with the land, then the eaters are suffering a kind of cultural amnesia that is misleading and dangerous. The current version of the "dream home" of the future involves "effortless" shopping from a list of available goods on a television monitor and heating precooked food by remote control. Of course, this implies and depends on, a perfect ignorance of the history of the food that is consumed. It requires that the citizenry should give up their hereditary and sensible aversion to buying a pig in a poke. It wishes to make the selling of pigs in pokes an honorable and glamorous activity. The dreamer in this dream home will perforce know nothing about the kind or quality of this food, or where it came from, or how it was produced and prepared, or what ingredients, additives, and residues in contains—unless, that is, the dreamer undertakes a close constant study of the food industry, in which case he or she might as well wake up and play an active and responsible part in the economy of food.

There is, then, a politics of food that, like any politics, involves our freedom. We still (sometimes) remember that we cannot be free if our minds and voices are controlled by someone else. But we have neglected to understand that we cannot be free if our food and its sources are con-trolled by someone else. The condition of the passive consumer of food is not a democratic condition. One reason to eat responsibly is to live free.

But if there is a food politics, there are also a food esthetics and a food ethics, neither of which is dissociated from politics. Like industrial sex, industrial eating has become a degraded, poor, and paltry thing. Our kitch-ens and other eating places more and more resemble filling stations, as our homes more and more resemble motels. "Life is not very interesting," we seem to have decided. "Let its satisfactions be minimal, perfunctory, and fast." We hurry through our meals to go to work and hurry through our work in order to "recreate" ourselves in the evenings and on weekends and vacations. And then we hurry, with the greatest possible speed and noise and violence, through our recreation—for what? To eat the billionth hamburger at some fast-food joint hellbent on increasing the "quality" of our life? And all this is carried out in a remarkable obliviousness to the causes and effects, the possibilities and the purposes, of the life of the body in this world.

One will find this obliviousness represented in virgin purity in the advertisements of the food industry, in which food wears as much makeup as the actors. If one gained one's whole knowledge of food from these advertisements (as some presumably do), one would not know that the various edibles were ever living creatures, or that they all come from the soil, or that they were produced by work. The passive American consumer, sitting down to a meal of pre-prepared or fast food, confronts a platter covered with inert, anonymous substances that have been processed, dyed, breaded, sauced, gravied, ground, pulped, strained, blended, prettified, and sanitized beyond resemblance to any part of any creature that ever lived. The products of nature and agriculture have been made, to all appearances, the products of industry. Both eater and eaten are thus in exile from biological realty. And the result is a kind of solitude, unprecedented in human experience, in which the eater may think of eating as, first, a purely commercial transaction between him and a supplier and then as a purely appetitive transaction between him and his food.

And this peculiar specialization of the act of eating is, again, of obvious benefit to the food industry, which has good reasons to obscure the connection between food and farming. It would not do for the consumer to know that the hamburger she is eating came from a steer who spent much of his life standing deep in his own excrement in a feedlot, helping to pollute the local streams, or that the calf that yielded the veal cutlet on her plate spent its life in a box in which it did not have room to turn around. And, though her sympathy for the slaw might be less tender, she should not be encouraged to meditate on the hygienic and biological implications of mile-square fields of cabbage, for vegetables grown in huge monocultures are dependent on toxic chemicals—just as animals in close confinement are dependent on antibiotics and other drugs.

The consumer, that is to say, must be kept from discovering that, in the food industry—as in any other industry—the overriding concerns are not quality and health, but volume and price. For decades now the entire industrial food economy, from the large farms and feedlots to the chains of supermarkets and fast-food restaurants, has been obsessed with volume. It has relentlessly increased scale in order to increase volume in order (presumably) to reduce costs. But as scale increases, diversity declines; as diversity declines, so does health; as health declines, the dependence on drugs and chemicals necessarily increases. As capital replaces labor, it does so by substituting machines, drugs, and chemicals for human workers and for the natural health and fertility of the soil. The food is produced by any means or any shortcut that will increase profits. And the business of the cosmeticians of advertising is to persuade the consumer that food so produced is good, tasty, healthful, and a guarantee of marital fidelity and long life.

It is possible, then, to be liberated from the husbandry and wifery of the old household food economy. But one can be thus liberated only by entering a trap (unless one sees ignorance and helplessness as the signs of privilege, as many people apparently do). The trap is the ideal of industrialism: a walled city surrounded by valves that let merchandise in but no consciousness out. How does one escape this trap? Only voluntarily, the same way that one went in: by restoring one's consciousness of what is involved in eating; by reclaiming responsibility for one's own part in the food economy. One might begin with the illuminating principle of Sir Albert Howard's *The Soil and Health*, that we should understand "the whole problem of health in soil, plant, animal, and man as one great subject." Eaters, that is, must understand that eating takes place inescapably in the world, that it is inescapably an agricultural act, and that how we eat determines, to a considerable extent, how the world is used. This is a simple way of describing a relationship that is inexpressibly complex. To eat responsibly is to understand and enact, so far as one can, this complex relationship. What can one do? Here is a list, probably not definitive:

1. Participate in food production to the extent that you can. If you have a yard or even just a porch box or a pot in a sunny window, grow something to eat in it. Make a little compost of your kitchen scraps and use it for fertilizer. Only by growing some food for yourself can you become acquainted with the beautiful energy cycle that revolves from soil to seed to flower to fruit to food to offal to decay, and around again. You will be fully responsible for any food that you grow for yourself, and you will know all about it. You will appreciate it fully, having known it all its life.

2. Prepare your own food. This means reviving in your own mind and life the arts of kitchen and household. This should enable you to eat more cheaply, and it will give you a measure of "quality control": you will have some reliable knowledge of what has been added to the food you eat.

3. Learn the origins of the food you buy, and buy the food that is produced closest to your home. The idea that every locality should be, as much as possible, the source of its own food makes several kinds of sense. The locally produced food supply is the most secure, the freshest, and the easiest for local consumers to know about and to influence.

4. Whenever possible, deal directly with a local farmer, gardener, or orchardist. All the reasons listed for the previous suggestion apply here. In addition, by such dealing you eliminate the whole pack of merchants, transporters, processors, packagers, and advertisers who thrive at the expense of both producers and consumers.

5. Learn, in self-defense, as much as you can of the economy and technology of industrial food production. What is added to food that is not food, and what do you pay for these additions?

6. Learn what is involved in the *best* farming and gardening.

7. Learn as much as you can, by direct observation and experience if possible, of the life histories of the food species.

The last suggestion seems particularly important to me. Many people are now as much estranged from the lives of domestic plants and animals (except for flowers and dogs and cats) as they are from the lives of the wild ones. This is regrettable, for these domestic creatures are in diverse ways attractive; there is much pleasure in knowing them. And farming, animal husbandry, horticulture, and gardening, at their best, are complex and comely arts; there is much pleasure in knowing them, too.

It follows that there is great *dis*pleasure in knowing about a food economy that degrades and abuses those arts and those plants and animals and the soil from which they come. For anyone who does know something of the modern history of food, eating away from home can be a chore. My own inclination is to eat seafood instead of red meat or poultry when I am traveling. Though I am by no means a vegetarian, I dislike the thought that some animal has been made miserable in order to feed me. If I am going to eat meat, I want it to be from an animal that has lived a pleasant, uncrowded life outdoors, on bountiful pasture, with good water nearby and trees for shade. And I am getting almost as fussy about food plants. I like to eat vegetables and fruits that I know have lived happily and healthily in good soil, not the products of the huge, bechemicaled factory-fields that I have seen, for example, in the Central Valley of California. The industrial farm is said to have been patterned on the factory production line. In practice, it looks more like a concentration camp.

The pleasure of eating should be an *extensive* pleasure, not that of the mere gourmet. People who know the garden in which their vegetables have grown and know that the garden is healthy will remember the beauty of the growing plants, perhaps in the dewy first light of morning when gardens are at their best. Such a memory involves itself with the food and is one of the pleasures of eating. The knowledge of the good health of the garden relieves and frees and comforts the eater. The same goes for eating meat. The thought of the good pasture and of the calf contentedly grazing flavors the steak. Some, I know, will think it bloodthirsty or worse to eat a fellow creature you have known all its life. On the contrary, I think it means that you eat with understanding and with gratitude. A significant part of the pleasure of eating is in one's accurate consciousness of the lives and the world from which food comes. The pleasure of eating, then, may be the best available standard of our health. And this pleasure, I think, is pretty fully available to the urban consumer who will make the necessary effort.

I mentioned earlier the politics, esthetics, and ethics of food. But to speak of the pleasure of eating is to go beyond those categories. Eating with the fullest pleasure—pleasure, that is, that does not depend on ignorance—is perhaps the profoundest enactment of our connection with the world. In this pleasure we experience and celebrate our dependence and our gratitude, for we are living from mystery, from creatures we did not make and powers we cannot comprehend. When I think of the meaning of food, I always remember these lines by the poet William Carlos Williams, which seem to me merely honest:

> There is nothing to eat,
>   seek it where you will,
>   but the body of the Lord.
> The blessed plants
>   and the sea, yield it
>   to the imagination
> intact.

1989

Index

Abjection, 70ff.
Absent referent, 217
Absolutism, 251, 253, 256, 261, 359
Absolutism/relativism dichotomy, 254, 256
Abstract, the, xiv, 126, 241
Action, 212, 235, 302, 305–314 *passim,* 319, 321, 323, 325, 339, 363; practical, 236, 301; rational, 236; food-centered, 301, 321; social, 303, 310; charitable, 304, 307; political, 310; industrial, 321; solidary, 321
Activity, 206, 227, 230, 231, 240, 254, 302; agricultural, 10, 321, 374–378 *passim;* manual, 203, 204, 214, 224; mental, 203, 204, 219, 224, 225; of appetite, 209; leisure, 213; theoretical, 213, 214, 216, 227; human, 214, 216, 219, 222, 224; practical, 214, 215, 223, 227; bodily, 219, 220, 227; community, 220, 253; women's, 255; men's, 255; political, 266; productive, 337
Adams, Carol, 133, 217, 316
Addams, Jane, 43
Adorno, Theodor, 5, 20
Agribusiness, xiii, 332, 343
Agriculture, 318, 321, 330, 332, 343, 360–369, 374–379. *See also* Farming; Gardening; Growing food
Aid, 305, 307, 308, 309, 319, 324, 325; food, 305, 318; "tied," 305, 306, 318, 324; self-interested, 308
Aid organizations, 304, 307, 309, 324–325; nongovernmental, 301, 302, 305, 309, 325; progressive, 302, 309; political, 305; charitable, 308; governmental, 308, 325
Altruism, 15, 17, 139, 303–304, 306–310, 324, 326
American Beef Council, 13
Animal Liberation Movement, 186
Animals, 13, 30, 32, 217, 266, 267, 268, 269, 304, 313–322 *passim,* 329, 338, 343, 351, 357, 361, 363, 372, 376, 377, 378. *See also* Meat
Anorexia nervosa, xiv, 7, 9, 11, 14, 28–55, 56–67
Anorexic, the, 33–36, 226
Anthology versus reader, xiii, xv
Anti-essentialism, 251, 256
Anzaldúa, Gloria, 225
Appetite, 33–34, 209, 211, 220, 225–226, 352
Aristotle, 235, 236, 242
Ariyaratne, A. T., 36
Arrogant perception, 85–86, 98–99

Arts, 203, 214, 215, 224, 230, 231, 232, 239, 246, 296; fine, xiii, 125, 132; applied, 125; and crafts, 203, 205, 224; culinary, 222, 245, 250, 294. *See also* Cuisine, as a normative art
Ātman, 18, 100
Attitudes, 204; cultural, 222; epistemological, 227, 252, 264
Augustine, 32
Awad, Mubarak, 136
Ayurveda, 12

Bacon, Francis, 316, 363, 364
Beauty: female, 29, 30, 47
Becoming, 214
Being, 214
Bernstein, Richard, 252
Berry, Wendell, 17, 129, 130, 321–322
Bhagavadgītā, 101
Body, the, 72, 217, 219, 220, 269, 292, 376; and Cartesianism, xiv; and food, 4, 28–55, 56–67, 210, 232; purification of, 26, 27; disdain for, 29, 36; and culture, 31; erotic, 31; and bodybuilding, 37–39; and breastfeeding, 68–69; sacred, 75–77, 284, 379; and sexual difference, 114–115; and soul, 210, 213, 231. *See also* Mind/body dichotomy
Bordo, Susan, xiv, 7, 11, 226
Bread, 203, 206, 217, 218, 261, 263, 309, 351
Bread for the World, 305
Brown, Lester, 177
Buddha, the, 18, 19, 100–107, 159–163, 280, 283, 284
Buddhism, 363
Buddhist rules for meals, 153–163
Buffalo Bird Woman, 221
Bulimia, 29
Burger King, 212, 233–234

Care, 15, 17, 124, 135
Carême, Antonin, 150
Cartesianism, 7, 10, 364, 365, 366, 368; and the body, xiv, 9, 33; and the "external" world, 19; in cooking methods, 218, 219; as anxiety, 252
Cash crops, 331, 332, 337, 343
Caste, 101
Change, 126, 204, 205, 207, 227, 242, 309, 365
Charity, 304–306, 307–310, 310–314 *passim,* 317, 319–320, 321, 323, 324, 353
Chavez, Cesar, 175
Chefs. *See* Cooks

DEANE W. CURTIN, Professor of Philosophy at
Gustavus Adolphus College, has published in the areas of
philosophy of art and environmental ethics.

LISA M. HELDKE, Assistant Professor of Philosophy at
Gustavus Adolphus College, writes and teaches in the area of
pragmatist feminism.